# ACCA

## Paper P4

## Advanced financial management

## Complete text

## British library cataloguing-in-publication data

A catalogue record for this book is available from the British Library.

Published by:
Kaplan Publishing UK
Unit 2 The Business Centre
Molly Millars Lane
Wokingham
Berkshire
RG41 2QZ

ISBN  978-1-84710-737-4

© Kaplan Financial Limited, 2009

The text in this material and any others made available by any Kaplan Group company does not amount to advice on a particular matter and should not be taken as such. No reliance should be placed on the content as the basis for any investment or other decision or in connection with any advice given to third parties. Please consult your appropriate professional adviser as necessary. Kaplan Publishing Limited and all other Kaplan group companies expressly disclaim all liability to any person in respect of any losses or other claims, whether direct, indirect, incidental, consequential or otherwise arising in relation to the use of such materials.

Printed in the UK by CPI William Clowes, Beccles NR34 7TL.

### Acknowledgements

We are grateful to the Association of Chartered Certified Accountants and the Chartered Institute of Management Accountants for permisssion to reproduce past examination questions.  The answers have been prepared by Kaplan Publishing.

# Contents

KAPLAN PUBLISHING

# Paper Introduction

# How to Use the Materials

These Kaplan Publishing learning materials have been carefully designed to make your learning experience as easy as possible and to give you the best chances of success in your examinations.

The product range contains a number of features to help you in the study process. They include:

(1)  Detailed study guide and syllabus objectives

(2)  Description of the examination

(3)  Study skills and revision guidance

(4)  Complete text or essential text

(5)  Question practice

The sections on the study guide, the syllabus objectives, the examination and study skills should all be read before you commence your studies. They are designed to familiarise you with the nature and content of the examination and give you tips on how to best to approach your learning.

The **complete text or essential text** comprises the main learning materials and gives guidance as to the importance of topics and where other related resources can be found. Each chapter includes:

- The **learning objectives** contained in each chapter, which have been carefully mapped to the examining body's own syllabus learning objectives or outcomes. You should use these to check you have a clear understanding of all the topics on which you might be assessed in the examination.

- The **chapter diagram** provides a visual reference for the content in the chapter, giving an overview of the topics and how they link together.

- The **content** for each topic area commences with a brief explanation or definition to put the topic into context before covering the topic in detail. You should follow your studying of the content with a review of the illustration/s. These are worked examples which will help you to understand better how to apply the content for the topic.

- **Test your understanding** sections provide an opportunity to assess your understanding of the key topics by applying what you have learned to short questions. Answers can be found at the back of each chapter.

- **Summary diagrams** complete each chapter to show the important links between topics and the overall content of the paper. These diagrams should be used to check that you have covered and understood the core topics before moving on.

- **Question practice** is provided at the back of each text.

## Icon Explanations

**Definition -** Key definitions that you will need to learn from the core content.

**Key Point -** Identifies topics that are key to success and are often examined.

**Expandable Text -** Expandable text provides you with additional information about a topic area and may help you gain a better understanding of the core content. Essential text users can access this additional content on-line (read it where you need further guidance or skip over when you are happy with the topic)

**Illustration -** Worked examples help you understand the core content better.

**Test Your Understanding -** Exercises for you to complete to ensure that you have understood the topics just learned.

**Tricky topic -** When reviewing these areas care should be taken and all illustrations and test your understanding exercises should be completed to ensure that the topic is understood.

## On-line subscribers

Our on-line resources are designed to increase the flexibility of your learning materials and provide you with immediate feedback on how your studies are progressing. Ask your local customer services staff if you are not already a subscriber and wish to join.

If you are subscribed to our on-line resources you will find:

(1) On-line referenceware: reproduces your Complete or Essential Text on-line, giving you anytime, anywhere access.

(2) On-line testing: provides you with additional on-line objective testing so you can practice what you have learned further.

(3) On-line performance management: immediate access to youron-line testing results. Review your performance by key topics and chart your achievement through the course relative to your peer group.

## Syllabus

### Paper background

The aim of ACCA Paper P4, Advanced financial management, is to apply relevant knowledge, skills and to exercise professional judgement as expected of a senior financial executive or advisor, in taking or recommending decisions relating to the financial management of an organisation.

### Objectives of the syllabus

- Explain the role and responsibility of the senior financial executive or advisor in meeting conflicting needs of stakeholders.

- Evaluate potential investment decisions and assess their financial and strategic consequences, both domestically and internationally.

- Assess and plan acquisitions and mergers as an alternative growth strategy.

- Evaluate and advise on alternative corporate re-organisation strategies.

- Apply and evaluate alternative advanced treasury and risk management techniques.

- Evaluate the impact of macro-economics and recognise the role of international financial institutions in the financial management of multinationals.

- Identify and assess the potential impact of emerging issues in finance and financial management.

### Core areas of the syllabus

- Role and responsibility towards stakeholders.

- Advanced investment appraisal.

- Acquisitions and mergers.

- Corporate reconstruction and re-organisation.

- Treasury and advanced risk management techniques.

- Economic environment for multinationals.

- Emerging issues in finance and financial management.

### Syllabus objectives

We have reproduced the ACCA's syllabus below, showing where the objectives are explored within this book. Within the chapters, we have broken down the extensive information found in the syllabus into easily digestible and relevant sections, called Content Objectives. These correspond to the objectives at the beginning of each chapter.

# A ROLE AND RESPONSIBILITY TOWARDS SHAREHOLDERS

## 1 Conflicting stakeholder interests

(a) Assess the potential sources of the conflict within a given corporate governance/ stakeholder framework informed by an understanding of the alternative theories of managerial behaviour. [3]**Ch. 1** Relevant underpinning theory for this assessment would be:

    (i) the separation of ownership and control

    (ii) transaction cost economics and comparative governance structures

    (iii) agency theory.

(b) Recommend, within specified problem domains, appropriate strategies for the resolution of stakeholder conflict and advise on alternative approaches that may be adopted. [3]**Ch. 1**

(c) Compare the emerging governance structures and policies with respect to corporate governance (with particular emphasis upon the European stakeholder and the US/UK shareholder model) and with respect to the role of the financial manager. [3]**Ch. 1**

## 2 The role and responsibility of senior financial executive/ advisor

(a) Advise the board of directors of the firm in setting the financial goals of the business and in its financial policy development [2] with particular reference to: [2]**Ch. 1**

    (i) investment selection and capital resource allocation

    (ii) minimising the firm's cost of capital

    (iii) distribution and retention policy

    (iv) communicating financial policy and corporate goals to internal and external stakeholders

    (v) financial planning and control

    (vi) the management of risk.

(b) Develop strategies for the achievement of the firm's goals in line with its agreed policy framework. [3]**Ch. 1**

(c) Recommend strategies for the management of the financial resources of the firm such that they are utilised in an efficient, effective and transparent way. [3]**Ch. 1**

(d) Establish an ethical financial policy for the financial management of the firm which is grounded in good governance, the highest standards of probity and is fully aligned with the ethical principles of the Association. [3]**Ch. 1**

(e) Explore the areas within the ethical framework of the firm which may be undermined by agency effects and/or stakeholder conflicts and establish strategies for dealing with them. [3]**Ch. 1**

(f) Prepare advice on personal finance to individual as well as groups of investors, covering areas such as investment and financing. [3]**Ch. 1**

### 3 Impact of environmental issues on corporate objectives and on governance

(a) Assess the issues which may impact upon corporate objectives and governance from: [3]**Ch. 1**
   (i) sustainability and environmental risk
   (ii) the carbon-trading economy and emissions
   (iii) the role of the environment agency
   (iv) environmental audits and the triple bottom line approach.

### 4 Financial strategy formulation

(a) Recommend the optimum capital mix and structure within a specified business context and capital asset structure. [3]**Ch. 5**

(b) Recommend appropriate distribution and retention policy. [3]**Ch. 6**

(c) Establish capital investment monitoring and risk management systems. [3]**Ch. 12**

(d) Develop a framework for risk management comparing and contrasting risk mitigation, hedging and diversification strategies. [3]**Ch. 12**

### 5 Ethical issues in financial management

(a) Assess the ethical dimension within business issues and decisions and advise on best practice in the financial management of the firm. [3]**Ch. 1**

(b) Demonstrate an understanding of the interconnectedness of the ethics of good business practice between all of the functional areas of the firm. [2]**Ch. 1**

(c) Recommend an ethical framework for the development of a firm's financial policies and a system for the assessment of their ethical impact upon the financial management of the firm. [3]**Ch. 1**

# B ADVANCED INVESTMENT APPRAISAL

## 1 Discounted cash flow techniques and the use of free cash flows

(a) Evaluate the potential value added to a firm arising from a specified capital investment project or portfolio using the net present value model. [3]**Ch. 2** Project modelling should include explicit treatment of:

   (i) inflation and specific price variation

   (ii) taxation and the assessment of fiscal risk

   (iii) multi-period capital rationing to include the formulation of programming methods and the interpretation of their output.

(b) Establish the potential economic return (using internal rate of return and modified internal rate of return) and advise on a project's return margin and its vulnerability to competitive action. [3]**Ch. 2**

(c) Forecast a firm's free cash flow and its free cash flow to equity (pre- and post-capital reinvestment). [2]**Ch. 2**

(d) Advise, in the context of a specified capital investment programme, on a firm's current and projected dividend capacity. [3]**Ch. 2,6**

(e) Advise on the value of a firm using its free cash flow and free cash flow to equity under alternative horizon and growth assumptions. [3]**Ch. 10**

## 2 Impact of financing on investment decisions and adjusted present values

(a) Assess the impact of financing upon investment decisions of: [3]**Ch. 5**

   (i) pecking order theory

   (ii) static trade-off theory

   (iii) agency effects and capital structure.

(b) Apply the adjusted present value technique to the appraisal of investment decisions that entail significant alterations in the financial structure of the firm, including their fiscal and transactions cost implications. [3]**Ch. 4**

(c) Outline the application of Monte Carlo simulation to investment appraisal. [2]**Ch. 12** Candidates will not be expected to undertake simulations in an examination context but will be expected to demonstrate an understanding of:

   (i) simple model design

   (ii) the different types of distribution controlling the key variables within the simulation

   (iii) the significance of the simulation output and the assessment of the likelihood of project success

   (iv) the measurement and interpretation of project value

### 3 Application of option pricing theory in investment decisions

(a) Demonstrate an understanding of option pricing theory: [2]**Ch. 8**
   (i) determine, using published data, the five principal drivers of option value (value of the underlying, exercise price, time to expiry, volatility and the risk-free rate)

   (ii) discuss the underlying assumptions, structure, application and limitations of the Black-Scholes model.

(b) Evaluate embedded real options within a project, classifying them into one of the real option archetypes. [3]**Ch. 8**

(c) Assess and advise on the value of options to delay, expand, redeploy and withdraw using the Black Scholes model. [3]**Ch. 8**

### 4 International investment and financing decisions

(a) Assess the impact upon the value of a project of alternative exchange rate assumptions. [3]**Ch. 7**

(b) Forecast project or firm free cash flows in any specified currency and determine the project's net present value or firm value under differing exchange rate, fiscal and transaction cost assumptions. [2]**Ch. 7**

(c) Evaluate the significance of exchange controls for a given investment decision and strategies for dealing with restricted remittance. [3]**Ch. 7**

(d) Assess the impact of a project upon a firm's exposure to translation, transaction and economic risk. [3]**Ch. 7**

(e) Assess and advise upon the costs and benefits of alternative sources of finance available within the international equity and bond financial markets. [3]**Ch. 7**

### 5 Impact of capital investment on financial reporting

(a) Assess the impact of a significant capital investment project upon the reported financial position and performance of the firm taking into account: [3]**Ch. 2,6**
   (i) alternative financing strategies

   (ii) foreign exchange translation

   (iii) taxation and double taxation

   (iv) capital allowances and the problem of tax exhaustion.

# C ACQUISITIONS AND MERGERS

## 1 Acquisitions and mergers versus other growth strategies

(a) Discuss the arguments for and against the use of acquisitions and mergers as a method of corporate expansion. [2]**Ch. 9**

(b) Evaluate the corporate and competitive nature of a given acquisition proposal. [3]**Ch. 9**

(c) Advise upon the criteria for choosing an appropriate target for acquisition. [3]**Ch. 9**

(d) Compare the various explanations for the high failure rate of acquisitions in enhancing shareholder value. [3]**Ch. 9**

(e) Evaluate, from a given context, the potential for synergy,
   (i) revenue synergy
   (ii) cost synergy
   (iii) financial synergy.

## 2 Valuation for acquisitions and mergers

(a) Outline the argument and the problem of overvaluation. [1]**Ch. 10**

(b) Estimate the potential near-term and continuing growth levels of a firm's earnings using both internal and external measures. [3]**Ch. 3**

(c) Assess the impact of an acquisition or merger upon the risk profile of the acquirer distinguishing: [3]**Ch. 10**
   (i) type 1 acquisitions that do not disturb the acquirer's exposure to financial or business risk
   (ii) type 2 acquisitions that impact upon the acquirer's exposure to financial risk
   (iii) type 3 acquisitions that impact upon the acquirer's exposure to both financial and business risk.

(d) Advise on the valuation of a type 1 acquisition of both quoted and unquoted entities using: [3]**Ch. 10**
   (i) 'book value-plus' models
   (ii) market relative models
   (iii) cash flow models, including EVATM, MVA.

(e) Advise on the valuation of type 2 acquisitions using the adjusted net present value model. [3]**Ch. 10**

(f) Advise on the valuation of type 3 acquisitions using iterative revaluation procedures. [3]**Ch. 10**

(g) Demonstrate an understanding of the procedure for valuing high growth start-ups. [2]**Ch. 10**

### 3 Regulatory framework and processes

(a) Demonstrate an understanding of the principal factors influencing the development of the regulatory framework for mergers and acquisitions globally and, in particular, be able to compare and contrast the shareholder versus the stakeholder models of regulation. [2]**Ch. 9**

(b) Identify the main regulatory issues which are likely to arise in the context of a given offer, and:

   (i) assess whether the offer is likely to be in the shareholders' best interests

   (ii) advise the directors of a target company on the most appropriate defence if a specific offer is to be treated as hostile. [3]**Ch. 9**

### 4 Financing acquisitions and mergers

(a) Compare the various sources of financing available for a proposed cash-based acquisition. [3]**Ch. 9**

(b) Evaluate the advantages and disadvantages of a financial offer for a given acquisition proposal using pure or mixed mode financing and recommend the most appropriate offer to be made. [3]**Ch. 9**

(c) Assess the impact of a given financial offer on the reported financial position and performance of the acquirer. [3]**Ch. 9**

### D Corporate reconstruction and reorganisation

### 1 Predicting corporate failure

(a) Assess the risk of corporate failure within the short to medium term using a range of appropriate financial evaluation methods (this will require an ability to use multivariate techniques such as the Z and Zeta score models). [3]**Ch. 11**

(b) Advise on the application of financial distress models to firms in emerging markets given local regulatory and financial market conditions. [3]**Ch. 11**

### 2 Financial reconstruction

(a) Assess a company situation and determine whether a financial reconstruction is the most appropriate strategy for dealing with the problem as presented. [3]**Ch. 11**

(b) Assess the likely response of the capital market and/or scheme and the impact their response is likely to have upon the value of the firm. [3]**Ch. 11**

(c) Recommend a reconstruction scheme from a given business situation, justifying the proposal in terms of its impact upon the reported performance and financial position of the firm. [3]**Ch. 11**

## 3 Business reorganisation

(a) Recommend, with reasons, strategies for unbundling parts of a quoted company. [3]**Ch. 11**

(b) Evaluate the likely financial and other benefits of unbundling. [3]**Ch. 11**

(c) Advise on the financial issues relating to a management buy-out and buy-in. [3]**Ch. 11**

## E Treasury and advanced risk management techniques

## 1 The role of the treasury function in multinationals

(a) Describe the role of the money markets in: [1] **Ch. 16**
   (i) providing short-term liquidity to industry and the public sector
   (ii) providing short-term trade finance
   (iii) allowing a multinational firm to manage its exposure to FOREX and interest rate risk.

(b) Explain the role of the banks and other financial institutions in the operation of the money markets. [1]**Ch. 16**

(c) Describe the characteristics and role of the principal money market instruments: [1]**Ch. 16**
   (i) coupon bearing
   (ii) discount instruments
   (iii) derivatives.

(d) Outline the role of the treasury management function within: [2]**Ch. 16**
   (i) the short term management of the firm's financial resources
   (ii) the longer term maximisation of shareholder value
   (iii) the management of risk exposure.

## 2 The use of financial derivatives to hedge against FOREX risk

(a) Demonstrate an understanding of the operations of the derivatives market, including: [3]**Ch. 12**
   (i) the relative advantages and disadvantages of exchange traded versus OTC agreements
   (ii) key features, such as standard contracts, tick sizes, margin requirements and margin trading
   (iii) the source of basis risk and how it can be minimised.

(b) Evaluate, for a given hedging requirement, which of the following is the most appropriate strategy, given the nature of the underlying position and the risk exposure: [3]**Ch. 13**

    (i)   the use of the forward exchange market and the creation of a money market hedge

    (ii)  synthetic foreign exchange agreements (SAFEs)

    (iii) exchange-traded currency futures contracts

    (iv) currency swaps

    (v)  FOREX swaps

    (vi) currency options.

(c) Advise on the use of bilateral and multilateral netting and matching as tools for minimising FOREX transactions costs and the management of market barriers to the free movement of capital and other remittances. [3]**Ch. 13**

## 3 The use of financial derivatives to hedge against interest rate risk

(a) Evaluate, for a given hedging requirement, which of the following is the most appropriate given the nature of the underlying position and the risk exposure:[3]**Ch. 14**

    (i)   forward rate agreements

    (ii)  interest rate futures

    (iii) interest rate swaps

    (iv) options on FRA's (caps and collars), interest rate futures and interest rate swaps.

## 4 Other forms of risk

(a) Assess the firm's exposure to political, economic, regulatory and fiscal risk and the strategies available for the mitigation of such risk.[3]**Ch. 12**

(b) Assess the firm's exposure to credit risk, including: [2]**Ch. 3**

    (i)   explain the role of, and the risk assessment models used by, the principal rating agencies

    (ii)  estimate the likely credit spread over risk free

    (iii) estimate the firm's current cost of debt capital using the appropriate term structure of interest rates and the credit spread.

(c) Explain the role of option pricing models in the assessment of default risk, the value of debt and its potential recoverability. [1]**Ch. 8**

## 5 Dividend policy in multinationals and transfer pricing

(a)  Determine a firm's dividend capacity and its policy given: [3]**Ch. 6**
   (i)   the firm's short- and long-term reinvestment strategy

   (ii)  the impact of any other capital reconstruction programmes on free cash flow to equity such as share repurchase agreements and new capital issues

   (iii) the availability and timing of central remittances

   (iv)  the corporate tax regime within the host jurisdiction.

(b)  Develop company policy on the transfer pricing of goods and services across international borders and be able to determine the most appropriate transfer pricing strategy in a given situation reflecting local regulations and tax regimes. [3]**Ch. 6**

## F ECONOMIC ENVIRONMENT FOR MULTINATIONALS

### 1 Management of international trade and finance

(a)  Advise on the theory and practice of free trade and the management of barriers to trade. [3]**Ch. 15**

(b)  Demonstrate an up-to-date understanding of the major trade agreements and common markets and, on the basis of contemporary circumstances, advise on their policy and strategic implications for a given business. [3]**Ch. 15**

(c)  Discuss the objectives of the World Trade Organisation. [2]**Ch. 15**

(d)  Discuss the role of international financial institutions within the context of a globalised economy, with particular attention to the International Monetary Fund, the Bank of International Settlements, The World Bank and the principal Central Banks (the Fed, Bank of England, European Central Bank and the Bank of Japan). [2]**Ch. 15**

(e)  Assess the role of the international financial markets with respect to the management of global debt, the financial development of the emerging economies and the maintenance of global financial stability. [2]**Ch. 15**

## 2 Strategic business and financial planning for multinationals

(a) Advise on the development of a financial planning framework for a multinational taking into account: [3]**Ch. 15**

   (i) compliance with national governance requirements (for example, the LSE requirements for admission for trading)

   (ii) the mobility of capital across borders and national limitations on remittances and transfer pricing

   (iii) the pattern of economic and other risk exposures in the different national markets

   (iv) agency issues in the central coordination of overseas operations and the balancing of local financial autonomy with effective central control.

## G EMERGING ISSUES

### 1 Developments in world financial markets

(a) Demonstrate awareness, and discuss the significance to the firm, of the latest developments in the world financial markets with particular reference to the removal of barriers to the free movement of capital and the international regulations on money laundering. [2]**Ch. 17**

### 2 Financial engineering and emerging derivative products

A Demonstrate awareness, and discuss the significance to the firm, of latest derivative products with particular emphasis on the risks in derivative trading and the application of the following in their management: [2]**Ch. 17**

   (i) value at risk

   (ii) scenario analysis

   (iii) stress testing.

### 3 Developments in international trade and finance

Demonstrate an awareness of new developments in the macroeconomic environment, establishing their impact upon the firm, and advising on the appropriate response to those developments both internally and externally. [2]**Ch. 17**

The superscript numbers in square brackets indicate the intellectual depth at which the subject area could be assessed within the examination. Level 1 (knowledge and comprehension) broadly equates with the Knowledge module, Level 2 (application and analysis) with the Skills module and Level 3 (synthesis and evaluation) to the Professional level. However, lower level skills can continue to be assessed as you progress through each module and level.

## The examination

## Examination format

The P4 **Advanced Financial Management** paper builds upon the skills and knowledge examined in the F9 Financial Management paper. At this stage candidates will be expected to demonstrate an integrated knowledge of the subject and an ability to relate their technical understanding of the subject to issues of strategic importance to the firm. The study guide specifies the wide range of contextual understanding that is required to achieve a satisfactory standard at this level. In particular the ethical and managerial aspects of the role of the senior financial manager or advisor will regularly feature in examination papers.

The examination will be a three hour paper in two sections:

Section A has two compulsory questions worth 60 marks in total. This section will normally cover significant issues relevant to the senior financial manager or advisor and will be set in the form of a short case study or scenario. The requirements of the section A questions are such that candidates will be expected to show a comprehensive understanding of issues from across the syllabus. Each question will contain a mix of computational and discursive elements. Normally, approximately 50 per cent of the marks will be apportioned to each of the two elements. A maximum of 40 marks will be available for either question in Section A.

Section B questions are designed to provide a more focused test of the syllabus with, normally, at least one question being wholly discursive. Candidates will be expected to provide answers in a specified form such as a short report or board memorandum commensurate with the professional level of the paper.

Candidates will be provided with a formulae sheet as well as present value, annuity and standard normal distribution tables.

|  | **Number of marks** |
|---|---|
| Section A | |
| Answer both questions | 60 |
| Section B | 40 |
| Two from three questions, 20 marks each | |
| | ——— |
| Total time allowed: 3 hours plus 15 minutes reading time | **100** |

## Examination tips

Spend the reading time reading the paper and planning your answers. You are allowed to annotate the question paper, so make use of this – e.g. highlighting key issues in the questions, planning calculations, brainstorming requirements – ensure that you understand the question. A key issue is to decide which questions you wish to attempt from section B – it is worth planning all three in outline before deciding.

**Divide the time** you spend on questions in proportion to the marks on offer. One suggestion **for this examination** is to allocate 1 and 4/5$^{ths}$ minutes to each mark available, so a 10-mark question should be completed in approximately 18 minutes. A danger in P4 is that you spend too long on the calculation aspects and neglect the written elements, so allocate your time within questions as well as between them.

Stick to the question and **tailor your answer** to what you are asked. Pay particular attention to the verbs in the question.

Spend the last five minutes reading through your answers and making any additions or corrections.

If you **get completely stuck** with a question, leave space in your answer book and **return to it later**.

If you do not understand what a question is asking, state your assumptions. Even if you do not answer in precisely the way the examiner hoped, you should be given some credit, if your assumptions are reasonable.

You should do everything you can to make things easy for the marker. The marker will find it easier to identify the points you have made if your answers are legible.

**Essay questions**: Your essay should have a clear structure. It should contain a brief introduction, a main section and a conclusion. Be concise. It is better to write a little about a lot of different points than a great deal about one or two points.

**Computations**: It is essential to include all your workings in your answers. Many computational questions require the use of a standard format. Be sure you know these formats thoroughly before the exam and use the layouts that you see in the answers given in this book and in model answers.

**Scenario-based questions**: Most questions will contain a hypothetical scenario. To write a good case answer, first identify the area in which there is a problem, outline the main principles/theories you are going to use to answer the question, and then apply the principles/theories to the case. It is vital that you relate your answer to the specific circumstances given.

**Reports, memos and other documents**: some questions ask you to present your answer in the form of a report or a memo or other document. So use the correct format - there could be easy marks to gain here.

## Study skills and revision guidance

This section aims to give guidance on how to study for your ACCA exams and to give ideas on how to improve your existing study techniques.

## Preparing to study

### Set your objectives

Before starting to study decide what you want to achieve - the type of pass you wish to obtain. This will decide the level of commitment and time you need to dedicate to your studies.

### Devise a study plan

Determine which times of the week you will study.

Split these times into sessions of at least one hour for study of new material. Any shorter periods could be used for revision or practice.

Put the times you plan to study onto a study plan for the weeks from now until the exam and set yourself targets for each period of study - in your sessions make sure you cover the course, course assignments and revision.

If you are studying for more than one paper at a time, try to vary your subjects as this can help you to keep interested and see subjects as part of wider knowledge.

When working through your course, compare your progress with your plan and, if necessary, re-plan your work (perhaps including extra sessions) or, if you are ahead, do some extra revision/practice questions.

## Effective studying

### Active reading

You are not expected to learn the text by rote, rather, you must understand what you are reading and be able to use it to pass the exam and develop good practice. A good technique to use is SQ3Rs - Survey, Question, Read, Recall, Review:

(1) **Survey the chapter** - look at the headings and read the introduction, summary and objectives, so as to get an overview of what the chapter deals with.

(2) **Question** - whilst undertaking the survey, ask yourself the questions that you hope the chapter will answer for you.

(3) **Read** through the chapter thoroughly, answering the questions and making sure you can meet the objectives. Attempt the exercises and activities in the text, and work through all the examples.

(4) **Recall** - at the end of each section and at the end of the chapter, try to recall the main ideas of the section/chapter without referring to the text. This is best done after a short break of a couple of minutes after the reading stage.

(5) **Review** - check that your recall notes are correct.

You may also find it helpful to re-read the chapter to try to see the topic(s) it deals with as a whole.

### Note-taking

Taking notes is a useful way of learning, but do not simply copy out the text. The notes must:

- be in your own words
- be concise
- cover the key points
- be well-organised
- be modified as you study further chapters in this text or in related ones.

Trying to summarise a chapter without referring to the text can be a useful way of determining which areas you know and which you don't.

**Three ways of taking notes:**

**Summarise the key points of a chapter.**

**Make linear notes** - a list of headings, divided up with subheadings listing the key points. If you use linear notes, you can use different colours to highlight key points and keep topic areas together. Use plenty of space to make your notes easy to use.

**Try a diagrammatic form** - the most common of which is a mind-map. To make a mind-map, put the main heading in the centre of the paper and put a circle around it. Then draw short lines radiating from this to the main sub-headings, which again have circles around them. Then continue the process from the sub-headings to sub-sub-headings, advantages, disadvantages, etc.

**Highlighting and underlining**

You may find it useful to underline or highlight key points in your study text - but do be selective. You may also wish to make notes in the margins.

**Revision**

The best approach to revision is to revise the course as you work through it. Also try to leave four to six weeks before the exam for final revision. Make sure you cover the whole syllabus and pay special attention to those areas where your knowledge is weak. Here are some recommendations:

**Read through the text and your notes again** and condense your notes into key phrases. It may help to put key revision points onto index cards to look at when you have a few minutes to spare.

**Review any assignments** you have completed and look at where you lost marks - put more work into those areas where you were weak.

**Practise exam standard questions** under timed conditions. If you are short of time, list the points that you would cover in your answer and then read the model answer, but do try to complete at least a few questions under exam conditions.

Also practise producing answer plans and comparing them to the model answer.

If you are stuck on a topic find somebody (a tutor) to explain it to you.

**Read good newspapers and professional journals**, especially ACCA's **Student Accountant** - this can give you an advantage in the exam.

Ensure you **know the structure of the exam** - how many questions and of what type you will be expected to answer. During your revision attempt all the different styles of questions you may be asked.

### Further reading

You can find further reading and technical articles under the student section of ACCA's website. Also, you may find it useful to read "Corporate Finance and Valuation" by Bob Ryan (the P4 examiner). Several theories and methods from this book appear in this Kaplan Text with the kind permission of the author.

# Formulae and tables

### Modigliani and Miller Proposition 2 (with tax)

$$k_e = k_e^i + (1 - T)(k_e^i - k_d)\frac{V_d}{V_e}$$

### Two asset portfolio

$$s_p = \sqrt{w_a^2 s_a^2 + w_b^2 s_b^2 + 2w_a w_b r_{ab} s_a s_b}$$

### The Capital Asset Pricing Model

$$E(r_i) = R_f + \beta_i(E(r_m) - R_f)$$

### The asset beta formula

$$\beta_a = \left[\frac{V_e}{(V_e + V_d(1-T))}\beta_e\right] + \left[\frac{V_d(1-T)}{V_e + V_d(1-T)}\beta_d\right]$$

### The Growth Model

$$P_o = \frac{D_o(1+g)}{(r_e - g)}$$

### Gordon's growth approximation

$$g = br_e$$

### The weighted average cost of capital

$$WACC = \left[\frac{V_e}{V_e + V_d}\right]k_e + \left[\frac{V_d}{V_e + V_d}\right]k_d(1-T)$$

### The Fisher formula

$$(1+i) = (1+r)(1+h)$$

### Purchasing power parity and interest rate parity

$$s_1 = S_o x \frac{(1+h_c)}{(1+h_b)} \qquad f_0 = s_o x \frac{(1+i_c)}{(1+i_b)}$$

| The Black-Scholes option pricing model | The forex modified Black-Scholes option pricing model |
|---|---|
| $c = P_a N(d_1) - P_e N(d_2) e^{-rt}$ <br><br> Where: <br><br> $d_1 = \dfrac{\ln(P_a/P_e) + (r + 0.5s^2)t}{s\sqrt{t}}$ <br><br> $d_2 = d_1 - s\sqrt{t}$ | $c = e^{-rt}\left[F_0 N(d_1) - X N(d_2)\right]$ <br><br> Or <br><br> $p = e^{-rt}\left[X N(-d_2) - F_0 N(-d_1)\right]$ <br><br> Where: <br><br> $d_1 = \dfrac{\ln(F_0/X) + s^2 T/2}{s\sqrt{T}}$ <br><br> and <br><br> $d_2 = d_1 - s\sqrt{T}$ |

The Put Call Parity relationship

$$p = c - P_a + P_e e^{-rt}$$

MIRR equation

$$MIRR = \left[\frac{PV_R}{PV_I}\right]^{\frac{1}{n}} (1 + r_e) - 1$$

KAPLAN PUBLISHING

# Present value table

Present value of 1 i.e. $(1 + r)^{-n}$

Where  r = discount rate
       n = number of periods until payment

### Discount rate (r)

| Periods (n) | 1% | 2% | 3% | 4% | 5% | 6% | 7% | 8% | 9% | 10% | |
|---|---|---|---|---|---|---|---|---|---|---|---|
| 1 | 0.990 | 0.980 | 0.971 | 0.962 | 0.952 | 0.943 | 0.935 | 0.926 | 0.917 | 0.909 | 1 |
| 2 | 0.980 | 0.961 | 0.943 | 0.925 | 0.907 | 0.890 | 0.873 | 0.857 | 0.842 | 0.826 | 2 |
| 3 | 0.971 | 0.942 | 0.915 | 0.889 | 0.864 | 0.840 | 0.816 | 0.794 | 0.772 | 0.751 | 3 |
| 4 | 0.961 | 0.924 | 0.888 | 0.855 | 0.823 | 0.792 | 0.763 | 0.735 | 0.708 | 0.683 | 4 |
| 5 | 0.951 | 0.906 | 0.863 | 0.822 | 0.784 | 0.747 | 0.713 | 0.681 | 0.650 | 0.621 | 5 |
| 6 | 0.942 | 0.888 | 0.837 | 0.790 | 0.746 | 0.705 | 0.666 | 0.630 | 0.596 | 0.564 | 6 |
| 7 | 0.933 | 0.871 | 0.813 | 0.760 | 0.711 | 0.665 | 0.623 | 0.583 | 0.547 | 0.513 | 7 |
| 8 | 0.923 | 0.853 | 0.789 | 0.731 | 0.677 | 0.627 | 0.582 | 0.540 | 0.502 | 0.467 | 8 |
| 9 | 0.914 | 0.837 | 0.766 | 0.703 | 0.645 | 0.592 | 0.544 | 0.500 | 0.460 | 0.424 | 9 |
| 10 | 0.905 | 0.820 | 0.744 | 0.676 | 0.614 | 0.558 | 0.508 | 0.463 | 0.422 | 0.386 | 10 |
| 11 | 0.896 | 0.804 | 0.722 | 0.650 | 0.585 | 0.527 | 0.475 | 0.429 | 0.388 | 0.350 | 11 |
| 12 | 0.887 | 0.788 | 0.701 | 0.625 | 0.557 | 0.497 | 0.444 | 0.397 | 0.356 | 0.319 | 12 |
| 13 | 0.879 | 0.773 | 0.681 | 0.601 | 0.530 | 0.469 | 0.415 | 0.368 | 0.326 | 0.290 | 13 |
| 14 | 0.870 | 0.758 | 0.661 | 0.577 | 0.505 | 0.442 | 0.388 | 0.340 | 0.299 | 0.263 | 14 |
| 15 | 0.861 | 0.743 | 0.642 | 0.555 | 0.481 | 0.417 | 0.362 | 0.315 | 0.275 | 0.239 | 15 |

| (n) | 11% | 12% | 13% | 14% | 15% | 16% | 17% | 18% | 19% | 20% | |
|---|---|---|---|---|---|---|---|---|---|---|---|
| 1 | 0.901 | 0.893 | 0.885 | 0.877 | 0.870 | 0.862 | 0.855 | 0.847 | 0.840 | 0.833 | 1 |
| 2 | 0.812 | 0.797 | 0.783 | 0.769 | 0.756 | 0.743 | 0.731 | 0.718 | 0.706 | 0.694 | 2 |
| 3 | 0.731 | 0.712 | 0.693 | 0.675 | 0.658 | 0.641 | 0.624 | 0.609 | 0.593 | 0.579 | 3 |
| 4 | 0.659 | 0.636 | 0.613 | 0.592 | 0.572 | 0.552 | 0.534 | 0.516 | 0.499 | 0.482 | 4 |
| 5 | 0.593 | 0.567 | 0.543 | 0.519 | 0.497 | 0.476 | 0.456 | 0.437 | 0.419 | 0.402 | 5 |
| 6 | 0.535 | 0.507 | 0.480 | 0.456 | 0.432 | 0.410 | 0.390 | 0.370 | 0.352 | 0.335 | 6 |
| 7 | 0.482 | 0.452 | 0.425 | 0.400 | 0.376 | 0.354 | 0.333 | 0.314 | 0.296 | 0.279 | 7 |
| 8 | 0.434 | 0.404 | 0.376 | 0.351 | 0.327 | 0.305 | 0.285 | 0.266 | 0.249 | 0.233 | 8 |
| 9 | 0.391 | 0.361 | 0.333 | 0.308 | 0.284 | 0.263 | 0.243 | 0.225 | 0.209 | 0.194 | 9 |
| 10 | 0.352 | 0.322 | 0.295 | 0.270 | 0.247 | 0.227 | 0.208 | 0.191 | 0.176 | 0.162 | 10 |
| 11 | 0.317 | 0.287 | 0.261 | 0.237 | 0.215 | 0.195 | 0.178 | 0.162 | 0.148 | 0.135 | 11 |
| 12 | 0.286 | 0.257 | 0.231 | 0.208 | 0.187 | 0.168 | 0.152 | 0.137 | 0.124 | 0.112 | 12 |
| 13 | 0.258 | 0.229 | 0.204 | 0.182 | 0.163 | 0.145 | 0.130 | 0.116 | 0.104 | 0.093 | 13 |
| 14 | 0.232 | 0.205 | 0.181 | 0.160 | 0.141 | 0.125 | 0.111 | 0.099 | 0.088 | 0.078 | 14 |
| 15 | 0.209 | 0.183 | 0.160 | 0.140 | 0.123 | 0.108 | 0.095 | 0.084 | 0.074 | 0.065 | 15 |

## Annuity table

Present value of an annuity of 1 i.e.

$$\frac{1 - (1 + r)^{-n}}{r}$$

Where   r = discount rate and  n = number of periods until payment

*Discount rate (r)*

| Periods (n) | 1% | 2% | 3% | 4% | 5% | 6% | 7% | 8% | 9% | 10% | |
|---|---|---|---|---|---|---|---|---|---|---|---|
| 1 | 0.990 | 0.980 | 0.971 | 0.962 | 0.952 | 0.943 | 0.935 | 0.926 | 0.917 | 0.909 | 1 |
| 2 | 1.970 | 1.942 | 1.913 | 1.886 | 1.859 | 1.833 | 1.808 | 1.783 | 1.759 | 1.736 | 2 |
| 3 | 2.941 | 2.884 | 2.829 | 2.775 | 2.723 | 2.673 | 2.624 | 2.577 | 2.531 | 2.487 | 3 |
| 4 | 3.902 | 3.808 | 3.717 | 3.630 | 3.546 | 3.465 | 3.387 | 3.312 | 3.240 | 3.170 | 4 |
| 5 | 4.853 | 4.713 | 4.580 | 4.452 | 4.329 | 4.212 | 4.100 | 3.993 | 3.890 | 3.791 | 5 |
| 6 | 5.795 | 5.601 | 5.417 | 5.242 | 5.076 | 4.917 | 4.767 | 4.623 | 4.486 | 4.355 | 6 |
| 7 | 6.728 | 6.472 | 6.230 | 6.002 | 5.786 | 5.582 | 5.389 | 5.206 | 5.033 | 4.868 | 7 |
| 8 | 7.652 | 7.325 | 7.020 | 6.733 | 6.463 | 6.210 | 5.971 | 5.747 | 5.535 | 5.335 | 8 |
| 9 | 8.566 | 8.162 | 7.786 | 7.435 | 7.108 | 6.802 | 6.515 | 6.247 | 5.995 | 5.759 | 9 |
| 10 | 9.471 | 8.983 | 8.530 | 8.111 | 7.722 | 7.360 | 7.024 | 6.710 | 6.418 | 6.145 | 10 |
| 11 | 10.37 | 9.787 | 9.253 | 8.760 | 8.306 | 7.887 | 7.499 | 7.139 | 6.805 | 6.495 | 11 |
| 12 | 11.36 | 10.58 | 9.954 | 9.385 | 8.863 | 8.384 | 7.943 | 7.536 | 7.161 | 6.814 | 12 |
| 13 | 12.13 | 11.35 | 10.63 | 9.986 | 9.394 | 8.853 | 8.358 | 7.904 | 7.487 | 7.103 | 13 |
| 14 | 13.00 | 12.11 | 11.30 | 10.56 | 9.899 | 9.295 | 8.745 | 8.244 | 7.786 | 7.367 | 14 |
| 15 | 13.87 | 12.85 | 11.94 | 11.12 | 10.38 | 9.712 | 9.108 | 8.559 | 8.061 | 7.606 | 15 |

| (n) | 11% | 12% | 13% | 14% | 15% | 16% | 17% | 18% | 19% | 20% | |
|---|---|---|---|---|---|---|---|---|---|---|---|
| 1 | 0.901 | 0.893 | 0.885 | 0.877 | 0.870 | 0.862 | 0.855 | 0.847 | 0.840 | 0.833 | 1 |
| 2 | 1.713 | 1.690 | 1.668 | 1.647 | 1.626 | 1.605 | 1.585 | 1.566 | 1.547 | 1.528 | 2 |
| 3 | 2.444 | 2.402 | 2.361 | 2.322 | 2.283 | 2.246 | 2.210 | 2.174 | 2.140 | 2.106 | 3 |
| 4 | 3.102 | 3.037 | 2.974 | 2.914 | 2.855 | 2.798 | 2.743 | 2.690 | 2.639 | 2.589 | 4 |
| 5 | 3.696 | 3.605 | 3.517 | 3.433 | 3.352 | 3.274 | 3.199 | 3.127 | 3.058 | 2.991 | 5 |
| 6 | 4.231 | 4.111 | 3.998 | 3.889 | 3.784 | 3.685 | 3.589 | 3.498 | 3.410 | 3.326 | 6 |
| 7 | 4.712 | 4.654 | 4.423 | 4.288 | 4.160 | 4.039 | 3.922 | 3.812 | 3.706 | 3.605 | 7 |
| 8 | 5.146 | 4.968 | 4.799 | 4.639 | 4.487 | 4.344 | 4.207 | 4.078 | 3.954 | 3.837 | 8 |
| 9 | 5.537 | 5.328 | 5.132 | 4.946 | 4.772 | 4.607 | 4.451 | 4.303 | 4.163 | 4.032 | 9 |
| 10 | 5.889 | 5.650 | 5.426 | 5.216 | 5.019 | 4.833 | 4.659 | 4.494 | 4.339 | 4.192 | 10 |
| 11 | 6.207 | 5.938 | 5.687 | 5.453 | 5.234 | 5.029 | 4.836 | 4.656 | 4.486 | 4.327 | 11 |
| 12 | 6.492 | 6.194 | 5.918 | 5.660 | 5.421 | 5.197 | 4.988 | 4.793 | 4.611 | 4.439 | 12 |
| 13 | 6.750 | 6.424 | 6.122 | 5.842 | 5.583 | 5.342 | 5.118 | 4.910 | 4.715 | 4.533 | 13 |
| 14 | 6.982 | 6.628 | 6.302 | 6.002 | 5.724 | 5.468 | 5.229 | 5.008 | 4.802 | 4.611 | 14 |
| 15 | 7.191 | 6.811 | 6.462 | 6.142 | 5.847 | 5.575 | 5.324 | 5.092 | 4.876 | 4.675 | 15 |

## Standard normal distribution table

| | 0.00 | 0.01 | 0.02 | 0.03 | 0.04 | 0.05 | 0.06 | 0.07 | 0.08 | 0.09 |
|---|---|---|---|---|---|---|---|---|---|---|
| **0.0** | 0.0000 | 0.0040 | 0.0080 | 0.0120 | 0.0160 | 0.0199 | 0.0239 | 0.0279 | 0.0319 | 0.0359 |
| **0.1** | 0.0398 | 0.0438 | 0.0478 | 0.0517 | 0.0557 | 0.0596 | 0.0636 | 0.0675 | 0.0714 | 0.0753 |
| **0.2** | 0.0793 | 0.0832 | 0.0871 | 0.0910 | 0.0948 | 0.0987 | 0.1026 | 0.1064 | 0.1103 | 0.1141 |
| **0.3** | 0.1179 | 0.1217 | 0.1255 | 0.1293 | 0.1331 | 0.1368 | 0.1406 | 0.1443 | 0.1480 | 0.1517 |
| **0.4** | 0.1554 | 0.1591 | 0.1628 | 0.1664 | 0.1700 | 0.1736 | 0.1772 | 0.1808 | 0.1844 | 0.1879 |
| **0.5** | 0.1915 | 0.1950 | 0.1985 | 0.2019 | 0.2054 | 0.2088 | 0.2123 | 0.2157 | 0.2190 | 0.2224 |
| **0.6** | 0.2257 | 0.2291 | 0.2324 | 0.2357 | 0.2389 | 0.2422 | 0.2454 | 0.2486 | 0.2517 | 0.2549 |
| **0.7** | 0.2580 | 0.2611 | 0.2642 | 0.2673 | 0.2703 | 0.2734 | 0.2764 | 0.2794 | 0.2823 | 0.2852 |
| **0.8** | 0.2881 | 0.2910 | 0.2939 | 0.2967 | 0.2995 | 0.3023 | 0.3051 | 0.3078 | 0.3106 | 0.3133 |
| **0.9** | 0.3159 | 0.3186 | 0.3212 | 0.3238 | 0.3264 | 0.3289 | 0.3315 | 0.3340 | 0.3365 | 0.3389 |
| **1.0** | 0.3413 | 0.3438 | 0.3461 | 0.3485 | 0.3508 | 0.3531 | 0.3554 | 0.3577 | 0.3599 | 0.3621 |
| **1.1** | 0.3643 | 0.3665 | 0.3686 | 0.3708 | 0.3729 | 0.3749 | 0.3770 | 0.3790 | 0.3810 | 0.3830 |
| **1.2** | 0.3849 | 0.3869 | 0.3888 | 0.3907 | 0.3925 | 0.3944 | 0.3962 | 0.3980 | 0.3997 | 0.4015 |
| **1.3** | 0.4032 | 0.4049 | 0.4066 | 0.4082 | 0.4099 | 0.4115 | 0.4131 | 0.4147 | 0.4162 | 0.4177 |
| **1.4** | 0.4192 | 0.4207 | 0.4222 | 0.4236 | 0.4251 | 0.4265 | 0.4279 | 0.4292 | 0.4306 | 0.4319 |
| **1.5** | 0.4332 | 0.4345 | 0.4357 | 0.4370 | 0.4382 | 0.4394 | 0.4406 | 0.4418 | 0.4429 | 0.4441 |
| **1.6** | 0.4452 | 0.4463 | 0.4474 | 0.4484 | 0.4495 | 0.4505 | 0.4515 | 0.4525 | 0.4535 | 0.4545 |
| **1.7** | 0.4554 | 0.4564 | 0.4573 | 0.4582 | 0.4591 | 0.4599 | 0.4608 | 0.4616 | 0.4625 | 0.4633 |
| **1.8** | 0.4641 | 0.4649 | 0.4656 | 0.4664 | 0.4671 | 0.4678 | 0.4686 | 0.4693 | 0.4699 | 0.4706 |
| **1.9** | 0.4713 | 0.4719 | 0.4726 | 0.4732 | 0.4738 | 0.4744 | 0.4750 | 0.4756 | 0.4761 | 0.4767 |
| **2.0** | 0.4772 | 0.4778 | 0.4783 | 0.4788 | 0.4793 | 0.4798 | 0.4803 | 0.4808 | 0.4812 | 0.4817 |
| **2.1** | 0.4821 | 0.4826 | 0.4830 | 0.4834 | 0.4838 | 0.4842 | 0.4846 | 0.4850 | 0.4854 | 0.4857 |
| **2.2** | 0.4861 | 0.4864 | 0.4868 | 0.4871 | 0.4875 | 0.4878 | 0.4881 | 0.4884 | 0.4887 | 0.4890 |
| **2.3** | 0.4893 | 0.4896 | 0.4898 | 0.4901 | 0.4904 | 0.4906 | 0.4909 | 0.4911 | 0.4913 | 0.4916 |
| **2.4** | 0.4918 | 0.4920 | 0.4922 | 0.4925 | 0.4927 | 0.4929 | 0.4931 | 0.4932 | 0.4934 | 0.4936 |
| **2.5** | 0.4938 | 0.4940 | 0.4941 | 0.4943 | 0.4945 | 0.4946 | 0.4948 | 0.4949 | 0.4951 | 0.4952 |
| **2.6** | 0.4953 | 0.4955 | 0.4956 | 0.4957 | 0.4959 | 0.4960 | 0.4961 | 0.4962 | 0.4963 | 0.4964 |
| **2.7** | 0.4965 | 0.4966 | 0.4967 | 0.4968 | 0.4969 | 0.4970 | 0.4971 | 0.4972 | 0.4973 | 0.4974 |
| **2.8** | 0.4974 | 0.4975 | 0.4976 | 0.4977 | 0.4977 | 0.4978 | 0.4979 | 0.4979 | 0.4980 | 0.4981 |
| **2.9** | 0.4981 | 0.4982 | 0.4982 | 0.4983 | 0.4984 | 0.4984 | 0.4985 | 0.4985 | 0.4986 | 0.4986 |
| **3.0** | 0.4987 | 0.4987 | 0.4987 | 0.4988 | 0.4988 | 0.4989 | 0.4989 | 0.4989 | 0.4990 | 0.4990 |

This table can be used to calculate $N(d_i)$, the cumulative normal distribution functions needed for the Black-Scholes model of option pricing. If $d_i > 0$, add 0.5 to the relevant number above. If $d_i < 0$, subtract the relevant number above from 0.5.

# The role and responsibility of the financial manager

## Chapter learning objectives

Upon completion of this chapter you will be able to:

- describe the relationship between strategy development and the goals and policies of a firm

- explain the role and responsibility of senior financial executives/advisors with regard to strategy development

- identify and explain a firm's reasons and objectives for developing a policy with regard to investment selection and capital resource allocation

- identify and explain the goal of minimising a firm's cost of capital

- identify and explain the reasons and objectives for developing a distribution and retention policy

- identify and explain the reasons and objectives for communicating financial policy and corporate goals to external stakeholders

- identify and explain the reasons and objectives for communicating financial policy and corporate goals to internal stakeholders

- explain the purpose of financial planning and control as part of financial policy

- explain the reasons and objectives for developing a policy with regard to risk management

- advise the board of directors in a scenario on the setting the financial goals of the business and in its financial policy development

- explain the importance of using financial resources in an efficient, effective and transparent manner and the role of senior financial executives in recommending to management strategies to achieve it.

- explain the ways in which the behaviour of those charged with corporate governance may give rise to a conflict of interest with stakeholders

- identify the potential conflicts between stakeholders and those charged with corporate governance in a specific scenario

- identify, explain and recommend the alternative approaches that may be adopted to resolve the conflicts of interests between those charged with governance and stakeholders

- describe, compare and contrast the emerging governance structures and policies in the UK, the US and Europe, with respect to corporate governance in general and the role of the financial manager in particular

- list and define the ethical principles governing members of the association

- explain the importance of establishing an ethical financial policy for the financial management of the firm (incorporating the ethical principles of the association and the principles of good corporate governance) and describe the role and responsibility of senior financial executives/advisors with regard to its development

- describe the ways in which the ethical framework of a firm could be undermined by agency effects and/or stakeholder conflicts

- identify and analyse the areas in a scenario where the ethical framework of the firm may be undermined by agency effects and/or stakeholder conflicts and recommend strategies for dealing with them

- identify and explain the ethical issues which may arise within business issues and decisions of a firm in a scenario question

- advise a firm, in a scenario question, on the best ethical practice in its financial management

- explain the interconnectedness of the ethics of good business practice between all of the functional areas of the firm

- recommend, in a scenario question, an ethical framework for the development of a firm's financial policies and a system for the assessment of their ethical impact upon the financial management of the firm

- analyse the potential impact of the following on corporate objectives and governance

    - of sustainability and environmental risk issues
    - the carbon-trading economy and emissions
    - environmental audits and the triple bottom line approach.

## 1 Key roles and responsibilities of the financial manager

The financial manager is responsible for making decisions which will increase the wealth of the company's shareholders.

The specific areas of responsibility are listed below.

However, it is also important that the financial manager considers the impact of his role on the other stakeholders of the firm.

You may be asked in the exam to assess the

- strategic impact
- financial impact
- regulatory impact
- ethical impact
- environmental impact

of a financial manager's decisions.

### Expandable Text - Link between strategy & financial mgr's role

You will remember from your earlier studies that the process of strategy selection starts with the development of a mission statement. A mission statement:

- is the overriding purpose of the firm
- guides and directs all decisions taken.

The mission is then broken down into broad-based goals, and then further, into detailed objectives. Strategies can then be developed to bridge the gap between current forecast performance and the targets set.

### Policy framework

The mission will also provide the basis for the development of a **policy framework**.

The purpose of this framework is:

- to govern the way in which decisions are taken, and
- specify the criteria to be considered in the evaluation of any potential strategy.

At a broad level, this framework will incorporate guidance on issues such as:

### Ethics and social responsibility

A consideration of the role of business in society. It covers responsibilities towards society as a whole, the extent to which the company should fulfil or exceed its legal obligations towards stakeholders and the behaviour expected of individuals within the firm itself.

### Stakeholder protection

The extent to which the needs and wishes of individual stakeholders are incorporated into decisions and the development of a framework to ensure their needs are met and their rights upheld.

### Corporate governance

The system by which companies are directed and controlled, including issues of risk management.

### Sustainable development

Ensuring that projects and developments that meet the needs of the present, do not compromise the ability of future generations to meet their own needs.

This guidance is often formulated as a general principle:

e.g. all suppliers used must demonstrate commitment to employee welfare,

but may also form the basis for the generation of specific targets:

e.g. increase by 10% the amount of raw materials sourced locally in the next 12 months.

### Financial policy

Policies will also be developed to govern decisions within each operational area of the business. These policies specify generally applicable processes or procedures to be followed when decisions are being made, or state one overarching principle which the sets the boundaries for all decisions taken.

For example, within the finance function, policies will be developed over areas such as:

- investment selection
- overall cost of finance
- distribution and retentions
- communication with stakeholders
- financial planning and control
- risk management
- efficient and effective use of resources.

## Key areas of responsibility for the financial manager

The main roles and responsibilities of the financial manager can be summarised by the following headings:

- investment selection and capital resource allocation
- raising finance and minimising the cost of capital
- distribution and retentions
- communication with stakeholders
- financial planning and control
- risk management
- efficient and effective use of resources.

The Advanced Financial Management syllabus (and the rest of this Text) covers these areas in detail. This chapter gives a brief introduction to each of them.

## Investment selection and capital resource allocation

The primary goal of a company should be the maximisation of shareholder wealth, but any number of stakeholders may have views on the objectives a company should pursue.

Therefore, key policy decisions need to be made:

- How to incorporate ethical issues, such as minimising potential pollution or refusal to trade with unacceptable regimes, into the investment appraisal process?

- What method of investment appraisal should be used?
    - NPV?
    - IRR?

- In times of capital rationing, how are competing projects to be evaluated?
    - use of theoretical methods
    - incorporation of non-financial factors such as:

    (1) closeness of match to objectives

    (2) degree to which all goals will be achieved.

- As markets are not truly efficient, and investors treat earnings and dividend announcements as new information, to what extent should the impact on, for example:
    - ROCE
    - EPS
    - DPS

    be considered when evaluating a project?

### Expandable Text - More on investment selection

### Incorporation of corporate policy issues

If for example, a decision has been taken to pay a 'fair' wage to all employees regardless of the legal minimum requirement in the country where the business is operating, this rule must be applied to the wages figure used in any project evaluation.

The financial executive must be aware of the policy requirement and ensure that sufficient research is carried out in advance that the correct figure is used.

### Methods of investment appraisal

Assuming that the discounted cash flow techniques are preferred over Payback and ARR (which do not assure the maximisation of shareholder wealth), it is still necessary to designate which of the DCF methods is to be applied. Although NPV is theoretically superior, it is not as well liked by non-financial managers. IRR as a percentage is deemed clearer and simpler (although the point could be argued!). It is for the senior financial executive to decide on a method and ensure it is applied correctly.

## Capital rationing

The rule for an NPV evaluation states that all projects with a positive NPV should be accepted. However, this presupposes no limits on the available funds. Where restrictions exist, theoretical models can be applied:

- Shortages in one period only – use limiting factor analysis (covered in Paper F9).
- Shortages in multiple periods – see chapter 6

However, these methods do not build in evaluation of non-financial factors such as how well each strategy will meet the objectives set and practical difficulties that might be encountered along the way.

Forms of evaluation such as Cost Benefit Analysis and Weighted Benefit Scoring can be used where these factors are significant. These methods, pioneered by the public sector where such problems are commonplace, include techniques to assign money values to non-financial factors and to weight subjective factors against each other. Detailed knowledge of such methods is outside the syllabus.

## Earning and dividend measures

Even where improving shareholder wealth is the primary concern of the financial executive, the impact of the investment decisions on the reported position and perceived performance of the firm cannot be ignored. In an imperfect market, the earnings of a company and the dividends paid, are treated as relevant information for evaluating a company's worth and may impact the share price. Yet it is the share price that the executive is trying to improve.

## Raising finance and minimising the cost of capital

A key aspect of financial management is the raising of funds to finance existing and new investments. As with investment decisions, the main objective with raising finance is assumed to be the maximisation of shareholder wealth.

The following issues thus need to be considered when setting criteria for future finance and deciding policies:

- Is the firm at its optimal gearing level with associated minimum cost of capital?
- What gearing level is required?
- What sources of finance are available?

- Tax implications.
- The risk profile of investors and management.
- Restrictions such as debt covenants.
- Implications for key ratios.

## Distribution and retention policy

When deciding how much cash to distribute to shareholders, the company directors must keep in mind that the firm's objective is to maximise shareholder value:

- Shareholder value arises from the current value of the shares which in turn is derived from the cash flows from investment decisions taken by the company's management.
- Retained earnings are a significant source of finance for companies and therefore directors need to ensure that a balance is struck:
  - Paying out too much may require alternative finance to be found to finance any capital expenditure or working capital requirements.
  - Paying out too little may fail to give shareholders their required income levels.
- The dividend payout policy, therefore, should be based on investor preferences for cash dividends now or capital gains in future from enhanced share value resultant from re-investment into projects with a positive NPV.

It is the task of the financial manager to decide on the appropriate policy for determining distributions and retentions.

## Communication with stakeholders

A vital role for those running a company is to keep both external and internal stakeholders informed of all significant matters.

## External stakeholders

External stakeholders to be kept informed would include:

- shareholders
- government
- suppliers
- customers
- community at large.

## Internal stakeholders

Corporate goals and financial policies must be communicated to all those involved within the organisation, whether at a senior level or in operational positions.

- managers/directors
- employees.

### Test your understanding 1

**Suggest reasons why it would be important to keep each of the above stakeholders informed of general corporate goals and intentions.**

In addition to information about corporate goals, key matters of financial policy will also need to be communicated to stakeholders:

- Shareholders will need information about:
    - dividend policy
    - expected returns on new investment projects
    - gearing levels
    - risk profile.

- Suppliers and customers will need information about:
    - payment policies
    - pricing policies.

## Financial planning and control

Financial planning and control is the main role of the management accountant within a company.

The senior financial executive will need to oversee the development of policies to govern the way in which the process is carried out.

KAPLAN PUBLISHING

Policies will be needed over areas such as:

- the planning process
- business plans
- budget setting
- monitoring and correcting activities
- evaluating performance.

## The management of risk

One of the key matters to consider when developing a financial policy framework is the way risk and risk management is to be incorporated into the decision making process.

A number of policy decisions must be made:

- What is the firm's appetite for risk?
- How should risk be monitored?
- How should risk be dealt with?

A major part of the P4 syllabus involves the choice and use of many alternative methods and products to manage risk exposure.

### Expandable Text - More detail on risk management

**Appetite for risk**

Shareholders will invest in companies with a risk profile that matches that required for their portfolio. Management should be wary of altering the risk profile of the business without shareholder support. An increase in risk will bring about an increase in the required return and may lead to current shareholders selling their shares and so depressing the share price.

Inevitably management will have their own attitude to risk. Unlike the well-diversified shareholders, the directors are likely to be heavily dependent on the success of the company for their own financial stability and be more risk averse as a consequence.

### Monitoring risk

The essence of risk is that the returns are uncertain. As time passes, so the various uncertain events on which the forecasts are based will occur. Management must monitor the events as they unfold, reforecast predicted results and take action as necessary. The degree and frequency of the monitoring process will depend on the significance of the risk to the project's outcome.

### Dealing with risk

Risk can be either accepted or dealt with. Possible solutions for dealing with risk include:

- mitigating the risk – reducing it by setting in place control procedures

- hedging the risk – taking action to ensure a certain outcome

- diversification – reducing the impact of one outcome by having a portfolio of different ongoing projects.

Policy decisions about which methods are to be preferred should be made in advance of specific actions being required.

## Use of resources

It will be important to develop a framework to ensure all resources (inventory, labour and non-current assets as well as cash) are used to provide value for money. Spending must be:

- economic

- efficient

- effective

- transparent.

Performance measures can be developed in each area to set targets and allow for regular monitoring.

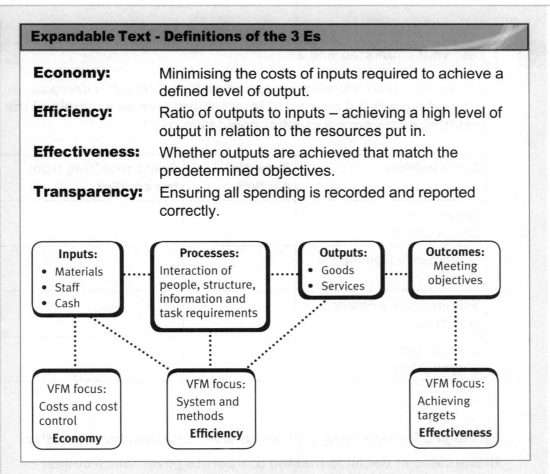

**Expandable Text - Definitions of the 3 Es**

**Economy:** Minimising the costs of inputs required to achieve a defined level of output.

**Efficiency:** Ratio of outputs to inputs – achieving a high level of output in relation to the resources put in.

**Effectiveness:** Whether outputs are achieved that match the predetermined objectives.

**Transparency:** Ensuring all spending is recorded and reported correctly.

## 2 Incorporating the interests of other stakeholders

We usually assume that the primary objective of a business is to maximise shareholder wealth.

However, a company is unlikely to be successful unless it also aims to satisfy the needs of its other stakeholders. The financial manager will have to identify potential conflicts between stakeholders' objectives and aim to resolve these conflicts.

## Test your understanding 2

For each of the following groups of stakeholders in a company, suggest a potential conflict of interest and give an example of the resulting costs such a conflict could give rise to.

| Stakeholders | Potential conflict | Costs resulting from the conflict |
|---|---|---|
| Employees v Shareholders | | |
| Customers v Community at large | | |
| Shareholders v Finance providers | | |
| Government v Shareholders | | |

## Strategies for managing conflict between stakeholders - practical

## Hierarchies of decision making (corporate governance codes)

In order to prevent abuse of decision-making power by the executive, control over decisions tends to be distributed between:

- the full board
- individual executive directors making operational decisions
- non-executive directors
  - audit committee
  - remuneration committee.
- shareholders in general meeting
- specific classes of shareholders where particular rights are concerned.

In addition, a company may elect to take some key decisions in consultation with the employees.

## Expandable Text - More on Corporate Governance

### The full board

Whilst for most operational matters, decisions may be taken by the appropriate functional director, matters of corporate policy, investment decisions over a certain limit, sensitive decisions etc. are likely to require the consent of the full board. This ensures that all salient factors are considered when the decision is taken.

### Non-executive directors

Whilst executive directors are employees involved in the day-to-day running of the business, non-executives are independent of the company, and appointed to monitor and challenge the executives as well as to advise and support them.

Removing decisions such as director remuneration and appointment from the remit of the executive, mitigates the likelihood of directors making self serving decisions contrary to the interests of other stakeholders.

In addition, creating an audit committee to provide an independent reporting line for internal auditors and external auditors alike, provides a safeguard for shareholders against potential cover-ups of poor management practices.

### Shareholders in general meeting

Legislation reserves for the shareholders certain key corporate decisions such as the appointment and removal of auditors and directors. When taking decisions, the directors will be aware that ignoring the wishes of the shareholders would put them at risk of removal. Shareholders may also use the company general meetings as an opportunity to express their concerns and remind the directors of their voting control.

### Specific classes of share

In order to protect the rights of non-voting shareholders such as those holding preference shares, it is common to allow them voting rights in particular circumstances such as where their dividend goes into arrears.

### The principles of corporate governance

Corporate governance is usually defined as 'the system by which companies are directed and controlled'. The concept encompasses issues of ethics, risk management and stakeholder protection.

The Organisation for Economic Cooperation and Development (OECD) issues specific guidelines for national legislation and regulation in the form of the Principles of Corporate Governance. These were explored in great depth in the P1 paper.

### Practical implications

The implications of the guidelines for companies in all countries are a need for the:

- Separation of the supervisory function and the management function.
- Transparency in the recruitment and remuneration of the board.
- Appointment of non-executive directors.
- Establishment of an audit committee.
- Establishment of risk control procedures to monitor strategic, business and operational activities.

However, different countries have adopted different techniques for dealing with these issues. A common distinction is made between:

- the **outsider system** developed in the US and the UK
- the **insider system** used in continental Europe and Japan.

The differences can be explained by the different economic environments in which they developed.

| | Anglo-American Model | European Model |
|---|---|---|
| Implications/impact | • gives priority to the interest of stakeholders<br>• pressure to deliver high returns to stakeholders<br>• relies on the market and outside investors for corporate control | • gives a higher priority to the interests of workers, managers, suppliers, customers, and the community<br>• management focused on stability of the firm and market growth, together with adequate profits<br>• uses a system of networks and committees to control the company |

KAPLAN PUBLISHING

| Governance Structures | • single **unitary** boards <br> • audit committees | • two-tier board system consisting of **management board** and **supervisory board** |
| --- | --- | --- |

## Implications for investment policy

The differing corporate governance structures above have practical implications for investment policy.

In the US/UK model the primary responsibility of management is to earn high returns for shareholders, therefore financial managers are more likely to:

- adopt new technologies
- consider high risk investments.

## Performance monitoring and evaluation systems

Managers are more likely to act in accordance with shareholders' wishes when their performance is regularly monitored and appraised against prescribed targets. To be of real value, the targets must be congruent with the maximisation of shareholder value.

### Test your understanding 3

**List ways in which management performance may be appraised and for each method consider the extent to which it is congruent with the maximisation of shareholder wealth.**

## Strategies for managing conflict between stakeholders - theoretical

### Methods of managing conflict (Thomas & Kilmann)

| | Uncooperative | Cooperative |
|---|---|---|
| **Assertive** | Competition | Collaboration |
| | | Compromise |
| **Unassertive** | Avoidance | Accommodation |

Desire to satisfy one's own concerns (vertical axis)

Desire to satisfy the concerns of others (horizontal axis)

### Expandable Text - More on Thomas & Kilmann

#### Competition

Involves stressing your position without considering opposing points of view.

This style is highly assertive with minimal cooperativeness; the goal is to win.

Useful when:

- action must be taken quickly
- the decision is necessary but will be unpopular
- the issue at hand is vital.

#### Avoidance

Involves failing to satisfy your concerns or the concerns of the other person.

This style is low assertiveness and low on cooperation. The goal is to delay.

Useful when:

- issues are of minor importance
- tensions need to be reduced

- to buy time. This is valuable where:
    - you need to enlist the support of others
    - the problem is symptomatic of a much larger issue which will need to be resolved first.

## Compromise

Involves finding a middle ground or forgoing some of your concerns and committing to other's concerns.

This style is moderately assertive and moderately cooperative; the goal is to find middle ground.

Useful when:

- issues are of moderate importance
- both parties are equally powerful and equally committed to opposing views
- the issue needs to be resolved promptly.

## Collaboration

Involves attempting to satisfy both sides.

It is highly assertive and highly cooperative; the goal is to find a 'win/win' solution.

Useful when:

- working in teams
- solutions must integrate a number of perspectives
- support and commitment is needed from all parties
- time is not a key priority.

## Accommodation

Involves foregoing your concerns in order to satisfy the concerns of others.

This style is low assertiveness and high cooperativeness; the goal is to yield.

Useful when:

*   need to demonstrate goodwill
*   issues are of low importance.

## Mapping stakeholders

**Mendelow's stakeholder mapping matrix**

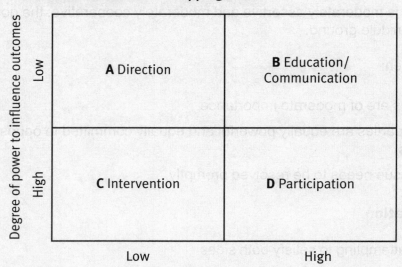

*Degree of power to influence outcomes* (Low / High)

| | | |
|---|---|---|
| | **A** Direction | **B** Education/ Communication |
| | **C** Intervention | **D** Participation |

Low — High
**Level of interest in the project**

### Expandable Text - More on Mendelow's matrix

**Box A – Direction**

**Suitable for:** Stakeholders who do not stand to lose or gain much from the project AND whose actions cannot affect the project's ability to meet its objectives.

They may require limited monitoring or informing of progress but are of low priority. They are unlikely to be the subject of project activities or involved in project management.

**Method:** Simply provide instructions as necessary. These stakeholders are likely to accept what they are told.

### Box B – Education and communication

**Suitable for:** Stakeholders who stand to lose or gain significantly from the project BUT whose actions cannot affect the project's ability to meet its objectives.

KAPLAN PUBLISHING

The project needs to ensure that their interests are fully represented. The positively disposed groups from this box may lobby others to support the strategy. In addition, if the strategy is presented as rational or inevitable to the dissenters, or a show of consultation gone through, this may stop them joining forces with more powerful dissenters in boxes C and D.

**Method:** Management should brief all groups on the reasonableness of project and of any provisions being made for those affected by the decisions. Advance notice will give each more time for adjustment.

### Box C – Intervention

**Suitable for:** Stakeholders whose actions can affect the project's ability to meet its objectives BUT who do not stand to lose or gain much from the project.

They may be a source of risk; means of monitoring and managing that risk should be explored. The key here is to keep the occupants satisfied to avoid them gaining interest and shifting into box D.

**Method:** Usually this is done by reassuring them of the likely outcomes of the strategy well in advance.

### Box D – Participation

Suitable for: Stakeholders who stand to lose or gain significantly from the project AND whose actions can affect the project's ability to meet its objectives.

These stakeholders can be major drivers of the change and major opponents of the strategy. The project needs to ensure that their interests are fully represented in the coalition. Overall impact of the project will require good relationships to be developed with these stakeholders.

**Method:** Initially there should be education/communication to assure them that the change is necessary, followed by discussion of how to implement it. Key stakeholders will be consulted throughout and will be part of the decision making process.

### Test your understanding 4

**For each of the scenarios below suggest the likely source of conflict and how such a conflict could have been avoided/could be resolved.**

(1)  The directors are keen to invest in new equipment for use in the production process to replace work currently done by hand.

(2)  The directors are considering a contract which will significantly increase the size of the company within just a few months.

(3)  The marketing director intends to run a month long TV campaign which will cost twice the allocated marketing budget.

## 3 The strategic impact of the financial manager's decisions

Strategic issues are those which impact the whole business in the long term.

Key strategic issues which may arise from decisions made by the financial manager are:

### Does the new investment project help to enhance the firm's competitive advantage?

For example, if the firm has traditionally competed on the basis of cost leadership, the financial manager needs to ensure that new projects maintain this position, and that any new finance is raised at the lowest possible cost.

### Fit with environment

A knowledge of the main Political, Economic, Social and Technological factors which impact the business will help the financial manager to identify likely opportunities.

### Use of resources

The financial manager should identify new investment opportunities which make the best use of the firm's key resources. Knowledge of the firm's current strengths (core competencies) and weaknesses is critical in assessing which new projects are most likely to be successful.

## Stakeholder reactions

As discussed above, it is critical that the views of all stakeholders are considered when financial management decisions are made. Theoretically, the directors have a primary objective to maximise shareholder wealth. However, decisions which appear to satisfy this requirement by ignoring other stakeholders' views in the short term can damage the firm's prospects for longer term shareholder wealth maximisation.

## Impact on risk

Investors will have been attracted to the firm because they deem its risk profile to be acceptable. Making decisions which change the overall risk of the firm may alienate shareholders and damage the firm's long term prospects.

## 4 The financial impact of the financial manager's decisions

It is common to assess the financial impact of a financial manager's decision by focussing on the likely Net Present Value (NPV) of investment projects undertaken. After all, the primary aim of a company is to maximise the wealth of its shareholders, and NPV represents the increase in shareholder wealth if a project is undertaken.

However, it is also important to consider the following issues:

## Likely impact on share price

In a perfect capital market, the NPV of the project would immediately be reflected in the company's share price. In the real world, unless the details of the project are communicated effectively to the market, the share price will not be impacted.

## Likely impact on financial statements

In theory, a positive NPV project should increase shareholder wealth. However, if the project has low (or negative) cashflows in the early years, the negative impact on the financial statements in the short term may give a negative signal to the market, thus causing the share price to fall.

## Impact on cost of capital

As discussed in detail elsewhere, raising new finance causes the firm's cost of capital to change. However, undertaking projects of different business risk from the firm's existing activities can also impact cost of capital. Projects will be more valuable when discounted at a low cost of capital, so the financial manager should avoid high risk projects unless it is felt that they are likely to deliver a high level of return.

### Test your understanding 5

The directors of Ribs Co, a listed company, are reviewing the company's current strategic position. The firm makes high quality garden tools which it sells in its domestic market but not abroad.

Over the last few years, the share price has risen significantly as the firm has expanded organically within its domestic market. Unfortunately, in the last 12 months, the influx of cheaper, foreign tools has adversely impacted the firm's profitability. Consequently, the share price has dropped sharply in recent weeks and the shareholders expressed their displeasure at the recent AGM.

The directors are evaluating two alternative investment projects which they hope will arrest the decline in profitability.

Project 1: This would involve closing the firm's domestic factory and switching production to a foreign country where labour rates are a quarter of those in the domestic market. Sales would continue to be targeted exclusively at the domestic market.

Project 2: This would involve a new investment in machinery at the domestic factory to allow production to be increased by 50%. The extra tools would be exported and sold as high quality tools in foreign market places.

Both projects have a positive Net Present Value (NPV) when discounted at the firm's current cost of capital.

**Discuss the strategic and financial issues that this case presents.**

### 5 The regulatory impact of the financial manager's decisions

The extent to which the financial manager's actions are scrutinised by regulators is determined by:

- the type of industry - some industries (in particular the privatised utility industries in the UK) are subject to high levels of regulation.

- whether the company is listed - listed companies are subject to high levels of scrutiny. The Regulator for Public Companies has the primary objective of ensuring clarity for all investors.

### The UK City Code

The City Code applies to takeovers in the UK. It stresses the vital importance of absolute secrecy before any takeover announcement is made. Once an announcement is made, the Code stipulates that the announcement should be as clear as possible, so that all shareholders (and potential shareholders) have equal access to information.

### 6 The ethical impact of the financial manager's decisions

Ethics, and the company's ethical framework, should provide a basis for all policy and decision making. The financial manager must consider whether an action is ethical at a:

- society level
- corporate level
- individual level.

---

### Expandable Text - Explanation of levels of ethics

#### Society level

The extent to which the wishes of all stakeholders both internal and external should be taken into account, even where there is no legal obligation to do so.

#### Corporate level

The extent to which companies should exceed legal obligations to stakeholders, and the approach they take to corporate governance and stakeholder conflict.

#### Individual level

The principles that the individuals running the company apply to their own actions and behaviours.

---

As key members of the decision-making executive, financial managers are responsible for ensuring that all the actions of the company for which they work:

- are ethical
- are grounded in good governance
- achieve the highest standards of probity.

In addition to general rules of ethics and governance, members of the ACCA have additional guidance to support their decision making.

### Expandable Text - ACCA Code of Ethics

### ACCA code of ethics

At an individual level, members of the ACCA are governed by a set of fundamental ethical principles. These principles are binding on all members and members review and agree to them each year when they renew their ACCA membership and submit their CPD return.

The fundamental principles are:

- integrity
- objectivity
- professional competence and due care
- confidentiality
- professional behaviour.

### Integrity

Members should be straightforward and honest in all professional and business relationships.

### Objectivity

Members should not allow bias, conflicts of interest or undue influence of others to override professional or business judgements.

### Professional competence and due care

Members have a continuing duty to maintain professional knowledge and skill at a level required to ensure that a client or employer receives competent professional service based on current developments in practice, legislation and techniques. Members should act diligently and in accordance with applicable technical and professional standards when providing professional services.

**Confidentiality**

Members should respect the confidentiality of information acquired as a result of professional and business relationships and should not disclose any such information to third parties without proper and specific authority or unless there is a legal or professional right or duty to disclose. Confidential information acquired as a result of professional and business relationships should not be used for the personal advantage of members or third parties.

**Professional behaviour**

Members should comply with relevant laws and regulations and should avoid any action that discredits the profession.

In working life, a financial manager may:

- have to deal with a conflict between stakeholders
- face a conflict between their position as agent and the needs of the shareholders for whom they act.

An ethical framework should provide a strategy for dealing with the situation.

### Ethical financial policy

All senior financial staff would be expected to sign up and adhere to an ethical financial policy framework. A typical code would cover matters such:

- acting in accordance with the ACCA principles
- disclosure of any possible conflicts of interest at the first possible opportunity to the appropriate company member
- ensuring full, fair, accurate, complete, objective, timely and understandable disclosure in all reports and documents that the company files
- ensuring all company financial practices concerning accounting, internal accounting controls and auditing matters meet the highest standards of professionalism, transparency and honesty
- complying with all internal policy all external rules and regulations
- responsible use and control of assets and other resources employed
- promotion of ethical behaviour among subordinates and peers and ensuring an atmosphere of continuing education and exchange of best practices.

## Assessing the ethical impact of decisions

Once a framework has been developed it is essential that all decisions are made in accordance with it.

This will involve:

- all employees explicitly signing up to the framework
- providing employees with guidelines to apply to ethical decisions
- offering resources for consultation in ethical dilemma
- ensuring unethical conduct can be reported without reprisal
- taking disciplinary action where violations have occured.

Guidelines for making ethical decisions often take the form of a series of questions which employees are encouraged to ask themselves before implementing a decision. For example:

- Have colleagues been properly consulted?
- Are actions legal and in compliance with professional standards?
- Is individual or company integrity being compromised?
- Are company values being upheld?
- Is the choice of action the most ethical one?
- If the decision were documented would a reviewer agree with the decision taken?

In addition to written ethical guidelines firms often provide employees with a list of people who can be consulted in the case of an ethical dilemma. For example:

- Line manager.
- Appointed quality and risk leaders.
- Firm legal team.
- Ethics hotline within the firm (obviously only in larger companies is this likely to be affordable).
- Professional hotline – the ACCA for example, provides its members with ethical advice and support, as do many other professional organisations.

### Test your understanding 6

Suggest ways in which ethical issues would influence the firm's financial policies in relation to the following:

- shareholders
- suppliers
- customers
- investment appraisal
- charity.

## 7 The environmental impact of the financial manager's decisions

In the last few years, the issue of sustainable development has taken on greater urgency as concerns about the long-term impact of business on the planet have grown.

The United Nations defines sustainable development as:

**Development that meets the needs of the present without compromising the ability of future generations to meet their own needs.**

The underlying principle for firms is that environmental, social and economic systems are interdependent and decisions must address all three concerns coherently.

In developing corporate policies and objectives, specific attention should be given to matters of sustainability and environmental risk.

### Expandable Text - Specific examples of environmental issues

#### Carbon-trading and emissions

Firms with high energy use may need to set objectives for their emissions of greenhouse gases in order to achieve targets set by governments under the Kyoto Protocol.

This may include:

- reducing emissions to reduce liability for energy taxes
- entering a carbon emissions trading scheme.

## The Kyoto Protocol

The Kyoto Protocol was negotiated by 160 nations in 1997. It is an attempt to limit national emissions of greenhouse gases in order to slow or halt an associated change of climate. The agreement sets emission targets for the individual nations. Australia, for instance, has agreed to limit its annual emission by the year 2012 to no more than 108% of its emission in 1990. For the world as a whole, the aim of the Protocol is to reduce the global emission of carbon dioxide to 5% below the 1990 value by the year 2012.

The Protocol was negotiated based on an economic mechanism of 'carbon trading' evolving; i.e. nations issuing permits for carbon emission, set to match the targets set by the Kyoto Protocol or its follow-on agreements. The permits, tradeable, both nationally and internationally, are intended to operate such that market forces ultimately replace government direction in the process of encouraging more efficient use of fossil fuel.

Individual companies will be able to decide whether to spend money on new 'carbon efficient' technology or on the acquisition of carbon credits from those industries or countries which have a surplus.

In the UK for example, there is a carbon emissions trading scheme, which was set up in 2002. Details are provided here only to provide a clear picture of how such a scheme works.

### The UK scheme

Organisations can enter the scheme directly, by volunteering to reduce emissions in return for a financial incentive provided by the government. They will be set emissions targets based on a formula. If they overachieve they can sell or bank the excess allowances. If they underachieve they must buy the allowances they need.

Some firms already have targets as a result of Climate Change Levy Agreements (CCLAs – see below) set up to help businesses with intensive energy use mitigate the effects of the UK energy tax. These firms can sell their surpluses or buy needed credits.

Other firms, even if they do not emit greenhouse gases, may set up an account to trade in the allowances.

The climate change levy is a tax on the use of energy in industry, commerce and the public sector, with offsetting cuts in employers' National Insurance Contributions – NICs – and additional support for energy efficiency schemes and renewable sources of energy. The levy forms a key part of the Government's overall Climate Change Programme.

## The role of an environment agency

Government environment agencies (in the UK – Defra – the Department for the environment, food and rural affairs) work to ensure that business meets the environmental targets set internationally. They set local business targets in key areas such as:

- energy conservation
- recycling
- protection of the countryside
- sustainable development

which will need to be taken into account when setting objectives for the business as a whole.

## Environmental audits and the triple bottom line approach

First coined in the mid-1990's, the phrase triple bottom line, refers to the need for companies to focus on the:

- economic value and
- environmental value and
- social value

both added and destroyed by the firm.

Providing stakeholders with corporate performance data in each of these areas is known as **triple bottom line reporting**.

In order to provide credible data, companies will need to:

- set up a suitable management system to capture the information
- ensure the reports are subject to an appropriate audit scrutiny.

## Triple bottom line reporting

A triple bottom line approach requires a shift in culture and focus, and the development of appropriate policies and objectives. It can also be used as a framework for measuring and reporting corporate performance.

Many leading companies are now publishing environmental and sustainability reports – demonstrating to stakeholders that they are addressing these issues.

In order to provide meaningful data, a business must be able to assess the environmental and social impact of their operations. One way to do this is to adopt the framework provided by ISO 14000. ISO 14000 is a series of international standards on environmental management. It provides a framework for the development of an environmental management system and a supporting audit programme.

Environmental auditing is a systematic, documented, periodic and objective process in assessing an organisation's activities and services in relation to:

- Assessing compliance with relevant statutory and internal requirements.

- Facilitating management control of environmental practices.

- Promoting good environmental management.

- Maintaining credibility with the public.

- Raising staff awareness and enforcing commitment to departmental environmental policy.

- Exploring improvement opportunities.

- Establishing the performance baseline for developing an Environmental Management System (EMS).

## 8 Chapter summary

**FINANCIAL STRATEGY DEVELOPMENT**

**Policy development**
- Mission
- Policy framework
- Financial policy
- Policy setting

**Policy issues**
- Investment selection
- Raising finance
- Dividend policy
- Communication
- Planning and control
- Risk management
- Use of resources

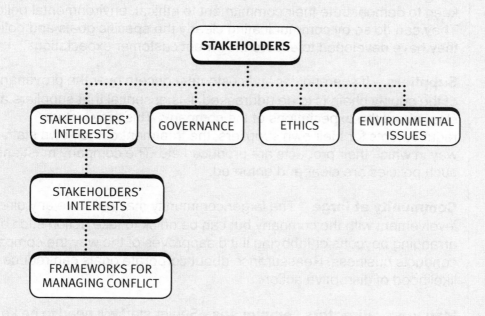

**STAKEHOLDERS**

STAKEHOLDERS' INTERESTS

GOVERNANCE

ETHICS

ENVIRONMENTAL ISSUES

STAKEHOLDERS' INTERESTS

FRAMEWORKS FOR MANAGING CONFLICT

## Test your understanding answers

### Test your understanding 1

**Shareholders** – The support of shareholders is necessary for the smooth running of the business. Actions from awkward questions at AGMs through to (in the worst case) a vote to remove the directors, are available to aggrieved shareholders. The goals set by a company should reflect their concerns as key stakeholders, and communication of them should reassure shareholders that the firm is acting as they would wish.

**Government** – Government targets and policies often include specific expectations of the business community. Keeping government departments informed of activities and consulting in key areas can help prevent later government intervention, or punitive action from regulators.

**Customers** – A business will struggle to continue without the support of its customers. Today, consumers are increasingly concerned about how the goods and services they buy are provided. Companies are therefore keen to demonstrate their commitment to ethical, environmental polices. They can do so by communicating clearly the specific goals and policies they have developed to ensure they meet customer expectations.

**Suppliers** – If shareholder and customer concern over the provenance of the supply chain is to be addressed, it is essential that suppliers are clear about the expectations of the company. This may include requirements for their own suppliers, the treatment of their own staff, the way in which their products are produced etc. The company must ensure such policies are clear and enforced.

**Community at large** – The larger community may not have any direct involvement with the company but can be quick to take action such as arranging boycotts or lobbying if it disapproves of the way the company conducts business. Reassurance about corporate goals can reduce the likelihood of disruptive action.

**Managers / directors / employees** - Senior staff will need to be kept fully up-to-date about all goals and policies set by the firm, so they can apply them when taking decisions. Explaining to employees why decisions are being taken can help to ensure co-operation in their implementation.

### Test your understanding 2

| Stakeholders | Potential conflict | Costs resulting from the conflict |
| --- | --- | --- |
| Employees v Shareholders | Employees may resist the introduction of automated processes which would improve efficiency but cost jobs. | Costs of strike or work to rule from employees. Costs of additional compensation to redundant staff. |
| | Shareholders may resist wage rises demanded by employees as uneconomical. | Costs of strikes etc. as above. Costs of reassuring shareholders – additional meetings for example. |
| Customers v Community at large | Customers may demand lower prices and greater choice, but in order to provide them a company may need to squeeze vulnerable suppliers or import products at great environmental cost. | Costs of overcoming negative publicity<br><br>Time spent renegotiating supplier contracts/sourcing new suppliers. |
| Shareholders v Finance providers | Shareholders may encourage management to pursue risky strategies in order to maximise potential returns, whereas finance providers prefer stable lower risk policies that ensure liquidity for the payment of debt interest. | Agency costs: loan covenants restricting further borrowing, dividend payouts, investment policy etc. |
| Government v Shareholders | Government will often insist upon levels of welfare (such as the minimum wage and Health and Safety practices) which would otherwise be avoided as an unnecessary expense. | Costs of complying with legislation. |

**N.B**. You may have come up with different suggestions. The point is to recognise that there are a huge range of potential conflicts of interest and each one results in additional costs for the business and therefore a reduction in returns to shareholders.

## Test your understanding 3

### Financial measures

Accounting ratios:

- EPS/ROCE/RI – both suffer from the same criticism – that earnings are not directly related to shareholder wealth and therefore may encourage non-goal congruent behaviour.

- DPS – is a measure of immediate improvement in wealth but must be looked at in conjunction with the company share price. Dividends may be reduced in order to invest in positive NPV projects, but in that case, the gain should be reflected in the share price.

- Economic value added – EVA is a more sophisticated method of residual income (registered as a trademark by Stern, Stewart & Co.), which more accurately measures improvements in shareholder wealth by adjusting the accounting data to eliminate much of the subjectivity and incorporating the company's WACC into the calculation.

Stock market figures:

- Share price – reflects the expectations of the investors. Is a direct measure of company success but is hard to link directly to directors' performance as it is affected by so many outside factors.

- PE ratio – as a multiple of share price over earnings it does reflect investors' view of the investment potential of the company but suffers from the same weakness as all other earnings related measures and is not easy to relate to directors activities.

### Shareholder value added

A calculation of the present value free cash flows, this method is a more accurate measure of improvements in shareholder wealth, but its complexity makes it of little use as a regular performance measure.

### Specific cost/revenue targets

A vast array of financial targets may be set around the levels of spending and investment, or around revenues earned. Care must be taken to ensure that the targets are achievable and within the control of the person being assessed. Particular attention must be paid to the interdependence of the various aspects of performance. If managers are incentivised to achieve a reduction in purchase spending for example, alternative measures must also confirm that quality is maintained.

### Non-financial measures

Balanced scorecard

Many businesses operate a balanced scorecard approach to management appraisal. This involves setting targets in all of those aspects of the business where success is necessary if positive NPVs are to be earned. In addition to financial targets, managers are measured on the satisfaction of customers, improvement of business practices and levels of innovation. Since achieving these targets should lead to improved project returns and greater cost efficiency, a balanced scorecard approach should lead to improved shareholder wealth.

Employee/satisfaction

In addition, some businesses specifically set management targets related to employee satisfaction ratings, or related targets such as absenteeism or staff turnover.

### Test your understanding 4

#### 1 – Conflict

Many directors will want to purchase the equipment to reduce costs – this should improve profits and potentially their own financial rewards if they are linked.

Employees (and possibly also) their unions may well resist the investment because of the associated job losses.

Customers may be unhappy if the quality of mass produced products is not as good as the hand made versions.

Marketing and sales directors may resist the change if they believe that quality will be undermined, and thereby revenue affected.

#### Solutions

Potential conflict my have been avoided if **reward packages** were linked to a range of measures (such as those used by the Balanced Scorecard Approach) ensuring directors considered quality, customer satisfaction and employee welfare in any decisions.

Equally employees could have been **consulted** in advance about any potential changes – perhaps at a works council meeting.

Management must consider whether the workforce is likely to take action such as strikes over the investment. The likelihood increases if they are unionised.

If they are unlikely to take any specific action then a campaign of **education and communication** may be sufficient. Management should explain to all the workers why the investment is being made and how they will deal with any job losses. Advance notice will give each more time for workers to adjust.

If the unions become involved, it may be necessary to reach a **compromise** solution to avoid wholesale disruption to the firm. This may involve phasing in the new equipment over a longer period or offering more generous redundancy packages than had been planned.

#### 2 – Conflict

Directors of large companies often earn better rewards packages than those of small ones so they are likely to support the change.

Employees should have more job opportunities and are likely to support the change.

Fast growth can be very expensive and put a strain on working capital – shareholders may be unhappy if returns are not sufficiently high. In addition, lenders may be concerned by the impact on key financial ratios.

## Solutions

Debt holders may well avoid later conflict by including **covenants** over gearing or other key ratios in the loan agreement.

Directors' **reward packages** will encourage goal congruence with shareholders if they are linked directly to shareholders' wealth.

Potentially high-risk strategies should be carefully evaluated as part of the **risk management** process required by good corporate governance. This should mean that any later concerns raised by shareholders can be answered.

The **audit committee** of non-executive directors may advise against the decision if they feel it would put too great a strain on resources.

Shareholders, although unlikely to get involved, could take action if they were sufficiently unhappy by threatening the directors with removal if they continue with the plan. This would be seen as a **competition** approach where a direct confrontation is taken.

## 3 – Conflict

A conflict may arise between the marketing director and the finance director over the allocation of resources since the proposed campaign exceeds the budget.

## Solutions

Decisions about spending over a certain limit may be referred to the **full board** for approval, to avoid conflict between individual directors.

If the matter is to be decided between the two directors, it would be better if they could **collaborate** to find a mutually satisfactory solution. It will be important to maintain a good working relationship and to set up a policy framework for such decisions in the future.

## Test your understanding 5

### Strategic issues

**Competitive advantage** - currently the firm is a differentiator (it competes on quality rather than cost). The new entrants into the market seem to be cost leaders. Undertaking Project 1 might reduce the quality of the Ribs Co tools and undermine the firm's long standing competitive advantage.

**Fit with environment** - clearly the environment has changed in the last 12 months. The new imports indicate that perhaps the economic environment has changed (movement in exchange rates? removal of import tariffs?), and also that customers are seemingly looking for cheaper tools (social factor). Ribs Co is right to try to find new projects which enable it to compete in this new environment.

**Stakeholder reactions** - the shareholders are not happy, so they will welcome the new projects (providing the directors communicate the positive NPV information effectively). However, other stakeholders are likely to be less impressed. For example, under Project 1 there are likely to be job cuts in the domestic market, so the employees, local community and domestic government are likely to be unhappy about this option. The directors must consider the long term consequences of upsetting these key stakeholders in the short term.

**Risk** - Project 2 appears to be the more risky option - it involves exporting goods into a foreign market where Ribs Co currently has no operations. There is no guarantee that the Ribs tools will be a success in the new market. However, there is huge potential under this option. Clearly the domestic market is becoming saturated, so perhaps now is the time for Ribs to seek out new opportunities abroad.

# Financial issues

**Positive NPVs** - both prospective projects have positive NPVs, so theoretically shareholder wealth should increase whichever is undertaken. However, the cash flow estimates need to be analysed and sensitivity analysis should be performed to see what changes in estimates can be tolerated.

**Impact on cost of capital** - Ribs Co's current cost of capital has been used for discounting the projects. However the change in risk (caused by the exposure to foreign factors in both projects) is likely to change the cost of capital.

**Financing** - both projects are likely to require significant short term capital expenditure. The directors will have to consider the size of investment required, and the firm's target gearing ratio, as they assess whether debt or equity funding should be sought.

## Test your understanding 6

Shareholders:

- Providing timely and accurate information to shareholders on the company's historical achievements and future prospects.

Suppliers:

- paying fair prices
- attempting to settle invoices promptly
- co-operating with suppliers to maintain and improve the quality of inputs
- not using or accepting bribery or excess hospitality as a means of securing contracts with suppliers.

Customers:

- charging fair prices
- offering fair payment terms
- honouring quantity and settlement discounts
- ensuring sufficient quality control process are built in that goods are fit for purpose.

Investment appraisal:

- payment of fair wages
- upholding obligations to protect, preserve and improve the environment
- only trading (both purchases and sales) with countries and companies that themselves have appropriate ethical frameworks.

Charity:

- Developing a policy on donations to educational and charitable institutions.

# Investment appraisal – DCF and the use of free cash flows

## Chapter learning objectives

Upon completion of this chapter you will be able to:

- define and calculate basic free cash flows for a specified capital investment project

- calculate free cash flows for a specified capital investment project incorporating general inflation and specific price variation

- calculate free cash flows for a specified capital investment project incorporating taxation and consider the potential impact of changes in tax rates

- prepare a basic linear programming formulation consisting of named variables, an objective function and a series of constraints

- define multi-period capital rationingprepare an NPV linear programming formulation to deal with a multi-period capital rationing problem

- interpret output provided resulting from a NPV linear programming formulation

- prepare a PV of dividends linear programming formulation to deal with a multi-period capital rationing problem

- interpret output provided resulting from an PV of dividends linear programming formulation

- calculate the economic return of a specified capital investment project by calculating the IRR

- use the IRR of a specified capital investment project to advise on a project's return margin

- calculate the economic return of a specified capital investment project by calculating the modified IRR

- forecast a firms' free cash flow and its free cash flow to equity (i.e. after deduction of debt interest and repayments and addition of new debt finance)

- calculate the dividend cover for a firm using free cash flows to equity and interpret the resultforecast a firms' terminal (or residual value) assuming cash flows are discounted in perpetuity with no growth

- forecast a firm's terminal (or residual value) assuming cash flows are discounted in perpetuity with growth

- forecast a firm's terminal (or residual value) assuming cash flows can be expressed as a lump sum using a PE ratio

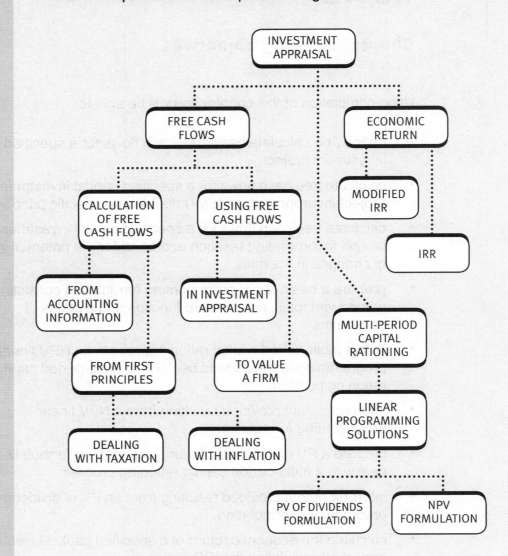

## 1 Free cash flows

Cash that is not retained and reinvested in the business is called free cash flow.

It represents cash flow available:

- to all the providers of capital of a company
- to pay dividends or finance additional capital projects.

### Uses of free cash flows

Free cash flows are used frequently in financial management:

- as a basis for evaluating potential investment projects using the NPV technique
- as an indicator of company performance
- to calculate the value of a firm and thus a potential share price.

### Calculating free cash flows for investment appraisal

Free cash flows can be calculated simply as:

Free cash flow = Revenue - Costs - Investments

The free cash flows used to evaluate investment projects are therefore essentially the **net relevant cash flows** you will recall from your earlier NPV studies. They are the net cash flows generated by the investment which are then discounted to find the project NPV.

## 2 Free cash flows and project appraisal

Capital investment projects are best evaluated using the net present value (NPV) technique. You should recall from earlier studies that this involved discounting the **relevant cash flows** for each year of the project at an appropriate cost of capital.

As mentioned above the net relevant cash flows associated with the project are the free cash flows it generates. The discounted free cash flows are totalled to provide the NPV of the project.

Some basic NPV concepts are revised as follows:

## Relevant costs and revenues

Relevant flows are those costs and revenues, which are:

- future
- incremental.

You should therefore ignore:

- sunk costs
- committed costs
- non-cash items
- apportioned overheads.

## Discounting

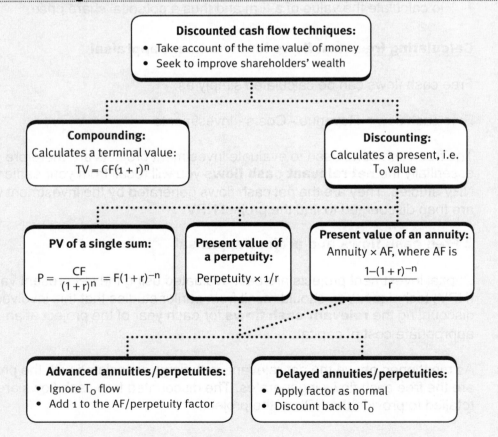

**Discounted cash flow techniques:**
- Take account of the time value of money
- Seek to improve shareholders' wealth

**Compounding:**
Calculates a terminal value:
$$TV = CF(1 + r)^n$$

**Discounting:**
Calculates a present, i.e. $T_0$ value

**PV of a single sum:**
$$P = \frac{CF}{(1 + r)^n} = F(1 + r)^{-n}$$

**Present value of a perpetuity:**
Perpetuity $\times 1/r$

**Present value of an annuity:**
Annuity $\times$ AF, where AF is
$$\frac{1-(1 + r)^{-n}}{r}$$

**Advanced annuities/perpetuities:**
- Ignore $T_0$ flow
- Add 1 to the AF/perpetuity factor

**Delayed annuities/perpetuities:**
- Apply factor as normal
- Discount back to $T_0$

## 3 Project appraisal – dealing with inflation

The treatment of inflation was introduced in Paper F9. A brief recap follows:

### The impact of inflation

Inflation is a general increase in prices leading to a general decline in the real value of money.

In times of inflation, the fund providers will require a return made up of two elements:

- Real return for the use of their funds.
- Additional return to compensate for inflation.

The overall required return is called the **money or nominal rate of return.**

Real and nominal rates are linked by the formula:

$$(1 + i) = (1 + r)(1 + h)$$

Or

$$(1 + r) = (1 + i) / (1 + h)$$

in which :

r = real rate
i = money/nominal interest rate
h = general inflation rate.

In investment appraisal two types of inflation need consideration:

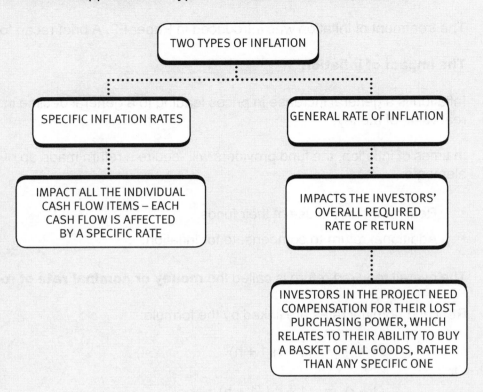

This inflationary impact can be dealt with in two different ways – both methods give the same NPV.

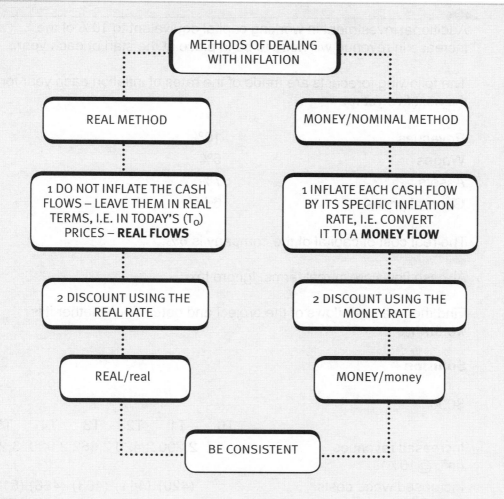

**Note:**

- as stated above, the real method can only be used if all cash flows are inflating at the general rate of inflation.

- in questions involving specific inflation rates, taxation or working capital, the money / nominal method is usually more reliable.

## Calculating the free cash flows of a project under inflation

In project appraisal the impact of inflation must therefore be taken into account when calculating the free cash flows to be discounted.

### Expandable Text - Illustration: Inflation in investment appraisal

A company is considering investing $4.5m in a project to achieve an annual increase in revenues over the next five years of $2m.

The project will lead to an increase in wage costs of $0.4m pa and will also require expenditure of $0.3m pa to maintain the level of existing assets to be used on the project.

Additional investment in working capital equivalent to 10% of the increase in revenue will need to be in place at the start of each year.

The following forecasts are made of the rates of inflation each year for the next five years:

| Revenues | 10% |
| Wages | 5% |
| Assets | 7% |
| General prices | 6.5% |

The real cost of capital of the company is 8%.

All cash flows are in real terms. Ignore tax.

Find the free cash flows of the project and determine whether it is worthwhile.

### Solution

$000

| | T0 | T1 | T2 | T3 | T4 | T5 |
|---|---|---|---|---|---|---|
| Increased revenues (infl. @10%) | | 2,200 | 2,420 | 2,662 | 2,928 | 3,221 |
| Increased wage costs (infl. @5%) | | (420) | (441) | (463) | (486) | (510) |
| Operating cash flows | | 1,780 | 1,979 | 2,199 | 2,442 | 2,711 |
| New investment | (4,500) | | | | | |
| Asset replacement spending (infl. @7%) | | (321) | (343) | (367) | (393) | (421) |
| Working capital injection (W1) | (220) | (22) | (24) | (27) | (29) | 322 |
| Free cash flows | (4,720) | 1,437 | 1,612 | 1,805 | 2,020 | 2,612 |
| PV factor @15% (W2) | 1.000 | 0.870 | 0.756 | 0.658 | 0.572 | 0.497 |
| PV of free cash flows | (4,720) | 1,250 | 1,219 | 1,187 | 1,155 | 1,298 |

The NPV = $1,389,000 which suggests that the project is worthwhile.

W1 working capital injection

| | T0 | T1 | T2 | T3 | T4 | T5 |
|---|---|---|---|---|---|---|
| Increased revenues | | 2,200 | 2,420 | 2,662 | 2,928 | 3,221 |
| Working capital required 10% in advance | 220 | 242 | 266 | 293 | 322 | |
| Working capital injection | (220) | (22) | (24) | (27) | (29) | 322 |

> **W2 cost of capital**
>
> $(1 + i) = (1 + r)(1 + h) = (1.08)(1.065) = 1.15$, giving $i = 15\%$

## Test your understanding 1

A company plans to invest $7m in a new product. Net contribution over the next five years is expected to be $4.2m pa in real terms.

Marketing expenditure of $1.4m pa will also be needed.

Expenditure of $1.3m pa will be required to replace existing assets which will now to be used on the project but are getting to the end of their useful lives. This expenditure will be incurred at the start of each year.

Additional investment in working capital equivalent to 10% of contribution will need to be in place at the start of each year. Working capital will be released at the end of the project.

The following forecasts are made of the rates of inflation each year for the next five years:

| | |
|---|---|
| Contribution | 8% |
| Marketing | 3% |
| Assets | 4% |
| General prices | 4.7% |

The real cost of capital of the company is 6%.

All cash flows are in real terms. Ignore tax.

**Find the free cash flows of the project and determine whether it is worthwhile.**

## 4 Project appraisal – dealing with taxation

The treatment of taxation was also introduced in Paper F9. There are two main impacts of taxation in an investment appraisal:

- tax is charged on operating cashflows, and

- capital allowances / writing down allowances can be claimed, thus generating tax relief

## Expandable Text - Revision of taxation on operating cashflows

### Tax on operating flows

Corporation tax charged on a company's profits is a relevant cash flow for NPV purposes. It is assumed that:

- operating cash inflows will be taxed at the corporation tax rate

- operating cash outflows will be tax deductible and attract tax relief at the corporation tax rate

- tax is paid in the same year the related operating cash flow is earned unless otherwise stated

- investment spending attracts capital or writing down allowances which get tax relief (see the section below)

- the company is earning net taxable profits overall.

## Expandable Text - Revision of Writing Down Allowances

### Capital allowances/writing down allowances (WDAs)

For tax purposes, a business may not deduct the cost of an asset from its profits as depreciation (in the way it does for financial accounting purposes). Instead the cost must be deducted in the form of capital or writing down allowances (WDAs).

The basic rules that follow are based on the current UK tax legislation:

- Writing down allowances are calculated on a reducing balance basis (usually at a rate of 25%).

- The total WDAs given over the life of an asset equate to their fall in value over the period (i.e. the cost less any scrap proceeds).

- Writing down allowances are claimed as early as possible.

- WDAs are given for every year of ownership except the year of disposal.

- In the year of sale or scrap a balancing allowance or charge arises.

KAPLAN PUBLISHING

| | $ |
|---|---|
| Original cost of asset | X |
| Cumulative capital allowances claimed | (X) |
| Written down value of the asset | X |
| Disposal value of the asset | (X) |
| Balancing allowance or charge | X |

You should carefully check the information given in the question however, since the examiner could ask you to examine the impact on the project of potential changes in the rules, for example:

- giving a 50% WDA in the first year of ownership and 25% thereafter

- giving 100% first year allowances (these are sometimes available to encourage investment in certain areas or types of assets)

- changing the calculation method from reducing balance to straight line.

## Calculating the free cash flows of a project taking account of taxation

In project appraisal the effects of taxation must be taken into account when calculating the free cash flows to be discounted.

### Expandable Text - Illustration: Taxation in investment appraisal

A company buys an asset for $26,000. It will be used on a project for three years after which it will be disposed of on the final day of year 3. Tax is payable at 30% and capital allowances are available at 25% reducing balance.

A    Calculate the writing down allowance and hence the tax savings for each year if the proceeds on disposal of the asset are $12,500.

B    If net trading income from the project is $16,000 pa and the cost of capital is 8% calculate the free cash flows and hence the net present value (NPV) of the project.

## Solution

| Time | | $ | Tax saving $ | Timing of tax relief |
|------|---|---|---|---|
| $T_0$ | Initial investment | 26,000 | | |
| $T_1$ | WDA @25% | (6,500) | 1,950 | $T_1$ |
| | Written down value | 19,500 | | |
| $T_2$ | WDA @25% | (4,875) | 1,463 | $T_2$ |
| | Written down value | 14,625 | | |
| | Sale proceeds | (12,500) | | |
| $T_3$ | Balancing allowance | 2,125 | 638 | $T_3$ |

| Time | $T_0$ | $T_1$ | $T_2$ | $T_3$ |
|------|---|---|---|---|
| Net trading inflows | | 16,000 | 16,000 | 16,000 |
| Tax payable (30%) | | (4,800) | (4,800) | (4,800) |
| Post tax operating flows | | 11,200 | 11,200 | 11,200 |
| Initial investment | (26,000) | | | |
| Scrap proceeds | | | | 12,500 |
| Tax relief on WDAs | | 1,950 | 1,463 | 638 |
| Free cash flows | (26,000) | 13,150 | 12,663 | 24,338 |
| Discount factor @ 8% | 1.000 | 0.926 | 0.857 | 0.794 |
| Present Value | (26,000) | 12,177 | 10,852 | 19,324 |
| NPV | 16,353 | | | |

### Test your understanding 2

A project will require an investment in a new asset of $10,000. It will be used on a project for four years after which it will be disposed of on the final day of year 4. Tax is payable at 30% one year in arrears, and capital allowances are available at 25% reducing balance.

Net operating flows from the project are expected to be $4,000 pa.

The company's cost of capital is 10%. Ignore inflation.

A  **Calculate the writing down allowance and hence the tax savings for each year if the proceeds on disposal of the asset are $2,500.**

B  **Identify the free cash flows for the project and calculate its net present value (NPV).**

## 5 Calculating free cash flows from accounting information

So far we have been considering the use of free cash flows in investment appraisal. However as mentioned above they are often calculated to appraise company performance or as a basis for share valuation.

When appraising an individual project, the free cash flows can usually be estimated quite easily. However, identifying free cash flows for an entire company or business unit is much more complex, since there are potentially far more of them.

In these situations, the level of free cash flows is more usually determined from the already prepared accounting information and therefore is found by working back from profits:

|  |  | Comment |
|---|---|---|
| Net operating profit (before interest and tax) | **X** | For future years, expected profits are predicted based on expected growth rates |
| Plus depreciation | **X** | Not a cash flow and therefore added back to profit |
| Less taxation | **(X)** | A relevant cash flow and therefore deducted from profit |
| Operating cash flow | **X** | |

| | | |
|---|---|---|
| Less investment: | | |
| Replacement non-current asset investment (RAI) | **(X)** | Needed in order to continue operations at current levels. If no information available about amounts, it  is assumed to be equal to current levels of depreciation |
| Incremental non-current asset investment (IAI) | **(X)** | Needed to sustain expected growth asset investment |
| Incremental working capital investment (IWCI) | **(X)** | Needed to sustain expected growth |
| Free cash flow | **X** | |

This method gives the level of free cash flow to the firm as a whole.

When calculated over a number of years, investors may draw conclusions from the emerging trends:

- Increase in free cash flows – often an indicator that increased earnings are to follow.

- Decrease in free cash flows – often an indicator of problems ahead.

## Free cash flow to equity

The above approach calculates free cash flows before deducting either interest or dividend payments.

The **free cash flow to equity only** can be calculated by taking the free cash flow calculated above and:

- deducting debt interest paid

- deducting any debt repayments

- adding any cash raised from debt issues.

In practical terms, the free cash flow to equity determines the dividend capacity of a firm i.e. the amount the firm can afford to pay out as a dividend.

Therefore, free cash flow to equity provides an alternative, arguably more meaningful, figure than earnings in the calculation of dividend cover:

Dividend cover in cash terms = Free cash flow to equity/Dividends paid

### Expandable Text - Free Cash Flow for one year only

#### Free cash flows for one year only

If the free cash flow is required for one year only, the calculation would usually be simplified to omit:

* the change in working capital
* discretionary non-maintenance capital spending

as the benefit from those investments is not yet included in the operating cash flow.

### Expandable Text - More details on Free Cash Flow

Cash, which is not retained and then reinvested in a business, is called free cash flow. This in effect represents the cash flow available to all the providers of capital of a company, whether these be debtholders or shareholders. This could be used to pay dividends or finance additional capital projects, if the necessary organisational criteria were met. Free cash flow is a very good measure of performance and an indicator of value.

Some would suggest that it is a better indicator of performance than measures based on net income. Forecast free cash flow is the most theoretically sound way to place a fair value on a company. Apparently Warren Buffet, the world's richest investor, uses historic and forecast free cash flow to value the businesses that he buys.

Growing free cash flows are frequently a prelude to increased earnings and hence may be a positive sign for investors. Conversely a shrinking free cash flow may be an indicator of problems ahead, and a sign that companies are unable to sustain earnings growth. This may not always be the case, as many young companies put a lot of their cash into investments, which diminish their free cash flow. However, in this case questions might be rasied about the sufficiency of short- and long-term capital.

There can be variations in the definition. When calculating free cash flow over a number of years it is sensible to include the change in working capital and all investment spending. Over a long period of time the cash flow resulting from all investment is likely to be realised and so such a measure would be useful to those undertaking business valuations and using data forecast into the future.

However, when calculating free cash flow for a single year it would be sensible to omit the change in working capital and discretionary non-maintenance capital spending, because the ultimate payoff from those investments is not yet included in the operating cash flow. However, this in turn may give rise to debate about what represents the level of sustaining capital expenditure that should be deducted. When analysing figures for free cash flow it is also important to be aware of any unusual events in a particular year, which may impact on the cash flow.

Figures calculated for free cash flow can be used in determining a company's cash flow ratios.

For example:

Dividend cover in cash terms = Free cash flow to equity/Dividends paid

It is argued that this measure of dividend cover is better than the conventional ratio of earnings divided by dividends paid, since dividends are paid in cash, and with no cash there can't be any dividends.

### Expandable Text - Illustration of calculations of Free Cash Flow

Calculate the free cash flow based on the following figures:

A    using the standard approach

B    assuming the calculation is for this year only

C    to show the free cash flow to equity.

|  | $000 |
| --- | --- |
| Operating profit | 300 |
| Depreciation | 120 |
| Increase in working capital | 50 |
| Capital expenditure to replace existing assets | 10 |
| Capital expenditure on new investments | 15 |
| Interest paid | 5 |
| Loans repaid | 20 |
| Tax paid | 140 |

## Solution

### A    Standard approach

| | $000 |
|---|---:|
| Net operating profit (before interest and tax) | 300 |
| Plus depreciation | 120 |
| Less taxation | (140) |
| | —— |
| Operating cash flow | 280 |
| Less investment: | |
| Replacement non-current asset investment | (10) |
| Incremental non-current asset investment | (15) |
| Incremental working capital investment | (50) |
| | —— |
| Free cash flow | 205 |
| | —— |

### B    Calculation for one year only

| | $000 |
|---|---:|
| Net operating profit (before interest and tax) | 300 |
| Plus depreciation | 120 |
| Less taxation | (140) |
| | —— |
| Operating cash flow | 280 |
| | —— |
| Less investment: | |
| Replacement non-current asset investment | (10) |
| | —— |
| Free cash flow | 270 |
| | —— |

### C    Free cash flows to equity

| | $000 |
|---|---:|
| Free cash flow to the firm | 205 |
| Less debt interest paid | (5) |
| Less loans repaid | (20) |
| | —— |
| Free cash flows to equity | 180 |
| | —— |

### Test your understanding 3

(a) **Calculate the free cash flow based on the following figures:**

    (i)   using the standard approach

    (ii)  to show the free cash flow to equity.

| | $000 |
|---|---|
| Capital expenditure on new investments | 25 |
| Capital expenditure to replace existing assets | 60 |
| Depreciation | 75 |
| Funds raised from new debenture issue | 30 |
| Increase in working capital | 55 |
| Interest paid | 10 |
| Loans repaid | 15 |
| Operating profit | 470 |
| Tax paid | 180 |
| Ordinary (25¢) shares at par | 460 |
| Dividend paid 5¢ per share | |

(b) **Calculate the dividend cover based on the free cash flow to equity and interpret your result.**

## 6 Economic return – the IRR

The other DCF technique used to appraise investment projects, which you should recall from earlier studies, is the calculation of the internal rate of return or the IRR.

A brief recap follows:

### IRR – the basics

The IRR of a project has the following features:

- It represents the discount rate at which the NPV of an investment is zero.

- It can be found by linear interpolation.

- Standard projects (outflow followed by inflows) should be accepted if the IRR is greater than the firm's cost of capital.

The steps in linear interpolation are:

(1) Calculate two NPVs for the project at two different costs of capital.

(2) Use the following formula to find the IRR:

$$IRR = L + \frac{N_L}{(N_L - N_H)} \times (H - L)$$

where:

L = Lower rate of interest.

H = Higher rate of interest.

$N_L$ = NPV at lower rate of interest.

$N_H$ = NPV at higher rate of interest.

(3) Compare the IRR with the company's cost of borrowing.

If the IRR is higher than the cost of capital, the project should be accepted.

### Test your understanding 4

An initial investment of $2,000 in a project yields cash inflows of $500, $500, $600, $600 and $440 at 12 months intervals. There is no scrap value. Funds are available to finance the project at 12%.

**Decide whether the project is worthwhile, using:**

A   **net present value approach**

B   **internal rate of return approach.**

## Interpreting the IRR

The IRR provides a decision rule for investment appraisal, but also provides information about the riskiness of a project – i.e. the sensitivity of its returns.

The project will only continue to have a positive NPV whilst the firm's cost of capital is lower than the IRR.

A project with a positive NPV at 14% but an IRR of 15% for example, is clearly sensitive to:

- an increase in the cost of finance
- an increase in investors' perception of the potential risks
- any alteration to the estimates used in the NPV appraisal.

### Expandable Text

Increases in interest rates will clearly increase the company's costs of finance as will concerns affecting the stock market as a whole and hence the returns demanded by investors.

However, other, company specific factors – such as the actions of competitors may affect the firm's position in the market place and the viability of its business model. This could impact the level of systematic risk it faces and result in an increase in the required return of shareholders.

Where the IRR is close to the company cost of capital, any changes to estimates in the NPV calculation will have a significant impact on the viability of the project. Any unexpected changes such as an increase in the costs of raw materials, or an aggressive advertising campaign run by a competitor will erode the return margin and may make the project unacceptable to investors.

## 7 The modified IRR (MIRR)

### Problems with using IRR

There are a number of problems with the standard IRR calculation:

- The decision rule is not always clear cut. For example, if a project has 2 IRRs (or more), it is difficult to interpret the rule which says "accept the project if the IRR is higher than the cost of capital".

- The assumptions. IRR is often mistakenly assumed to be a measure of the return from a project, which it is not. The IRR only represents the return from the project if funds can be reinvested at the IRR for the duration of the project.

- Choosing between projects. Since projects can have multiple IRRs (or none at all) it is difficult to usefully compare projects using IRR.

It is therefore usually considered more reliable to calculate the NPV of projects for investment appraisal purposes.

## Expandable Text

For conventional projects (those with a cash outflow at time 0 followed by inflows over the life of the project), the decision rule states that projects should be accepted if the IRR exceeds the cost of capital.

However unconventional projects with different cash flow patterns may have no IRR, more than one IRR, or a single IRR but the project should only be accepted if the cost of capital is greater.

The IRR calculates the discount rate that would cause the project to break-even assuming it:

- is the cost of financing the project
- is the return that can be earned on all the returns earned by the project.

Since, in practice, these rates are likely to be different, the IRR is unreliable.

A project with a high IRR is not necessarily the one offering the highest return in NPV terms and IRR is therefore an unreliable tool for choosing between mutually exclusive projects.

A more useful measure is the modified internal rate of return or MIRR.

This measure has been developed to counter the above problems since it:

- is unique
- can deal with different borrowing and reinvestment rates
- is a simple percentage.

It is therefore more popular with non-financially minded managers, as a simple rule can be applied:

MIRR = Project's return

If Project return > company cost of finance ⇒ Accept project

### The interpretation of MIRR

MIRR measures the economic yield of the investment under the assumption that any cash surpluses are reinvested at the firm's current cost of capital.

Although MIRR, like IRR, cannot replace net present value as the principle evaluation technique it does give a measure of the maximum cost of finance that the firm could sustain and allow the project to remain worthwhile. For this reason it gives a useful insight into the margin of error, or room for negotiation, when considering the financing of particular investment projects.

## Calculating the MIRR

Method:

(1)  Find the terminal value of the cash inflows from the project if invested at the company's reinvestment rate.

(2)  Find the present value of the cash outflows, discounted at the company's cost of finance.

(3)  The MIRR is then found by taking the n th root of (TV inflows / PV outflows) and subtracting 1 (Note that n is the length of the project in years.)

## Student Accountant article

Read the examiner's April 2008 article in Student Accountant magazine for more details on MIRR.

### Expandable Text - Illustration of NPV, IRR and MIRR

A project requires an initial investment of $24,000 and will generate annual cash flows as follows:

| Year | Cash flow $ |
|------|-------------|
| 1 | 7,800 |
| 2 | 6,000 |
| 3 | 4,200 |
| 4 | 7,400 |
| 5 | 9,200 |

The cost of capital is 10%.

A   Find the NPV and the IRR of the project.

B   Show the overall net cash position for the project if:

–   the company had a cost of capital equivalent to the IRR

–   and all cash flows earned were invested for the duration of the project at that rate.

C   Assume now that funds can be borrowed at 10% whilst the reinvestment rate for positive cash flows is 12%. What is the MIRR?

## Solution

### NPV

| Time | Cash flow | DF @10% | PV |
|------|-----------|---------|-----|
| 0 | (24,000) | 1 | (24,000) |
| 1 | 7,800 | 0.909 | 7,090.2 |
| 2 | 6,000 | 0.826 | 4,956 |
| 3 | 4,200 | 0.751 | 3,154.2 |
| 4 | 7,400 | 0.683 | 5,054.2 |
| 5 | 9,200 | 0.621 | 5,713.2 |
| | | | ———— |
| | | NPV = | 1,967.8 |
| | | | ———— |

### IRR

| Time | Cash flow | DF@10% | PV | DF @14% | PV |
|------|-----------|--------|-----|---------|-----|
| 0 | (24,000) | 1 | (24,000) | 1 | (24,000) |
| 1 | 7,800 | 0.909 | 7,090.2 | 0.877 | 6,840.6 |
| 2 | 6,000 | 0.826 | 4,956.0 | 0.769 | 4,614.0 |
| 3 | 4,200 | 0.751 | 3,154.2 | 0.675 | 2,835.0 |
| 4 | 7,400 | 0.683 | 5,054.2 | 0.592 | 4,380.8 |
| 5 | 9,200 | 0.621 | 5,713.2 | 0.477 | 4,774.8 |
| | | | ———— | | ———— |
| | | NPV = | 1,967.8 | | (554.8) |
| | | | ———— | | ———— |

This gives an IRR of:

IRR = 10 + [1,967.8/(1,967.8 - 555.8)] × (14 - 4) = 13.12%

Using a spreadsheet a more accurate IRR can be shown to be 13.07% and it is this will use for demonstration purpose:

**Net cash position**

| Time | Cash inflow | Invested for | Invested at 13.07% | |
|------|-------------|--------------|--------------------|---|
| 1 | 7,800 | 4 years | $\times 1.1307^4$ | 12,749.24 |
| 2 | 6,000 | 3 years | $\times 1.1307^3$ | 8,673.48 |
| 3 | 4,200 | 2 years | $\times 1.1307^2$ | 5,369.63 |
| 4 | 7,400 | 1 year | $\times 1.1307$ | 8,367.18 |
| 5 | 9,200 | – | | 9,200.00 |
| | | | | 44,359.53 |

Total amount invested at end of project The time 5 value of the cost of the investment: $\$24,000 \times (1.1307)^5 = \$44,356$ which matches the value of the income from the returns.

Or alternatively

Time 0 value of the income from the returns = $44,360/1.1307^5 = \$24,002$ which matches the initial cost of the project.

The net cash position for the project is therefore effectively zero – i.e. an IRR of 13.07% means that if the cost of borrowing and the return earned on investments were both 13.07%, the project would break even.

## MIRR

To calculate the MIRR, we restate the project cash flows to be equivalent to an outflow at time 0 and a single inflow at the end of the project life (the 'terminal value'), using the assumed reinvestment rate.

| Year | Cash flow at time 0 $ | Equivalent cash flow at time 5 $ |
|---|---|---|
| 0 | (24,000) | |
| 1 | $7,800 \times 1.12^4 =$ | 12,273 |
| 2 | $6,000 \times 1.12^3 =$ | 8,430 |
| 3 | $4,200 \times 1.12^2 =$ | 5,268 |
| 4 | $7,400 \times 1.12 =$ | 8,288 |
| 5 | $9,200 \times 1 =$ | 9,200 |
| | | ———— |
| | | 43,459 |
| | | ———— |

Thus, what is the IRR of a cash outflow of $24,000 at time 0 followed by an inflow of $43,459 at time 5?

$$43,459/(1 + r)^5 = 24,000$$

$$43,459/24,000 = (1 + r)^5$$

$$\sqrt[5]{\left(\frac{43,459}{24,000}\right)} - 1 = r$$

$$r = 0.126$$

so the MIRR is 12.6%. This is therefore the return on the project.

Since the return on the project exceeds the cost of finance, the project should be accepted.

### Test your understanding 5

A project requires an initial investment of $20,000 and will generate annual cash flows as follows:

| Year | Cash flow $ |
| --- | --- |
| 1 | 4,000 |
| 2 | (2,000) |
| 3 | 6,000 |
| 4 | 7,600 |
| 5 | 10,000 |

The firm's financing rate (for negative cashflows) is 9%, and its reinvestment rate for positive cashflows is 6%..

### What is the MIRR?

### Alternative calculation of MIRR

To avoid having to calculate the terminal value of the project inflows, there is an alternative way of computing MIRR which only uses present value calculations.

$$1 + MIRR = (1+re) \times [PVR/PVI]^{1/n}$$

where

PVR = the present value of the "return phase" of the project

PVI = the present value of the "investment phase" of the project

re  = the firm's cost of capital

This formula is given on the exam formula sheet.

**Illustration 1**

A project with the following cash flows is under consideration:

| $000 | $T_0$ | $T_1$ | $T_2$ | $T_3$ | $T_4$ |
|------|-------|-------|-------|-------|-------|
| | (20,000) | 8,000 | 12,000 | 4,000 | 2,000 |

Cost of capital 8%

Calculate the MIRR.

**Solution**

PVR = 22,340 (this is the present value of the year 1-4 cash flows).

PVI = 20,000

$1 + MIRR = (1+re) \times (PVR/PVI)^{1/n} = 1.08 \times (22,340/20,000)^{1/4} = 1.1103$, giving MIRR = 11% pa.

Check: MIRR calculated the "long way":

| Year | | TV |
|------|------|------|
| 1 | $8,000 \times (1.08)^3$ | 10,077 |
| 2 | $12,000 \times (1.08)^2$ | 13,997 |
| 3 | $4,000 \times (1.08)^1$ | 2,000 |
| 4 | | |
| | | 30,394 |

$1 + MIRR = (30,394/20,000)^{1/4} = 1.1103$, as before

## 8 Investment appraisal and capital rationing

Capital rationing was first introduced in Paper F9. A brief recap follows:

**Capital rationing – the basics**

Shareholder wealth is maximised if a company undertakes all possible positive NPV projects.

**Capital rationing** is where there are insufficient funds to do so.

This shortage of funds may be for:

- a single period only – dealt with as in limiting factor analysis by calculating profitability indexes (PIs)

  PI = NPV/ PV of capital invested

- more than one period – extending over a number of years or even indefinitely.

## Test your understanding 6

Peel Co has identified 4 positive NPV projects, as follows:

| Project | NPV ($m) | Investment at $t_0$ ($m) |
|---------|----------|--------------------------|
| A | 60 | 9 |
| B | 40 | 12 |
| C | 35 | 6 |
| D | 20 | 4 |

Peel Co can only raise $12m of finance to invest at $t_0$.

**Advise the company which project(s) to accept if the projects are:**

**(i) independent and divisible**

**(ii) independent and indivisible**

**(iii) mutually exclusive**

## Multi-period capital rationing

A solution to a multi-period capital rationing problem cannot be found using PIs. This method can only deal with one limiting factor (i.e. one period of shortage). Here there are a number of limiting factors (i.e. a number of periods of shortage) and linear programming techniques must therefore be applied.

In the exam you will **not** be expected to produce a solution to a linear programming problem. However, in the following illustrations, you will see how to formulate a linear programming model.

In practice, long term capital rationing is a signal that the firm should be looking to expand its capital base through a new issue of finance to the markets.

KAPLAN PUBLISHING

## Expandable text - Revision of linear programming

In your previous studies, (Papers F2 and F5), you were introduced to the details of linear programming. In this paper, we are interested only in formulating the linear programming problem and this revision example therefore only reviews those first key stages.

Linear programming is a technique for dealing with scarce or rationed resources. The solution calculated identifies the optimum allocation of the scarce resources between the products/projects being considered.

A brief recap follows:

The linear programme is formulated in three stages:

(1)  Define the unknowns.

(2)  Formulate the objective function.

(3)  Express the constraints in terms of inequalities including the non-negativities.

## Expandable Text - Simple Linear Programming Example

A company makes two products, brooms and mops. Each product passes through two departments, manufacture and packaging. The time spent in each department is as follows:

| | Departmental time (hours) | |
| --- | --- | --- |
| | Manufacture | Packaging |
| Brooms | 3 | 2 |
| Mops | 4 | 6 |

There are 4,800 hours available in the manufacturing department and 3,600 available in the packaging department. Production of brooms must not exceed 1,100 units.

The contribution earned from one broom is $15 and from a mop is $10.

Formulate the linear programme needed to identify the optimum use of the scarce labour resource.

## Solution

### (1) Define the unknowns

Let m = number of mops to be produced.

Let b = number of brooms to be produced.

Let z = contribution earned from the products made.

### (2) Formulate the objective function

The aim is to maximise contribution:

$z = 15b + 10m$.

### (3) Express the constraints in terms of inequalities including the non-negativities

| | |
|---|---:|
| Manufacturing | $3b + 4m \leq 4,800$ |
| Packaging | $2b + 6m \leq 3,600$ |
| Production | $b \leq 1,100$ |
| b, m ≥ 0 | |

The main constraints simply say that you cannot use any more of the resource than you have available.

Since only 4,800 hours of manufacturing time is available, the constraint shows that the number of hours taken to make a broom times the number of brooms made (3b) plus the number of hours needed to make a mop times the number of mops made (4m) must not exceed 4,800.

The same principle is applied to packaging time.

The third constraint restricts the production of brooms to 1,100.

The non-negative constraints at the end, prevent negative quantities from being produced. (If this seems unnecessary, remember that a computer solving the problem does not have a sense of this being ridiculous and producing negative quantities would, on paper, actually contribute scarce resource!)

The linear programming method can be applied to a multi-period capital rationing problem in one of two ways. The objective of the solution can be either:

- to maximise the total NPV from the investment in available projects
- to maximise the present value of cash flow available for dividends.

Both techniques result in the same project selections.

## Expandable Text - Example of the NPV formulation

A company has identified the following independent investment projects, all of which are divisible and exhibit constant returns to scale. No project can be delayed or done more than once.

| Project | Cash flows at time: | 0 | 1 | 2 | 3 | 4 |
|---|---|---|---|---|---|---|
| | | $000 | $000 | $000 | $000 | $000 |
| A | | -10 | -20 | +10 | +20 | +20 |
| B | | -10 | -10 | +30 | – | – |
| C | | -5 | +2 | +2 | +2 | +2 |
| D | | – | -15 | -15 | +20 | +20 |
| E | | -20 | +10 | -20 | +20 | +20 |
| F | | -8 | -4 | +15 | +10 | – |

There is only $20,000 of capital available at $T_0$ and only $5,000 at $T_1$, plus the cash inflows from the projects undertaken at $T_0$. In each time period thereafter, capital is freely available. The appropriate discount rate is 10%.

Formulate the NPV linear programme.

### Solution

Since our objective is to maximise the total NPV from the investments the first (additional) stage will be to calculate those NPVs at a discount rate of 10%.

| Project | NPV @10% |
|---|---|
| | $000 |
| A | +8.77 |
| B | +5.70 |
| C | +1.34 |
| D | +2.65 |
| E | +1.25 |
| F | +8.27 |

We now progress as for a standard linear programme:

## (1) Define the unknowns

The linear programme will then select the combination of projects, which will maximise total NPV.

Therefore:

Let a = the proportion of project A undertaken

Let b = the proportion of project B undertaken

Let c = the proportion of project C undertaken

Let d = the proportion of project D undertaken

Let e = the proportion of project E undertaken

Let f = the proportion of project F undertaken

And

Let z = the NPV of the combination of projects selected.

## (2) Formulate the objective function

The objective function to be maximised is:

$z = 8.77a + 5.70b + 1.34c + 2.65d + 1.25e + 8.27f.$

## (3) Express the constraints in terms of inequalities including the non-negativities

| Time 0 | $10a + 10b + 5c + 20e + 8f \leq 20$ |
| Time 1 | $20a + 10b + 15d + 4f \leq 5 + 2c + 10e$ |
| Also | $0 \leq a, b, c, d, e, f \leq 1$ |

## (4) Interpret the results

The linear programme when solved will give values for a, b, c, d, e and f. These will be the proportions of each project which, should be undertaken to maximise the NPV – an amount given by z.

KAPLAN PUBLISHING

Further details on interpretation

The objective function (z) is the maximum NPV earned. This will be the sum of the NPVs earned from each product. Since they may each be done only in part, the full NPV from each one is multiplied by the proportion of it to be undertaken (a, b, c etc.) and these are then summed together to give the objective function.

The main constraints simply say that you cannot spend any more money than you have available.

- The first constraint relates to the limited capital available at $T_0$.

- How much of the $T_0$ capital for each project will actually be needed, depends on the proportions of each project undertaken. The full $T_0$ amounts are therefore multiplied by the proportions to be undertaken, and the sum of those amounts must not exceed the $20,000 available.

- The second constraint relates to the limited capital available at $T_1$.

- Here the financial situation is eased because projects C and E have positive cash inflows at $T_1$ and these flows can be used to fund investment needs at that time.

- The funds required by projects using limited cash (A, B, D, and F) are therefore multiplied by the proportions to be undertaken. This amount must be less than what is available – the $5,000 plus the funds brought it by whatever proportions of C and E we end up choosing to do.

The third constraint is a summarised one. It shows that none of the projects can be done more than once (i.e. must be ≤1) and that is not possible to do a negative amount of any project (they must be ≥ 0). This second non-negative rule is essential. If it were not included, a computer model may well compute that effectively 'undoing' a project frees up cash and include it in a solution!

### Expandable Text - Example of the PV of dividends formulation

### Linear programming and capital rationing – the PV of dividends formulation

This method is more flexible and removes the need to calculate the NPVs of the projects as this is taken care of by the linear programme itself.

The objective is to maximise the cash flows for dividends during the life span of the available projects.

The same information will be used as for the last example in order to provide a clear comparison.

## Example

A company has identified the following independent investment projects, all of which are divisible and exhibit constant returns to scale. No project can be done more than once.

| Project | Cash flows at time: | 0 | 1 | 2 | 3 | 4 |
|---------|------|------|------|------|------|------|
| | | $000 | $000 | $000 | $000 | $000 |
| A | | -10 | -20 | +10 | +20 | +20 |
| B | | -10 | -10 | +30 | – | – |
| C | | -5 | +2 | +2 | +2 | +2 |
| D | | – | -15 | -15 | +20 | +20 |
| E | | -20 | +10 | -20 | +20 | +20 |
| F | | -8 | -4 | +15 | +10 | – |

There is only $20,000 of capital available at $T_0$ and only $5,000 at $T_1$, plus the cash inflows from the projects undertaken at $T_0$. In each time period thereafter, capital is freely available. The appropriate discount rate is 10%.

Formulate the PV of dividends linear programme.

## Solution

### (1) Define the unknowns

As before the amount of each project to be undertaken is shown as:

Let a = the proportion of project A undertaken.

Let b = the proportion of project B undertaken.

Let c = the proportion of project C undertaken.

Let d = the proportion of project D undertaken.

Let e = the proportion of project E undertaken.

Let f = the proportion of project F undertaken.

But for the objective function:

Let z = the PV of dividends.

In addition, the dividend flows must be defined:

Let $d_0$ = dividend flow generated at $T_0$ by the projects selected.

Let $d_1$ = dividend flow generated at $T_1$ by the projects selected.

Let $d_2$ = dividend flow generated at $T_2$ by the projects selected.

Let $d_3$ = dividend flow generated at $T_3$ by the projects selected.

Let $d_4$ = dividend flow generated at $T_4$ by the projects selected.

## (2) Formulate the objective function

The objective function to be maximised is:

$$z = d_0/1 + d_1/1.1 + d_2/1.1^2 + d_3/1.1^3 + d_4/1.1^4$$

or

$$z = d_0 + 0.909 \, d_1 + 0.826 \, d_2 + 0.751 \, d_3 + 0.683 \, d_4$$

## (3) Express the constraints in terms of inequalities including the non-negativities

| | |
|---|---|
| Time 0 | $10a + 10b + 5c + 20e + 8f + \mathbf{d_0} \le 20$ |
| Time 1 | $20a + 10b + 15d + 4f + \mathbf{d_1} \le 5 + 2c + 10e$ |
| Time 2 | $15d + 20e + \mathbf{d_2} \le 10a + 30b + 2c + 15f$ |
| Time 3 | $\mathbf{d_3} \le 20a + 2c + 20d + 20e + 10f$ |
| Time 4 | $\mathbf{d_4} \le 20a + 2c + 20d + 20e$ |
| Also | $0 \le a, b, c, d, e, f \le 1$ |
| And | $d_0, d_1, d_2, d_3, d_4, \ge 0$ |

## (4) Interpret the results

The linear programme when solved will give values for a, b, c, d, e and f.

These will be the proportions of each project, which should be undertaken to maximise the PV of dividends – an amount given by z.

Note that the only difference in the value of z in these formulations is:

- PV of dividends formulation – z gives the PV of the project returns gross of the investment cost.

- NPV formulation – z gives the PV of the project returns net of the investment cost.

Note that the dividend flows are defined for each of the periods in which there are projects under consideration. Where the projects are for varying durations, the flows are defined for each year up to the point where the cash flow from the longest-lived investment opportunity stops.

The cost of capital is 10%. Since it is the present value of dividends to be maximised, the cash flow for each year is discounted at 10%. The first version shows z using the formula to give the present value of each year. The second version uses the discount factors from the formula sheets.

As before the main constraints express the fact that we cannot spend more than we have.

Whilst for an NPV formulation, we will have as only as many main constraints as there are periods of capital rationing, in the PV of dividends formulation we need a constraint for every year for which we have potential project cash flows.

As before, the outflows include the funds required for the projects, but now also include the dividend flow for the period. The available funds are as before – the cash supplied by the company plus any income from the projects.

Therefore:

- The first two constraints are amended to include the dividend flow as an additional payment to be funded.

- Then, further constraints are formulated for the remaining three years.

The additional constraint, for the proportion of the projects to be undertaken, is as before, but we now need an additional non-negative constraint – the dividends cannot be negative amounts – they must exceed or equal zero. Again, if it seems unnecessary, consider a computer program solving the formulation – if permitted, it may indeed make the dividend payments negative, as they would represent income and fund more projects!

## Dual values

Dual values are the change in the objective function from having one more or less unit of scarce resource available.

In capital rationing, the scarce resource is cash and dual values can be used to calculate:

- the impact of raising funds to facilitate further investment or

- diverting funds away from current projects to newly discovered ones.

Dual values can be used to filter newly discovered investment projects. The cash flows they would generate can be compared with the impact of diverting funds away from the current investment plan. The dual values can be used quickly to calculate the effect of diverting the funds.

### Expandable Text - More on dual values

The dual price is:

- the amount by which one additional unit of scarce resource would increase the value of the objective function, or alternatively

- the amount by which one fewer unit of scarce resource would decrease the value of the objective function.

In capital rationing, the scarce resource is available funds, so the dual value expresses the increase in the objective function gained if one more dollar became available, or the reduction if one less dollar were invested.

The amount of the dual value varies depending on which method is used to formulate the linear programme:

- NPV method – the dual mquals the change in NPV earned if $1 more or less is available.

- PV of dividends method – the dual equals the change in the PV of cash available to pay dividends if $1 more or less is available.

An example is given here for clarity.

A company under capital rationing has developed an investment plan using linear programming. It has a cost of capital of 10%. The dual values have been calculated as:

- NPV method: $T_0 = 0.2$, $T_1 = 0.07$, $T_2 = 0$.
- PV of dividends method: $T_0 = 1.2$, $T_1 = 0.979$, $T_2 = 0.826$.

A new project has come to light with the following flows:

| Time | Cash flow $000 |
|------|----------------|
| 0    | (30)           |
| 1    | 20             |
| 2    | 20             |

### Appraisal using NPV duals

(1)  Calculate the NPV of the new project

| Time | Cash flow $000 | DF @10% | PV $000 |
|---|---|---|---|
| 0 | (30) | 1 | (30.00) |
| 1 | 20 | 0.909 | 18.18 |
| 2 | 20 | 0.826 | 16.52 |
| | | | _____ |
| | Net present value | | 4.70 |
| | | | _____ |

(2)  Find dual value of the project – i.e. the impact on the current investment plan of diverting funds

| Time | Cash flow $000 | Dual value | Opportunity cost of the cash flow $000 |
|---|---|---|---|
| 0 | (30) | 0.200 | (6.00) |
| 1 | 20 | 0.070 | 1.40 |
| 2 | 20 | 0.000 | |
| | | | _____ |
| | Net dual value | | (4.60) |
| | | | _____ |

The NPV of the current investment plan would therefore fall by $4,600 if the new project were taken on.

(3)  Compare the two

| | $000 |
|---|---|
| Net present value | 4.70 |
| Net dual value | (4.60) |
| Net benefit | 0.10 |

The project is therefore worthy of further consideration as it should increase the overall NPV of the investments by $100.

### Appraisal using PV of dividend duals

This method is far simpler but will always give the same result.

| Time | Cash flow | Dual value | Opportunity cost of the cash flow |
|------|-----------|------------|-----------------------------------|
| | $000 | | $000 |
| 0 | (30) | 1.200 | (36.00) |
| 1 | 20 | 0.979 | 19.58 |
| 2 | 20 | 0.826 | 16.52 |
| | | | ——— |
| | Net dual value | | 0.10 |
| | | | ——— |

The increase in funds will be $100 as before.

## 9 The impact of corporate reporting on investment appraisal

The main approach to evaluating capital investment projects and financing options, for a profit-maximiser, is their impact on shareholder value. However, the impact on the reported financial position and performance of the firm must also be considered. In particular, you may need to examine the implications for:

- the share price
- gearing
- ROCE
- earning per share.

### Timing differences between cash flows and profits

For NPV purposes, the timing of the cash flows associated with a project is taken account of through the discounting process. It is therefore irrelevant if the cash flows in the earlier years are negative, provided overall the present value of the cash inflows outweighs the costs.

However, the impact on reported profits may be significant. Major new investment will bring about higher levels of depreciation in the earlier years, which are not yet matched by higher revenues. This will reduce reported profits and the EPS figure.

This reduction could impact:

- the share price – if the reasons for the fall in profit are not understood
- key ratios such as:
  - ROCE
  - asset turnover
  - profit margins.
- the meeting of loan covenants.

## 10 Chapter Summary

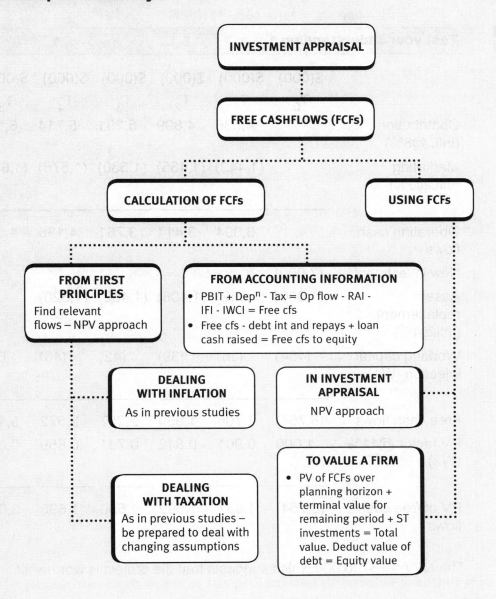

INVESTMENT APPRAISAL

FREE CASHFLOWS (FCFs)

CALCULATION OF FCFs

USING FCFs

**FROM FIRST PRINCIPLES**

Find relevant flows – NPV approach

**FROM ACCOUNTING INFORMATION**
- PBIT + Dep$^n$ - Tax = Op flow - RAI - IFI - IWCI = Free cfs
- Free cfs - debt int and repays + loan cash raised = Free cfs to equity

**DEALING WITH INFLATION**

As in previous studies

**IN INVESTMENT APPRAISAL**

NPV approach

**DEALING WITH TAXATION**

As in previous studies – be prepared to deal with changing assumptions

**TO VALUE A FIRM**
- PV of FCFs over planning horizon + terminal value for remaining period + ST investments = Total value. Deduct value of debt = Equity value

## Test your understanding answers

### Test your understanding 1

| | $(000) T_0 | $(000) T_1 | $(000) T_2 | $(000) T_3 | $(000) T_4 | $(000) T_5 |
|---|---|---|---|---|---|---|
| Contribution (infl. @8%) | | 4,536 | 4,899 | 5,291 | 5,714 | 6,171 |
| Marketing (infl.@3%) | | (1,442) | (1,485) | (1,530) | (1,576) | (1,623) |
| Operating cash flows | | 3,094 | 3,414 | 3,761 | 4,138 | 4,548 |
| New investment | (7,000) | | | | | |
| Asset replacement (infl@4%) | (1,300) | (1,352) | (1,406) | (1,462) | (1,520) | |
| Working capital injection (W1) | (454) | (36) | (39) | (42) | (46) | 617 |
| Free cash flows | (8,754) | 1,706 | 1,969 | 2,257 | 2,572 | 5,165 |
| PV factor @11% (W2) | 1.000 | 0.901 | 0.812 | 0.731 | 0.659 | 0.593 |
| PV of free cash flows | (8,754) | 1,537 | 1,599 | 1,650 | 1,695 | 3,063 |

The NPV = +$790,000 which suggests that the project is worthwhile.

W1 Working capital injection

| | $T_0$ | $T_1$ | $T_2$ | $T_3$ | $T_4$ | $T_5$ |
|---|---|---|---|---|---|---|
| Increased revenues | | 4,536 | 4,899 | 5,291 | 5,714 | 6,171 |
| Working capital required 10% in advance | 454 | 490 | 529 | 571 | 617 | |
| Working capital injection | (454) | (36) | (39) | (42) | (46) | 617 |

W2 Cost of capital

$(1 + i) = (1 + r)(1 + h) = (1 + 0.06)(1 + 0.047) = 1.11$, giving $i = 11\%$

## Test your understanding 2

(a)

| Time | | $ | Tax saving $ | Timing of tax relief |
|---|---|---|---|---|
| $T_0$ | Initial investment | 10,000 | | |
| $T_1$ | WDA @25% | (2,500) | 750 | $T_2$ |
| | Written down value | 7,500 | | |
| $T_2$ | WDA @25% | (1,875) | 563 | $T_3$ |
| | Written down value | 5,625 | | |
| $T_3$ | WDA @25% | (1,406) | 422 | $T_4$ |
| | Written down value | 4,219 | | |
| | Sale proceeds | (2,500) | | |
| $T_4$ | Balancing allowance | 1,719 | 516 | $T_5$ |

**Note**

- total WDAs = 2,500 + 1,875 + 1,406 + 1,719 = 7,500 = fall in value of the asset
- total tax relief = 750 + 563 + 422 + 516 = 2251 = 7,500 × 30%

(b)

| Time | $T_0$ | $T_1$ | $T_2$ | $T_3$ | $T_4$ | $T_5$ |
|---|---|---|---|---|---|---|
| Net trading inflows | | 4,000 | 4,000 | 4,000 | 4,000 | |
| Tax payable (30%) | | | (1,200) | (1,200) | (1,200) | (1,200) |
| Post tax operating flows | | 4,000 | 2,800 | 2,800 | 2,800 | (1,200) |
| Initial investment | (10,000) | | | | | |
| Scrap proceeds | | | | | 2,500 | |
| Tax relief on WDAs | | | 750 | 563 | 422 | 516 |
| Free cash flows | (10,000) | 4,000 | 3,550 | 3,363 | 5,722 | (684) |
| Discount factor @10% | 1.000 | 0.909 | 0.826 | 0.751 | 0.683 | 0.621 |
| Present value | (10,000) | 3,636 | 2,932 | 2,526 | 3,908 | (425) |
| | | | | | NPV | 2,577 |

## Test your understanding 3

(a)

### 1 Standard approach

|  | $000 |
|---|---|
| Net operating profit (before interest and tax) | 470 |
| Plus depreciation | 75 |
| Less taxation | (180) |
| Operating cash flow | 365 |
| Less investment: | |
| Replacement non-current asset investment | (60) |
| Incremental non-current asset investment | (25) |
| Incremental working capital investment | (55) |
| Free cash flow | 225 |

### 2 Free cash flow to equity

|  | $000 |
|---|---|
| Free cash flow to the firm | 225 |
| Less debt interest paid | (10) |
| Less loans repaid | (15) |
| Plus new debt finance raised | 30 |
| Free cash flow to equity | 230 |

### (b) Dividend cover in cash terms

The standard dividend cover calculation uses earnings after interest and tax and would give an answer of:

(470,000 - 10,000 - 180,000)/92,000 = 3 times

This high result suggests a good level of security for the ordinary shareholders but could be misleading since it is not earnings that are used to pay dividends, but cash.

However, calculation of the cash cover gives:

Dividend cover in cash terms = (Free cash flow to equity)/dividends paid

= 230,000/92,000 = 2.5 times

where

dividends paid = 0.05 × (460,000 × 4)

This offers reassurance as the available resources could pay the dividend 2½ times, which would generally be considered a safe level of cover.

## Test your understanding 4

It is useful to set out the cash flows in a table:

| Time | 0 | 1 | 2 | 3 | 4 | 5 |
|------|-----|-----|-----|-----|-----|-----|
|  | -$2,000 | +$500 | +$500 | +$600 | +$600 | +$440 |

### A    Net present value approach

| Year | Cash flow $ | PV factor @12% | Present value $ |
|------|------|------|------|
| 0 | -2,000 | 1.000 | -2,000 |
| 1 | +500 | 0.893 | +446 |
| 2 | +500 | 0.797 | +398 |
| 3 | +600 | 0.712 | +427 |
| 4 | +600 | 0.636 | +382 |
| 5 | +440 | 0.567 | +249 |
|  |  |  | -98 |

Since the net present value at 12% is negative, the project should be rejected.

### B    Internal rate of return approach

Calculating IRR requires a trial and error approach. Since we have already calculated in (a) that NPV at 12% is negative, we must decrease the discount rate to bring the NPV towards zero – try 8%.

| Year $ | Cash flow | PV factor @12% $ | Present value | PV factor @8% $ | Present value |
|------|------|------|------|------|------|
| 0 | -2,000 | 1.000 | -2,000 | 1.000 | -2,000 |
| 1 | +500 | 0.893 | +446 | 0.926 | +463 |
| 2 | +500 | 0.797 | +398 | 0.857 | +428 |
| 3 | +600 | 0.712 | +427 | 0.794 | +476 |
| 4 | +600 | 0.636 | +382 | 0.735 | +441 |
| 5 | +440 | 0.567 | +249 | 0.681 | +300 |
|  |  |  | -98 |  | +108 |

See above: NPV is +$108.

Thus, the IRR lies between 8% and 12%. We may estimate it by interpolation, as before.

IRR = 8% +[`108/(108 - (-98))] × (12% - 8%)

= 10.1%

The project should be rejected because the IRR is less than the cost of borrowing, which is 12%, i.e. the same conclusion as with NPV analysis above.

### Test your understanding 5

| Year | Equivalent cashflow at time 0 $ | | Equivalent cash flow at time 5 $ | |
|---|---|---|---|---|
| 0 | | (20,000) | | |
| 1 | | | $4,000 \times 1.06^4 =$ | 5,050 |
| 2 | $(2,000) \times 1/1.09^2 =$ | (1,683) | | |
| 3 | | | $6,000 \times 1.06^2 =$ | 6,742 |
| 4 | | | $7,600 \times 1.06 =$ | 8,056 |
| 5 | | | $10,000 \times 1 =$ | 10,000 |
| | | (21,683) | | 29,848 |

$$\sqrt[5]{\frac{29{,}848}{21{,}683}} - 1 = 6.6\%$$

Since the MIRR, the return on the project, is less than the cost of finance, the project should be rejected.

## Test your understanding 6

(i) when projects are independent and divisible, th PI method can be used.

| Project | PI (NPV/Investment) | Ranking |
|---------|---------------------|---------|
| A | 6.67 | 1 |
| B | 3.33 | 4 |
| C | 5.83 | 2 |
| D | 5.00 | 3 |

So, first do Project A (cost $9m), then do half of project C (cost $6m / 2 = $3m) to use the $12m of capital.

Total NPV = $60m (from A) + $17.5m (from half of C) = **$77.5m**

(ii) if projects are indivisible, a trial and error approach has to be used.

Choices for $12m investment are:

Either do A, or B, or (C+D).

By inspection, the best option is A, with an NPV of **$60m**.

(iii) if projects are mutually exclusive, pick the one with the highest positive NPV, i.e. A, with an NPV of **$60m**.

# The weighted average cost of capital (WACC)

## Chapter learning objectives

Upon completion of this chapter you will be able to:

- calculate a cost of equity using Dividend Valuation Model (DVM), the Capital Asset Pricing Model (CAPM) and Modigliani and Miller's Proposition 2 formula

- calculate a cost of debt using DVM, CAPM and credit spreads.

- understand how lenders set their interest rates on debt finance.

- calculate a weighted average cost of capital.

- understand the circumstances in which the WACC can be used as a project discount rate.

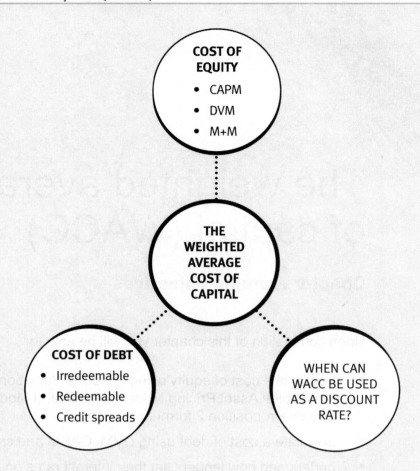

# 1 The weighted average cost of capital (WACC)
## Overview of the WACC

A key consideration in financial management is the firm's WACC. The WACC is derived by finding a firm's cost of equity and cost of debt and averaging them according to the market value of each source of finance. The formula for calculating WACC is given on the exam formula sheet as:

$$\text{WACC} = \left[\frac{V_e}{V_e + V_d}\right]k_e + \left[\frac{V_d}{V_e + V_d}\right]k_d(1-T)$$

### Expandable Text - Explanation of terms

$V_e$ and $V_d$ are the market values of equity and debt respectively.

$k_e$ and $k_d$ are the returns required by the equity holders and the debt holders respectively.

T is the corporation tax rate

$k_e$ is the cost of equity

$k_d(1-T)$ is the cost of debt

This chapter reviews the basic techniques for deriving cost of equity and cost of debt from the F9 paper, and adds some more advanced techniques too.

# 2 The cost of equity (ke)
## Methods of calculating $k_e$

The three main methods of calculating $k_e$ are:

- the Capital Asset Pricing Model (CAPM)
- the Dividend Valuation Model (DVM)
- Modigliani and Miller's Proposition 2 formula

The formulae for these methods are all given on the exam formula sheet.

### The Capital Asset Pricing Model (CAPM)

The CAPM derives a required return for an investor by relating return to the level of systematic risk faced by an investor - note that the CAPM is based on the assumption that all investors are well diversified, so only systematic risk is relevant.

The CAPM formula is:

Required return ( $k_e$ ) = $R_f$ + $\beta_i$ ($E(R_m)$ - $R_f$)

where:

$R_f$ = risk free rate

$E(R_m)$ = expected return on the market

N.B. ($E(R_m)$ - $R_f$) is called the equity risk premium

$\beta_i$ = beta factor = systematic risk of the firm or project compared to market.

### Expandable Text - The beta factor

The beta factor indicates the level of systematic risk faced by an investor.

A beta > 1 indicates above average risk, while beta < 1 means relatively low risk.

Beta factors are derived by statistically analysing returns from a particular share over a period compared to the overall market returns. If the returns on the individual share are more volatile than the overall market, the firm's beta will be greater than 1.

### Which beta factor to use?

To calculate the current cost of equity of a firm, the current beta factor can be used.

However, if the firm's current beta factor cannot be derived easily, a proxy beta may be used.

A proxy beta is usually found by identifying a quoted company with a similar business risk profile and using its beta. However, when selecting an appropriate beta from a similar company, account has to be taken of the gearing ratios involved.

The beta values for companies reflect both:

- business risk (resulting from operations)
- finance risk (resulting from their level of gearing).

There are therefore two types of beta:

- "Asset" or "ungeared" beta, $\beta_a$, which reflects purely the systematic risk of the business area.
- "Equity" or "geared" beta, $\beta_e$, which reflects the systematic risk of the business area and the company specific gearing ratio.

In the exam, you will often have to degear the proxy equity beta (using the gearing of the quoted company) and then regear to reflect the gearing position of the company in question.

The formula to regear and degear betas is:

$$\beta_a = \left[\frac{V_e}{(V_e + V_d(1-T))}\beta_e\right] + \left[\frac{V_d(1-T)}{V_e + V_d(1-T)}\beta_d\right]$$

However, $\beta_d$ (beta value for debt) is often assumed to be zero, because of the low risk of being a debt holder, so this equation often simplifies to give

$$\beta_a = \left[\frac{V_e}{(V_e + V_d(1-T))}\beta_e\right]$$

**Test your understanding 1**

The directors of Moorland Co, a company which has 75% of its operations in the retail sector and 25% in manufacturing, are trying to derive the firm's cost of equity. However, since the company is not listed, it has been difficult to determine an appropriate beta factor. Instead, the following information has been researched:

**Retail industry** - quoted retailers have an average equity beta of 1.20, and an average gearing ratio of 20:80 (debt:equity).

**Manufacturing industry** - quoted manufacturers have an average equity beta of 1.45 and an average gearing ratio of 45:55 (debt:equity).

The risk free rate is 3% and the equity risk premium is 6%. Tax on corporate profits is 30%. Moorland Co has gearing of 50% debt and 50% gearing by market values. Assume that the risk on corporate debt is negligible.

**Required:**

**Calculate the cost of equity of Moorland Co using the CAPM model.**

## The dividend valuation model (DVM)

**Theory:** The value of the company/share is the present value of the expected future dividends discounted at the shareholders' required rate of return.

Assuming a constant growth rate in dividends, g:

$$P_0 = D_0(1 + g) / (k_e - g)$$

(this formula is given on the formula sheet)

### Expandable Text - Explanation of terms

$D_0$ = current level of dividend

$P_0$ = current share price

g = estimated growth rate

If we need to derive ke the formula can be rearranged to:

ke = $[D_n (1+g) / P_n] + g$

### Expandable Text - Deriving g in the DVM formula

There are two ways of estimating the likely growth rate of dividends:

- Extrapolating based on past dividend patterns.
- Assuming growth is dependent on the level of earnings retained in the business.

## Estimating dividend growth from past dividend patterns

This method assumes that the past pattern of dividends is a fair indicator of the future.

The formula for extrapolating growth can therefore be written as:

$$g = \sqrt[n]{\frac{Do}{\text{Dividend n yrs ago}}} - 1 = \left(\frac{Do}{\text{Dividend n yrs ago}}\right)^{\left(\frac{1}{n}\right)} - 1$$

where:

n = number of years of dividend growth

This method can only be used if:

- recent dividend pattern is considered typical
- historical pattern is expected to continue.

As a result, this method will usually only be appropriate to predict growth rates over the short term.

### Illustration of the calculation

A company currently pays a dividend of 32¢; five years ago the dividend was 20¢.

Estimate the annual growth rate in dividends.

### Solution

Since growth is assumed to be constant, the growth rate, g, can be assumed to have been the same in each of the 5 years, i.e. the 20¢ will have become 32¢ after 5 years of constant growth.

$20¢ \times (1 + g)^5 = 32¢$

or $(1 + g)^5 = 32/20 = 1.6$

$1 + g = 1.6^{1/5} \approx 1.1$, so g = 0.1 or 10%.

### Estimating growth using the earnings retention model (Gordon's growth model)

This model is based on the assumption that:

* growth is primarily due to the reinvestment of retained earnings

The formula is therefore:

$g = r \times b$

where:

$b$ = earnings retention rate

$r$ = rate of return to equity

### What is r?

At F9 level, r was considered to be the Accounting Rate of Return on equity calculated as:

$r$ = PAT / opening shareholders' funds

However, at P4 we need to re-examine this assumption. The weakness of the ARR as a measure of return is that:

* it ignores the level of investment in intangible assets
* in the long run, the return on new investment tends to the cost of equity.

Hence, if a short term growth rate is required, the ARR provides a fair approximation for use in the growth model. However, if a long term growth rate is needed, $k_e$ should be used as the percentage return. To avoid a recursion problem, this should be derived using CAPM.

### Modigliani and Miller's Proposition 2 formula

Modigliani and Miller's gearing theory is covered in the later chapter on Capital Structure and Financing.

As part of their theory, they derived a formula which can be used to derive a firm's cost of equity:

$k_e = k_e^i + (1-T)(k_e^i - kd)(Vd / Ve)$

(this formula is given on the formula sheet)

## Expandable Text - Explanation of terms

$V_e$ and $V_d$ are the market values of equity and debt respectively.

$k_d$ is the (pre tax) return required by the debt holders.

T is the corporation tax rate

$k_e^i$ is the cost of equity in an equivalent ungeared firm

$k_e$ is the cost of equity in the geared firm

## Test your understanding 2

Moondog Co is a company with a 20:80 debt:equity ratio. Using CAPM, its cost of equity has been calculated as 12%.

It is considering raising some debt finance to change its gearing ratio to 25:75 debt to equity. The expected return to debt holders is 4% per annum, and the rate of corporate tax is 30%.

**Calculate the theoretical cost of equity in Moondog Co after the refinancing.**

## 3 The cost of debt (kd(1-T))

### Methods of calculating $k_d$(1-T)

The company's cost of debt is found by taking the return required by debt holders / lenders ($k_d$) and adjusting it for the tax relief received by the firm as it pays debt interest.

In paper F9, $k_d$ (1-T) was generally estimated using the principles of the dividend valuation model.

## Expandable Text - The use of DVM to estimate cost of debt

As seen above, the basic theory of the DVM is:

The value of a share = the present value of the future dividends discounted at the shareholders' required rate of return

Using the same logic,

The value of a bond = the present value of the future receipts (interest and redemption amount) discounted at the lenders' required rate of return.

This theory gives rise to two alternative calculations of $k_d$ (1-T):

**Irredeemable debt**

$K_d$ (1-T) = I (1-T) / MV

where

I = the annual interest paid,

T = corporation tax rate,

MV = the current bond price

**Redeemable debt**

$k_d$ (1-T) = the Internal Rate of Return (IRR) of

the bond price

the interest (net of tax)

the redemption payment

**Illustration of method**

Dodgy Co's 6% coupon bonds are currently priced at $89%. The bonds are redemable at par in 5 years. Corporation tax is 30%. Calculate the cost of debt.

To calculate IRR, we discount at 2 rates (5% and 10% here) and then interpolate:

PV at 5% = 89 - (6 × 5 yr 5% annuity factor) - (100 × 5 yr 5% discount factor) = -15.37

PV at 10% = 89 - (6 × 5 yr 10% annuity factor) - (100 × 5 yr 10% discount factor) = 4.15

Hence IRR (cost of debt) is approximately 8.9%

**Credit spread**

However, the main technique used in Paper P4 for deriving cost of debt is based on an awareness of **credit spread** (sometimes referred to as the "default risk premium"), and the formula:

$k_d$ (1-T) = (Risk free rate + Credit spread) (1-T)

The credit spread is a measure of the credit risk associated with a company. Credit spreads are generally calculated by a credit rating agency and presented in a table like the one below: To understand how credit spreads are derived, see the section on how lenders set their interest rates at the end of this chapter.

### Expandable Text - Credit risk, rating agencies and spread

#### What is credit risk?

Credit or default risk is the uncertainty surrounding a firm's ability to service its debts and obligations.

It can be defined as the risk borne by a lender that the borrower will default either on interest payments, the repayment of the borrowing at the due date or both.

#### The role of credit rating agencies

If a company wants to assess whether a firm that owes them money is likely to default on the debt, a key source of information is a credit rating agency.

They provide vital information on creditworthiness to:

- potential investors
- regulators of investing bodies
- the firm itself.

#### The assessment of creditworthiness

A large number of agencies can provide information on smaller firms, but for larger firms credit assessments are usually carried out by one of the international credit rating agencies. The three largest international agencies are Standard and Poors, Moodys and Fitch.

Certain factors have been shown to have a particular correlation with the likelihood that a company will default on its obligations:

- The magnitude and strength of the company's cash flows.
- The size of the debt relative to the asset value of the firm.
- The volatility of the firm's asset value.
- The length of time the debt has to run.

Using this and other data, firms are scored and rated on a scale, such as the one shown here:

| Fitch/S&P | Grade | Risk of default |
|---|---|---|
| AAA | Investment | Highest quality – zero risk |
| AA | Investment | High quality – v little risk |
| A | Investment | Strong – minimal risk |
| **BBB** | **Investment** | **Medium grade – low but clear risk** |
| BB | Junk | Speculative – marginal |
| B | Junk | Significant risk exposure |
| CCC | Junk | Considerable risk exposure |
| CC | Junk | Highly speculative – v high risk |
| C | Junk | In default – v high likelihood of failure |

## Calculating credit scores

The credit rating agencies use a variety of models to assess the creditworthiness of companies.

In the popular Kaplan Urwitz model, measures such as firm size, profitability, type of debt, gearing ratios, interest cover and levels of risk are fed into formulae to generate a credit score.

These scores are then used to create the rankings shown above. For example a score of above 6.76 suggests a AAA rating.

## Credit spread

There is no way to tell in advance which firms will default on their obligations and which won't. As a result, to compensate lenders for this uncertainty, firms generally pay a spread or premium over the risk-free rate of interest, which is proportional to their default probability.

The yield on a corporate bond is therefore given by:

Yield on corporate bond = Yield on equivalent treasury bond + credit spread

**Table of credit spreads for industrial company bonds:**

| Rating | 1 yr | 2 yr | 3 yr | 5 yr | 7 yr | 10 yr | 30 yr |
|---|---|---|---|---|---|---|---|
| AAA | 5 | 10 | 15 | 22 | 27 | 30 | 55 |
| AA | 15 | 25 | 30 | 37 | 44 | 50 | 65 |
| A | 40 | 50 | 57 | 65 | 71 | 75 | 90 |
| BBB | 65 | 80 | 88 | 95 | 126 | 149 | 175 |
| BB | 210 | 235 | 240 | 250 | 265 | 275 | 290 |
| B+ | 375 | 402 | 415 | 425 | 425 | 440 | 450 |

## Expandable Text - Examples of calculations of yield

### Simple illustration

The current return on 5-year treasury bonds is 3.6%. C plc has equivalent bonds in issue but has an A rating. What is the expected yield on C's bonds?

### Solution

From the table the credit spread for an A rated, 5-year bond is 65.

This means that 0.65% must be added to the yield on equivalent treasury bonds.

So yield on C's bonds = 3.6% + 0.65% = 4.25%

### More advanced illustration

The current return on 8-year treasury bonds is 4.2%. X plc has equivalent bonds in issue but has a BBB rating. What is the expected yield on X's bonds?

### Solution

From the table the credit spread for an BBB rated, 7-year bond is 126. The spread for a 10-year bond is 149.

This would suggest an adjustment of

$$126 + \frac{(149 - 126)}{3}$$

$= 126 + 7.67 = 133.67$

So 1.34% must be added to the yield on equivalent treasury bonds.

So yield on X's bonds = 4.2% + 1.34% = 5.54%

### Test your understanding 3

The current return on 4-year treasury bonds is 2.6%. F plc has equivalent bonds in issue but has a AA rating.

(i)  **calculate the expected yield on F's bonds**

(ii) **find F's cost of debt associated with these bonds if the rate of corporation tax is 30%**

(Use the information in the table of credit spreads above).

### Test your understanding 4

Landline Co has an A credit rating.

It has $30m of 2 year bonds in issue, which are trading at $90%, and $50m of 10 year bonds which are trading at $108%.

The risk free rate is 2.5% and the corporation tax rate is 30%.

**Calculate the company's cost of debt capital.**

(Use the information in the table of credit spreads above).

## Using the CAPM to calculate cost of debt

The CAPM can be used to derive a required return as long as the systematic risk of an investment is known. Earlier in the chapter we saw how to use an equity beta to derive a required return on equity. We also said that the risk on debt is usually relatively low, so the debt beta is often zero. However, if the debt beta is not zero (for example if the company's credit rating shows that it has a credit spread greater than zero) the CAPM can also be used to derive $k_d$ as follows:

$$kd = R_f + ß_{debt} (E(R_m) - R_f)$$

Then, the cost of debt is kd (1-T) as usual.

## 4 How do lenders set their interest rates?

### Link to credit spreads

The table of credit spreads shown above showed the premium over risk free rate which a company would have to pay in order to satisfy its lenders. Another way of looking at the issue of yield on a bond is to look at it from the perspective of the lender. How lenders set their interest rates was the subject of an article written by the examiner for Student Accountant magazine in August 2008.

### Overview of the method

Lenders set their interest rates after assessing the likelihood that the borrower will default. The basic idea is that the lender will assess the likelihood (using normal distribution theory) of the firm's cash flows falling to a level which is lower than the required interest payment in the coming year. If it looks likely that the firm will have to default, the interest rate will be set at a high level to compensate the lender for this risk.

**Expandable Text - Introduction to normal distribution theory**

The exam formula sheet contains a normal distribution table. Normal distributions have several applications in the P4 syllabus.

A normal distribution is often drawn as a "bell shaped" curve, with its peak at the mean in the centre, as shown:

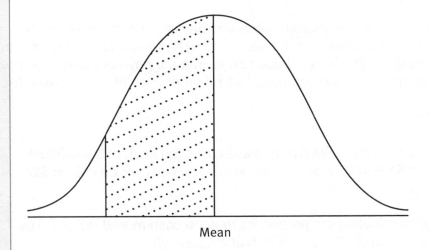

Mean

The figure from the normal distribution table gives the size of an area (shaded on the diagram) between the mean and a point z standard deviations away.

## Example of a simple normal distribution

The height of adult males is normally distributed with a mean of 175 cm and a standard deviation of 5cm.

What is the probability of a man being shorter than 168cm?

## Solution

168cm is 7cm away from the mean.

This represents 7/5 = 1.40 standard deviations.

From tables, 0.4192 of the normal curve lies between the mean and 1.40 standard deviations.

Hence, the probability of a man being shorter than 168cm is 0.5 - 0.4192 = 0.0808 (approximately 8%)

### Illustration 1

Villa Co has $2m of debt, on which it pays annual interest of 6%.

The company's operating cash flow in the coming year is forecast to be $140,000, and currently the company has $12,000 cash on deposit.

Given that the annual volatility (standard deviation) of the company's cash flows (measured over the last 5 years) has been 25%, calculate the probability that Villa Co will default on its interest payment within the next year (assuming that the company has no other lines of credit available).

### Solution

The key here is that Villa Co will have expected cash of $140,000 + $12,000 = $152,000, and its interest commitment will be 6% on $2m, i.e. $120,000.

We need to calculate the probability that the cash available will fall by $152,000 - $120,000 = $32,000 over the next year.

Assuming that the annual cash flow is normally distributed, a volatility (standard deviation) of 25% on a cash flow of $140,000 represents a standard deviation of 0.25 × $140,000 = $35,000.

Thus, our fall of $32,000 represents 32,000 / 35,000 = 0.91 standard deviations.

From the normal distribution tables, the area between the mean and 0.91 standard deviations = 0.3186.

Hence, there must be a 0.5 - 0.3186 = 0.1814 chance of the cashflow being insufficient to meet the interest payment.

i.e. the probability of default is approximately 18%.

Calculating the credit spread from this probability of default will be covered in the later chapter on Option Pricing.

## 5 The use of WACC as a discount rate in project appraisal
### Link to project appraisal

When evaluating a project, it is important to use a cost of capital which is appropriate to the risk of the new project. The existing WACC will therefore be appropriate as a discount rate if **both**:

(1)  the new project has the same level of business risk as the existing operations. If business risk changes, required returns of shareholders will change (to compensate them for the new level of risk), and hence WACC will change.

(2)  undertaking the new project will not alter the firm's gearing (financial risk). The values of equity and debt are key componenets in the calculation of WACC, so if the values change, clearly the existing WACC will no longer be applicable.

If one or both of these factors do not apply when undertaking a new project, the existing WACC cannot be used as a discount rate. The next chapter explores the alternative methods available in these situations.

# 6 Chapter overview

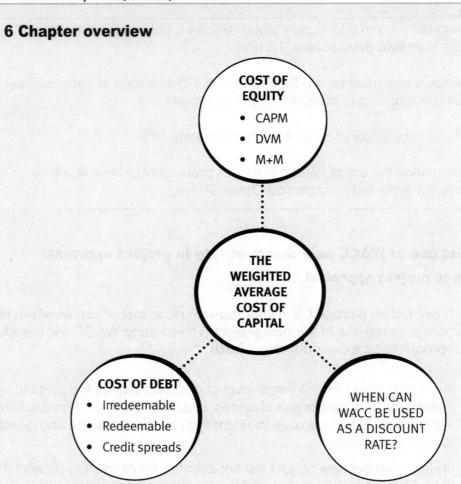

# Test your understanding answers

## Test your understanding 1

In order to use CAPM we shall need to derive a suitable equity beta for Moorland Co.

This will be done by first finding a suitable asset beta (based on the asset betas of the 2 parts of the business) and gearing up to reflect Moorland Co's 50:50 gearing level.

### Retail industry

the asset beta of retail operations can be found from the industry information as follows: (assuming the debt beta is zero)

$$\beta_a = \beta_e \times \frac{V_e}{V_e + V_d(1 - T)}$$

$$= 1.20 \times (80/(80 + 20(1 - 0.30)))$$

$$= 1.02$$

### Manufacturing industry

Similarly, the asset beta for manufacturing operations is:

$$\beta_a = \beta_e \times \frac{V_e}{V_e + V_d(1 - T)}$$

$$= 1.45 \times (55/(55 + 45(1 - 0.30)))$$

$$= 0.92$$

### Moorland Co asset beta

Hence, the asset beta of Moorland will be a weighted average of these two asset betas:

$ß_a$ (Moorland) = $(0.75 × 1.02) + (0.25 × 0.92) = 1.00$

### Moorland Co equity beta

So, regearing this asset beta now gives:

$1.00 = ß_e × [50/(50 + 50(1-0.30))]$

So, $ß_e = 1.00/0.59 = 1.69$

### Moorland Co cost of equity

Using CAPM:

$K_e = R_F + ß (E(R_M) - R_F) = 3\% + (1.69 × 6\%) = 13.1\%$

### Test your understanding 2

Using M+M's Proposition 2 equation, we can degear the existing $k_e$ and then regear it to the new gearing level:

### Degearing:

$k_e = k_e^i + (1-T)(k_e^i - kd)(Vd / Ve)$

$12\% = k_e^i + (1-0.30)(k_e^i - 4\%)(20 / 80)$

Rearranging carefully gives $k_e^i = 10.8\%$

### Now regearing:

$k_e = 10.8\% + (1-0.30)(10.8\%-4\%)(25/75)$

$k_e = 12.4\%$

KAPLAN PUBLISHING

## Test your understanding 3

From the table the credit spread for an AA rated, 3-year bond is 30. The spread for a 5-year bond is 37.

This would suggest an adjustment of:

30 + (37 - 30)/2 = 33.5 basis points

The yield is therefore found by adding 0.335% to the yield on equivalent treasury bonds.

So yield on F's bonds =

2.6% + 0.335% = 2.935%

The cost of debt = 2.935 × (1 − 0.3) = 2.05%

## Test your understanding 4

The overall cost of debt will be the weighted average of the costs of the two types of debt (weighted according to market values).

**2 year bonds**

Market value = $30m × 0.90 = $27m

kd = 2.5% + 50 credit spread (from table) = 3.00%

**10 year bonds**

Market value = $50m × 1.08 = $54m

kd = 2.5% + 75 credit spread (from table) = 3.25%

**Overall cost of debt**

Therefore the weighted average cost of debt (given that the ratio of market values is 1:2) is

[((1/3) × 3.00%) + ((2/3) × 3.25%)] × (1-0.30) = 2.22%

# Risk adjusted WACC and adjusted present value

## Chapter learning objectives

Upon completion of this chapter you will be able to:

- calculate a suitable project equity beta by degearing and re-gearing betas as appropriate, and use to calculate an appropriate WACC for investment appraisal

- explain the weaknesses of the traditional forms of discounting used in project appraisal where the investment decision will entail significant alterations in the financial structure of the firm and identify when they may not be appropriate

- apply the adjusted present value technique to the appraisal of investment decisions that entail significant alterations in the financial structure of the firm, including the calculation of transaction costs and the tax shield

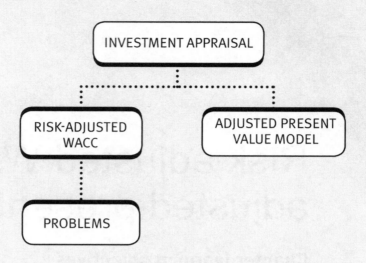

## 1 Introduction - the quadrant diagram

### Alternative methods of investment appraisal

As seen in the previous chapter, the company's existing WACC should not be used as a discount rate unless the business risk and financial risk are expected to stay constant when a new project is undertaken. If business risk and / or financial risk change when a new project is undertaken, the method of investment appraisal needs to be changed according to the following "quadrant diagram":

| | | Business risk | |
|---|---|---|---|
| | | **Same** | **Different** |
| **Financial risk** | **Same** | Existing WACC | Risk-adj. WACC |
| | **Different** | Use APV | Use APV |

## 2 The risk adjusted WACC

### Basic principle

If the business risk of the new project is different from the business risk of a company's existing operations, the company's shareholders will expect a different return to compensate them for this new level of risk.

Hence, the appropriate WACC which should be used to discount the new project's cashflows is not the company's existing WACC, but a "risk adjusted" WACC which incorporates this new required return to the shareholders (cost of equity).

## Calculating a risk-adjusted WACC

(1) Find the appropriate equity beta from a suitable quoted company.

(2) Adjust the available equity beta to convert it to an asset beta – degear it.

(3) Readjust the asset beta to reflect the project (i.e. its own) gearing levels – regear the beta.

(4) Use beta to find Ke.

(5) Use this Ke to find the WACC.

(6) Evaluate the project.

### Test Your Understanding 1

B plc is a hot air balloon manufacturer whose equity:debt ratio is 5:2. The corporate debt, which is assumed to be risk free, has a gross redemption yield of 11%. The beta value of the company's equity is 1.1. The average return on the stock market is 16%. The corporation tax rate is 30%.

The company is considering a waterbed-manufacturing project. S plc is a waterbed-manufacturing company. It has an equity beta of 1.59 and a $V_e$:$V_d$ ratio of 2:1. B plc will finance the project to maintain its existing capital structure.

**What would be a suitable cost of capital to apply to the project?**

## Using the risk-adjusted WACC

The risk-adjusted WACC calculated above reflects the business risk of the project and the current capital structure of the business, so it is wholly appropriate as a discount rate for the new project.

Two other issues also need to be considered:

- The method used to gear and degear betas is based on the assumption that debt is perpetual. This overvalues the tax shield where debt is finite.

- Issue costs on equity are ignored.

**Expandable Text - Theoretical points re: risk adjusted WACC**

The degearing and regearing procedure is a product of the M&M 1963 position. To use these equations debt must be perpetual and risk-free. If it is not perpetual, to ignore that it is for a shorter period will overvalue the tax shield on debt.

The value $V_e + V_d$ used in the WACC equation should represent market values of debt and equity after the project has been adopted (i.e. the equity value should include the NPV of the project).

By using the ratio of the company before the project we have assumed that the project has a zero NPV – this is unlikely to be the case. If the project has a positive NPV the calculation will assume that borrowing is proportional to the present value of future cash flows rather than the initial value of the asset.

## 3 The adjusted present value (APV) technique

### Basic principle

The APV method evaluates the project and the impact of financing separately. Hence, it can be used if a new project has a different financial risk (debt-equity ratio) from the company, i.e. the overall capital structure of the company changes.

APV consists of two different decisions:

| APV | = | Investment decision | + | Financing decision |
|---|---|---|---|---|
| (3) Value of a geared project | = | (1) Value of an all equity financed project | + | (2) Present value of financing side effects |

### The investment decision

The project is evaluated as though it were being undertaken by an all equity company with all financing side effects ignored. The financial risk is quantified later in the second part of the APV analysis – the financing decision. Therefore:

- ignore the financial risk in the investment decision process

- use a beta that reflects just the business risk, i.e.ß asset.

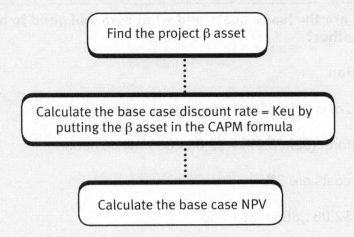

Find the project β asset

Calculate the base case discount rate = Keu by putting the β asset in the CAPM formula

Calculate the base case NPV

Once the base case NPV is identified, the PV of the financing package is evaluated.

## The financing decision

Financing cash flows consist of:

- issue costs
- tax reliefs.

As all financing cash flows are low risk they are discounted at either:

- the Kd or
- the risk free rate.

### Expandable Text - Examples of exam tricks on APV

#### APV tricks

In exam questions, you may see the following tricks when calculating the "financing decision" part. All these tricks are covered in the next "Test your understanding" questions:

#### Grossing up

A firm will know how much finance is required for the investment. Issue costs of finance will usually be quoted on top. It will therefore be necessary to gross up the funds to be raised.

#### Grossing up illustration

The finance required for a planned investment is $2m (net of issue costs). Issue costs are 3%. And the finance raised will also have to cover the issue costs.

**What are the issue costs and what sum will need to be raised altogether?**

**Solution**

The $2m is 97% of the amount to be raised:

Therefore, ($2m/0.97) = $2,061,856 will be needed.

Issue costs are 3%

3% × $2,061,856 = $61,856

Issue costs can be calculated in one stage as:

$2m × 3/97 = $61,856

### PV of debt issue costs

As always, calculations involving debt must take account of the tax effects.

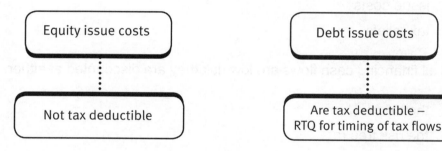

Method:

| | |
|---|---|
| Issue costs at $T_n$ | (X) |
| Tax relief at the CT rate (issue costs × CT rate) | X |
| PV of the tax relief (RTQ for timing of tax flows) | X |
| **PV of the issue costs** | **(X)** |
| (issue costs – PV of tax relief) | |

### PV of the tax relief on interest payment

The PV of the tax relief on interest payments is also known as the PV of the tax shield.

The method adopted depends on the information given:

## Simple scenario: Debentures – interest paid at a fixed amount each year

| | |
|---|---|
| Annual tax relief = Total loan × interest rate × tax rate | X |
| Annuity factor for n years | X |
| Year one discount factor (if tax is delayed one year) | X |
| **PV of the tax shield** | X |

## More complex scenario: Bank loans – repayments are for equal amounts

The repayments will be made up of both interest and capital elements.

### Step 1

Find the amount of the repayment

Annual amount = (Amount of the loan/Relevant annuity factor)

### Step 2

Compute the annual interest charge.

### Illustration of the more complex scenario

$400,000 is to be borrowed for 3 years and repaid in equal instalments. The risk-free rate is 10% and all debt is assumed to be risk free. Calculate the present value of the tax relief on the debt interest if the corporation tax rate is 30%. Assume that tax is delayed 1 year.

### Solution

Equal annual repayment = 400,000 / 3yr AF@10% = 400,000/2.487 = $160,836

| Year | Opening balance | Interest at 10% | Repayment | Closing balance |
|---|---|---|---|---|
| | $ | $ | $ | $ |
| 1 | 400,000 | 40,000 | 160,836 | 279,164 |
| 2 | 279,164 | 27,916 | 160,836 | 146,244 |
| 3 | 146,244 | 14,624 | 160,836 | 32 (diff due to rounding) |

The tax relief on the interest can now be calculated:

| Year | Interest cost | Tax relief @ 30% | Timing of tax | 10% DCF | PV |
|------|------|------|------|------|------|
| | $ | $ | $ | $ | $ |
| 1 | 40,000 | 12,000 | Year 2 | 0.826 | 9,912 |
| 2 | 27,916 | 8,375 | Year 3 | 0.751 | 6,290 |
| 3 | 14,624 | 4,387 | Year 4 | 0.683 | 2,932 |
| PV of tax relief = | | | | | 19,134 |

## Calculation of APV (in detail)

The base case NPV (investment decision) is used as a starting point. The costs and benefits of the financing are then added to find a final adjusted present value:

| | |
|------|------|
| Base case NPV | X |
| | |
| PV of the issue costs | |
| Equity | (X) |
| Debt | (X) |
| PV of the tax shield | X |
| | |
| | ___ |
| Adjusted Present Value | X |

A fully worked example now follows.

## Test your understanding 2

Rounding plc is a company currently engaged in the manufacture of baby equipment. It wishes to diversify into the manufacture of snowboards.

### The investment details

The company's equity beta is 1.27 and is current debt to equity ratio is 25:75, however the company's gearing ratio will change as a result of the new project.

Firms involved in snowboard manufacture have an average equity beta of 1.19 and an average debt to equity ratio of 30:70.

Assume that the debt is risk free, that the risk free rate is 10% and that the expected return from the market portfolio is 16%.

The new project will involve the purchase of new machinery for a cost of $800,000 (net of issue costs), which will produce annual cash inflows of $450,000 for 3 years. At the end of this time it will have no scrap value.

Corporation tax is payable in the same year at a rate of 33%. The machine will attract writing down allowances of 25% pa on a reducing balance basis, with a balancing allowance at the end of the project life when the machine is scrapped.

**The financing details:**

The new investment will be financed as follows:

Debentures (redeemable in three years time) :     40%
Rights issue of equity :     60%

The issue costs are 4% on the gross equity issued and 2% on the gross debt issued.

**Estimate the adjusted present value of the project.**

## Test Your Understanding 3

Blades plc is considering diversifying its operations away from its main area of business (food manufacturing) into the plastics business. It wishes to evaluate an investment project, which involves the purchase of a moulding machine that costs $450,000. The project is expected to produce net annual operating cash flows of $220,000 for each of the three years of its life. At the end of this time its scrap value will be zero.

The assets of the project will support debt finance of 40% of its initial cost (including issue costs).

The loan is to be repaid in three equal annual instalments. The balance of finance will be provided by a placing of new equity. Issue costs will be 5% of funds raised for the equity placing and 2% for the loan. Debt issue costs are allowable for corporation tax.

The plastics industry has an average equity beta of 1.368 and an average debt:equity ratio of 1:5 at market values. Blade's current equity beta is 1.8 and 20% of its long-term capital is represented by debt which is generally regarded to be risk-free.

The risk-free rate is 10% pa and the expected return on an average market portfolio is 15%.

Corporation tax is at a rate of 30%, payable in the same year. The machine will attract a 70% initial capital allowance and the balance is to be written off evenly over the remainder of the asset life and is allowable against tax. The firm is certain that it will earn sufficient profits against which to offset these allowances.

**Calculate the adjusted present value and determine whether the project is worthwhile.**

### Expandable Text - Additional factors regarding the APV method

#### Additional factors – subsidised/cheap loans

If a loan is cheap, the interest cost is lower. However, the benefit is reduced since the tax shield will also be lower:

PV of the cheap loan (opportunity benefit):

| | |
|---|---|
| PV of the interest saved | X |
| Less: PV of the tax relief lost | (X) |
| **PV of the cheap loan** | X |

**Example**: A plc requires $1 million in debt finance for 5 years.

It has borrowed $700,000 in the form of 10% debentures redeemable in 5 years and the remainder under a government subsidised loan scheme at 6%. The tax rate is 30%. Assume that tax is delayed one year.

Calculate the PV of the tax shields and the PV of the cheap loan.

(a) *PV of the tax shields*

Although the cheap loan has a cost of 6% it has the same risk as a normal loan, therefore the appropriate discount rate is 10% pa.

| | Normal loan | Cheap loan |
|---|---|---|
| Annual tax relief = Total loan × interest rate × tax rate | | |
| 700,000 × 0.10 × .30 = | 21,000 | |
| 300,000 × 0.06 × .30 = | | 5,400 |
| Annuity factor for 5 years @10% | 3.791 | 3.791 |
| Discount factor for 1 year @10% | 0.909 | 0.909 |
| **PV of the tax shield** | **72,366** | **18,609** |

**(b)** *PV of the cheap loan*

| | | 0 | 1 | 2 | 3 | 4 | 5 | 6 |
|---|---|---|---|---|---|---|---|---|
| Annuity | PV of the interest saved | | X | X | X | X | X | |
| Deferred annuity | PV of the tax relief lost | • | • | (X) | (X) | (X) | (X) | (X) |

| | Interest saved | Tax relief lost |
|---|---|---|
| **Annual amount** | | |
| 300,000 × (10% - 6%) = | 12,000 | |
| 12,000 × .30 = | | 3,600 |
| Annuity factor for 5 years | 3.791 | 3.791 |
| Present value factor – | | 0.909 |
| **PV of the cheap loan** | **45,492** | **(12,406)** |

The APV calculation is therefore amended as follows:

| | |
|---|---|
| Base case NPV | X/(X) |
| PV of the issue costs: | |
| Equity | (X) |
| Debt | (X) |
| PV of the tax shield: | |
| Normal loan | X |
| Cheap loan | X |
| PV of the cheap loan: | |
| Interest saved | X |
| Tax relief lost | (X) |
| Adjusted present value | X/(X) |

**Additional factors – debt capacity**

Debt finance benefits a project because of the associated tax shield. If a project brings about an increase in the borrowing capacity of the firm, it will increase the potential tax shield available.

An occasional exam trick is to give both the amount of debt actually raised and the increase in debt capacity brought about by the project. It is this theoretical debt capacity on which the tax shield should be based.

A project's debt capacity denotes its ability to act as security for a loan. It is the tax relief available on such a loan, which gives debt capacity its value.

When calculating the present value of the tax shield (tax relief on interest) it should be based on the project's theoretical debt capacity and not on the actual amount of the debt used.

The tax benefit from a project accrues from each pound of debt finance that it can support, even if the debt is used on some other project. We therefore use the theoretical debt capacity to match the tax benefit to the specific project.

For example, if a question stated that actual debt raised is $800,000 but you are told in the question 'The investment is believed to add $1 million to the company's debt capacity.' The present value of the tax shield is based on the £1 million – the theoretical amount.

## Advantages and disadvantages of APV

The APV technique has practical advantages and theoretical disadvantages.

### Advantages

- Step-by-step approach gives clear understanding of the elements of the decision

- Can evaluate any type of financing package

- More straightforward than adjusting the WACC which can be very complex

### Disadvantages

- Based on M&M's with-tax theory. Therefore ignores:
    - Bankruptcy risk
    - Tax exhaustion
    - Agency costs

- Based on M&M's with-tax theory. Therefore assumes:
    - Debt is risk free and irredeemable

## 4 Chapter summary

**Beta revisited**

Asset beta – reflects pure systematic business risk

Equity beta – reflects business and gearing risk

Betas can be geared and ungeared:

$$\beta \text{ asset} = \beta \text{ equity} \times \frac{V_e}{V_e + V_d(1-T)}$$

**INVESTMENT APPRAISAL**

**Problems with the risk-adjusted WACC**

- Can't cope if gearing ratio changed by project
- Over-values tax shield where debt not permanent
- Ignore costs of raising finance.

**Adjusted present value model**

Two-part approach:

- Find base NPV:
  PV of project flows using asset beta in the CAPM
- Find PV of financing
  PV of issue costs on equity
  PV of issue costs on debt
  PV of tax relief

## Test your understanding answers

### Test Your Understanding 1

**Step 1**

B Plc has selected an appropriate equity beta for waterbed-manufacturing of 1.59

**Step 2**

Based on new industry information:

*   the ß equity (1.59)
*   gearing ratio of the new industry (2:1)

de-gear the equity beta of the company in the new industry and find the business risk asset beta of the new project/industry.

$$\beta_a = \beta_e \times \frac{V_e}{V_e + V_d(1 - T)}$$

$$= 1.59 \times (2/(2 + 1(1 - 0.3)))$$

$$= 1.18$$

**Step 3**

Calculate the equity beta of the new project, by re-gearing:

*   incorporate the financial risk of our company using our gearing ratio (5:2)

$$\beta_a = \beta_e \times \frac{V_e}{V_e + V_d(1 - T)}$$

$$1.18 = \beta_e \times [5/(5 + 2(0.70))]$$

$$1.18 = 0.78 \, \beta_e$$

$$\beta_e = 1.18/0.78 = 1.51$$

**Now proceed as usual**

Calculate the cost of equity of the project based on CAPM:

$K_e = R_F + ß \ (E(R_M) - R_F) = 11\% + 1.51 (16\% - 11\%) = 18.55\%$

Find the cost of debt:

$K_d = I (1 - T)$

$K_d = 11\% (1 - 0.3) = 7.70\%$

Calculate the WACC of the project.

(Use our company's D:E ratio)

WACC = 18.55% × 5/7 + 7.70 × 2/7 = 15.45%

We have calculated a discount rate, which reflects the systematic risk of this particular project.

## Test your understanding 2

### The investment decision

Estimate the base case NPV.

Firstly compute the asset beta of the project. This is achieved by degearing the equity beta from the snowboard industry average.

$ß_a = ß_e \times [V_e/(V_e + V_d(1 - T))]$

$ß_a = 1.19 \times (70/(70 + 30(1 - 0.33)))$

$ß_a = 0.92$

The next task is to determine the base case discount rate for the project.

$E(R_i) = R_f + (E(R_m) - R_f) ß_a$

$= 10\% + (16\% - 10\%) 0.92$

$= 15.52\%$ – round to the nearest % point so we can use the tables.

Therefore we will use **16%**.

### Base case NPV calculation

| Time | 0 | 1 | 2 | 3 |
|---|---|---|---|---|
| | $000 | $000 | $000 | $000 |
| Receipts | | 450 | 450 | 450 |
| Corporation tax | | (149) | (149) | (149) |
| @33% | | | | |
| Tax relief on capital allowances (W1) | | 66 | 50 | 149 |
| Initial outlay | (800) | | | |
| | ――― | ――― | ――― | ――― |
| Net cash flow | (800) | 367 | 351 | 450 |
| Discount rate (16%) | 1 | 0.862 | 0.743 | 0.641 |
| | ――― | ――― | ――― | ――― |
| Present value | (800) | 316 | 261 | 288 |
| **Base case NPV** | **65** | | | |

## Capital allowances computation W1

|  | W.D.A. | Tax relief at 33% | Timing |
|---|---|---|---|
| Investment | 800 | | |
| Y1 WDA | (200) | 66 | Time 1 |
| | 600 | | |
| Y2 WDA | (150) | 50 | Time 2 |
| | 450 | | |
| Y3 Proceeds | 0 | | |
| | 450 | | |
| Balancing allowance | 450 | 149 | Time 3 |

## (2) The financing decision

Lay out the financing package:

| | $ | Issue costs |
|---|---|---|
| Equity – 60% × 800,000 | 480,000 | 4% |
| Debt – 40% × 800,000 | 320,000 | 2% |
| | 800,000 | |

### A   PV of issue costs on equity

The question states that the $800k is net of issue costs therefore we need to gross up.

Equity issue cost: $480,000 × 4/96 = ($20,000)

### B   PV of issue costs on debt

Debt issue cost: $320,000 × (2 /98) ($6,531)

| | |
|---|---|
| Issue costs of debt at $T_0$ | ($6,531) |
| Tax relief at 33% | $2,155 |
| **PV of the issue costs on debt** | **($4,376)** |

### C  PV of the tax shield

Total amount raised by loan – don't forget to add the issue costs

= $320,000 + $6,531 = **$326,531**

| | |
|---|---:|
| Annual tax relief = $326,531 × 0.10 × 0.33 | 10,776 |
| | × |
| Annuity factor for 3 years | 2.487 |
| PV of the tax shield | **$26,800** |

### (3)  The APV calculation

| | |
|---|---:|
| Base cost NPV | 65,000 |
| Less: PV of issue costs: | |
|     Equity | (20,000) |
|     Debt | (4,376) |
| Plus PV of tax shield | 26,800 |
| Therefore adjusted present value is | $67,424 |

Based upon these estimates the project appears financial viable.

KAPLAN PUBLISHING

## Test Your Understanding 3

### Step 1: Base case net present value

First compute the ungeared (asset) beta for this project type (based on the equity beta for the plastics industry).

$$\beta_a = \beta_e \times \frac{V_e}{V_e + V_d(1 - T)}$$

$$= 1.368 \times [5/(5 + 1(1 - 0.30))]$$
$$= 1.2$$

Required return of project
$$= 10\% + (15\% - 10\%)\,1.2$$
$$= 16\% \text{ pa.}$$

Then discount the project cash flows at 16%

| Time | 0 | 1 | 2 | 3 |
|---|---|---|---|---|
| | $000 | $000 | $000 | $000 |
| Equipment | (450) | | | |
| Capital allowances (W1) | | 94.5 | 20.25 | 20.25 |
| Operating cash flows | | 220.00 | 220.00 | 220.00 |
| Tax on operating cash flows | | (66.00) | (66.00) | (66.00) |
| | (450) | 31248.5 | 174.25 | 174.25 |
| 16% factors | 1 | 0.862 | 0.743 | 0.641 |
| PV | (450) | 214.21 | 129.47 | 111.69 |
| Base case NPV = | $5,370 | | | |

**Workings**

**W1 – Capital allowances**

|  | Tax @30% |  |
|---|---|---|
|  | $ | $ |
| Cost of machine | 450,000 |  |
| First year allowances (70%) | 315,000 | 94,500 |
|  | ——— |  |
|  | 135,000 |  |
|  | ——— |  |
| Writing down allowances (straight line) |  |  |
| (for each of next three years) | 67,500 | 20,250 |

**Step 2: Adjusted present value (the side effects)**

Lay out the financing package:

|  | $ |
|---|---|
| Capital requirements: |  |
| Equity (60%) | 270,000 |
| Debt (40%) | 180,000 |
|  | ——— |
|  | 450,000 |
|  | ——— |

|  | $ |
|---|---|
| Issue costs: |  |
| (i) Equity 5/95 × 270,000 | 14,210 |
| (ii) Debt 2/98 × 180,000 | 3,673 |
| Issue costs on debt at $T_0$ | ($3,673) |
| Tax relief at 30% | $1,102 |
|  | ——— |
| **PV of the issue costs on debt** | **($2,571)** |

(iii) Tax relief on loan interest

Gross value of loan = $180,000 + $3,673 (issue costs) = $183,673

Annual repayments = $183,673/2.487 = $73,853

Loan schedule

| Year | Opening balance | Interest | Repayment | Closing balance |
|------|-----------------|----------|-----------|-----------------|
|      | $ | $ | $ | $ |
| 1 | 183,673 | 18,367 | 73,853 | 128,187 |
| 2 | 128,187 | 12,819 | 73,853 | 67,153 |
| 3 | 67,153 | 6,715 | 73,853 | 15 (rounding diff) |

Tax relief at 30% on interest:

| Year | Cash | 10% factor | PV |
|------|------|------------|-----|
|      | $ |  | $ |
| 1 | 5,510 | 0.909 | 5,009 |
| 2 | 3,846 | 0.826 | 3,177 |
| 3 | 2,015 | 0.6751 | 1,513 |
|   |   |   | ––––– |
|   |   |   | 9,699 |
|   |   |   | ––––– |

## Step 3: Adjusted present value

|  | $ |
|--|---|
| Base case NPV | 5,370 |
| Issue costs – equity | (14,210) |
| Issue costs – debt | (2,571) |
| Tax shield | 9,699 |
|  | ––––– |
| The project APV is | (1,712) |
|  | ––––– |

The project will reduce shareholder wealth by $1,712 and is not acceptable.

# 5

# Capital structure (gearing) and financing

## Chapter learning objectives

Upon completion of this chapter you will be able to:

- explain the basic principles of capital structure theory and identify the major factors which would influence the optimum capital mix and structure for a firm

- in a scenario question, within a specified business context and capital asset structure, recommend the optimum capital mix and structure for a firm

- describe pecking order theory and assess the impact it has on the financing of investment decisions

- describe static trade-off theory (that the optimal capital structure involves a trade off between the tax benefits of debt and the increased bankruptcy costs of debt) and assess the impact it has on the financing of investment decisions

- describe the agency effects on capital structure and assess the impact it has on the financing of investment decisions.

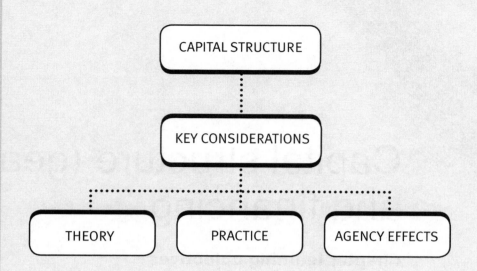

## 1 Introduction

A financial manager often has to decide what type of finance to raise in order to fund the investment in a new project.

This chapter covers the key practical and theoretical considerations which influence the basic financing decision i.e. should debt or equity finance be used?

Then, the chapter explains the main features of the key debt and equity financing options.

## 2 The basic financing decision - debt or equity

### Practical considerations

The following diagram summarises the main practical factors which must be considered when choosing between debt and equity finance.

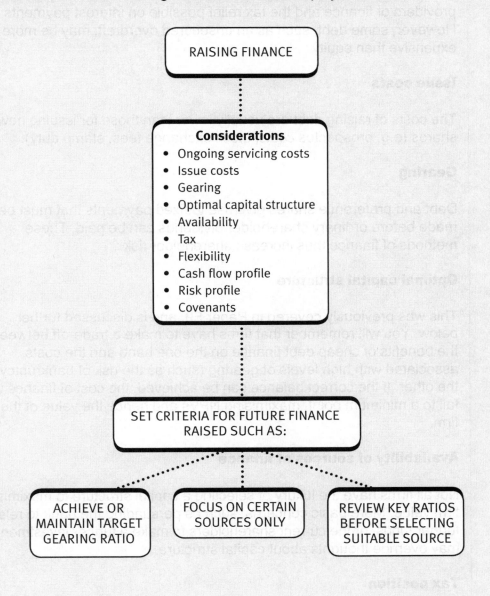

**Expandable Text - More detail on practical considerations**

### Ongoing servicing costs

Debt is usually cheaper than equity due to lower risk faced by the providers of finance and the tax relief possible on interest payments. However, some debt, such as an unsecured overdraft, may be more expensive than equity.

### Issue costs

The costs of raising debt are usually lower than those for issuing new shares (e.g. prospectus costs, stock exchange fees, stamp duty).

### Gearing

Debt and preference shares give rise to fixed payments that must be made before ordinary shareholder dividends can be paid. These methods of finance thus increase shareholder risk.

### Optimal capital structure

This was previously covered in Paper F9, and is discussed further below. You will remember that firms have to make a trade-off between the benefits of cheap debt finance on the one hand and the costs associated with high levels of gearing (such as the risk of bankruptcy) on the other. If the correct balance can be achieved, the cost of finance will fall to a minimum point, maximising NPVs and hence the value of the firm.

### Availability of sources of finance

Not all firms have the luxury of selecting a capital structure to maximise firm value. More basic concerns, such as persuading the bank to release further funds, or the current shareholders to make a further investment, may override thoughts about capital structure.

### Tax position

The tax benefits of debt only remain available whilst the firm is in a tax paying position.

### Flexibility

Some firms operating in high risk industries use mainly equity finance to gain the flexibility not to have to pay dividends should returns fall.

## Cash flow profile

Cash flow forecasts are central to financing decisions – e.g. ensuring that two sources of finance do not mature at the same time.

## Risk profile

Business failure can have a far greater impact on directors than on a well-diversified investor. It may be argued that directors have a natural tendency to be cautious about borrowing.

## Covenants

There may be restrictions imposed on the level of gearing, either by the company's Articles of Association (the internal regulations that govern the way the company must be run), or by previous loan agreements.

## Theoretical considerations

The main capital structure theories assess the way in which a change in gearing / capital structure impacts on the firm's weighted average cost of capital (WACC).

The theories consider the relative sizes of the following two opposing forces:

First, debt is (usually) cheaper than equity:

- Lower risk.
- Tax relief on interest.

so we might expect that increasing proportion of debt finance would **reduce WACC**.

## BUT:

Second, increasing levels of debt makes equity more risky:

- Fixed commitment paid before equity – finance risk.

so increasing gearing (proportion of finance in the form of debt) increases the cost of equity and that would **increase WACC.**

The theories attempt to answer the question:

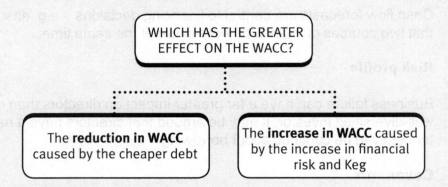

WHICH HAS THE GREATER EFFECT ON THE WACC?

The **reduction in WACC** caused by the cheaper debt

The **increase in WACC** caused by the increase in financial risk and Keg

## The traditional view

Also known as the intuitive view, the traditional view has no theoretical basis but common sense. It concludes that a firm should have an optimal level of gearing, where WACC is minimised, BUT it does not tell us where that optimal point is. The only way of finding the optimal point is by trial and error.

### Expandable Text - The traditional view explained

At low levels of gearing:

Equity holders see risk increases as marginal as gearing rises, so the cheapness of debt issue dominates resulting in a lower WACC.

At higher levels of gearing:

Equity holders become increasingly concerned with the increased volatility of their returns (debt interest paid first). This dominates the cheapness of the extra debt so the WACC starts to rise as gearing increases.

At very high levels of gearing:

Serious bankruptcy risk worries equity and debt holders alike so both $K_e$ and $K_d$ rise with increased gearing, resulting in the WACC rising further.

This can be shown diagrammatically:

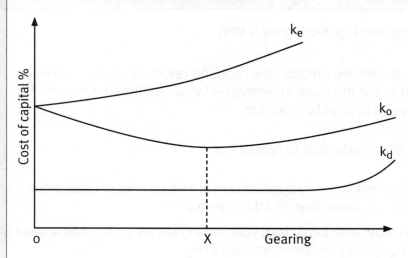

where:

$K_e$ is the cost of equity

$K_d$ is the cost of debt, and

$K_o$ is the overall or weighted average cost of capital.

Conclusion:

There is an optimal level of gearing – point X.

Problem:

There is no method, apart from trial and error, available to locate the optimal point.

## Modigliani and Miller's theory (with tax)

Modigliani and Miller's "with tax theory" concluded that because of the tax advantages of issuing debt finance (tax relief on debt interest) firm's should increase their gearing as much as possible. The theory is based on assumptions such as perfect capital markets.

**↑gearing = ↑Ke**

## Expandable Text - Modigliani and Miller's theory explained

The starting point for the theory is that:

*   as investors are rational, the required return of equity is directly linked to the increase in gearing – i.e. as gearing increases, $K_e$ increases in direct proportion.

However, this is adjusted to reflect that:

*   debt interest is tax deductible so the overall cost of debt to the company is lower than in MM – no tax

*   lower debt costs imply less volatility in returns for the same level of gearing, giving smaller increases in $K_e$

*   the increase in $K_e$ does not offset the benefit of the cheaper debt finance and therefore the WACC falls as gearing is increased.

Conclusion:

Gearing up reduces the WACC, and the optimal capital structure is 99.9% gearing.

This is demonstrated in the following diagrams:

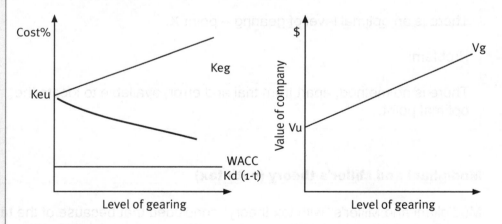

In practice firms are rarely found with the very high levels of gearing as advocated by MM. This is because of:

*   bankruptcy risk

*   agency costs

*   tax exhaustion

*   the impact on borrowing/debt capacity

*   differences in risk tolerance levels between shareholders and directors

- restrictions in the Articles of Association
- increases in the cost of borrowing as gearing increases.

As a result, despite the theories, gearing levels in real firms tend to be based on more practical considerations. These matters are discussed below.

In practice firms are rarely found with the very high levels of gearing as advocated by Modigliani and Miller. This is because of:

- bankruptcy risk
- agency costs
- tax exhaustion
- the impact on borrowing/debt capacity
- differences in risk tolerance levels between shareholders and directors
- restrictions in the Articles of Association
- increases in the cost of borrowing as gearing increases.

As a result, despite the theories, gearing levels in real firms tend to be based on more practical considerations.

**Expandable Text - Key practical arguments against M+M**

**Bankruptcy risk**
As gearing increases so does the possibility of bankruptcy. If shareholders become concerned, this will reduce the share price and increase the WACC of the company.

**Agencycosts: restrictive conditions**
In order to safeguard their investments lenders/debentures holders often impose restrictive conditions in the loan agreements that constrains management's freedom of action.

E.g. restrictions:

- on the level of dividends
- on the level of additional debt that can be raised
- on management from disposing of any major fixed assets without the debenture holders' agreement.

## Tax exhaustion

After a certain level of gearing companies will discover that they have no tax liability left against which to offset interest charges.

$K_d(1-t)$ simply becomes $K_d$.

## Borrowing/debt capacity

High levels of gearing are unusual because companies run out of suitable assets to offer as security against loans. Companies with assets, which have an active second-hand market, and low levels of depreciation such as property companies, have a high borrowing capacity.

## Difference risk tolerance levels between shareholders and directors

Business failure can have a far greater impact on directors than on a well-diversified investor. It may be argued that directors have a natural tendency to be cautious about borrowing.

### Test your understanding 1

X Co, an unquoted manufacturing company, has been experiencing a growth in demand, and this trend is expected to continue. In order to cope with the growth in demand, the company needs to buy further machinery and this is expected to cost 30% of the current company value.

In the past, a high proportion of earnings has been distributed by way of dividends so few cash reserves are available. 51% of the shares in X Co are still owned by the founding family.

A decision must now be taken about how to raise the funds. The firm has already raised some loan finance and this is secured against the company land and buildings.

**Suggest the issues that should be considered by the board in determining whether debt would be an appropriate source of finance.**

## 3 Real world approaches to the gearing question

### Static trade-off theory

It is possible to revise M and M's theory to incorporate bankruptcy risk and so to arrive at the same conclusion as the traditional theory of gearing – i.e. that an optimal gearing level exists.

Given this, firms will strive to reach the optimum level by means of a trade-off.

Static trade-off theory argues that firms in a stable (static) position will adjust their current level of gearing to achieve a target level:

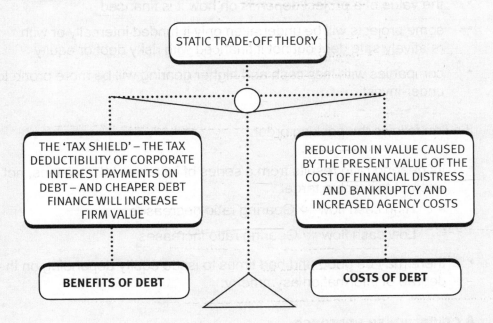

Above target debt ratio the value of the firm is not optimal:

- Financial distress and agency costs exceed the benefits of debt.

- Firms decrease their debt levels.

Below the target debt ratio can still increase the value of the firm because:

- marginal value of the benefits of debt are still greater than the costs associated with the use of debt

- firms increase their debt.

**NB:** Research suggests that this theory is not backed up by empirical evidence.

## Pecking order theory

Pecking order theory tries to explain why firms do not behave the way the static trade-off model would predict. It states that firms have a preferred hierarchy for financing decisions:

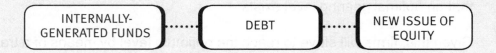

INTERNALLY-GENERATED FUNDS ······ DEBT ······ NEW ISSUE OF EQUITY

The implications for investment are that:

- the value of a project depends on how it is financed

- some projects will be undertaken only if funded internally or with relatively safe debt but not if financed with risky debt or equity

- companies with less cash and higher gearing will be more prone to under-invest.

If a firm follows the pecking order:

- its gearing ratio results from a series of incremental decisions, not an attempt to reach a target
  - High cash flow $\Rightarrow$ Gearing ratio decreases
  - Low cash flow $\Rightarrow$ Gearing ratio increases

- there may be good and bad times to issue equity depending on the degree of information asymmetry.

## A compromise approach

The different theories can be reconciled to encourage firms to make the correct financing decisions:

(1) Select a long run target gearing ratio.

(2) Whilst far from target, decisions should be governed by static trade-off theory.

(3) When close to target, pecking order theory will dictate source of funds.

### Test your understanding 2

**What factors about the raising and servicing the various sources of funds may explain the order of preference of most companies?**

## Expandable Text - More on pecking order v static trade off

Pecking order theory was developed to suggest a reason for this observed inconsistency in practice between the static trade-off model and what companies actually appear to do.

### Issue costs ✓

Internally generated funds have the lowest issue costs, debt moderate issue costs and equity the highest. Firms issue as much as they can from internally generated funds first then move on to debt and finally equity.

*[handwritten notes in margin: Cheapest Issue Cost ① Internally generated funds (R-E) ② Debt (Moderate) ③ Equity (Expensive)]*

### Asymmetric information

Myers has suggested asymmetric information as an explanation for the heavy reliance on retentions. This may be a situation where managers, because of their access to more information about the firm, know that the value of the shares is greater than the current market value based on the weak and semi-strong market information.

In the case of a new project, managers forecast maybe higher and more realistic than that of the market. If new shares were issued in this situation there is a possibility that they would be issued at too low a price, thus transferring wealth from existing shareholders to new shareholders. In these circumstances there might be a natural preference for internally generated funds over new issues. If additional funds are required over and above internally generated funds, then debt would be the next alternative.

If management is against making equity issues when in possession of favourable inside information, market participants might assume that management would be more likely to favour new issues when they are in possession of unfavourable inside information. This leads to the suggestion that new issues might be regarded as a signal of bad news! Managers may therefore wish to rely primarily on internally generated funds supplemented by borrowing, with issues of new equity as a last resort.

Myers and Majluf (1984) demonstrated that with asymmetric information, equity issues are interpreted by the market as bad news, since managers are only motivated to make equity issues when shares are overpriced. Bennett Stewart (1990) puts it differently: 'Raising equity conveys doubt. Investors suspect that management is attempting to shore up the firm's financial resources for rough times ahead by selling over-valued shares.'

> Asquith and Mullins (1983) empirically observed that announcements of new equity issues are greeted by sharp declines in stock prices. Thus, equity issues are comparatively rare among large established companies.

### Dealing with 'gearing drift'

Profitable companies will tend to find that their gearing level gradually reduces over time as accumulated profits help to increase the value of equity. This is known as "gearing drift".

Gearing drift can cause a firm to move away from its optimal gearing position.

The firm might have to occasionally increase gearing (by issuing debt, or paying a large dividend or buying back shares) to return to its optimal gearing position.

### Signalling to investors

In a perfect capital market, investors fully understand the reasons why a firm chooses a particular source of finance.

However, in the real world it is important that the firm considers the signalling effect of raising new finance. Generally, it is thought that raising new finance gives a positive signal to the market: the firm is showing that it is confident that it has identified attractive new projects and that it will be able to afford to service the new finance in the future.

Investors and analysts may well assess the impact of the new finance on a firm's income statement and balance sheet (statement of financial position) in order to help them assess the likely success of the firm after the new finance has been raised.

## Test your understanding 3

A company is considering a number of funding options for a new project. The new project may be funded by $10m of equity or debt. Below are the financial statements under each option.

**Statement of financial position (Balance sheet) extract**

|  | Equity finance $m | Debt finance $m |
|---|---|---|
| Long term liabilities |  |  |
| Debentures (10%) | 0.0 | 10.0 |
|  |  |  |
| Capital |  |  |
| Share capital (50¢) | 11.0 | 3.5 |
| Share premium | 4.0 | 1.5 |
| Reserves | 5.0 | 5.0 |
|  | 20.0 | 10.0 |

**Income statement extract**

|  | £m |
|---|---|
| Revenue | 100.0 |
| Gross profit | 20.0 |
| Less expenses (excluding finance charges) | (15.0) |
| Operating profit | 5.0 |

Corporation tax is charged at 30%.

(a) **Calculate ROCE and return on equity (ROE) and compare the financial performance of the company under the two funding options.**

(b) **What is the impact on the company's performance of financing by debt rather than equity?**

## 4 Agency effects

Agency costs have a further impact on a firm's practical financing decisions.

Where gearing is high, the interests of management and shareholders may conflict with those of creditors.

Management may for example:

- gamble on high-risk projects to solve problems
- pay large dividends to secure company value for themselves
- hide problems and cut back on discretionary spending
- invest in higher risk business areas than the loan was designated to fund.

In order to safeguard their investments lenders/debentures holders often impose restrictive conditions in the loan agreements that constrains management's freedom of action: these may include restrictions:

- on the level of dividends
- on the level of additional debt that can be raised
- on acceptable working capital and other ratios
- on management from disposing of any major asset without the debenture holders' agreement.

These effects may:

- encourage use of retained earnings
- restrict further borrowing
- make new issues less attractive to investors.

### Expandable Text - More on agency effects

In a situation of high gearing, shareholder and creditor interests are often at odds regarding the acceptability of investment projects.

Shareholders may be tempted to gamble on high-risk projects as if things work out well they take all the 'winnings' whereas if things turn out badly the debenture holders will stand part of the losses, the shareholders only being liable up to their equity stake.

There are further ways in which managers (appointed by shareholders) can act in the interests of the shareholders rather than the debt holders:

## Dividends

We have seen how shareholders may be reluctant to put money into an ailing company. On the other hand they are usually happy to take money out. Large cash dividends will secure part of the company's value for the shareholders at the expense of the creditors.

## Playing for time

In general, because of the increasing effect of the indirect costs of bankruptcy, if a firm is going to fail, it is better that this happens sooner rather than later from the creditors' point of view. However, managers may try to hide the extent of the problem by cutting back on research, maintenance, etc. and thus make 'this year's' results better at the expense of 'next year's'.

## Changing risks

The company may change the risk of the business without informing the lender. For example, management may negotiate a loan for a relatively safe investment project offering good security and therefore carrying only modest interest charges and then use the funds to finance a far riskier investment. Alternatively management may arrange further loans which increase the risks of the initial creditors by undercutting their asset backing. These actions will once again be to the advantage of the shareholders and to the cost of the creditors.

It is because of the risk that managers might act in this way that most loan agreements contain restrictive covenants for protection of the lender, the costs of these covenants to the firms in terms of constraints upon managers' freedom of action being a further example of **agency costs**.

Covenants used by suppliers of debt finance may place restrictions on:

- issuing new debt – with a superior claim on assets
- dividends – growth to be linked to earnings
- merger activity – to ensure post-merger asset backing of loans is maintained at a minimum prescribed level
- investment policy.

Contravention of these agreements will usually result in the loan becoming immediately repayable, thus allowing the debenture holders to restrict the size of any losses.

## 5 Equity financing options

The main options for companies wishing to raise equity finance are:

- rights issue to existing shareholders - this option is the simplest method, providing the existing shareholders can afford to invest the amount of funds required. The existing shareholders' control is not diluted.

- public issue of shares - gaining a public listing increases the marketability of the company's shares, and makes it easier to raise further equity finance from a large number of investors in the future. Becoming a listed company is an expensive and time-consuming process, and once listed, the company has to face a higher level of regulation and public scrutiny. Also, since the company's shares are likely to become widely distributed between many investors, the threat of takeover increases when a company becomes listed.

- private placing - "private equity finance" is the name given to finance raised from investors organised through the mediation of a venture capital company or private equity business. These investors do not operate through the formal equity market, so raising private equity finance does not expose the company to the same level of scrutiny and regulation that a stock market listing would. Private equity is often perceived as a relatively high risk investment, so investors usually demand higher rates of return than they would from a stock market listed company. Business Angels are a source of private equity finance for small companies.

Read Peter Atrill's March 2009 article in Student Accountant magazine ("Being an Angel") for more details on Business Angels.

## 6 Debt financing options

A company seeking to raise long term debt finance will be constrained by its size, its debt capacity and its credit rating.

Small and medium sized enterprises (SMEs) may make use of private lending through family, friends and other small business investors. The usual starting point is to approach a bank, who will make a lending decision based on the company's business plan.

Larger companies have the following additional options:

- bond issue - this is an attractive way of raising large amounts of debt finance, at a low rate of interest. There are however significant issue costs and there is a risk that the issue might not be fully subscribed (unless it is underwritten). Bonds may be issued in the domestic, or an overseas, capital market.

- debenture issue - debentures are asset backed securities (i.e. lower risk for investors).

- convertible bond issue - convertibles carry the right of conversion to equity at some future date. This makes the bond more attractive to a potential investor.

- mezzanine finance - the most risky type of debt from the lender's point of view. The holder of mezzanine debt is ranked after all the other debt holders on a liquidation, and the debt is unsecured. A high coupon rate has to be paid to compensate the investor for this risk.

- syndicated loan - for large amounts of debt finance, where one bank is not prepared to take the risk of lending such a large amount, a loan may be raised from a syndicate of banks. Rates of interest tend to be slightly higher than those in the bond market, but transaction costs are low and loans can be arranged much quicker than a bond issue.

## 7 Chapter summary

```
                          ┌─────────────────────────┐
                          │    CAPITAL STRUCTURE     │
                          └─────────────────────────┘
                                     ┊
                          ┌─────────────────────────┐
                          │   KEY CONSIDERATIONS     │
                          │  • Ongoing servicing costs│
                          │  • Issue costs           │
                          │  • Gearing               │
                          │  • Optimal capital structure│
                          │  • Availability          │
                          │  • Tax                   │
                          │  • Flexibility           │
                          │  • Cash flow profile     │
                          │  • Risk profile          │
                          │  • Covenants             │
                          └─────────────────────────┘
```

**THEORY**
- Traditional theory – find the optimal gearing level
- MM with tax – gear up as much as possible
- Bankruptcy risk changes MM to give similar result to traditional

**PRACTICE**
- Static trade-off
- Pecking order
- Compromise

**AGENCY EFFECTS**

# Test your understanding answers

## Test your understanding 1

Issues to raise would include:

- Retained earnings – often a preferred source of funds for smaller firms, these cannot be easily used here as the family shareholders expect significant dividends. This means that outside finance must be considered.

- High level of required funding relative to the size of the firm – could be perceived by potential investors as increasing business risk even though the expansion is in the same industry. This would increase required returns of equity investors before the increase in debt funding is even considered.

- Assets for loan security – since land and buildings are already mortgaged, the machinery will have to be used as security. The attractiveness of this depends on whether they are specialised or would have a ready resale market.

- Gearing levels – the company is already geared but it is not clear whether the current level is optimum. Raising further debt finance, subject to the taxation considerations below, should reduce the overall cost of capital, but such a significant sum is likely to be seen as high risk. The fixed interest payments could bankrupt the firm if the expected growth does not occur. This is likely to increase the required returns of shareholders and may mean that debt lenders demand higher returns than are being paid on the current loans.

- Taxation – the high levels of investment will attract capital allowances. Depending on the current tax position of the firm and the treatment of those allowances by the revenue, the company may find itself in a non tax-paying position. This would negate the benefits of the cheaper debt finance.

- Agency costs – lenders often impose restrictive covenants on the company. This is particularly likely where such a significant level of funds is to be raised. A company largely in family control may be reluctant to have such restrictions, especially on dividend payments for example, which are appear to be used here to provide the family members with a source of income.

- Risk profile – the family members may be reluctant to take on further debt. The risk of bankruptcy mentioned above, is of greater concern to undiversified family owners than to the typically well diversified outside investor.

- Control – since the family retain voting control, the choice may be between debt finance and a rights issue, unless they are willing to give up control. If they do not have the funds to inject, a loan may be the only choice.

- Consideration should be given to alternatives such as leasing the machinery, or seeking venture capital funding (although that too may also require a loss of absolute family control).

## Test your understanding 2

### Internally generated funds – i.e. retained earnings

- Already have the funds.
- Do not have to spend any time persuading outside investors of the merits of the project.
- No issue costs.

### Debt

- The degree of questioning and publicity associated with debt is usually significantly less than that associated with a share issue.
- Quicker to raise than equity.
- Moderate issue costs.
- Seen as cheaper to service.

### New issue of equity

- Perception by stock markets that it is a possible sign of problems.
- Extensive questioning and publicity associated with a share issue.
- Takes time to raise.
- Expensive issue costs.

**Test your understanding 3**

|  | | Equity finance | Debt finance |
|---|---|---|---|
| (a) | Return on capital employed | = $5m/$20m × | = $5m/$20m × |
|  |  | 100 | 100 |
|  |  | = 25% | = 25% |

| Working | | Equity finance | Debt finance |
|---|---|---|---|
|  |  | $m | $m |
| PB FC & T | | 5.0 | 5.0 |
| Finance charges | | 0.0 | (1.0) |
| PBT | | 5.0 | 4.0 |
| Tax (@30%) | | (1.5) | (1.2) |
| PAT | | 3.5 | 2.8 |
| Return on equity | | =$3.5m/$20m × 100 =17.5% | =$2.8m/$10m × 100 =28% |

The financial performance of the two funding options is exactly the same for ROCE. This should not be a surprise given that ROCE is an indication of performance before financing, or underlying performance.

(b) When considering the ROE we see that the geared option achieves a higher return than the equity option. This is because the debt (10%) is costing less than the return on capital (25%). The excess return on that part funded by debt passes to the shareholder enhancing their return. The only differences between ROCE and ROE will be due to taxation and gearing.

# 6

# Dividend policy

## Chapter learning objectives

Upon completion of this chapter you will be able to:

- list and explain the factors, which affect distribution and retention policy

- recommend an appropriate distribution and retention policy in a scenario question.

- explain the potential objectives of a firm's dividend policy and explain how this may be affected by its dividend capacity

- identify a firm's short- and long-term reinvestment strategy and discuss the implications for a firm's dividend policy

- identify the impact of capital reconstruction programmes such as share repurchase agreements and new capital issues on a firm's free cash flows and explain the implications for a firm's dividend capacity

- discuss the impact of the availability and timing of central remittances on a firm's dividend capacity

- identify the factors in a corporate tax regime within the host jurisdiction of a firm which would impact dividend capacity and policy and discuss how it would affect them

- explain the importance of transfer prices to multinational firms

- list, explain and evaluate the transfer pricing strategies available to multinational firms

- explain the impact of local regulations and tax regimes on the selection of suitable transfer pricing policies by multinational firms

- advise a given firm on the appropriate transfer pricing strategy in a given situation reflecting local regulations and tax regimes.

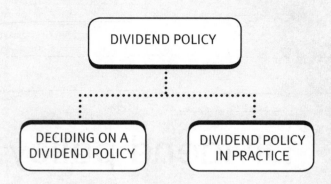

## 1 Deciding on a distribution and retention policy
### Dividend irrelevancy theory (Modigliani and Miller)

In an efficient market, dividend irrelevancy theory suggests that, provided all retained earnings are invested in positive NPV projects, existing shareholders will be indifferent about the pattern of dividend payouts.

However, practical influences, including market imperfections, mean that changes in dividend policy, particularly reductions in dividends paid, can have an adverse effect on shareholder wealth:

- Reductions in dividend can convey 'bad news' to shareholders (dividend signalling).

- Changes in dividend policy, particularly reductions, may conflict with investor liquidity requirements (selling shares to 'manufacture dividends' is not a costless alternative to being paid the dividend).

- Changes in dividend policy may upset investor tax planning (e.g. income v capital gain if shares are sold). Companies may have attracted a certain clientele of shareholders precisely because of their preference between income and growth.

As a result, most companies prefer to predetermine dividend policy.

**Expandable Text - More details on Modigliani and Miller's theory**

## The classic view of the irrelevance of the source of equity finance

This view was developed by Modigliani and Miller and may now be regarded as the classic position:

- Their argument is that the source of equity finance is in itself irrelevant.

- Since ultimately it represents a sacrifice of consumption (or other investment opportunities) by the investor at identical risk levels, it makes no difference whether dividends are paid to the investor, or equity is raised as new issues, or profits are simply retained.

- The only differences would arise due to institutional frictional factors, such as issue costs, taxation and so on.

- If both new equity and retained earnings have the same cost then it should be irrelevant, in terms of shareholder wealth, where equity funds come from.

- Provided any cash retained is invested at the shareholders' required return, a cut in dividend of any size should not adversely affect the investor – the cash lost now is exactly compensated by an increase in the value of their shares. If the funds were actually invested at higher than the expected return for the level of risk, this would in fact increase shareholders' wealth.

- It theoretically makes no difference whether the new investment is funded by retention of dividend or new equity raised.

- The key issue is thus the investment policy not the dividend policy.

## Arguments for the relevance of dividend policy

It was shown above that in theory the level of dividend is irrelevant.

In a perfect capital market it is difficult to challenge the dividend irrelevance position. However, once these assumptions are relaxed, certain practical influences emerge and the arguments need further review.

### *Dividend signalling*

In reality, investors do not have perfect information concerning the future prospects of the company. Many authorities claim, therefore, that the pattern of dividend payments is a key consideration on the part of investors when estimating future performance.

*Preference for current income*

Many investors require cash dividends to finance current consumption. This does not only apply to individual investors needing cash to live on but also to institutional investors, such as pension funds and insurance companies, who require regular cash outflows to meet day to day outgoings such as pension payments and insurance claims. This implies that many shareholders will prefer companies who pay regular cash dividends and will therefore value their shares more highly.

*Resolution of uncertainty*

One argument often put forward for high dividend payout is that income in the form of dividend is more secure than income in the form of capital gain. This, therefore, leads investors to place more value on high payout shares (sometimes referred to as the 'Bird in the Hand' theory).

*Taxation*

In many situations income in the form of dividend is taxed in a different way from income in the form of capital gains. This distortion in the personal tax system can have an impact on investors' preferences.

From the corporate point of view this further complicates the dividend decision, as different groups of shareholders are likely to prefer different payout patterns.

**Conclusions on dividend irrelevance arguments**

Once market imperfections are introduced dividend policy does appear to have an impact upon shareholder wealth. If the clientele theory is taken into account three major points should be noted.

## Practical influences on dividend policy

Before developing a particular dividend policy, a company must consider the following:

- legal position
- levels of profitability and free cash flow
- expectations of shareholders
- optimal gearing position - paying a large dividend reduces the value of equity in the firm, so can help a firm move towards its optimal gearing position.
- inflation

KAPLAN PUBLISHING

- control

- tax

- liquidity/cash management in the short and long term

- other sources of finance and the necessary servicing costs.

These factors limit the 'dividend capacity' of the firm.

## Dividend capacity

This can be simply defined as the ability at any given time of a firm's ability to pay dividends to its shareholders. This will clearly have a direct impact on a company's ability to implement its dividend policy (i.e. can the company actually pay the dividend it would like to).

Legally, the firm's dividend capacity is determined by the amount of accumulated distributable profits.

However, more practically, the dividend capacity can be calculated as the Free Cash Flow to Equity (after reinvestment), since in practice, the level of cash available will be the main driver of how much the firm can afford to pay out.

### Expandable Text - Legal position in relation to dividends

### Legal position in relation to dividends

Many countries will place legal restrictions on the amount of dividend that can be paid out relative to a company's earnings.

In addition, governments have operated policies of dividend restraint over various periods.

### Profitability

Profit is obviously an essential requirement for dividends. All other things being equal, the more stable the profit the greater the proportion that can be safely paid out as dividends. If profits are volatile it is unwise to commit the firm to a higher dividend payout ratio.

### Inflation

In periods of inflation, paying out dividends based on historic cost profits can lead to erosion of the operating capacity of the business. For example, insufficient funds may be retained for future asset replacement. Current cost accounting recalculates profit taking into consideration inflation, asset values and capital maintenance. Firms would then ensure that the dividend is limited to the CCA profit.

### Growth

Rapidly growing companies commonly pay very low dividends, the bulk of earnings being retained to finance expansion.

### Control

The use of internally generated funds does not alter ownership or control. This can be advantageous particularly in family owned firms.

### Liquidity

Sufficient liquid funds need to be available to pay the dividend.

### Tax

The personal tax position of investors may put them in a position of preferring either dividend income or capital gains though growing share prices. If the clientele of investors in the company have a clear preference for one or the other, the company should be wary of altering dividend policy and upsetting investors.

### Other sources of finance

If a firm has limited access to other sources of funds, retained earnings become a very important source of finance. Dividends will therefore tend to be small. This situation is commonly experienced by unquoted companies that have very limited access to external finance.

## 2 Dividend policy in practice

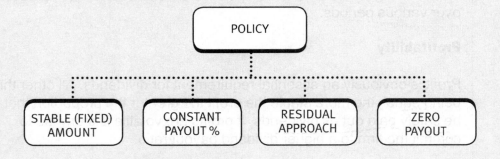

In practice, there are a number of commonly adopted dividend policies:

- stable dividend policy
- constant payout ratio
- zero dividend policy
- residual approach to dividends.

## Expandable Text - Explanation of practical dividend policies

### Stable dividend policy

Paying a constant or constantly growing dividend each year:

- offers investors a predictable cash flow
- reduces management opportunities to divert funds to non-profitable activities
- works well for mature firms with stable cash flows.

However, there is a risk that reduced earnings would force a dividend cut with all the associated difficulties.

### Constant payout ratio

Paying out a constant proportion of equity earnings:

- maintains a link between earnings, reinvestment rate and dividend flow but
- cash flow is unpredictable for the investor
- gives no indication of management intention or expectation.

### Zero dividend policy

All surplus earnings are invested back into the business. Such a policy:

- is common during the growth phase
- should be reflected in increased share price.

When growth opportunities are exhausted (no further positive NPV projects are available):

- cash will start to accumulate
- a new distribution policy will be required.

### Residual dividend policy

A dividend is paid only if no further positive NPV projects available. This may be popular for firms:

- in the growth phase
- without easy access to alternative sources of funds.

However:

- cash flow is unpredictable for the investor
- gives constantly changing signals regarding management expectations.

### Ratchet patterns

Most firms adopt a variant on the stable dividend policy – a **ratchet pattern** of payments. This involves paying out a stable, but rising dividend per share:

- Dividends lag behind earnings, but can then be maintained even when earnings fall below the dividend level.
- Avoids 'bad news' signals.
- Does not disturb the tax position of investors.

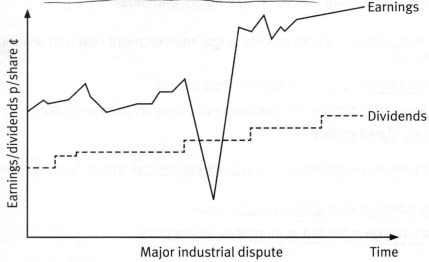

### Scrip dividends

A scrip dividend is where a company allows its shareholders to take their dividends in the form of new shares rather than cash.

Do not confuse a scrip issue (which is a bonus issue) with a scrip dividend.

- The advantage to the shareholder of a scrip dividend is that he can painlessly increase his shareholding in the company without having to pay broker's commissions or stamp duty on a share purchase.
- The advantage to the company is that it does not have to find the cash to pay a dividend and in certain circumstances it can save tax.

KAPLAN PUBLISHING

Some companies give shareholders the choice between cash and scrip dividends. In such cases the terms of the choice are usually designed so that the shareholder who chooses the scrip sees their wealth increase with a fall in wealth if cash is chosen. Such an arrangement is called 'an enhanced scrip'.

A scrip dividend effectively converts retained profits into permanent share capital.

There can be a number of advantages to 'paying' a scrip dividend rather than cash:

- Preservation of cash for re-investment.

- Unless significant, a scrip issue will not dilute the share price.

- More shares reduce the company's gearing and hence increase its borrowing capacity.

- Shareholders get more shares without incurring transaction costs.

- Shareholders may get a tax advantage if dividends in the form of shares rather than cash.

One major disadvantage in these scrip dividend plans is that shareholders receive no cash with which to pay taxes on the dividends.

## Test your understanding 1

A Inc, a listed company, has produced either trading losses or only small profits over the last few years and so has not recently paid any dividends. However following recent management changes and a company restructuring, the company is earning good profits and the directors are looking to formalise the future dividend policy at a forthcoming board meeting.

Particular concerns have been expressed by some directors:

- Director X has referred to the need to provide investors with stability, not reduce dividends and only increase them when it is clear that the increase can be maintained.

- Director Y has commented on the relationship between dividend payments and share price. The director believes that the dividend payout should therefore be as high as possible, with the company borrowing to pay them if necessary.

**Make notes on the relevant matters to raise at the board meeting including comments on the specific concerns raised.**

## 3 Share buyback schemes

If a company wishes to return a large sum of cash to its shareholders, then it might consider a share buyback (or repurchase) rather than a one-off special dividend.

> These are schemes through which a company 'buys back' its shares from shareholders and cancels them. The company's Articles of Association must allow it.

It often occurs when the company:

- has no positive NPV projects
- wants to increase the share price [cosmetic exercise]
- wants to reduce the cost of capital by increasing its gearing.
- wants to give a positive signal to the market. In the real world, since the directors have more information than the investors about the firm's financial position, buying the shares gives a signal to investors that the shares currently represent good value for money.

### Advantages and disadvantages of a share buyback

Advantages for the company might include:

- Giving flexibility where a firm's excess cash flows are thought to be only temporary. Management can make the distribution in the form of a share repurchase rather than paying higher cash dividends that cannot be maintained.
- Increasing EPS through a reduction in the number of shares in issue.
- Effective use of surplus funds where growth of business is poor, outlook is poor (i.e. adjusting the equity base to a more appropriate level).
- Buying out dissident shareholders.
- Creation of a 'market' where no active market exist for its shares (e.g. if the company is unquoted).
- Altering capital structure to reduce the cost of capital.
- Reducing likelihood of a takeover.

For the shareholders, advantages might include:

- Giving a choice, as they can sell or not sell. With cash dividend shareholders must accept the payment and pay the taxes.
- Saving transaction costs.

But constraints might include:

- Getting approval by general meeting (arguments about the price at which repurchase is to take place).

- The company may pay too high a price for the shares.

- The shareholders may feel they have received too small a price for their shares.

- Premiums paid are set first against share premium and then against distributable profits (if against distributable profits, this will reduce future dividend capacity).

- Might be seen as a failure of the current management/company to make better use of the funds through reinvesting them in the business.

- Shareholders may not be indifferent between dividends and capital gains due to their tax circumstances.

**Student Accountant article**

Read Peter Atrill's article in the February 2009 issue of Student Accountant magazine for more detail on share buybacks.

**4 Dividend policy in multinational companies**

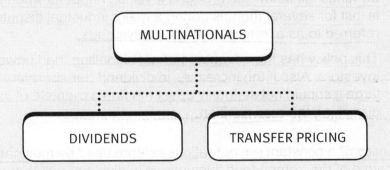

**Objectives of a firm's dividend policy**

As detailed above, when deciding how much cash to distribute to shareholders, the company directors must keep in mind that the firm's objective is to maximise shareholder value.

The dividend payout policy should be based on investor preferences for cash dividends now or capital gains in future from enhanced share value resultant from re-investment into projects with a positive NPV.

Many types of multinational company shareholder (for example, institutions such as pension funds and insurance companies) rely on dividends to meet current expenses and any instability in dividends would seriously affect them.

An additional factor for multinationals is that they have more than one dividend policy to consider:

- Dividends to external shareholders.
- Dividends between group companies, facilitating the movement of profits and funds within the group.

---

**Expandable Text - Alternative dividend policies used by MNCs**

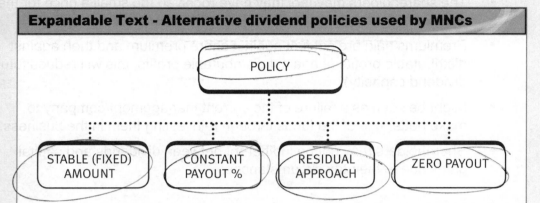

Probably the most common policy adopted by multinationals for external shareholders is a variant on stable dividend policy. Most companies go for a stable, but rising, dividend per share:

- Dividends lag behind earnings, but are maintained even when earnings fall below the dividend level, as happens when production is lost for several months during a major industrial dispute. This was referred to as a 'ratchet' pattern of dividends.

- This policy has the advantage of not signalling 'bad news' to investors. Also if the increases in dividend per share are not too large it should not seriously upset the firm's clientele of investors by disturbing their tax position.

A policy of a constant payout ratio is seldom used by multinationals because of the tremendous fluctuations in dividend per share that it could bring:

- Many firms, however, might work towards a long-run target payout percentage smoothing out the peaks and troughs each year.

- If sufficiently smoothed the pattern would be not unlike the ratchet pattern demonstrated above.

The residual approach to dividends contains a lot of financial commonsense:

- If positive NPV projects are available, they should be adopted, otherwise funds should be returned to shareholders.

---

- This avoids the unnecessary transaction costs involved in paying shareholders a dividend and then asking for funds from the same shareholders (via a rights issue) to fund a new project.

- The major problem with the residual approach to dividends is that it can lead to large fluctuations in dividends, which could signal 'bad news' to investors.

## 5 Dividend capacity and free cash flow to equity for multinational companies

### Dividend capacity for a multinational company

As for any company, dividend capacity is a major determinant of dividend policy for multinationals. Key factors include:

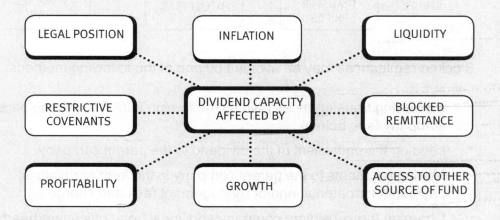

The additional factor that was not discussed above is remittance 'blocking'.

If, once a foreign direct investment has taken place, the government of the host country imposes a restriction on the amount of profit that can be returned to the parent company, this is known as a 'block on the remittance of dividends':

- Often done through the imposition of strict exchange controls.

- Limits the amount of centrally remitted funds available to pay dividends to parent company shareholders (i.e. restricts dividend capacity).

## How the parent company might try to avoid such a block on remittances

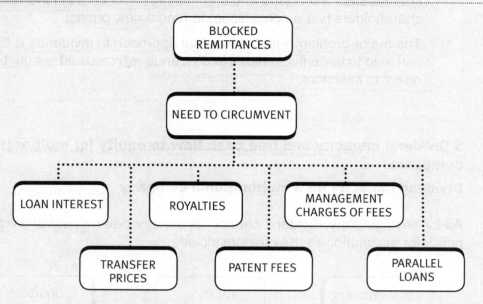

Blocked remittances may be avoided by one of the following methods:

- Increasing transfer prices paid by the foreign subsidiary to the parent company (see below).

- Lending the equivalent of the dividend to the parent company.

- Making payments to the parent company in the form of royalties, payments for patents, and/or management fees and charges.

- Charging the subsidiary company additional head office overheads.

- Parallel loans (currency swaps), whereby the foreign subsidiary lends cash to the subsidiary of another a company requiring funds in the foreign country. In return the parent company would receive the loan of an equivalent amount of cash in the home country from the other subsidiary's parent company.

The government of the foreign country might try to prevent many of these measures being used.

### Free cash flow to equity (FCFE)

- The gross free cash flow to equity of a multinational company can be defined as:

  Operating cash flow + dividends from joint ventures – net interest paid – tax.

- To determine the potential dividend capacity of the business, account needs to be taken of any capital re-investment. This is known as the net free cash flow to equity and can be defined as:

Gross free cash flow to equity – capital expenditure +/- disposals/acquisitions + new capital issued.

### Test your understanding 2

**What is the 20X6 net free cash flow to equity (i.e. the potential dividend capacity) for the following business?** [All figures are taken from the company's cash flow statement]

|  | 20X6 $m | 20X5 $m |
|---|---|---|
| Capital expenditure | 500 | 400 |
| Acquisition of new subsidiary company | 325 | 0 |
| Disposal of old subsidiary | 250 | 100 |
| Equity dividends paid | 75 | 70 |
| Taxation paid | 275 | 200 |
| Operating cash inflow | 1,000 | 800 |
| Interest paid | 315 | 295 |
| Dividend from joint venture | 150 | 80 |
| New ordinary shares issued | 100 | 100 |

### Expandable Text - FCFE: Reinvestment & capital reconstruction

#### Re-investment strategy

A company's re-investment strategy will have two strands:

- Short-term reinvestment - working capital requirements that will come from operating cash flow (for example, an investment in inventory).
- Long-term reinvestment - capital expenditure programmes:
    - Generally positive purpose (for example, an expansion plan) and positive expected NPV.
    - Sometimes negative purpose (for example, compliance with new legal requirements on emissions in a factory) and negative expected NPV.

Any re-investment of profits earned will restrict the capacity of a company to pay a dividend.

Management will require to show that the proposed reinvestment strategy will provide a return to shareholders (i.e. increase their wealth) more than an immediate payout in the form of dividends or share repurchase.

In these circumstances, a company may decide to give its shareholders a 'payout' using a scrip dividend, preserving the cash in the business for re-investment and at the same time rewarding its shareholders with a non-cash return in the form of additional shares.

## Capital reconstruction programmes

The nature of the capital reconstruction will determine its impact on both current and future free cash flow.

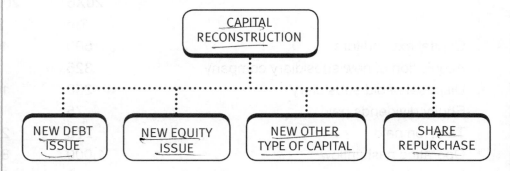

### Share repurchase scheme

- Reduces immediate free cash flow to give shareholders an alternative to a straight cash dividend.

- Potentially increases future free cash flows as there will be fewer shares to pay future dividends on but the company may decide to keep the absolute dividend payout the same as before, simply paying out a higher dividend per share than before the repurchase.

## New issue of debt for reinvestment purposes (i.e. working capital or capital expenditure)

- Reduces future free cash flow by interest costs and debt repayments.

## New issue of debt to pay current cash dividend or share repurchase

- Provides immediate cash to pay dividend or share repurchase.
- Reduces future free cash flow by interest costs and debt repayments.

### New issue of equity for reinvestment purposes (i.e. working capital or capital expenditure)

- Increases the number of shares on which dividends may have to be paid in the future but the company may decide to keep the absolute dividend payout the same as before, simply paying out a lower dividend per share than before the new issue.

*↑ no. of Shares*
*⇒ dividends was to paid in future, but*
*less before the new issue*

### Other

There may be other forms of capital issue, such as:

- special types of ordinary shares, perhaps with enhanced dividend rights or fixed dividend rights, both payable before 'normal' ordinary shares

- preference shares with a first dividend claim on the after tax profit.

Any negative impact that required payments for the type of finance have on free cash flow will reduce the company's dividend capacity.

## 6 Transfer Pricing

### Basic principles

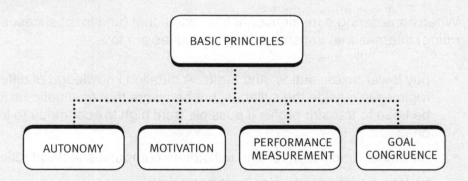

The transfer price is the price charged by one part of an organisation when supplying goods or services to another part of the same organisation.

Large diversified groups will be split into numerous smaller profit centres, each preparing accounts for its own sphere of activities and paying tax on its profits. Multinational groups are likely to own individual companies established in different countries throughout the world.

Multinational transfer pricing is the process of deciding on appropriate prices for the goods and services sold intra-group across national borders.

Remember the objectives of a good 'domestic' transfer pricing system:

- Maintain divisional autonomy.
- Maintain motivation for managers.
- Assess divisional performance objectively.
- Ensure goal congruence.

## Multinational aspects

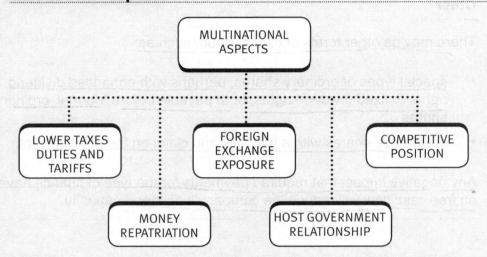

The setting of transfer prices is vital for multinational groups.

When considering a multinational firm, additional (and in most cases over-riding) international transfer pricing objectives are to:

- pay lower taxes, duties, and tariffs. A detailed knowledge of different tax regimes is outside the syllabus, but be aware that multinational firms will be keen to transfer profits if possible from high tax countries to low tax ones.
- repatriate funds from foreign subsidiary companies to head office
- be less exposed to foreign exchange risks
- build and maintain a better international competitive position
- enable foreign subsidiaries to match or undercut local competitors' prices
- have good relations with governments in the countries in which the multinational firm operates.

In particular, international transfer pricing requires careful consideration of multiple currency effects and multiple tax and legal regimes.

Illustration 1

Examples in practice of the objectives of international transfer pricing might include:

- reduction of overall corporate income taxes, primarily by manipulating the transfer price to divert taxable income from high tax countries to low tax countries

- minimisation of import duties by setting a low transfer price into a country with import duties will reduce the level of duty paid

- avoidance of exchange controls or other restrictions such as dividend remittance restrictions by setting a low transfer price to the parent company as an alternative to a dividend payment

- improvement of the appearance of the financial performance of a subsidiary by increasing profits through transfer pricing thus helping to:
  - satisfy any earnings criteria set by lenders to the subsidiary
  - make the acquisition of a new loan easier.

Transfer pricing (especially international transfer pricing) is not simply buying and selling products between divisions. The term is also used to cover, inter alia:

- head office general management charges to subsidiaries for various services

- specific charges made to subsidiaries by, for example, head office human resource or information technology functions

- royalty payments.
  - between parent company and subsidiaries
  - among subsidiaries.

- interest rate on borrowings between group companies.

## Expandable Text - The basics of transfer pricing

### A general rule for transfer pricing

Transfer price per unit = Standard variable cost in the producing division plus the opportunity cost to the company as a whole of supplying the unit internally.

The opportunity cost will be either the contribution forgone by selling one unit internally rather than externally, or the contribution forgone by not using the same facilities in the producing division for their next best alternative use.

The application of this general rule means that the transfer price equals:

- **the standard variable cost of the producing division**, if there is no outside market for the units manufactured and no alternative use for the facilities in that division

- **the market price**, if there is an outside market for the units manufactured in the producing division and no alternative more profitable use for the facilities in that division.

### Transfer pricing systems

A transfer pricing system should:

- be reasonably easy to operate and to understand

- be flexible in terms of a changing organisation structure

- allow divisional autonomy to be maintained, since continued autonomy should motivate divisional managers to give their best performance

- allow divisional performance to be assessed objectively

- ensure that divisional managers make decisions that are in the best interests both of the divisions and of the whole company.

There are broadly three types of transfer prices:

- Market-based prices.

- Cost-related prices.

- Negotiated prices and dual prices.

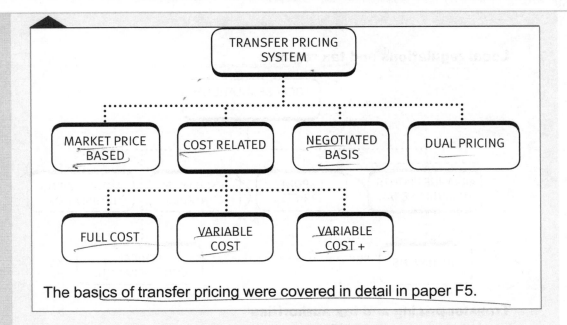

The basics of transfer pricing were covered in detail in paper F5.

## Choice of transfer price basis for the multinational company

| Basis | Comments |
|---|---|
| Market based | • Encouraged by tax and customs authorities in both multinational company and local subsidiary jurisdictions. |
| | • The profit split between the group companies is fair and therefore the authorities in each country receive their appropriate share of corporate tax and duties |
| | • Prices for the same goods in different countries could vary significantly |
| | • Exchange rate changes could have significant impact |
| | • Local taxes could have significant impact |
| | • Strategically, subsidiary will want to set its prices in accordance with local supply and demand conditions |
| Full cost | • Acceptable to tax and customs authorities in both multinational company and local subsidiary jurisdictions |
| | • The authorities in each country receive their appropriate share of corporate tax and duties as the transfer price approximates to the 'correct' cost of the goods |
| Variable cost | • Unacceptable to tax and customs authorities in the supplying company's jurisdiction |
| | • All profits allocated to the receiving company and thus no corporate tax payable by supplying company |
| Negotiated | • Could result in sub-optimal decision as no advantage taken of different corporate tax rates and duties |

## Local regulations and tax regimes

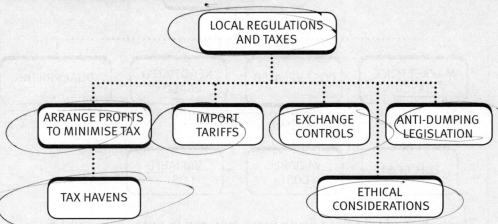

## Transfer pricing and tax authorities

One common approach to setting international transfer prices adopted by multinational companies is to seek to minimise the group's overall total tax liability. The objective is to set transfer prices in order to report:

- low profits in countries with high tax rates
- high profits in countries with low tax rates.

---

### Illustration 2

For example, if the taxation on corporate profits is:

- 35% in Wyland
- 25% in Exland.

A multinational company operating in both of these countries may try to 'manipulate' its results so that the majority of the profit is made by its subsidiary/division in Exland thereby saving corporate tax.

The aim is to minimise profits in Wyland and maximise profit in Exland. It could do this via:

- increasing or decreasing transfer prices between the subsidiaries/divisions as appropriate
- invoice services provided by the Exland subsidiary/division to the Wyland subsidiary/division.

---

This objective is frustrated in many countries whose governments require that transfer prices are set on an arm's length basis [i.e. using the prevailing market price]. The principle is still useful however as a broad objective and particularly valuable when transferring goods for which no external market price exists or when operating in countries without an arm's length transfer price requirement.

Alternatively many multinational businesses sited in high tax jurisdictions create marketing/promotional/distribution subsidiaries in low tax jurisdictions and transfer products to them at low transfer prices. Overall corporate tax will be reduced, as the profit from selling these products to the final customer will be taxed in the lower jurisdiction.

If transfer prices are set on the basis of minimising tax, this can have consequences for the whole company:

- Autonomy will be compromised if the parent company fixes transfer prices throughout the group to minimise total tax.

- This can have adverse motivational consequences.

## Expandable Text - Tax havens, import tariffs and local regulations

### The use of tax havens

A tax haven is a country that has a series of unique characteristics, the primary one being relatively low tax compared to other countries. Bank secrecy and strict privacy laws are also other common features of tax havens.

There are many tax havens throughout the world. Well-known examples are:

- Cayman Islands.
- Luxembourg.
- Liechtenstein.
- Bahamas.
- And closer to the UK, the Channel Islands.

From the perspective of a multinational company tax havens may provide opportunities to reduce corporate taxes by the quite legal use of subsidiaries in offshore tax havens like the Cayman Islands. Where tax regimes differ around the globe organisations can make use of differing tax rules to keep a larger proportion of their profits.

A defining feature of the tax haven is that normally little production takes place but many organisations are registered there. Many companies seek to lower their taxes by, for example, setting up foreign units and using internal lending so that profits are taken primarily in tax havens and costs are incurred in high tax countries.

Inevitably tax authorities in higher tax countries have sought to close tax loopholes, and potentially such changes could result in a heavily increased tax burden for multinationals and hence represents a significant risk to their post-tax earnings. However, advantages still exist.

A tax haven will be most attractive with the following criteria:

- Low rate of corporation tax.

- Low withholding tax on dividends paid to overseas holding companies.

- Comprehensive tax treaties with other countries.

- Stable economy with low political risk.

- Lack of exchange controls.

- Good communications with the rest of the world.

- Developed legal framework so that rights can be safeguarded.

## Import tariffs

An import tariff is a schedule of duties imposed by a country on imported goods. The tariff can be levied on a percentage of the value of the import, or as an amount per unit of import.

For example, if the government of Zedland imposes an import tariff of 10% on the value of all goods imported, a multinational company with a subsidiary/division in Zedland that imports goods from another subsidiary in another country may decide to minimise costs by minimising the transfer price.

That decision might, however, conflict with the objective of minimising corporate taxation if the subsidiary then sold the goods to the final customer and corporate taxation rate in Zedland was very high.

## Local regulations

There are other potential local rules and regulations that will impact on the transfer pricing policy of a multinational company.

## Exchange controls

Foreign exchange controls are various forms of controls imposed by a government on the purchase/sale of foreign currencies by residents or on the purchase/sale of local currency by non-residents. A common exchange control is a restriction on the amount of currency that may be imported or exported.

Profits made and cash flows earned in a foreign country are of no value to a multinational group if they cannot be repatriated to the home country for distribution to shareholders. Under exchange controls, capital invested into a country may often be repatriated, whereas remittance of the profits is strictly limited.

Charging management fees, royalties, fees for research and development, technical know-how and so on, will impact upon the profitability in a subsidiary abroad. Provided that even those fees and so on can be remitted, and do not become restricted also by the exchange controls, this is a way of releasing funds from a country, which has such controls.

Most governments are naturally well aware of these possibilities and respond by limiting repatriations in general. For example, a proportion of profit made may have to be retained and reinvested in the host country. Such 'blocked funds' may even have to be invested in government bonds, the cash from which may then be sent to the group but only upon maturity.

## Anti-dumping legislation

'Dumping' is the practice of selling goods/services in an overseas/foreign market at a price lower than the price or cost in the home market. It might be without motive or it might have an economic purpose such as trying to put competitors out of business. Anti-dumping legislation is designed to minimise the impact of this practice.

For example, many governments take action to protect domestic industries by preventing multinational companies from transferring goods cheaply into their countries. Forcing the use of market price based transfer pricing can do this.

### Ethical issues in transfer pricing

There are a number of potential ethical issues for the multinational company to consider when formulating its transfer pricing strategy:

- Social responsibility, reducing amounts paid in customs duties and tax.
- Bypassing a country's financial regulation via remittance of dividends.
- Not operating as a 'responsible citizen' in foreign country.
- Reputational loss.
- Bad publicity.
- Tax evasion.

### Summary – deciding on a transfer pricing strategy

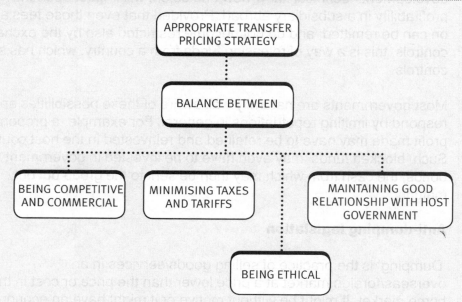

### Expandable Text - Comprehensive example 1

Colsan plc ['Colsan'] is a UK-based multinational company with two overseas subsidiaries. Colsan wishes to minimise its global tax bill, and part of its tax strategy is to try to take advantage of opportunities provided by transfer pricing.

Colsan has subsidiaries in Fraland and Serland

| Taxation and excise duty rates | UK | Fraland | Serland |
|---|---|---|---|
| Corporate tax on profits | 30% | 45% | 20% |
| Withholding tax on dividends | – | 10% | – |
| Import tariffs on all goods (not tax allowable) | – | – | 5% |

The Fraland subsidiary produces 100,000 sofa frames per annum, which are then sent to Serland for the upholstery to be added, and the furniture completed. The frames are sold to the Serland subsidiary at a transfer price equal to variable cost (which is £50) plus 50%. Annual fixed costs in Fraland are £1.5m.

The Serland subsidiary incurs additional variable costs of £72 per unit and sells the completed furniture for £200 per unit in Serland. Annual fixed costs in Serland are £1.7m.

All transactions between the companies are in £ sterling. Each year, the Fraland subsidiary remits 60% of its profit after tax and the Serland subsidiary remits 100% of its profit after tax to Colsan.

If Colsan instructs the Fraland subsidiary to sell the frames to the Serland subsidiary at full cost.

- Determine the potential effect of this on the group tax and tariff payments.

- Outline the consequences of this strategy.

Assume that bi-lateral tax agreements exist which allow Fraland and Serland tax paid to be credited against Colsan's UK tax liability.

| Potential effect 1 [under the current scheme] | Fraland | Serland |
|---|---|---|
| | £000 | £000 |
| Sales | 7,500 | 20,000 |
| Variable costs | (5,000) | (7,200) |
| Cost from Fraland | – | (7,500) |
| Fixed costs | (1,500) | (1,700) |
| Profit before tax | 1,000 | 3,600 |
| Local corporate tax [45% in Fraland, 20%in Serland] | (450) | (720) |
| Profit after local corporate tax | 550 | 2,880 |
| Import tariff [5% in Serland] | – | (375) |
| Gross remittance to UK [60% before withholding tax in Fraland, 100% in Serland] | 330 | 2,505 |
| With-holding tax [10% in Fraland] | (33) | – |
| Net remitted to UK | 297 | 2,505 |
| Retained locally | 220 | 0 |
| UK corporate tax: | | |
| Taxable profit | 1,000 | 3,600 |
| UK corporate tax @ 30% | 300 | 1,080 |
| Less: local corporate tax [allowed under bi-lateral agreement] | (300) | (720) |
| Additional UK corporate tax payable | 0 | 360 |

| Potential effect 1 [under the current scheme] | Fraland | Serland |
|---|---|---|
| | £000 | £000 |
| Sales | 6,500 | 20,000 |
| Variable costs | (5,000) | (7,200) |
| Cost from Fraland | – | (6,500) |
| Fixed costs | (1,500) | (1,700) |
| Profit before tax | 0 | 4,600 |
| Local corporate tax [45% in Fraland, 20% in Serland] | 0 | (920) |
| Profit after local corporate tax | 0 | 3,680 |
| Import tariff [5% in Serland] | – | (325) |
| Gross remittance to UK [60% before withholding tax in Fraland, 100% in Serland] | 0 | 3,355 |
| With-holding tax [10% in Fraland] | 0 | – |
| Net remitted to UK | 0 | 3,355 |
| Retained locally | 0 | 0 |
| UK corporate tax: | | |
| Taxable profit | 0 | 4,600 |
| UK corporate tax @ 30% | 0 | 1,380 |
| Less: local corporate tax [allowed under bi-lateral agreement] | 0 | (920) |
| Additional UK corporate tax payable | 0 | 460 |

| Summary of potential effects | Under the current scheme | Under the proposed scheme | Difference |
|---|---|---|---|
| | £000 | £000 | £,000 |
| Net amount remitted to UK | 2,802 | 3,355 | 553 |
| Retained locally in Fraland | 220 | 0 | (220) |
| Taxes payable: | | | |
| In UK [additional tax] | 360 | 460 | (100) |
| In Fraland | 483 | 0 | 483 |
| In Serland | 1,095 | 1,245 | (150) |
| Total taxes payable | 1,938 | 1,705 | 233 |

The proposed new scheme may be unacceptable to:

- The tax authorities in Fraland, where £483,000 in corporate taxes would be lost. The tax authorities might insist on an arms-length transfer price for transfers between Fraland and Serland.

- The subsidiary in Fraland, which would no longer make a profit, or have retentions available for future investment in Fraland. Dependent on how performance in Fraland was evaluated, this might adversely affect rewards and motivation for the employees in Fraland.

## 7 Chapter summary

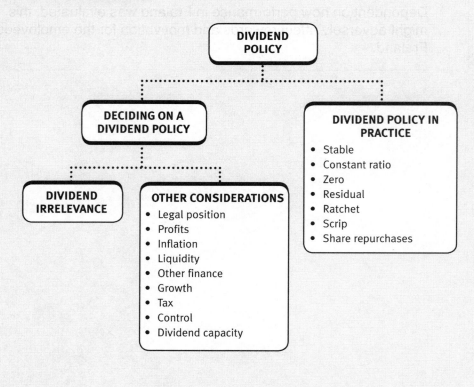

**DIVIDEND POLICY**

**DECIDING ON A DIVIDEND POLICY**

**DIVIDEND IRRELEVANCE**

**OTHER CONSIDERATIONS**
- Legal position
- Profits
- Inflation
- Liquidity
- Other finance
- Growth
- Tax
- Control
- Dividend capacity

**DIVIDEND POLICY IN PRACTICE**
- Stable
- Constant ratio
- Zero
- Residual
- Ratchet
- Scrip
- Share repurchases

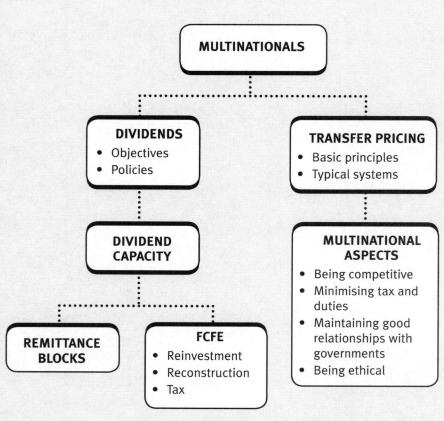

**MULTINATIONALS**

**DIVIDENDS**
- Objectives
- Policies

**TRANSFER PRICING**
- Basic principles
- Typical systems

**DIVIDEND CAPACITY**

**MULTINATIONAL ASPECTS**
- Being competitive
- Minimising tax and duties
- Maintaining good relationships with governments
- Being ethical

**REMITTANCE BLOCKS**

**FCFE**
- Reinvestment
- Reconstruction
- Tax

# Test your understanding answers

## Test your understanding 1

Notes would need to cover:

### Theoretical position on dividends

Provided a company invests in positive NPV projects, the pattern of dividend payments is not relevant to an investor. The company should therefore use the funds available to invest in all positive NPV opportunities and any remaining funds should be distributed as dividends. Dividends are a **residual decision**.

### Information content

In practice however, investors treat the level of dividends as a signal about the financial well being of the company, and believe that high dividends signal confidence about the future.

This contrasts directly with the theory which would suggest a confident company would be retaining dividends to invest in all the positive NPV projects.

### Clientele effect

Certain types of investor have a preference for certain types of income, and constantly changing the level of dividend payout will make it difficult for investors to plan their cash and tax positions.

### Liquidity

Whilst it is theoretically possible for a firm to borrow to pay dividends, taking out loan finance will alter the gearing level of the firm, which itself will be the subject of policy and cannot be altered arbitrarily.

### Cost of finance

If the firm needs funds for future investments, retained earnings are the cheapest source of funds available.

### Policy

A suitable policy would therefore be one that:

- leaves sufficient funds for investment and avoids the need to incur transaction costs raising funds in the near future
- has a fairly constant dividend pattern.

### Director X

This is the policy many companies do adopt in practice. The problem is that it ignores the availability of funds, and the investment projects that may require them.

### Director Y

Director Y is correct that the value of a share is, in part, dependent on the dividend stream. In theory, as mentioned above, it should not matter if a dividend is missed, provided the funds are invested in positive NPV projects. However, it is true that in practice, if shareholders are unhappy about the cut, and sell their shares the price fall.

### Test your understanding 2

Gross FCFE = \$(1,000 + 150 - 315 - 275) = \$560m

Net FCFE [potential dividend capacity] = \$(560 - 500 - 325 + 250 + 100) = \$85m

This potential can then be compared to the actual dividend to determine whether there has been an over or under distribution.

# International investment and financing decisions

## Chapter learning objectives

Upon completion of this chapter you will be able to:

- explain the principle of four-way equivalence and the impact on exchange rate fluctuations

- explain the impact of alternative exchange rate assumptions on the value of a project involving overseas cash flows

- forecast project or firm free cash flows in any specified currency

- for an international project use the net present value technique to determine the project's net present value or firm value under differing exchange rate, fiscal and transaction cost assumptions

- explain and apply the International CAPM equation

- for an international project or firm use the adjusted present value technique to determine the project's net present value or firm value under differing exchange rate, fiscal and transaction cost assumptions

- evaluate the significance of exchange controls for a given investment decision and strategies for dealing with restricted remittance

- assess the impact of a project upon a firm's exposure to translation, transaction and economic risk

- describe the costs and benefits of alternative sources of finance available within the international bond and equity markets

- in a scenario question, advise upon the costs and benefits of alternative sources of finance available within the international financial markets.

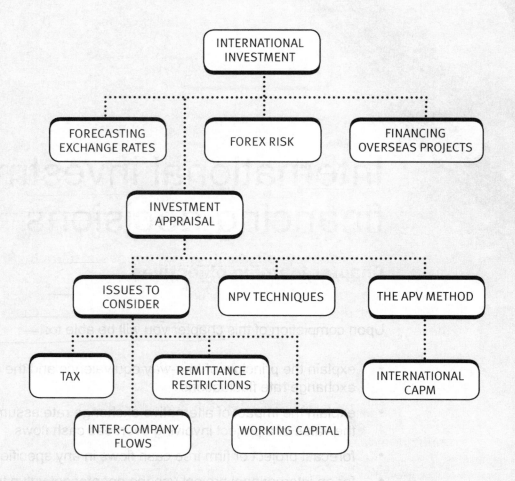

# 1 Forecasting foreign exchange rates

## The relationship between interest, inflation, spot and forward rates

The overall relationship between spot rates, interest rates, inflation rates and the forward and expected future spot rates was covered in Paper F9.

A feature of exam questions covering international investment decisions is often the need to calculate the relevant exchange rates over a number of years, and a summary of the key relationships is therefore given in the four-way equivalence table follows.

Note :

$F_0$ = forward rate

$S_0$ = spot rate

$S_1$ = expected future spot rate

$i_b$ = interest rate for base currency

$i_c$ = interest rate for counter currency

$h_b$ = inflation rate for base currency

$h_c$ = inflation rate for counter currency

| DIFFERENCE IN INTEREST RATES $$\frac{(1+i_c)}{(1+i_b)}$$ | EQUAL<br>International Fisher Effect | EXPECTED DIFFERENCE IN INFLATION RATES $$\frac{(1+h_c)}{(1+h_b)}$$ |
|---|---|---|

| EQUAL<br>Interest rate<br>parity theory | | EQUAL<br>Purchasing power<br>parity theory |
|---|---|---|

| DIFFERENCE BETWEEN FORWARD AND SPOT RATES $$\frac{F_1}{F_0}$$ | EQUAL<br>Expectations theory | EXPECTED CHANGE IN SPOT RATES $$\frac{S_1}{S_0}$$ |
|---|---|---|

## Expandable Text - Illustration of parity calculations

The current dollar sterling exchange rate is given as $/£1.7025 – 1.7075.

Expected inflation rates are:

| Year | USA | UK |
|---|---|---|
| 1 | 5% | 2% |
| 2 | 3% | 4% |
| 3 | 4% | 4% |

Use the relationships above to work out the expected spot rate for the next three years.

### Solution

Using the PPPT formula:

$$S_1 = S_0 \times \frac{(1+ h_c)}{(1+h_b)}$$

$$S_1 = S_0 \times \frac{(1+ \text{USA inflation})}{(1+ \text{UK inflation})}$$

and the mid point of the quoted spread as the exchange rate today:

$$\left(\frac{1.7075 + 1.7025}{2}\right) = 1.7050$$

The calculations for the next three years are:

Year 1    $1.7050 \times \left(\dfrac{1.05}{1.02}\right) = 1.7551$

Year 2    $1.7551 \times \left(\dfrac{1.03}{1.04}\right) = 1.7382$

Year 3    $1.7382 \times \left(\dfrac{1.04}{1.04}\right) = 1.7382$

Note that the exchange rate at the end of one year becomes the basis of the next year's calculation.

### Test your understanding 1

The current euro sterling exchange rate is given as 1.5274 – 1.5376.

Expected inflation rates are:

| Year | Europe | UK |
|:---:|:---:|:---:|
| 1 | 3% | 1% |
| 2 | 1% | 4% |
| 3 | 2% | 3% |

**Use the relationships above to work out the expected spot rate for the next three years.**

## Cross rates

You may not be given the exchange rate you need for a particular currency, but instead be given the relationship it has with a different currency. You will then need to calculate a **cross rate.**

For example, if you have a rate in $/£ and a rate in €/£, you can derive a cross rate for $/€ by dividing the $/£ rate by the €/£ rate.

## Expandable Text - Cross rate calculation

A UK company has a Greek subsidiary which is to purchase materials costing $100,000. The NPV of the overseas cash flows is being calculated in euros, but you have not been provided with the euro/dollar exchange rate. Instead you have the following information:

| | |
|---|---|
| $/£ | 1.90 |
| €/£ | 1.45 |

What is the value of the purchase in euros?

### Solution

The solution could be calculated in two stages:

1. Convert the purchase into sterling:

   $100,000/1.90 = £52,632

2. Convert the sterling value into euros

   £52,632 × 1.45 = €76,316

However an easier alternative, particularly if there are a number of transactions to convert, is to calculate a cross rate:

The $/€ rate will be 1.90/1.45 = 1.3103

The value of the transaction is therefore:

$100,000/1.3103 = €76,318

## Test your understanding 2

A UK company with an US office has to pay €100,000 for a machine. The NPV of the overseas cash flows is being calculated in dollars.

You have the following information:

| | |
|---|---|
| €/£ | 1.53 |
| $/£ | 1.87 |

**What is the cost of the machine in dollars?**

## Changing inflation rates

When finding exchange rates it might first be necessary to calculate the inflation rates expected in a foreign country.

### Illustration 1

Inflation is currently 80% in Brazil, although the government hopes to reduce it each year by 25% of the previous years rate. What will the inflation rate be in Brazil over the next four years?

**Solution**

| Year 1 | 80% × 0.75 | = 60% |
| Year 2 | 60% × 0.75 | = 45% |
| Year 3 | 45% × 0.75 | = 34% |
| Year 4 | 34% × 0.75 | = 26% |
| OR | 80% × $(0.75)^4$ | = 25.3% (more accurate) |

You should also comment in your answer that it is unlikely the government will achieve this reduction each year.

### Test your understanding 3

**The current rate of inflation in Costovia is 65%. Government action is helping to reduce this rate each year by 10% of the previous rate. The Costovian peso/dollar rate is currently 142 – 146, and the inflation rate in the US over the next three years is expected to be 4%, 3.5% and 3% respectively. Find the exchange rate for the Costovian peso against the dollar for the next three years.**

## 2 Foreign projects and investment appraisal

### NPV analysis

The appraisal of projects involving overseas investment, uses the same NPV model you have used in earlier sessions. It includes basics such as:

- identifying relevant cash flows

- calculating a project's corporation tax liability, including the calculation of tax relief on capital expenditure

- dealing with inflation and distinguishing money and real flows.

However, overseas investment appraisal includes additional challenges:

- Double taxation.

- Inter-company flows (e.g. management charges or royalties).

- Remittance restrictions.

- Forecasting future spot rates (dealt with in section 1 above).

## Taxation

The level of taxation on a project's profits will depend on the relationship between the tax rates in the home and overseas country.

There are three possible tax scenarios for an exam question.

The home country may have a tax rate that is:

- lower than

- the same as

- higher than the overseas country.

The question will always assume a double-tax treaty ⇒ project always taxed at the **highest** rate.

| **Illustration 2** | | | | |

What will be the rate of tax on a project carried out in the US by a UK company in each of the following scenarios?

|  | UK tax |  | US tax |
|---|---|---|---|
| (a) | 33% | < | 40% |
| (b) | 33% | = | 33% |
| (c) | 33% | > | 25% |

**Solution**

- Scenario (a) – no further UK tax to pay on the project's $ profits. Profits taxed at 40% in the US.

- Scenario (b) – no further UK tax to pay on the project's $ profits. Profits taxed at 33% in the US.

- Scenario (c) – project's profits would be taxed at 33% : 25% in the US and a further 8% tax payable in the UK.

## Inter-company cash flows

Inter-company cash flows, such as transfer prices, royalties and management charges, can also affect the tax computations.

Although complex in reality, in the exam:

- Assume inter-company cash flows are allowable for tax (and state it) unless the question says otherwise

- If an inter-company cash flow is allowable for tax relief overseas, there will be a corresponding tax liability on the income in the home country

- Assume that the tax authorities will only allow 'arm's length'/open-market prices for tax relief and will not allow an artificially high or low transfer price.

### Expandable Text - Transfer pricing

The transfer price is the price charged by one part of a company when supplying goods or services to another part of the company, e.g. overseas subsidiary.

Transfer prices are particularly problematical. By manipulating the transfer prices charged it may be possible to minimise the global taxation cost for the group, i.e. to report low profits in countries with high taxes and high profits in countries with low rates.

For instance, suppose we have two companies within a group that are based in different countries.

Company A sells components to Company B, whilst B sells marketing services to Company A.

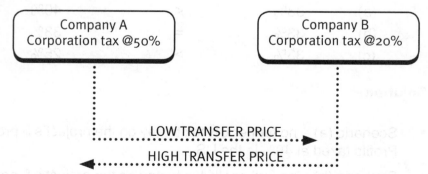

- Company A will report low income therefore limiting its tax charge.

  Company B will be reporting high income as it pays less tax.

By manipulating the transfer price the overall tax charge can be lowered. However, the government of country A will not look favourably on this action.

This objective is therefore frustrated in many countries, as the relevant tax authorities require the transfer price to be set on an arms length basis, i.e. the market price.

If a question tells you that a company is going to considerably increase its transfer price, you could incorporate the new price in you NPV calculations. However it is essential that you then state in your report that the policy may be unsuccessful, as most governments require the transfer price to be set on an arm's length basis, i.e. the market price.

Therefore it is preferable, for exam purposes, to assume that the tax authorities will only allow 'arm's length'/open-market prices for tax relief and will not allow an artificially high or low transfer price.

A second problem may also arise. Although the above may decrease the taxation, the profits will end up in country B. If the currency of country B is weak relative to the holding company, then loss from the depreciation of the currency may be more than the tax saving.

The issues of double taxation and the tax treatment of inter-company flows can be shown with an example:

## Illustration 3

A project carried out by a US subsidiary of a UK company is due to earn revenues of $100m in the US in Year 2 with associatedcosts of $30m. Royalty payments of $10m will be made by the US subsidiary to the UK. Assume tax is paid at 25% in the US and 33% in the UK; and assume a forecast $/£ spot rate of $1.50/£.

What are the cash flows associated with the project?

### Solution

| Year 2 | $m | |
|---|---|---|
| Revenues | 100 | |
| Costs | (30) | |
| Royalties | (10) | |
| Pre-tax profit | 60 | $10m |
| 25% US tax | (15) | ÷$/£1.50 |
| Remit to parent | 45 | = £6.7m |
| @$/£ Spot | ÷1.50 | |
| £ Cash flow | 30 | |
| Royalties | 6.7 | |
| UK tax | (5.4)* | |
| After tax cash flow | £31.3m | |

### UK tax computation

UK tax on $ profits = 33% - 25% = 8%

| | | |
|---|---|---|
| 8% UK tax on $ profits: | $60m ÷ 1.50 | £40m |
| | £40m × 0.08 = | = £3.2m |
| 33% UK tax on royalties: | £6.7m × 0.33 = | = £2.2m |
| UK tax payable | | £5.4m* |

## Remittance restrictions

Remittance restrictions occur where an overseas government places a limit on the funds that can be repatriated back to the holding company. This restriction may change the cash flows that are received by the holding company.

The actual amount received by the parent company (and therefore the shareholders) is the relevant flow for NPV purposes.

### Illustration 4

A project's after-US tax $ cash flow is as follows ($m):

A project's after-US tax $ cash flow is as follows ($m):

| Year | 0 | 1 | 2 | 3 |
|---|---|---|---|---|
| | (10) | 3 | 4 | 6 |

In any one year, only 50% of cash flows generated can be remitted back to the parent. The blocked funds can be released back to the parent in the year after the end of the project.

Find the cash flows to be evaluated for NPV purposes.

**Solution**

Cash flows to parent:

| Year | 1 | 2 | 3 | 4 |
|---|---|---|---|---|
| Net cash flow | 3 | 4 | 6 | |
| Blocked funds | (1.5) | (2) | (3) | |
| **Remit to parent** | **1.5** | **2** | **3** | **6.5** |

It is these remitted cash flows that have to be put through the NPV calculation.

The final cash flows for NPV purposes are therefore:

| Time | $m |
|------|-----|
| 0 | (10.0) |
| 1 | 1.5 |
| 2 | 2.0 |
| 3 | 3.0 |
| 4 | 6.5 |

## Working capital

It is a normally assumed that the working capital requirement for the overseas project will increase by the annual rate of inflation in that country.

### Expandable Text - Working capital calculation

Four million pesos in working capital are required immediately for a project running in South America. The inflation rates for the next six years in the South American country are expected to be:

| Year | 1 | 2 | 3 | 4 | 5 | 6 |
|------|----|----|----|----|----|----|
| | 6% | 4% | 5% | 4% | 3% | 4% |

Identify the working capital flows for the NPV calculation:

**Solution**

All cash flows in $000's

| Year | 0 | 1 | 2 | 3 | 4 | 5 | 6 | 7 |
|------|---|---|---|---|---|---|---|---|
| Working capital | 4,000 | | | | | | | |
| Inflation | 1 | 1.06 | 1.04 | 1.05 | 1.04 | 1.03 | 1.04 | |
| Total w/c | 4,000 | 4,240 | 4,410 | 4,631 | 4,816 | 4,960 | 5,158 | |
| W/c injection | (4,000) | (240) | (170) | (221) | (185) | (144) | (198) | 5,158 |

Working capital released

### Test your understanding 4

Four million pesos are required in working capital immediately. The inflation rate in the South American country is expected to remain constant for the next six years at a rate of 6%. Identify the working capital flows for the NPV calculation, assuming the working capital is released at t = 7.

## 3 NPV analysis for foreign projects

There are two methods for calculating the NPV of overseas projects:

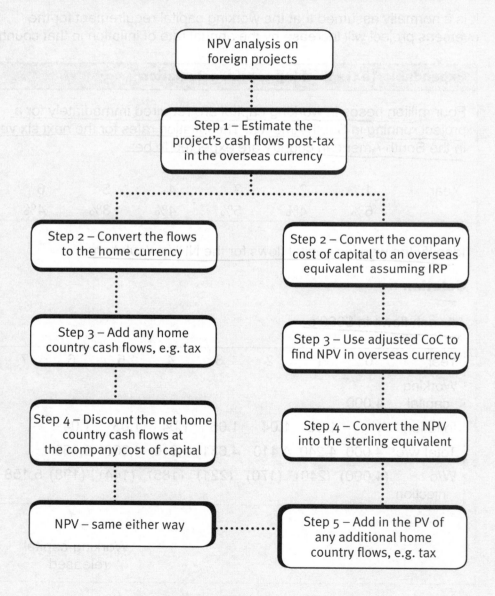

The simpler 4-step method is the more conventional one which is used in the majority of cases.

## Test your understanding 5: The standard method for foreign NPV

A manufacturing company based in the United Kingdom is evaluating an investment project overseas – in REBMATT a politically stable country. It will cost an initial 5.0 million REBMATT dollars (RM$) and it is expected to earn post-tax cash flows as follows:

| Year | 1 | 2 | 3 | 4 |
|---|---|---|---|---|
| Cash flow (RM$000) | 1,500 | 1,900 | 2,500 | 2,700 |

The following information is available:

• Real interest rates in the two countries are the same. They are expected to remain the same for the period of the project.

• The current spot rate is RM$ 2 per £1 Sterling.

• The risk-free rate of interest in REBMATT is 7% and in the UK 9%.

• The company requires a sterling return from this project of 16%.

**Calculate the £ Sterling net present value of the project using the standard method i.e. by discounting annual cash flows in £ Sterling.**

## Expandable Text - The alternative method for foreign NPV

In the previous Test Your Understanding, the NPV could have been calculated by discounting cashflows in REBMATT $ as follows:

**Calculate the adjusted discount rate using the interest rate parity formula:**

$$\frac{1 + i_{1st}}{1 + i_{2nd}} = \frac{spot}{forward\ spot} = \frac{spot}{expected\ future\ spot}$$

$$\frac{1 + 0.16}{1 + i_\$} = \frac{2.000}{1.9633}$$

$$1 + i_\$ = \frac{(1 + 0.16) \times 1.9633}{2.000}$$

$$i\$ = 13.87\%$$

| Year | Cash flow RM $ | DF 13.87% | PV |
|------|----------------|-----------|--------|
| 0 | (5,000) | 1.000 | (5,000) |
| 1 | 1,500 | 0.878 | 1,317 |
| 2 | 1,900 | 0.771 | 1,465 |
| 3 | 2,500 | 0.678 | 1,695 |
| 4 | 2,700 | 0.594 | 1,604 |
| | | | RM $1,081 |

PV = **1,081/2.000 = £541.**

The difference between the two results is due to rounding.

## Standard proforma for the conventional approach

| Year | 0 | 1 | 2 | 3 | 4 | 5 |
|---|---|---|---|---|---|---|
| | FC | FC | FC | FC | FC | FC |
| **Sales/receipts payments:** | | x | x | x | x | |
| Variable costs | | (x) | (x) | (x) | (x) | |
| Wages/materials | | (x) | (x) | (x) | (x) | |
| Incremental fixed costs | | (x) | (x) | (x) | (x) | |
| **Untaxed sub returns, e.g. royalties** | | (x) — | (x) — | (x) — | (x) — | |
| **Taxable profits** | | x | x | x | x | |
| **Foreign tax @ say 20%** | | (x) | (x) | (x) | (x) | |
| Initial outlay | (x) | | | | | |
| Realisable value | | | | | x | |
| Tax relief on capital allowances | x | x | x | x | x | |
| Working capital | (x) | (x) | (x) | (x) | (x) | x |
| **Net foreign CF** | (x) | x | x | x | x | x |
| **Exchange rate (based on PPPT)** | x | x | x | x | x | x |
| Home currency CF | (x) | x | x | x | x | x |
| Domestic tax on foreign taxable profits @30% − 20% = 10% | | (x) | (x) | (x) | (x) | |
| Untaxed sub returns, e.g. royalties | | x | x | x | x | |
| Domestic tax on royalties etc. @30% | | (x) | (x) | (x) | (x) | |
| **Net home currency CF** | (x) | x | x | x | x | x |
| DF (say 16%) | 1 | 0.862 | 0.743 | 0.641 | 0.552 | 0.476 |
| **Home currency PV** | (x) | x | x | x | x | x |
| **Home currency NPV** | | | x/(x) | | | |

## Performing the calculation

It will be necessary to do a number of subsidiary workings in order to reach the final NPV figure, so remember the basic rules:

- Lay out your table clearly and remember you will need one column more than the length of the project if tax is lagged by a year.

- Make sure all workings are clearly referenced.

- State any assumptions and be prepared to comment on them further in any written report that follows.

The following is a guideline order of approach for the conventional approach:

(1) Calculate all the relevant flows in the foreign currency.

(2) If tax is payable on the foreign flows, deduct it.

(3) Convert the net flows into the domestic currency – you may well need to predict future exchange rates to do so.

(4) Consider whether any restrictions are placed on remittances and if so, calculate the cash flows actually received by the parent.

(5) Add any other domestic cash flows to the remitted amounts from overseas.

(6) Discount the total net cash flows in the domestic currency at an appropriate cost of capital.

### Test your understanding 6: Exam standard question: foreign NPV

Puxty Plc is a specialist manufacturer of window frames. Its main UK manufacturing operation is based in the south of England, from where it distributes its products throughout the UK.

The directors are now considering whether they should open up an additional manufacturing operation in France – which they believe there will be a good market for their products.

A suitable factory has been located just outside Paris that could be rented on a 5-year lease at an annual charge of €3.8m, payable each year in advance. The manufacturing equipment would cost €75m, of which €60m would have to be paid at the start of the project, with the balance payable 12 months later.

At the start of each year the French factory would require working capital equal to 40% of that year's sales revenues. It is expected that the factory will be able to produce and sell 80,000 window units per year although, in the first year, because of the need to 'run in' the machinery and its new workforce, output is only expected to be 50,000 window units. Each window is likely to be sold for €750, a price that represents a 150% mark-up on cash production costs.

The French factory would be set up as a wholly-owned subsidiary of Puxty Plc. In France, 25% straight-line depreciation on cost is an allowable expense against company tax. Corporation tax is payable at 40% at each year-end without delay and any unused losses can be brought forward for set off against the following year's profits. No UK tax would be payable on the after-tax French profits.

All amounts in € are given in current terms. Annual inflation in French is expected to run at 6% per year in the foreseeable future. All FF cash flows involved are expected to increase in line with this inflation rate, with the exception of the factory rental and the cost of the manufacturing equipment, both of which would remain unchanged.

The French factory would be producing windows to a special design patented by Puxty. To protect its patent rights, Puxty Plc will charge its French subsidiary a fixed royalty of £20 per window. This cost would be allowable against the subsidiary's French tax liability.

The current €/£ spot rate is 1.5. Inflation in the UK is expected to be 4% per year over the period. There are no cash flow remittance restrictions between France and the UK.

Puxty Plc is an all-equity financed company that is quoted on the London Stock Exchange. Its shares have a beta value of 1.25. The current annual return on UK Government Treasury Bills is 10% and the expected return on the market is 18%. In the UK Corporation Tax is payable at 35%, one year in arrears.

Puxty operates on a 5-year planning horizon. At the end of five years, assume that working capital would be fully recovered and the production equipment would have a scrap value, at that time, of €70m before tax. Proceeds on asset sales are taxed at 40%. Assume all cash flows arise at the end of the year to which they relate, unless otherwise stated.

**Required**

**Evaluate the proposed investment in France and recommend what investment decision should be made by Puxty plc. State clearly any assumptions you make and work all calculations rounded to nearest 10,000 (either € or £) – i.e. €0.01m or £0.01m.**

## Expandable Text - International CAPM and APV

### A recap of the basics

The APV method of investment appraisal was introduced in a previous chapter in the context of domestic investments. There are essentially three steps to the technique:

**Step 1** Estimate the base case NPV assuming that the project is financed entirely by equity.

**Step 2** Estimate the financial "side effects" of the actual method of financing.

**Step 3** Add the values from steps 1 and 2 to give the APV.

If the APV is positive, accept the project.

We now examine the applicability of the method in appraising international investments.

### Mechanics of the International APV method

The normal procedure of determining the relevant cash flows and discounting at a rate of return commensurate with the project's risk should be followed as before, but taking account of the international factors as discussed above.

The steps therefore become

**Step 1**The base case NPV assumes that the project is financed entirely by equity, so the discount rate must be the cost of equity allowing for the project risk but excluding financial risk – using the international CAPM equation with an ungeared 'world' β ( **see below**).

**Step 2**Adjustments should be made for:

- tax relief on debt interest and issue costs
- subsidies from overseas governments
- projects financed by loans raised locally
- restriction on remittances.

**Step 3** Add the values from steps 1 and 2 to give the APV.

This is basically the same approach as for domestic appraisal, with a little more care needed in identifying the appropriate appraisal rates and adjustments.

## International CAPM

In the domestic context you should recall that the CAPM could be used to derive the return required as

$$Rj = R_f + \beta(R_m - R_f)$$

where Rj is the required return from the investment

$R_f$ is the risk-free rate of return

$R_m$ is the expected return from the whole market

$\beta$ is a measure of the systematic risk of the investment

However, where a company operates:

- internationally
- in integrated markets

investors should therefore consider applying the international cost of capital to investment appraisal, rather than a domestic CAPM.

The logic:

(1) A company involved in international operations, will, in addition to the usual risk, be exposed to:

- currency risk
- political risk.

These are mainly unsystematic and can be diversified away by holding an internationally diversified portfolio.

(2) For example, a fully diversified UK investor can achieve further risk reduction by investing in other countries. Part of the systematic risk of the UK market is in fact unsystematic risk from an international viewpoint.

The international CAPM equation will therefore read:

$$Rj = R_f + \beta_w (R_w - R_f)$$

where

Rj is the required return

$R_w$ is the expected return from the whole world portfolio

$\beta_w$ is a measure of the project's world systematic risk, i.e. how returns on the investment correlate with those on the world market.

In the UK, for example, the return from the whole market could be estimated from looking at domestic stock market indexes such as the FTSE Actuaries All-Share index, which covers about 700 of the top shares listed in the UK.

This basic CAPM model is valid for:

- a company or investor with domestic investments only, or
- investments in a country with segmented markets, as opposed to integrated markets.

Integrated capital markets exist if investors can invest in any country that does not impose restrictions on capital movements. Segmented markets are associated with a closed economy, or markets where switching investments from country to country is not easily achieved, such as in many service industries.

It is argued that:

Investors can diversify their risk more effectively in an integrated market, because more investments are available and returns on domestic and foreign assets are not perfectly correlated.

The cost of capital is lower if markets are integrated than in a closed economy. Companies whose shareholders are international investors should therefore consider applying the international cost of capital to investment appraisal, rather than a domestic CAPM.

This can be done by looking at the international CAPM.

In practice it is impossible to hold a share of the whole world portfolio, but significant international diversification can be achieved by:

- direct holdings in overseas companies
- holdings in unit trusts specialising in overseas companies
- investing in multinational companies.

You should appreciate that in principle risk reduction can be achieved either by investing directly in an international portfolio of shares or investing in local companies with significant overseas activities.

KAPLAN PUBLISHING

Implications of the international capital asset pricing model (or IAPM) are that:

When setting a cost of capital, a company should assess the nature of its investors and their investment portfolios.

If markets are segmented, investments that are profitable for an international/foreign company might not be profitable for a domestic company, because the international company will have a lower cost of capital.

However, the validity of the international capital asset pricing model rests on the assumption that capital markets are fully integrated and investors are 'world' investors. In practice, this is not necessarily the case. Countries and capital markets are not fully integrated, since there are costs to foreign investment and domestic investors often have better access to information than foreign investors.

In conclusion, although the international capital asset pricing model can in theory be applied, there remain valid reasons for measuring the cost of equity on the basis of a domestic market portfolio and the basic CAPM.

# 4 Financing foreign projects

A firm planning to invest overseas may choose to raise the finance required in the international financial markets.

There is a variety of sources of finance available:

Short-term funding:

- Eurocurrency loans.
- Syndicated loans
- Short-term syndicated credit facilities.
- Multiple option facilities.
- Euronotes.

Long-term funding:

- Syndicated loans
- Eurobonds.

### Eurocurrency loans

Multinational companies and large companies, which are heavily engaged in international transactions, may require funds in a foreign currency.

A Eurocurrency loan is a loan by a bank to a company denominated in currency of a country other than that in which they are based.

> e.g. A UK company acquiring a dollar loan from a UK bank operating in the Eurocurrency market has acquired a Eurodollar loan.

Loans can take a variety of forms:

- Straight loans.
- Lines of credit.
- Revolving loans.

Borrowers looking to eurocurrency loans must have first class credit ratings and wish to deal in large sums of money.

A variety of factors will influence the decision over whether to borrow in the domestic currency or in a foreign currency. The most important are:

- the currency required
- cost and convenience
- the size of loans.

### Expandable Text

#### The currency required

Companies may have needs for foreign currency funds for either trading or financing purposes and the Eurocurrency market may be a more convenient or cheaper source of such funds than in the domestic market of the country whose currency is needed.

#### Cost and convenience

Eurocurrency loans may be:

A   cheaper if interest rates are lower; even if interest rate differentials are small this may be significant for large loans

B   quicker to arrange

C   unsecured and large companies can rely on their credit ratings rather than the security that can offer.

> ## The size of loans
>
> The Eurocurrency markets hold very large funds and for companies wishing to obtain very large loans this may be a viable alternative to domestic banking sources.

As well as a conventional Eurocurrency loans, the international money markets have developed alternative short-term credit instruments.

## Syndicated loans

For large loans a single bank may not be willing (due to risk exposure) or able to lend the whole amount.

A syndicated loan is a loan made to a borrower by two or more participants but is governed by a single loan agreement. The loan is structured by an arranger and each syndicate participant contributes a defined percentage of the loan and receives the same percentage of the repayments.

The syndicated loan market is made up of international lenders and was originally limited to global firms for acquisitions and other major investments. This is for the following reasons:

- Cost – being international, loans can often be raised avoiding national regulation and are thus cheaper.
- Speed – the market is very efficient so large loans can often be put together quickly if necessary.
- By diversifying lending sources borrowers may be able to eliminate foreign exchange rate risk.

However, the market has expanded rapidly with smaller and medium sized firms borrowing funds – syndicated loans as small as $10 million are now commonplace.

## Syndicated credits

Similar to syndicated loans, syndicated credits allow a borrower to borrow funds when it requires, but can choose not take up the full amount of the agreed facility. These are expensive funds used commonly:

- to fund takeovers
- to refinance debts incurred during a takeover.

## Multiple option facilities

Recently developed financial instruments, these are designed to give the borrower a choice of available funds.

Commonly this will combine:

- a panel of banks to provide a credit standby at a rate of interest linked to LIBOR
- another panel of banks to bid to provide loans when the borrower needs cash.

These funds can be in a variety of forms and denominated in a variety of currencies.

## Euronotes

Euronotes have the following features:

- Firms issue promissory notes which promise to pay the holder a fixed sum of money on a specific date or range of dates in the future.
- The Eurobond market acts as both a primary and secondary market often underwritten by banks through revolving underwriting facilities.
- Can be are short or medium term issued in single or multiple currencies. The medium-term notes bridge the gap between the short-term issues and the longer-term Eurobonds.

## Eurobonds

The most important source of longer term funding is the Eurobond.

Eurobonds are:

- long term (3–20 years)
- issued and sold internationally
- denominated in a single currency
- fixed or floating interest rate bonds.

They are suitable for organisations that require:

- large capital sums for long periods
- borrowing not subject to domestic regulations.

However, a currency risk may arise if the investment the bonds are funding generates net revenues in a currency different from that the bond is denominated in.

### Expandable Text - More details on Eurobonds

In addition to short-term credit, companies and government bodies may wish to raise long-term capital. For this there is an international capital market corresponding to the international money market but dealing in longer-term funding with a different range of financial instruments. The most important of these is the Eurobond.

Eurobonds are long-term loans, usually between 3 and 20 years duration, issued and sold internationally and denominated in a single currency, often not that of the country of origin of the borrower. They may be fixed or floating interest rate bonds. The latter were introduced since inflation, especially if unpredictable, made fixed rate bonds less attractive to potential borrowers.

Eurobonds are suitable sources of finance for organisations that require:

- large capital sums for long periods, e.g. to finance major capital investment programmes
- borrowing not subject to domestic regulations especially exchange controls which may limit their ability to export capital sums.

However, Eurobonds involves the borrower in currency risk. If the capital investment generates revenue in a currency other than that in which the bond is denominated and exchange rates change the borrower will:

- suffer losses if the currency in which the bond is denominated strengthens against the currency in which the revenues are denominated
- make gains if the currency in which the bond is denominated weakens against the currency in which the revenues are denominated.

### Expandable Text - Detailed example

Assume that 'now' is June 20X3.

#### Question part (a)

Somax plc wishes to raise 260 million Swiss francs in floating rate finance for a period of five years. Discuss the advantages and disadvantages of raising such funds through:

(1) Direct borrowing from a domestic banking system such as the Swiss domestic banking system. (Detailed knowledge of the Swiss banking system is not required.)

(2) The Euromarket.

## Question part (b)

The funds are to be used to establish a new production plant in Switzerland. Somax evaluates its investments using NPV, but is not sure what cost of capital to use in the discounting process.

The company is also proposing to increase its equity finance in the near future for UK expansion, resulting overall in little change in the company's market weighted capital gearing. The summarised financial data for the company before the expansion are shown below:

Income statement for the year ending 31 March 20X3.

|  | £ million |
|---|---|
| Turnover | 1,984 |
| Gross profit | 432 |
| Profit after tax | 81 |
| Dividends | 37 |
| Retained earnings | 44 |

Balance sheet (statement of financial position) as at 31 March 20X3

|  | £ million |
|---|---|
| Non-current assets (net) | 846 |
| Working capital | 350 |
|  | 1,196 |
| Medium and long-term loans[1] | (210) |
|  | 986 |

**Shareholders' funds**

|  |  |
|---|---|
| Issued ordinary shares (50 pence par) | 225 |
| Reserves | 761 |
|  | 986 |

[1] Including £75m 14% fixed rate bonds due to mature in five years time and redeemable at £100. The current market price of these bonds is £119.50. Other medium and long-term loans are floating rate UK bank loans at bank base rate plus 1%.

Corporate tax may be assumed to be at the rate of 33% in both the UK and Switzerland.

The company's ordinary shares are currently trading at 376 pence.

Somax's equity beta is estimated to be 1.18. The systematic risk of debt may be assumed to be zero.

The risk free rate is 7.75% and market return 14.5%. Bank base rate is currently 8.25%.

The estimated equity beta of the main Swiss competitor in the same industry as the new proposed plant in Switzerland is 1.5, and the competitor's capital gearing is 35% equity, 65% debt by book values, and 60% equity, 40% debt by market values.

### Exchange rates

|        | Spot             | 6 months forward |
|--------|------------------|------------------|
| Spot   | SFr2.3245–2.3300/£1 |                  |
| 6 months forward | SFr2.2955–2.3009/£1 |         |

Somax can borrow in Swiss francs at a floating rate of between 5.75% and 6% depending upon which form of borrowing is selected (i.e. in the Euromarkets or the Swiss domestic market).

SFr LIBOR is currently 5%.

The interest rate parity theorem may be assumed to hold.

### Required:

**Estimate the STERLING cost of capital that Somax should use as the discount rate for its proposed investment in Switzerland. State clearly any assumptions that you make.**

### Solution

(a) **Tutorial note:** The rates in this question might seem unusual, but you should answer the question on the basis of the data provided.

SFr260 million is approximately £110 million. This is a large sum to borrow from an individual bank. The largest domestic Swiss banks could handle individual loans of this size, but it is possible that the loan would be arranged through several Swiss banks, which spreads the default risk between them.

Domestic banking systems are normally subject to more regulation and reserve requirements than the Euromarkets, leading to wider spreads between borrowing and lending rates. The cost of borrowing on domestic markets is often slightly more expensive than the Euromarkets, and may involve fixed or floating charges on corporate assets as security for loans. Few Euromarket loans require security. Domestic market loans may be either fixed or floating rate, but bank loans are more likely to be at a floating rate.

If Euromarkets are used the main choices are:

(1)  Eurocurrency loans from the international banking system.

(2)  The issue of securities direct to the market by Somax.

A five year loan is quite long for the Eurocurrency market, which specialises in short to medium-term loans. Large loans can be raised quickly at little issue cost, often through investment syndicates of banks. However, medium-term to long-term international bank loans may be arranged by individual banks or syndicates of banks. Interest on these types of loan is normally floating rate, at SFr LIBOR plus a percentage dependent upon Somax's credit rating. Draw-down dates are often flexible, but commitment fees may be payable if the full amount of the loan is not drawn down immediately, and early redemption penalties are normal.

An argument in favour of using the banking system, whether domestic or international is that banks are specialists in analysing and monitoring debts. If large loans are agreed by banks this is a sign of good credit standing, and may facilitate access to cheaper funds on other capital markets.

Somax has a number of choices of issuing securities on the Euromarket. The Euronote market involves short to medium-term issue of paper such as Euro-commercial paper and Euro-medium term notes. Banks, for a fee, will arrange such issues and may underwrite their success.

Eurobonds (international bonds) are medium to long-term bonds sold in countries other than the country of the currency in which the issue is denominated. Both the eurobond and euronote market provide the opportunity to borrow either fixed or floating rate finance, depending upon which financial instrument is selected although most bond and note issues are at a fixed coupon.

Some eurobonds may be convertible or have warrants attached which can offer attractions to both issuers and investors. A disadvantage of the eurobond market is that issue costs are higher than the eurocurrency market, and it takes longer to arrange a eurobond issue. In addition, only very large companies with a good credit rating are likely to issue bonds successfully in the European market. The main advantage of issuing bonds, notes or commercial paper on the euromarket is that funds may normally be raised at a lower interest cost than borrowing from the domestic or international banking system.

(b) The discount rate should be a weighted average cost of capital, which takes into account the systematic risk of the new investment.

**Cost of equity**

Somax proposes to establish a new production plant in Switzerland. As this involves diversifying into a new industry, the company's existing equity beta is unlikely to reflect the systematic risk of the new investment. The project systematic risk may be estimated using the equity beta of the main Swiss competitor after allowing for differences in capital structure (financial risk) between the two companies.

Ungearing the equity beta of the Swiss competitor (using market values):

$$\beta_a = \beta_e \times \frac{V_e}{V_e + V_d(1-T)}$$

$$\beta_a = 1.5 \times \frac{60}{60 + 40(1-0.33)} = 1.037$$

The asset beta must be re-geared to reflect the capital structure of Somax. Using market values:

| | | £m |
|---|---|---|
| Equity: | 450 million shares at 376 pence | 1,692.00 |
| Debt: | Bank loans (210 – 75) | 135.00 |
| | 14% bonds (£75 million × 1.195) | 89.63 |
| | | 1,916.63 |

$$\beta_e = \beta_a \times \frac{V_e + V_d(1 - T)}{V_e}$$

$$\beta_e = 1.037 \times \frac{1,692 + 224.63(1 - 0.33)}{1,692} = 1.129$$

Using CAPM, the cost of equity is:

$$K_e = R_f + (R_m - R_f)\beta_e$$

$$K_e = 7.75\% + (14.5\% - 7.75\%)\,1.129 = 15.37\%.$$

## Cost of debt

Somax is considering the use of two alternative forms of SFr floating rate financing which involved differing interest costs, varying from 5.75% to 6%. Issuing securities on the Euromarket would normally be slightly cheaper than borrowing directly from international banks. It is assumed that the 5.75% rate refers to Euromarket borrowing.

Using interest rate parity we can derive the effective interest rates in sterling terms:

$$F_0 = S_0 \times \frac{(1 + i_{SFr})}{(1 + i_{\pounds})}$$

Using mid rate exchange rates, and taking the Swiss rate of 5.75% per annum initially:

$$2.2982 = 2.3273 \times \frac{(1 + (5.75\% \times 6/12))}{(1 + i_\pounds)}$$

so $i_\pounds$ = 4.18% from the formula (a 6 monthly rate), which corresponds to an annual rate of 8.36%.

(Similarly, using the Swiss rate of 6% would give an effective sterling rate of 8.60%.)

## WACC

Note that gearing levels are not expected to change the estimated weighted average cost of capital is:

(15.37% × 1,692 + 8.36% (1 − 0.33) 224.63)/(1,692 + 224.63)

= 14.23% or (14.24% using the 8.60% cost of debt).

## 5 Chapter summary

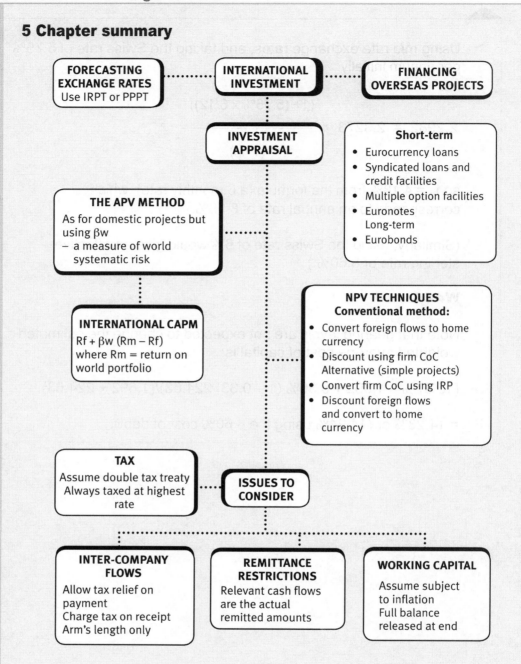

**FORECASTING EXCHANGE RATES**
Use IRPT or PPPT

**INTERNATIONAL INVESTMENT**

**FINANCING OVERSEAS PROJECTS**

**INVESTMENT APPRAISAL**

**Short-term**
- Eurocurrency loans
- Syndicated loans and credit facilities
- Multiple option facilities
- Euronotes
  Long-term
- Eurobonds

**THE APV METHOD**
As for domestic projects but using βw
– a measure of world systematic risk

**INTERNATIONAL CAPM**
Rf + βw (Rm – Rf)
where Rm = return on world portfolio

**NPV TECHNIQUES**
**Conventional method:**
- Convert foreign flows to home currency
- Discount using firm CoC Alternative (simple projects)
- Convert firm CoC using IRP
- Discount foreign flows and convert to home currency

**TAX**
Assume double tax treaty
Always taxed at highest rate

**ISSUES TO CONSIDER**

**INTER-COMPANY FLOWS**
Allow tax relief on payment
Charge tax on receipt
Arm's length only

**REMITTANCE RESTRICTIONS**
Relevant cash flows are the actual remitted amounts

**WORKING CAPITAL**
Assume subject to inflation
Full balance released at end

# Test your understanding answers

## Test your understanding 1

Using the formula:

$$\text{Future Spot} = \text{Spot} \times \frac{(1+h_c)}{(1+h_b)}$$

and the midpoint of the quoted spread as the exchange rate today:

1.5274 + (1.5376 – 1.5274)/2 = 1.5325

The calculations for the next three years are:

Year 1  $1.5325 \times \left(\dfrac{1.03}{1.01}\right) = 1.5628$

Year 2  $1.5628 \times \left(\dfrac{1.01}{1.04}\right) = 1.5177$

Year 3  $1.5177 \times \left(\dfrac{1.02}{1.03}\right) = 1.5030$

## Test your understanding 2

The €/$ cross rate will be calculated as:

1.53/1.87 = 0.8182

The cost of the machine is therefore:

€$100,000 / 0.8182 = $122,220

## Test your understanding 3

Step 1 – find the inflation rate in Costovia over the next three years:

Year 1           65%           × 0.9 = 58.5%
Year 2           58.5%         × 0.9 = 52.7%
Year 3           52.7%         × 0.9 = 47.4%

Step 2 – find the exchange rates:

Using the formula:

$$\text{Future Spot} = \text{Spot} \times \frac{(1+h_c)}{(1+h_b)}$$

expand the midpoint of the quoted spread as the exchange rate today:

142 + (146 – 142)/2 = 144

The calculations for the next three years are:

Year 1 144 × (1.585/1.04) = 220

Year 2 220 × (1.527/1.035) = 325

Year 3 325 × (1.474/1.03 ) = 465

## Test your understanding 4

| Year | 0 | 1 | 2 | 3 | 4 | 5 | 6 | 7 |
|---|---|---|---|---|---|---|---|---|
| Working capital | 4,000 | | | | | | | |
| Inflation | 1.00 | 1.06 | 1.06 | 1.06 | 1.06 | 1.06 | 1.06 | |
| Total money | 4,000 | 4,240 | 4,494 | 4,764 | 5,050 | 5,353 | 5,674 | |
| Movement | (4,000) | (240) | (254) | (270) | (286) | (303) | (321) | 5,674 |

Working capital
released

## Test your understanding 5: The standard method for foreign NPV

### Calculation of exchange rates

Using the interest rate parity theory:

| Year 1 | $2.00 \times 1.07/1.09 = 1.9633$ |
| Year 2 | $1.9633 \times 1.07/1.09 = 1.9273$ |
| Year 3 | $1.9273 \times 1.07/1.09 = 1.8919$ |
| Year 4 | $1.8919 \times 1.07/1.09 = 1.8572$ |

| Year | 0 | 1 | 2 | 3 | 4 |
|---|---|---|---|---|---|
| Cash flow (RM$000) | (5,000) | 1,500 | 1,900 | 2,500 | 2,700 |
| Exchange rate | 2.000 | 1.9633 | 1.9273 | 1.8919 | 1.8572 |
| Cash flow £ | (2,500) | 764 | 986 | 1,321 | 1,454 |
| PV factor 16% | 1.000 | 0.862 | 0.743 | 0.641 | 0.552 |
| PV | (2,500) | 659 | 733 | 847 | 803 |

**NPV = £542**

## Test your understanding 6: Exam standard question: foreign NPV

**Solution**

**Cash flow analysis (€m)**

|  | 0 | 1 | 2 | 3 | 4 | 5 | 6 |
|---|---|---|---|---|---|---|---|
| Revenues (W1) | – | 39.75 | 67.42 | 71.46 | 75.75 | 80.29 | – |
| Operating costs (W2) | – | (15.90) | (26.97) | (28.58) | (30.30) | (32.12) | – |
| Rental charges | (3.80) | (3.80) | (3.80) | (3.80) | (3.80) | – | – |
| Royalties (W3) | – | (1.53) | (2.50) | (2.54) | (2.59) | (2.64) | – |
| Tax charge (W5) | – | (0.00) | (6.07) | (7.12) | (8.12) | (16.69) | – |
| Equipment outlay | (60.00) | (15.00) | – | – | – | – | – |
| Scrap value | – | – | – | – | – | 70.00 | – |
| Tax on scrap | – | – | – | – | – | (28.00) | – |
| Working capital (W6) | (15.90) | (11.07) | (1.61) | (1.72) | (1.82) | 32.12 | – |
| Net €m c/f | (79.70) | (7.55) | 26.47 | 27.70 | 29.12 | 102.96 | – |
| €/£ (W4) | 1.50 | 1.53 | 1.56 | 1.59 | 1.62 | 1.65 | – |
| £m c/f | (53.13) | (4.93) | 16.97 | 17.42 | 17.98 | 62.40 | – |
| £m royalties (W3) | – | 1.00 | 1.60 | 1.60 | 1.60 | 1.60 | – |
| UK royalty tax 35% | – | – | (0.35) | (0.56) | (0.56) | (0.56) | (0.56) |
| Net £m c/f | (53.13) | (3.93) | 18.22 | 18.46 | 19.02 | 63.06 | (0.56) |
| 20% Discount (W7) | 1 | 0.833 | 0.694 | 0.579 | 0.482 | 0.402 | 0.335 |
|  | (53.13) | (3.27) | 12.64 | 10.69 | 9.17 | 25.35 | (0.19) |

NPV: + £1.26m.

## W1 €m Sales revenues

$50{,}000 \times 750 (1.06) = 39.75$ Year 1

$80{,}000 \times 750 (1.06)^2 = 67.42$ Year 2

$80{,}000 \times 750 (1.06)^3 = 71.46$ Year 3

$80{,}000 \times 750 (1.06)^4 = 75.75$ Year 4

$80{,}000 \times 750 (1.06)^5 = 80.29$ Year 5

## W2 €m Production costs

$39.75 \div 2.5 = 15.9$ Year 1

$67.42 \div 2.5 = 26.97$ Year 2

$71.46 \div 2.5 = 28.58$ Year 3

$75.75 \div 2.5 = 30.30$ Year 4

$80.29 \div 2.5 = 32.12$ Year 5

## W3 €m Royalty payments

$50{,}000 \times £20 = £1m \times 1.53 = €1.53m$ = Year 1 (exchange rate calculations – see W4).

$80{,}000 \times £20 = £1.6m \times 1.56 = €2.50m$ = Year 2

$80{,}000 \times £20 = £1.6m \times 1.59 = €2.54m$ = Year 3

$80{,}000 \times £20 = £1.6m \times 1.62 = €2.59m$ = Year 4

$80{,}000 \times £20 = £1.6m \times 1.65 = €2.64m$ = Year 5

## W4 €/£ Exchange rate

$$S_1 = S_0 \times \frac{(1+ h_c)}{(1+h_b)}$$

Year 1 = 1.50 × 1.06/1.04 = 1.53
Year 2 = 1.53 × 1.06/1.04 = 1.56
Year 3 = 1.56 × 1.06/1.04 = 1.59
Year 4 = 1.59 × 1.06/1.04 = 1.62
Year 5 = 1.62 × 1.06/1.04 = 1.65

## W5 Basic €m tax calculations

| | Years | | | | |
|---|---|---|---|---|---|
| | **1** | **2** | **3** | **4** | **5** |
| Revenues | 39.75 | 67.42 | 71.46 | 75.75 | 80.29 |
| Less: | | | | | |
| Operating costs | (15.90) | (26.97) | (28.58) | (30.30) | (32.12) |
| Depreciation | (18.75) | (18.75) | (18.75) | (18.75) | – |
| Rental charges | (3.80) | (3.80) | (3.80) | (3.80) | (3.80) |
| Royalties | (1.53) | (2.50) | (2.54) | (2.59) | (2.64) |
| Taxable cash flow | (0.23) | 15.40 | 17.79 | 20.31 | 41.73 |
| Loss b/f* | | (0.23) | | | |
| Tax at 40% (no lag) | **0.00** | **6.07** | **7.12** | **8.12** | **16.69** |

*No other business in France means no profits available to set off the loss in that year. Instead it is carried forward for set off in the following year.

## W6 €m Working capital requirement

Revenue × 40% Needed − Previous balance = Injection

39.75 × 0.4 = 15.90 − 0 = 15.90 Year 0

67.42 × 0.4 = 26.97 − 15.90 = 11.07 Year 1

71.46 × 0.4 = 28.58 − 26.97 = 1.61 Year 2

75.75 × 0.4 = 30.30 − 28.58 = 1.72 Year 3

80.29 × 0.4 = 32.12 − 30.30 = 1.82 Year 4

Recovery 32.12 Year 5

## W7 £ discount rate

Using the CAPM equation:

$$Rj = R_f + \beta(R_m - R_f)$$

The discount rate can be found as: 10% + (18% − 10%) × 1.25 = 20%.

## Conclusion

As the French manufacturing project generates a positive NPV it should be undertaken, provided the directors are happy with the estimates they have made.

**Assumptions**

Royalties are allowable against French tax.

Royalties are subject to UK tax.

Further information that might be useful to the analysis would include:

- Details as to how the estimates of the project's cash flows were made.

- Details about where the company derived its estimate of the future French inflation rate and the future rate of depreciation of the French franc.

- Details of how the estimate of the machinery's five-year scrap value was made.

- An analysis about whether or not country risk might be a significant factor.

- How sensitive is the NPV calculation to changes in some of the key estimates.

# Option pricing

## Chapter learning objectives

Upon completion of this chapter you will be able to:

- explain the principles of option pricing theory

- determine, using published data, the five principal drivers of option value (value of the underlying, exercise price, time to expiry, volatility and the risk-free rate)

- discuss the underlying assumptions, structure, application and limitations of the Black-Scholes model

- recognise real options embedded within a project, and classify them as one of the real option archetypes

- use the principles of the Black-Scholes model to explain the value of real options to delay, expand, redeploy and withdraw in investment projects and calculate the value of the options.

- use option pricing theory to calculate credit spreads.

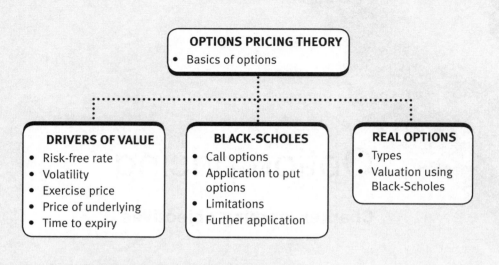

## 1 The principles of option pricing theory

### Option terminology

| | |
|---|---|
| **An option** | The right but not an obligation, to buy or sell a particular good at an exercise price, at or before a specified date. |
| **Call option** *right to buy* | The right but not an obligation to buy a particular good at an exercise price. |
| **Put option** *right to sell* | The right but not an obligation to sell a particular good at an exercise price. |
| **Exercise/strike price** | The fixed price at which the good may be bought or sold. |
| **American option** | An option that can be exercised on any day up until its expiry date. |
| **European option** | An option that can only be exercised on the last day of the option. |
| **Premium** | The cost of an option. |
| **Traded option** | Standardised option contracts sold on a futures exchange (normally American options). |
| **Over the counter (OTC) option** | Tailor-made option – usually sold by a bank (normally European options). |

### Option value

The key aspect to an option's value is that the buyer has a choice whether or not to use it. Thus the option can be used to avoid downside risk exposure without foregoing upside exposure.

The value of an option is made up of two components. These are illustrated below for a call option:

## The intrinsic value

The intrinsic value looks at the exercise price compared with the price of the underlying asset.

| Share price | $ | 80 | 90 | 100 | 110 | 120 |
|---|---|---|---|---|---|---|
| Exercise price | $ | 100 | 100 | 100 | 100 | 100 |
| **Intrinsic value** | $ | 0 | 0 | 0 | 10 | 20 |

Out of the money ← | ↑ | → In the money

At the money

- The value of the call option will increase as the share price increases. Conversely a lower exercise price would also give a higher option value.

- An option can never have a negative intrinsic value. If the option is out of the money, then the intrinsic value is zero.

- On the expiry date, the value of an option is equal to its intrinsic value.

## The time value

- Time to expiry.
  - As the period to expiry increases, the chance of a profit before the expiry date grows, increasing the option value.

- Volatility of the share price.
  - The holder of a call option does not suffer if the share price falls below the exercise price, i.e. there is a limit to the downside.

  - However the option holder gains if the share price increases above the exercise price, i.e. there is no limit to the upside.

  - Thus the greater the volatility the better, as this increases the probability of a valuable increase in share price.

- Risk-free interest rate.
  - As stated above, the exercise price has to be paid in the future, therefore the higher the interest rates the lower the present value of the exercise price. This reduces the cost of exercising and thus adds value to the current call option value.

  - Alternatively, since having a call option means that the share purchase can be deferred, owning a call option becomes more valuable when interest rates are high, since the money left in the bank will be generating a higher return.

Summary of the determinants of call option prices:

| Increase in | Value of a call |
|---|---|
| Share price | Increase |
| Exercise price | Decrease |
| Time to expiry | Increase |
| Volatility – s | Increase |
| Interest rate | Increase |

## Test your understanding 1

**Complete the following table for put options.**

Summary of the determinants of call option prices:

| **Increase in** | **Call** | **Put** |
|---|---|---|
| Share price | Increase | |
| Exercise price | Decrease | |
| Time to expiry | Increase | |
| Volatility – s | Increase | |
| Interest rate | Increase | |

## Test your understanding 2

**A pension fund manager is concerned that the value of the stock market will fall. Suggest an option strategy he could use to protect the fund value.**

## Expandable Text - The drivers of option value in practice

### Introduction

As discussed above, the main drivers of option value are as follows:

- value of the underlying asset
- exercise price
- time to expiry
- volatility
- risk-free rate.

Determining these figures in practice is discussed below.

## Value of the underlying asset

- For quoted underlying assets a value can be looked up on the market. Most markets give prices for buying and selling the underlying asset. A mid-price is usually used for option pricing.

  For example, if a price is quoted as 243–244 cents, then a mid-price of 243.5 cents should be used.

- In the case of unquoted underlying assets a separate exercise must be undertaken to value them.

  For example, suppose an unquoted company has issued share options to employees as part of their remuneration package. To value these call options (e.g. for disclosure or taxation purposes) one must first value the shares using, e.g. P/E ratios.

## Exercise price and time to expiry

Both the exercise price and expiry date are stated in the terms of the option contract.

## Volatility

- Volatility represents the standard deviation of day-to-day price changes in a security, expressed as an annualised percentage. Two measures of volatility are commonly used in options trading: historical and implied.
- Historical volatility can be measured by observing price changes of a security over a period of time. It is not necessarily a forecast of future volatility, but can be used to determine the option price.
- Implied volatility can be calculated by taking current quoted options prices and working backwards.

A common approach to calculating historical volatility is as follows:

(1) Calculate the daily return using (current price/previous day's price) or $P_n/P_{n-1}$.

(2) Take the log of each 'return' to convert into a continuous return.

(3) Calculate the standard deviation of the logs to get a daily volatility.

(4) Annualise the result.

### Volatility calculation

| Day | Price | $P_n/P_{n-1}$ | $\ln(P_n/P_{n-1})$ 'x' | $x^2$ |
|---|---|---|---|---|
| Monday | 100 | | | |
| Tuesday | 101 | 1.010000 | 0.009950 | 0.000099 |
| Wednesday | 105 | 1.039604 | 0.038840 | 0.001509 |
| Thursday | 103 | 0.980952 | −0.019231 | 0.000370 |
| Friday | 104 | 1.009709 | 0.009662 | 0.000093 |
| Sum | | | 0.039221 | 0.002071 |
| Average | | | 0.009805 | 0.000518 |

Daily volatility $=$ standard deviation $= \sqrt{\dfrac{\Sigma x^2}{n} - x^2}$

$= \sqrt{(0.000518 - 0.009805^2)}$

$= 0.0205$ or approximately 2%

Assuming 260 trading days on the market, Annualised volatility = daily volatility $\times \sqrt{260} = 0.33$ or 33%.

The method for calculating the continuous return in the above example may be unfamiliar to you. The basic idea is that instead of dividing a time period into years or weeks or days for discounting purposes we can discount continuously. To get the same answer either way, we need to set continuous rate = ln (1 + discrete rate)

For example, if the discrete rate is 10% p.a., then a continuous rate is given by

Continuous rate = ln1.10 = 0.0953 or 9.53%.

Discount factors using continuous rates are given by DF = $e^{-it}$ where i is the continuous rate and t the time period.

### Risk-free rate

- The risk-free rate is the minimum return required by investors from a risk-free investment.

- Treasury bills or other short-term (usually three months). Government borrowings are regarded as the safest possible investment and their rate of return is often given in a question to be used as a figure for the risk-free rate.

## 2 The Black-Scholes option pricing model

### Introduction

*Rigrid tobmy*

The **Black-Scholes** model values call options before the expiry date and takes account of all five factors that determine the value of an option.

### Using the Black-Scholes model to value call options

Value of a call option = $P_a N(d_1) - P_e e^{-rt} N(d_2)$

Where
$$d_1 = \frac{\ln (Pa/Pe) + (r + 0.5s^2)t}{S\sqrt{T}}$$

$d_2 = d_1 - s\sqrt{T}$    calculate $d_1$ and $d_2$ to two decimal places.

**Note:** The formula is daunting, but fortunately you do not need to learn it, as it will be given in the examination paper. You need to be aware only of the variables which it includes, to be able to plug in the numbers.

### The key:

$P_a$ = current price of underlying asset (e.g. share price)

$\dot{P}_e$ = exercise price

r = risk-free rate of interest

t = time until expiry of option in years

s = volatility of the share price (as measured by the standard deviation expressed as a decimal - see explanation below)

N(d) = equals the area under the normal curve up to d (see normal distribution tables)

e = 2.71828, the exponential constant

ln = the natural log (log to be base e)

$P_e e^{-rt}$ = present value of the exercise price calculated by using the continuous discounting factors.

### Measures of volatility - standard deviation and variance

The measure of volatility used in the Black-Scholes model is the annual standard deviation (s), expressed as a decimal.

Exam questions may quote volatility in terms of the "variance", which is the square of the standard deviation. In this case, take the square root of the given variance figure to give the volatility in the correct terms for the Black-Scholes formula.

Alternatively, monthly, or weekly, standard deviations may be quoted. To convert from a monthly standard deviation to an annual figure,

- square the monthly standard deviation
- multiply by 12
- take the square root of the result.

This will now be the annual standard deviation figure as required.

### Expandable Text - Normal distribution tables

### Recap of normal distributions

Extract from standard normal distribution table

|     | 0.00 | 0.01 | 0.02 | 0.03 | 0.04 | 0.05 | 0.06 | 0.07 | 0.08 | 0.09 |
|-----|------|------|------|------|------|------|------|------|------|------|
| 0.0 | .0000 | .0040 | .0080 | .0120 | .0159 | .0199 | .0239 | .0279 | .0319 | .0359 |
| 0.1 | .0398 | .0438 | .0478 | .0517 | .0557 | .0596 | .0636 | .0675 | .0714 | .0753 |
| 0.2 | .0793 | .0832 | .0871 | .0910 | .0948 | .0987 | .1026 | .1064 | .1103 | .1141 |
| 0.3 | .1179 | .1217 | .1255 | .1293 | .1331 | .1368 | .1406 | .1443 | .1480 | .1517 |
| 0.4 | .1554 | .1591 | .1628 | .1664 | .1700 | .1736 | .1772 | .1808 | .1844 | .1879 |
| 0.5 | .1915 | .1950 | .1985 | .2019 | .2054 | .2088 | .2123 | .2157 | .2190 | .2224 |
| 0.6 | .2257 | .2291 | .2324 | .2357 | .2389 | .2422 | .2454 | .2486 | .2518 | .2549 |
| 0.7 | .2580 | .2611 | .2642 | .2673 | .2704 | .2734 | .2764 | .2794 | .2823 | .2852 |
| 0.8 | .2881 | .2910 | .2939 | .2967 | .2995 | .3023 | .3051 | .3078 | .3106 | .3133 |
| 0.9 | .3159 | .3186 | .3212 | .3238 | .3264 | .3289 | .3315 | .3340 | .3365 | .3389 |
| 1.0 | .3413 | .3438 | .3461 | .3485 | .3508 | .3531 | .3554 | .3577 | .3599 | .3621 |
| 1.1 | .3643 | .3665 | .3686 | .3708 | .3729 | .3749 | .3770 | .3790 | .3810 | .3830 |
| 1.2 | .3849 | .3869 | .3888 | .3907 | .3925 | .3944 | .3962 | .3980 | .3997 | .4015 |
| 1.3 | .4032 | .4049 | .4066 | .4082 | .4099 | .4115 | .4131 | .4147 | .4162 | .4177 |
| 1.4 | .4192 | .4207 | .4222 | .4236 | .4251 | .4265 | .4279 | .4292 | .4306 | .4319 |
| 1.5 | .4332 | .4345 | .4357 | .4370 | .4382 | .4394 | .4406 | .4418 | .4430 | .4441 |
| 1.6 | .4452 | .4463 | .4474 | .4485 | .4495 | .4505 | .4515 | .4525 | .4535 | .4545 |
| 1.7 | .4554 | .4564 | .4573 | .4582 | .4591 | .4599 | .4608 | .4616 | .4625 | .4633 |
| 1.8 | .4641 | .4649 | .4656 | .4664 | .4671 | .4678 | .4686 | .4693 | .4699 | .4706 |
| 1.9 | .4713 | .4719 | .4726 | .4732 | .4738 | .4744 | .4750 | .4756 | .4762 | .4767 |

This table can be used to calculate $N(d_1)$, the cumulative normal distribution function needed for the Black-Scholes model of option pricing.

- If $d_1 > 0$, add 0.5 to the relevant number above.
- If $d_1 < 0$, subtract the relevant number above from 0.5.

For example if $d_1$ is 1.05, $N(d_1) = 0.3531 + 0.5 = 0.8531$.

**Note**

$N(d)$ = Is the area under the normal curve up to d in the shaped area of the figure below.

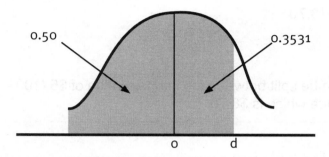

**Expandable Text - Illustration of the Black-Scholes model**

| The current share price of B plc shares | = $100 $P_a$ | | |
| The exercise price | = $95 $P_e$ | | |
| The risk-free rate of interest | = 10% pa ✓ | = | 0.1 |
| The standard deviation of return on the shares | = 50% $S$ | = | 0.5 |
| The time to expiry | = 3 months $t$ | = | 0.25 |

Calculate the value of the above call option.

**Solution**

**Step 1: Calculate $d_1$ and $d_2$.**

$$d_1 = \frac{\ln(P_a/P_e) + (r + 0.5s^2)t}{s\sqrt{t}}$$

$$d_1 = \frac{\ln(100/95) + (0.1 + 0.5 \times 0.5^2)0.25}{0.5 \times \sqrt{0.25}}$$

$d_1 = 0.43$

$d_2 = d_1 - s\sqrt{t} = 0.43 - 0.5 \times \sqrt{0.25} = 0.18$

**Step 2: Use normal distribution tables to find the value of $N(d_1)$ and $N(d_2)$.**

$N(d_1) = 0.5 + 0.1664 = 0.6664$

$N(d_2) = 0.5 + 0.0714 = 0.5714$

### Step 3: Plug these numbers into the Black-Scholes formula.

Value of a call option = $P_a N(d_1) - P_e N(d_2)e^{-rt}$

$$= 100 \times 0.6664 - 95 \times 0.5714 \times e^{-(0.1 \times 0.25)}$$

$$= \$13.70$$

### Note

This can be split between the intrinsic value of $5 (100 – 95) and the time value which is $8.70.

### Test your understanding 3

Suppose that the risk-free rate is 5% and the variance of the return on the share in the past has been estimated as 12%.

**Estimate the value of a six-month call option at an exercise price of $1.48 (current share price = $1.64).**

## Using the Black-Scholes model to value put options

If you have calculated the value of a call option using Black-Scholes, then the value of a corresponding put option can be found using the put call parity formula.

The put call parity equation is on the examination formula sheet:

**Put call parity** $P = c - P_a + P_e \times e^{-rt}$

Step 1: Value the corresponding call option using the Black-Scholes model.

Step 2: Then calculate the value the put option using the put call parity equation.

### Expandable Text - Black-Scholes model: value put options

Returning to the earlier example of B plc, where the current share price is $100, exercise price is $95, the risk-free rate of interest is 10%, the standard deviation of shares return is 50% and the time to expiry is three months, calculate the value of a put option.

### Solution

- Step 1: We have already calculated the value of the call option at $13.70.

- Step 2: Using put call parity equation:

**Put call parity** $P = c - P_a + P_e \times e^{-rt}$

Value of a put = 13.70 - 100.00 + 92.65

= $6.35

### Test your understanding 4

**Using the information given in TYU 3, calculate the value of the corresponding put option.**

## Underlying assumptions and limitations

The model assumes that:

- The options are European calls.
- There are no transaction costs or taxes.
- The investor can borrow at the risk-free rate.
- The risk-free rate of interest and the share's volatility is constant over the life of the option.
- The future share-price volatility can be estimated by observing past share price volatility.
- The share price follows a random walk and that the possible share prices are based on a normal distribution.
- No dividends are payable before the option expiry date.

In practice these unrealistic assumptions can be relaxed and the basic model can be developed to reflect a more complex situation.

## Application to American call options

One of the limitations of the **Black-Scholes** formula is that it assumes that the shares will not pay dividends before the option expires. If this holds true then the model can also be used to value American call options.

In fact, if no dividends are payable before the option expiry date, the American call option will be worth the same as a European call option.

You will not be asked to value American call options on shares that do pay dividends or American put options using the **Black-Scholes** model.

**Expandable Text - Application of Black-Scholes model**

Going back to our exercise about B plc, where we calculated that the value of the call option was $13.70 with three months to expiry and assuming that this is an American option and the holder wants to close the option today he has two basic choices:

(1)  exercise today and benefit by the intrinsic value of $5.00 or

(2)  sell the option back to the market and receive $13.70 (intrinsic value plus time value).

Therefore if the American option-holder exercises early he will forfeit the time value. Quite simply the option is 'worth more alive than dead'. The right to exercise an American call early is irrelevant and the option will be exercised on the expiry date just like a European option.

Therefore the values of European and American call options on shares not paying dividends are equal.

You will not be asked to value American call options on shares that do pay dividends or American put options using the **Black-Scholes** model.

**Application to shares where dividends are payable before the expiry date**

The **Black-Scholes** formula can be adapted to call options with dividends being paid before expiry by calculating a 'dividend adjusted share price':

•  Simply deduct the present value of dividends to be paid (before the expiry of the option) from the current share price.

•  $P_a$, becomes $P_a$ – PV (dividends) in the Black-Scholes formula.

## Illustration 1 – The Black-Scholes option pricing model

You have been asked to value call options in D plc.

- The options are due to expire in five months' time. However a dividend of 40 cents is due to be paid in three months' time.
- The current share price is $10.
- The risk-free rate is 10%.

What value should be used for the dividend-adjusted share price?

### Solution

Three months' time t = (3/12) = 0.25 of a year, r = 0.10.

- The present value of the dividends is equal to:

  $40e^{-rt} = 40e^{-(0.1 \times 0.25)} = 39.01$ say 39 cents.

- So $P_a$ – PV (dividends) = $10.00 – 0.39 = $9.61, is used in the Black-Scholes model.

## Test your understanding 5

A call option on V plc's shares has the following details:

- Exercise price $50
- Current share price $40
- Risk-free rate 8%
- Time to expiry 3 months
- Dividend of $2 per share to be paid in three months' time.

**Calculate a dividend-adjusted share price for use in the Black-Scholes option pricing model.**

## 3 Foreign currency options - the "Grabbe Variant" formula

### Application to foreign currency options – the 'Grabbe variant'

- The risk-free interest rate is a necessary component of the Black-Scholes model to incorporate the time value of money.

- A complication that arises with currency options is that there are now two interest rates – one for each currency. These can be incorporated by using the predicted forward rate in the formula as detailed below.

- The Black-Scholes formula can be adapted for forex as follows:

**Value of a currency call option** = $e^{-rT} [F N(d_1) - X N(d_2)]$

**Value of a currency put option** = $e^{-rT} [X N(-d_2) - F N(-d_1)]$

Where $d_1 = (\ln (F/X) + \tfrac{1}{2}s^2T)/s\sqrt{T}$

$d_2 = d_1 - s\sqrt{T}$.

F = forward rate, calculated using interest rate parity (see below)

X = exercise rate

r = domestic interest rate (as usual)

F and X need to be quoted as the price of the foreign currency (i.e. 'direct' quotes) but indirect rates are used in the interest rate parity formula:

Interest rate parity: $F_0 = S_0 \times \dfrac{(1 + i_c)}{(1 + i_b)}$.

### Expandable Text - Illustration of the Grabbe Variant formula

A UK firm is looking to build a factory in Germany and will find out in 3 months' time whether its tender has been successful, in which case an immediate payment in euros will be necessary. The treasurer has decided to hedge using currency options.

| | |
|---|---|
| Sterling/euro spot rate (direct) | £0.8 = €1 |
| Sterling/euro spot rate (indirect) | £1 = €1.25 |
| 3 month € LIBOR | 3% p.a. |
| 3 month £ LIBOR | 4.5% p.a. |
| Annual volatility of the Euro against Sterling | 20% |

**Required:**

Calculate the value of a 3 month Euro/sterling call option with an exercise price of £0.80 = €1 (i.e. currently 'at the money').

**Solution**

**Step 1: Calculate the forward rate using interest rate parity (usually used with indirect exchange rates).**

| | | |
|---|---|---|
| Forward rate | = | spot × (1 + foreign i)/(1 + domestic i) |
| | = | 1.25 × (1 + 3/12 × 3%)/(1 + 3/12 × 4.5%) |
| | = | 1.24536 |

Quoted as a direct rate this is 1/1.24536... = 0.8030

**Step 2: Calculate $d_1$ and $d_2$ using direct exchange rates.**

$$d_1 = \frac{\ln(F/X) + \frac{1}{2}s^2T}{s\sqrt{T}} = \frac{\ln(0.8030/0.8) + 0.5 \times 0.2^2 \times 0.25}{0.2 \times \sqrt{0.25}} = 0.0874$$

$$d_2 = d_1 - s\sqrt{T} = 0.0874 - 0.2 \times \sqrt{0.25} = -0.0126$$

Step 3: Use normal distribution tables to find the value of $N(d_1)$ and $N(d_2)$.

$N(d_1) = 0.5 + 0.0359 = 0.5359$

$N(d_2) = 0.5 - 0.0040 = 0.4960$

**Step 4: Plug these numbers into the Black- Scholes formula.**

| | | |
|---|---|---|
| Value of a call option | = | $e^{-rT}[F\,N(d_1) - X\,N(d_2)]$ |
| | = | $e^{-(0.045 \times 0.25)}$ [0.8030 × 0.5359 - 0.8 × 0.4960] |
| | = | 0.9888 × 0.033528 |
| | = | £0.03315 or 3.315 pence per euro |

### Test your understanding 6

A US firm is suing a French rival over patent infringement and will find out in 9 months' time whether it has been successful, in which case an immediate receipt in euros will crystallise. The treasurer has decided to hedge using currency options.

| | |
|---|---|
| Dollar/euro spot rate (direct) | $1.3249 = €1 |
| Dollar/euro spot rate (indirect) | $1 = €0.7548 |
| 3 month € LIBOR | 3% |
| 3 month $ LIBOR | 5% |

Annual volatility of the Euro against the dollar 25%.

**Calculate the value of a 9 month Euro/dollar put option with an exercise price of $1.3249 = €1 (i.e. currently "at the money").**

## Delta and delta hedges

The figure $N(d_1)$ is known as delta. Delta measures the change in option value which would result from a $1 change in the value of the underlying asset (e.g. share).

An investor can eliminate the risk of his shareholding by constructing a 'delta hedge'.

- An investor who holds a number of shares and sells (an option writer) a number of call options in the proportion dictated by the delta/ the hedge ratio ensures a hedged portfolio. N.B. A hedged portfolio is one where the gains and losses cancel out against each other.

- Number of option calls to sell = Number of shares held/$N(d_1)$.

- Alternatively, if you have already written call options, then a delta hedge can be constructed by buying shares.

- Number of shares to hold = Number of call options sold × $N(d_1)$.

Because share prices change continuously in the real world, the value of delta also changes continuously. Therefore, the investor who wants to maintain a risk neutral position will have to continuously adjust the balance of options and shares in his portfolio. This process is known as "dynamic delta hedging".

**Expandable Text - Example of a delta hedge**

Assuming a call option currently has a delta of 0.5, let use it to construct a hedged portfolio for an investor who holds 100 shares.

The investor in shares will find out how many call options he will have to (write) sell.

So if you had 100 shares we would need to sell (100 shares/.5) = 200 calls to construct a delta hedge. The number of options will exceed the number of shares unless the delta is 1, then they would be an equal number of each.

The call option writers (the seller of the call options) will find out how many shares they will have to buy.

If the share price increases by 10 cents, the call options increase by 5 cents. However as we have sold the call option our portfolio decreases by 5 cents for every call option sold.

| The Comfort Table: | Delta | Number of shares purchased | Number of call options sold | Overall gain or loss is zero. |
|---|---|---|---|---|
| | | | | Delta neutral |
| Current position | .5 | 100 | 200 | |
| Share price increases by 10c | | $10 | (-5c × 200) – $10 = | 0 |

However, the difficulty is that the delta value is not at a constant. It changes as the share price changes.

Suppose that the 10 cents move in the share price caused the delta to move to 0.7. The option writer will need to buy 200 calls × .7 = 140 shares in order to hedge the position, i.e. 40 extra shares.

The portfolio will need rebalancing as the delta value changes. The frequency of this depends on the rate of change of delta, measured by gamma.

## 4 Identifying real options in investment appraisal
### Introduction

- Flexibility adds value to an investment.

- Financial options are an example where this flexibility can be valued.

- Real options theory attempts to classify and value flexibilty in general by taking the ideas of financial options pricing and developing them.

- Conventional investment-appraisal techniques typically undervalue flexibilty within projects with high uncertainty.

### Expandable Text

- Flexibilty adds value to an investment:
  - For example, if an investment can be staggered, then future costs can be avoided if the market turns out to be less attractive than originally expected.

  - The core to this value lies in reducing downside risk exposure but keeping upside potential open – i.e. in making probability distributions asymmetric.

- Financial options are an example where this flexibility can be valued.
  - A call option on a share allows an investor to 'wait and see' what happens to a share price before deciding whether to exercise the option and will thus benefit from favourable price movements without being affected by adverse movements.

- Real options theory attempts to classify and value flexibility in general by taking the ideas of financial options pricing and developing them:
  - A financial option gives the owner the right, but not the obligation, to buy or sell a security at a given price. Analogously, companies that make strategic investments have the right, but not the obligation, to exploit these opportunities in the future.

  - As with financial options most real options involve spending more up front (analogous to the option premium) to give additional flexibility later.

- Conventional investment-appraisal techniques typically undervalue flexibility within projects with high uncertainty.
  - High uncertainty within a NPV context will result in a higher discount rate and a lower NPV. However, with such uncertainty any embedded real options will become more valuable.

## Different types of real option

There are many different classifications of real options. Most can be summarised under the following generic headings:

### Options to delay/defer

The key here is to be able to delay investment without losing the opportunity, creating a call option on the future investment.

**Illustration 2 – Identifying real options in investment appraisal**

For example, establishing a drugs patent allows the owner of the patent to wait and see how market conditions develop before producing the drug, without the potential downside of competitors entering the market.

(**Note:** drugs patents was the subject of a past examination question on this area. However, there is some debate whether or not patents are real options. This debate is outside the scope of the syllabus.)

### Options to switch/redeploy

It may be possible to switch the use of assets should market conditions change.

**Illustration 3 – Identifying real options in investment appraisal**

For example, traditional production lines were set up to make one product. Modern flexible manufacturing systems (FMS) allow the product output to be changed to match customer requirements.

Similarly a new plant could be designed with resale and/or other uses in mind, using more general-purpose assets than dedicated to allow easier switching.

**Illustration 4 – Identifying real options in investment appraisal**

For example, when designing a plant management can choose whether to have higher or lower operating gearing. By having mainly variable costs, it is financially more beneficial if the plant does not have to operate every month.

### Options to expand/contract

It may be possible to adjust the scale of an investment depending on the market conditions.

### Options to abandon

If a project has clearly identifiable stages such that investment can be staggered, then management have to decide whether to abandon or continue at the end of each stage.

**Illustration 5 – Identifying real options in investment appraisal**

When looking to develop their stadiums, many football clubs face the decision whether to build a one- or a two-tier stand:

- A one-tier stand would be cheaper but would be inadequate if the club's attendance improved greatly.

- A two-tier stand would allow for much greater fan numbers but would be more expensive and would be seen as a waste of money should attendance not improve greatly.

Some clubs (e.g. West Bromwich Albion in the UK) have solved this problem by building a one-tier stand with stronger foundations and designed in such a way (e.g. positioning of exits, corporate boxes, etc.) that it would be relatively straightforward to add a second tier at a later stage without knocking down the first tier.

Such a stand is more expensive than a conventional one-tier stand but the premium paid makes it easier to expand at a later date when (if!) attendance grows.

**Illustration 6 – Identifying real options in investment appraisal**

Amazon.com undertook a substantial investment to develop its customer base, brand name and information infrastructure for its core book business. This in effect created a portfolio of real options to extend its operations into a variety of new businesses such as CDs, DVDs, etc.

**Test your understanding 7**

**Comment on a strategy of vertical integration in the context of real options.**

**Test your understanding 8**

A film studio has three new releases planned for the Christmas period but does not know which will be the biggest hit for allocating marketing resources. It thus decides to do a trial screening of each film in selected cinemas and allocates the marketing budget on the basis of the results.

**Comment on this plan using real option theory.**

## 5 Valuing real options

### Introduction

Valuing real options is a complex process and currently a matter of some debate as to the most suitable methodology. Within the P4 syllabus you are expected to be able to apply the Black-Scholes model to real options.

### Using the Black-Scholes model to value real options

The **Black-Scholes** equation is well suited for simple real options, those with a single source of uncertainty and a single decision date. To use the model we need to identify the five key input variables as follows:

### Exercise price

For most real options (e.g. option to expand, option to delay), the capital investment required can be substituted for the exercise price. For an option to abandon, use the salvage value on abandonment.

### Share price

The value of the underlying asset is usually taken to be the PV of the future cash flows from the project (i.e. excluding any initial investment).

### Time to expiry

This is straightforward if the project involves a single investment.

### Volatility

The volatility of the underlying asset (here the future operating cash flows) can be measured using typical industry sector risk.

### Risk-free rate

Many writers continue to use the risk-free rate for real options. However, some argue that a higher rate be used to reflect the extra risks when replacing the share price with the PV of future cash flows.

## Illustration 7 – Valuing real options

A UK retailer is considering opening a new store in Germany with the following details:

- Estimated cost          •   €12m
- Present value of net receipts   •   €10m
- NPV                •   –€2m

These figures would suggest that the investment should be rejected. However, if the first store is opened then the firm would gain the option to open a second store (an option to expand).

Suppose this would have the following details:

- Timing (t)            •   5 years' time
- Estimated cost ($P_e$)      •   €20m
- Present value of net receipts ($P_a$)   •   €15m
- Volatility of cash flows (s)    •   28.3%
- Risk-free rate (r)        •   6%.

The value of the call option on the second store is then calculated as normal using **Black-Scholes**:

### Step 1: Compute $d_1$ and $d_2$

$$d_1 = \frac{\ln(P_a/P_e) + (r + 0.5s^2)t}{s\sqrt{t}}$$

$$d_1 = \frac{\ln(15/20) + (0.06 + 0.5 \times 0.283^2)5}{0.283 \times \sqrt{5}}$$

$d_1 = 0.33$

$d_2 = d_1 - s\sqrt{T} = 0.33 - 0.283 \times \sqrt{5} = -0.30$

### Step 2: Compute $N(d_1)$ and $N(d_2)$.

$N(d_1) = 0.5 + 0.1293 = 0.6293$

$N(d_2) = 0.5 - 0.1179 = 0.3821$

## Step 3: Use formula.

$$\text{Value of a call option} = P_a N(d_1) - P_e N(d_2)e^{-rt}$$

$$= 15 \times 0.6293 - 20 \times 0.3821 \times e^{-(0.06 \times 5)}$$

$$= €3.8m$$

## Summary

| | €m |
|---|---|
| Conventional NPV of first store | (2) |
| Value of call option on second store | 3.8 |
| | |
| **Strategic NPV** | **1.8** |

The project should thus be accepted.

## Test your understanding 9

An online DVD and CD retailer is considering investing $2m on improving its customer information and online ordering systems. This is justified on the grounds that it will allow the business to extend the range of products offered. In particular the board are interested in selling gadgets and have estimated the following:

- Timing
- Estimated cost
- Present value of net receipts
- Volatility of cash flows
- Risk-free rate

- 1 years' time
- $5m
- $4m
- 40%
- 5%

**Advise the firm.**

# 6 Using option pricing theory to calculate credit spreads

## Explanation of credit spreads

For any bond the lender's required/expected return will be made up of two elements:

- The risk free rate of return

- A premium ("the credit spread") based on the expected probability of default and the expected loss given default - covered in the earlier chapter on WACC (when looking at cost of debt).

Option pricing theory (OPT) can be used to calculate these credit spreads and the risk of default.

## Overview of the method

A key concept in this context is that shareholders can be viewed as having a call option on the company's assets. By redeeming the debt, shareholders effectively acquire the assets of the company. Default hands the assets to the lenders.

Shareholders exercise this option if the value of the firm's assets is at least equal to the redemption value. If not, then the option is allowed to lapse, the company is handed over to the debt holders and the shareholders walk away.

Not defaulting thus corresponds to the call option being in the money at expiry.

(A corresponding view is that the lenders have sold a put option under which the company is sold to them for more than its worth – they give up the full redemption value in exchange for the company assets)

### Illustration 8

Suppose OPT Inc has the following capital structure

| | |
|---|---|
| Asset value | 100 |
| Debt – 5 yr zero coupon rate, deep discounted bonds | 60 |
| Equity | 40 |

Furthermore, suppose that

- The (discrete) risk-free rate $r_f$ = 5%

- Volatility = s = 25%

Next, let us start by considering the case if the debt were risk free.

(1) The yield to the lender would be 5% and so the redemption value in 5 years should be $60 (1.05)^5 = 76.577$

(2) The equity can then be valued as a call option on the company's assets:

  – Value of underlying asset = 100

  – Exercise price = redemption value of debt = 76.577

  – Volatility = s = 25%

  – Continuous risk free rate = $\ln(1.05) = 0.04879 = 4.879\%$

  – t = 5

Using this with the Black Scholes formula gives a call value of 44

(3) The current value of debt can then be valued as the total asset value less the value of the equity:

Value of debt = 100 - 44 = 56

This is the wrong answer as we know the debt to be worth 60. The problem is that lenders will require a risk adjusted return higher than 5% and hence a higher redemption value than 76.577

(4) Using the "solver" or "goal-seek" function in a spreadsheet this calculation can be reversed to determine what redemption value does give the current value of debt as 60. The required redemption value is 84.

The required return of the lender is thus given by

$1 + r = (84/60)^{1/5} = 1.07$

The lender thus requires 7%, giving a credit spread of 2% over the risk free rate.

Note the return and spread have been calculated using discrete returns. A continuous approach would be as follows:

  – Required return of lender = $(1/5) \times \ln(84/60) = 0.06729$ or 6.729%

  – Credit spread = $0.06729 - 0.04879 = 0.0185$ or 1.85%.

## Expandable Text - OPT Inc continued - probability of default

### The probability of default

It can be shown that the probability of a call option ending in the money can be calculated as N(d*), where d* is given by

$$d^* = \frac{\ln(Pa/Pe) + [\mu - 0.5s^2]T}{s\sqrt{T}}$$

Where $\mu$ = (continuous return) on the company's assets

Suppose in our OPT Inc example that

- The (discrete) market return $r_m = 9^2/_3\%$
- Asset beta = $\beta_a$ = 0.6

From this data we can use CAPM to calculate a required return on the company's assets as

$$K_a = r_f + \beta_a(r_m - r_f) = 0.05 + 0.6(0.09666 - 0.05) = 0.078 \text{ or } 7.8\%$$

This can be converted into a continuous return as $\mu = \ln(1.078) = 0.0751$ or 7.51%

Substituting this into the above formula for d*:

$$d^* = \frac{\ln(100/84) + [0.0751 - 0.5 \times 0.25^2] \times 5}{0.25 \times \sqrt{5}} = 0.704$$

The probability of NOT defaulting is N(0.704) = 0.758

The probability of default is then 1 − 0.758 = 0.242 or 24.2%.

## Calculation of credit spreads using probability theory

Alternatively, credit spreads can be calculated using probability theory.

Based on the lender's assessment of credit risk and probability of default (covered in the above illustration and in the earlier chapter on WACC), the lender sets the interest rate such that the expected return from the debt is at the appropriate level for the level of perceived risk.

## Expandable Text - Using prob. theory to value credit spreads

Panda plc is a UK sportswear company which has expanded rapidly over the last 10 years. Its assets are now valued at £55m. In order to fund its most recent project, a new manufacturing facility in a deprived area of the West Midlands, the directors have decided to borrow £10m from the ITCD Bank plc. The money will be repayable in 1 year.

The interest rate quoted on the loan is 5.90% p.a., being base rate plus 65 basis points. The directors are unsure how this rate has been computed. The bank has provided them with the following information by way of explanation:

- Loan from ITCD Bank plc to Panda plc
- Loan value: £10m
- Asset value: £55m
- Standard deviation of returns: 40% p.a.
- Base rate: 5.25% p.a.
- Expected level of recovery on default: 70%
- Panda plc Credit Rating: AA
- Credit spread on a 1 year loan: 65 basis points

**Required**

**Show how the interest rate on the loan of 5.90% has been derived.**

**Solution**

With assets of £55m and a loan of £10m, the bank will have calculated the likelihood of Panda plc's assets falling below £10m in the next year, as follows:

Standard deviation = 40%, which (on an average asset value of £55m) translates to a value of £22m.

Hence, the loan value of £10m lies £45m, or 45/22 = 2.045 Standard Deviations below the mean.

Using normal distribution tables, the area under the normal curve between the mean and this point is 0.4796. Thus (including the proportion of the curve lying above the mean) there is a 0.9796 chance (97.96%) of Panda plc's asset values exceeding the £10m loan value in 1 year. This means that there is a 0.0204 chance (2.04%) of default, in which case the bank predicts that only 70% of the loan will be recoverable.

The bank will now calculate an interest rate such that the expected receipt in 1 year exactly covers the amount borrowed, as follows:

Assuming a base rate of 5.25%:

Value of £10m at time 1 (divide by 1.0525) = £9,501,188

Total expected receipt = Expected value if paid + Expected value on default

Expected value if paid = 0.9796 x £9,501,188 = £9,307,363
Expected value if default = 0.7 x 0.0204 x £9,501,188 = £135,677
Total expected receipt = £9,443,040

Hence £10m loan = £9,443,040 x [1 + i] hence i = 0.05898 or 5.90%, which is base rate plus 65 basis points as quoted.

## Student Accountant article

The examiner's August 2008 Student Accountant magazine article on "How lenders set their rates" covers this calculation in detail.

## 7 Chapter summary

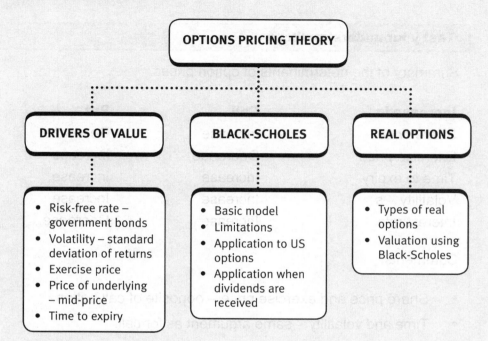

**OPTIONS PRICING THEORY**

**DRIVERS OF VALUE**

- Risk-free rate – government bonds
- Volatility – standard deviation of returns
- Exercise price
- Price of underlying – mid-price
- Time to expiry

**BLACK-SCHOLES**

- Basic model
- Limitations
- Application to US options
- Application when dividends are received

**REAL OPTIONS**

- Types of real options
- Valuation using Black-Scholes

## Test your understanding answers

### Test your understanding 1

Summary of the determinants of option prices.

| Increase in | Call | Put |
|---|---|---|
| Share price | Increase | Decrease |
| Exercise price | Decrease | Increase |
| Time to expiry | Increase | Increase |
| Volatility – s | Increase | Increase |
| Interest rate | Increase | Decrease |

Comments:

- Share price and exercise price – opposite of call option.

- Time and volatility – same argument as for call.

- Interest rate – a higher interest rate reduces the present value of deferred receipts making the option less valuable as an alternative to selling now.

### Test your understanding 2

Buying put options would allow the manager to limit the downside exposure.

## Test your understanding 3

**Step 1: Compute $d_1$ and $d_2$.**

$$d_1 = \frac{\ln(Ps/X) + (r+0.5s^2)t}{s\sqrt{T}}$$

$$d_1 = \frac{\ln(164/148) + (0.05+0.5 \times 0.12)0.5}{\sqrt{0.12} \times \sqrt{0.5}}$$

$$d_1 = 0.64$$

$$d_2 = d_1 - s\sqrt{T} = 0.64 - \sqrt{0.12} \times \sqrt{0.5} = 0.40$$

**Step 2: Compute $N(d_1)$ and $N(d_2)$.**

$N(d_1) = 0.5 + 0.2389 = 0.7389$

$N(d_2) = 0.5 + 0.1554 = 0.6554$

**Step 3: Use formula.**

$$\begin{aligned}
\text{Value of a call option} \quad &= \quad P_a N(d_1) - P_e N(d_2)e^{-rt} \\[2mm]
&= \quad 164 \times 0.7389 - 148 \times 0.6554 \times e^{-(0.05 \times 0.5)} \\[2mm]
&= \quad 26.4 \text{ cents}
\end{aligned}$$

## Test your understanding 4

$$\begin{aligned}
\text{Put call parity } p \quad &= \quad c - P_a + P_e e^{-rt} \\[2mm]
\text{Value of a put} \quad &= \quad 26.4 - 164 + 144.32 \\[2mm]
&= \quad 6.7 \text{ cents}
\end{aligned}$$

### Test your understanding 5

- The present value of the dividends is equal to: $2e^{-rt} = 2e^{-(0.08 \times 0.25)}$ = 1.96
- So $P_a$ – PV (dividends) = \$40.00 – 1.96 = \$38.04, is used in the Black-Scholes model.

### Test your understanding 6

**Step 1: Calculate the forward rate using interest rate parity (usually used with indirect exchange rates).**

Forward rate  = spot × (1 + Euro i)/(1 + US\$ i)

  = 0.7548 × (1 + 9/12 × 3%)/(1 + 9/12 × 5%)

  = 0.7439

Quoted as a direct rate this is 1/0.7439 = 1.3443

**Step 2: Calculate $d_1$ and $d_2$ using direct exchange rates.**

$$d_1 = \frac{\ln(F/X) + 1/2\, s^2 T}{s\sqrt{T}} = \frac{\ln(1.3443/1.3249) + 0.5 \times 0.25^2 \times 0.75}{0.25 \times \sqrt{0.75}} = 0.1754$$

$$d_2 = d_1 - s\sqrt{T} = 0.1754 - 0.25 \times \sqrt{0.75} = -0.0411$$

**Step 3: Use normal distribution tables to find the value of $N(-d_1)$ and $N(-d_2)$.**

$N(-d_1) = 0.5 - 0.0695 = 0.4305$

$N(-d_2) = 0.5 + 0.0164 = 0.5164$

**Step 4: Plug these numbers into the Black-Scholes formula.**

Value of a put option = $e^{-rt} [X\, N(-d_2) - F\, N(-d_1)]$

= $e^{-(0.05 \times 0.75)} [1.3249 \times 0.5164 - 1.3443 \times 0.4305]$

= 0.96319 × 0.105457

= \$0.10157 or 10.157 cents per euro.

### Test your understanding 7

- Vertical integration is usually evaluated in terms of cost, quality and barriers to entry.

- By outsourcing, the company can switch between different types of supply and different suppliers.

- Vertical integration loses this flexibility, effectively giving up a switching option.

### Test your understanding 8

The studio has effectively acquired a learning option allowing better subsequent decisions. The feedback generates a range of call options on future marketing investment.

### Test your understanding 9

The value of the call option on selling gadgets is calculated using **Black-Scholes**:

**Step 1: Compute $d_1$ and $d_2$.**

$$d_1 = \frac{\ln(P_a/P_e) + (r + 0.5s^2)t}{s\sqrt{t}}$$

$$d_1 = \frac{\ln(4/5) + (0.05 + 0.05 \times 0.4^2)1}{0.4 \times \sqrt{1}}$$

$$d_1 = -0.23$$

$$d_2 = d_1 - s\sqrt{t} = -0.23 - 0.4 \times \sqrt{1} = -0.63$$

### Step 2: Compute N(d$_1$) and N(d$_2$).

$N(d_1) = 0.5 - 0.0910 = 0.4090$

$N(d_2) = 0.5 - 0.2357 = 0.2643$

### Step 3: Use formula.

| Value of a call option | = | $Pa\,N(d_1) - P_e e^{-rt} N(d_2)$ |
|---|---|---|
| | = | $4 \times 0.4090 - 5 \times e^{-(0.05 \times 1)} \times 0.2643$ |
| | = | $1.636 - 4.756 \times 0.2643$ |
| | = | €0.38m. |

### Summary

| | €m |
|---|---|
| Investment in upgrading customer database and online ordering | (2) |
| Value of call option on gadgets | 0.38 |
| Strategic NPV | **(1.62)** |

The project should thus be rejected.

# chapter

# 9

# Strategic aspects of acquisitions

## Chapter learning objectives

Upon completion of this chapter you will be able to:

- explain the arguments for and against the use of acquisitions and mergers as a method of corporate expansion

- identify and explain the corporate issues arising on an acquisition

- evaluate the corporate nature of a given acquisition proposal in a scenario

- describe the competitive issues surrounding a given acquisition proposal in a scenario

- explain the criteria for choosing an appropriate target for acquisition

- list and compare the various explanations for the high failure rate of acquisitions in enhancing shareholder value

- list and explain potential sources of synergy

- describe and evaluate in a given context the potential for the various categories of synergy gains

- list and explain the principal factors influencing the development of the regulatory framework for mergers and acquisitions globally

- compare and contrast the shareholder versus the stakeholder models of regulation for mergers and acquisitions globally

- for a given offer in a scenario, identify the main regulatory issues which are likely to arise

- for a given offer in a scenario, assess whether the offer is likely to be in the shareholders' best interests

- list, explain and evaluate the available defence strategies available to the directors of a target company if offer is to be treated as hostile

- for a given offer in a scenario, advise the directors of a target company on the most appropriate defence if the offer is to be treated as hostile

- list and evaluate the various sources of financing available for a proposed cash-based acquisition

- evaluate the advantages and disadvantages of a financial offer for a given acquisition proposal using pure or mixed mode financing and recommend the most appropriate offer to be made

- explain the distinction between merger and acquisition accounting and assess the impact of a given financial offer on the reported financial position and performance of the acquirer.

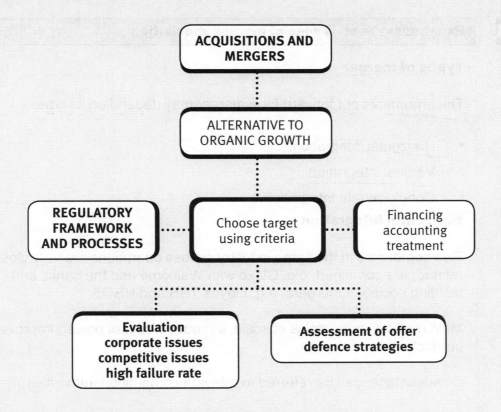

## 1 Mergers and acquisitions – the terms explained

### Merger or acquisition

- A merger is in essence the pooling of interests by two business entities which results in common ownership.

- An acquisition normally involves a larger company (a predator) acquiring a smaller company (a target).

- Generally both referred to as mergers for PR reasons:
  - It portrays a better message to the customers of the target company.
  - To appease the employees of the target company.

- An alternative approach is that a company may simply purchase the assets of another company rather than acquiring its business, goodwill, etc.

When studying P4 and taking the exam you should not be concerned with the strict definitions of mergers and acquisitions used in the corporate reporting papers – the terms are often used interchangeably in this area.

## Expandable Text - Types of merger/acquisition

### Types of merger

The arguments put forward for a merger may depend on its type:

- Horizontal integration.
- Vertical integration.
- Conglomerate integration.

### Horizontal integration

Two companies in the same industry, whose operations are very closely related, are combined, e.g. Glaxo with Welcome and the banks and building societies mergers, e.g. Lloyds TSB and HBOS.

Main motives: economies of scale, increased market power, improved product mix.

Disadvantage: can be referred to relevant competition authorities.

### Vertical integration

Two companies in the same industry, but from different stages of the production chain merger.

e.g. major players in the oil industry tend to be highly vertically integrated.

Main motives: increased certainty of supply or demand and just-in-time inventory systems leading to major savings in inventory holding costs.

### Conglomerate integration

A combination of unrelated businesses, there is no common thread and the main synergy lies with the management skills and brand name, e.g. General Electrical Corporation and Tomkins (management) or Virgin (brand).

Main motives: risk reduction through diversification and cost reduction (management) or improved revenues (brand).

## 2 Organic growth versus growth by acquisition

Organic growth is internally generated growth within the firm.

### Growth strategy

Assuming a standard profit maximising company, the primary purpose of any growth strategy should be to increase shareholder wealth.

- No external growth should be considered unless the organic alternative has been dismissed as inferior.

**Expandable Text - Adv's/disadv's of organic growth and acq'n**

**Advantages of organic growth (disadvantages of growth by acquisition)**

- Organic growth allows planning of strategic growth in line with stated objectives.

- It is less risky than growth by acquisition – done over time.

- The cost is often much higher in an acquisition – significant acquisition premiums.

- Avoids problems integrating new acquired companies – the integration process is often a difficult process due to cultural differences between the two companies.

- An acquisition places an immediate pressure on current management resources to learn to manage the new business.

**Advantages of growth by acquisition (disadvantages of organic growth)**

- Quickest way is to enter a new product or geographical market.

- Reduces the risk of over-supply and excessive competition.

- Fewer competitors.

- Increase market power in order to be able to exercise some control over the price of the product, e.g. monopoly or by collusion with other producers.

- Acquiring the target company's staff highly trained staff – may give a competitive edge.

### The reasons for acquisitions

*Two company* (handwritten)

Whilst the potential for synergy is a key reason given for growth by acquisitions other motives do exist:

- Entry to new markets and industries.

- To acquire the target company's staff and know-how.

- Managerial motives – conscious pursuit of self-interest by managers.

- Arrogance factor/Hubris hypothesis.

- Diversification.

- A defence mechanism to prevent being taken over.

- A means of improving liquidity.

- Improved ability to raise finance.

- A reduction of risk by acquiring substantial assets (if the predator has a high earnings to net asset ratio and is in a risky business).

- To obtain a growth company (especially if the predator's growth is declining).

- To create a situation where rationalisation (which would otherwise be shirked) may be carried out more acceptably.

### Expandable Text - Why a company may want to be acquired

Many combinations are by mutual agreement, so small companies being acquired may welcome such a move. Possible reasons for this include:

- Personal – e.g. to retire, for security, because of the problem of inheritance tax.

- Business – an expanding small company may find that it reaches a size where it is impossible to restrain growth, but funds or management expertise for this are lacking.

- Technical – increasing sophistication presents a problem for the small company, e.g:

  - cost of research and development may be prohibitive

  - inability to employ specialised expertise

  - inability to offer a complete range of services or products to customers.

- Can apply to companies that are quite large by most standards, e.g. Rolls-Royce Ltd was too small to absorb the research costs on one new engine.

**Expandable Text - Corporate and competitive aspects of mergers**

- Need to decide in an exam question what is happening – i.e. is it a:
  - merger
  - acquisition
  - simply a purchase of assets
  - demerger
  - spin-off
  - management buy out

## Methods of mergers and acquisitions

Though the terms are used loosely to describe a variety of activities, in every case the end result is that two companies become a single enterprise, in fact if not in name, the end result is achieved by:

- transfer of assets
- transfer of shares.

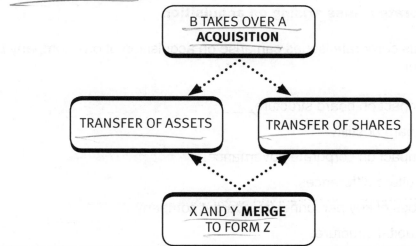

The two methods of undertaking acquisitions and mergers are summarised as follows:

|  | Transfer of assets | Transfer of shares |
|---|---|---|
| Acquisition (B takes over A) | B acquires trade and assets from A for cash. A is then liquidated, and the proceeds received by the old shareholders of A. | B acquires shares in A from A's shareholders in exchange for cash. A, as a subsidiary of B, may subsequently transfer its trade and assets to its new parent company (B). |
| Merger (X and Y merge to form Z) | Z acquires trade and assets from both X and Y in return for shares in Z. X and Y are then liquidated and the shares in Z distributed in specie to the shareholders of X and Y. | Z acquires shares in X and Y in return for its own shares. X and Y as subsidiaries of Z may subsequently transfer their trade and assets to their new parent company (Z). |

## Corporate issues arising on acquisition

Various corporate issues can arise on acquisition of one company by another:

- Impact on board structure.
- Board hostility.
- Impact on corporate governance.
- Culture differences.
- Loss of key personnel from target company.
- Capital structure.
- Integration difficulties – e.g. systems, operations.
- Adverse PR.

## Competitive issues

When considering acquisitions and mergers the competitive aspects need to be considered.

- One of the motives for acquiring a company is to remove competitive rivalry from the market.

For example, consolidation in the supermarket industry:

The purchase of Safeways by William Morrison in the UK in 2006 reduced the number of supermarket chains and as such the level of competition in this market.

## Test your understanding 1 - Fred's group

Fred's ironmongery was founded in 1845 by the Fred family and grew over the next century into a national chain with 1,005 stores. In 1975 it joined forces with Mary's which had 375 stores and there followed a period of rationalisation where several of Mary's stores closed, became departments of Fred's or were transferred to Fred's subsidiary company Fredrica's. In 2004 Fred's again joined forces – this time with Annette's – unlike Mary's, Annette's has maintained its own logo and brand names rather than using the distinctive Fred's 'F'. Both Annette's and Mary's operated in the same market as Fred's. Fred's also has a history of purchasing small shareholdings in related businesses and purchasing company assets. Annette's has maintained all its 976 stores and is due to open a further 15 in late 2008.

On amalgamation with Mary's – Matthew James the CEO of Fred's replaced nearly all the key personnel with Fred's staff – stating that:

'A new era needs a new approach'. However, this approach had altered by 2004 when Pippa John from Annette's was appointed Deputy CEO with the explanation – 'We need to utilise the expertise of all areas of the Group'.

**What is the corporate nature of the above two amalgamations of Fred's?**

In early 2007 Fred's indicated that it is considering joining with Moira's – in what is believed to be an attempt to obtain Moira's impressive property portfolio, we are at present awaiting developments in this situation.

**List some of the issues that may arise on the amalgamation of Moira's by Fred's.**

### Test your understanding 2 - Premier foods

The takeover of RHM by Premier foods will mean that Premier foods will be the largest food producer in the UK. The takeover means that Premier's Batchelors, Branston, Lloyd Grossman and Quorn brands and RHM's brands Mr Kipling, Sharwoods and Bisto are owned by the same group. There are likely to be factory closures and job cuts.

**What competitive issues arise from this scenario?**

## 3 Identifying possible acquisition targets

Suppose a company decides to expand. Its directors will produce criteria (size, location, finances, products, expertise, management) against which targets can be judged.

Directors and/or advisors then seek out prospective targets in the business sectors it is interested in.

The team then examines each prospect closely from both a commercial and financial viewpoint against criteria.

In general businesses are acquired as going concerns rather than the purchase of specific assets.

### Expandable Text - Steps in identifying acquisition targets

#### Steps to be taken

Assuming that external growth has been decided upon, the firm needs to consider the steps to be taken. A possible sequence of steps is as follows (given in the context of acquisitions, although much will apply to mergers as well):

- Strategic steps
    - Step 1: Appraise possible acquisitions.
    - Step 2: Select the best acquisition target.
    - Step 3: Decide on the financial strategy, i.e. the amount and the structure of the consideration.

- Tactical steps
    - Step 1: Launch a dawn raid subject to relevant regulation.
    - Step 2: Make a public offer for the shares not held.
    - Step 3: Success will be achieved if more than 50% of the target company's shares are acquired.

## Information required for the appraisal of acquisitions

The following needs to be considered when appraising a target for acquisition:

- Organisation.
- Sales and marketing.
- Production, supply and distribution.
- Technology.
- Accounting information.
- Treasury information.
- Tax information.

When considering a target for acquisition a company need to assess carefully the following – this information would only be available pre-acquisition where an agreed bid was negotiated.

| 1 **Organisation** | 2 **Sales and marketing** |
|---|---|
| Special requirements, e.g. | Special requirements, e.g. |
| • organisation chart, key management and quality<br><br>• employee analysis, terms and conditions<br><br>• unionisation and industrial relations<br><br>• pension arrangements.<br><br>Clearly, businesses are about people, and their quality and organisation requires examination. Further, comparison needs to be made with existing group remuneration levels and pensions, to determine the financial impact of their adoption, where appropriate, on the acquisition. | • historic and future sales volumes by product group and geographical location<br><br>• market position, including customers and competition for major product groups<br><br>• normal trading terms<br><br>• historic sales and promotions expenditure by product group.<br><br>This additional information should provide a detailed assessment of the market and customer base to be acquired. |

## 3 Production, supply and distribution

Special requirements, e.g.

- total capacity and current usage levels

- need for future capital investment to replace existing assets, or meet expanded volume requirements.

This would provide an assessment of the overhead burden due to under capacity production and of the potential future capital requirements to maintain the required productive capacity of the business.

## 4 Technology

Special requirements, e.g.

- details of particular technical skills inherent in the acquisition

- research and development organisation and historic expenditure.

Thus, an analysis would be made of the technical assets acquired, and their past and potential future maintenance costs.

## 5 Accounting information

Special requirements, e.g.

- company searches for all companies

- historic consolidated and individual company accounts

- detailed explanation of accounting policies

- explanation of major fluctuations in sales, gross margins, overheads and capital employed.

These provide the background for basic financial analysis.

## 6 Treasury information

Special requirements, e.g.

- amounts, terms and security of bank facilities and all other external loans and leasing facilities (including capitalised value, if not capitalised)

- details of restrictive covenants and trust deeds for such facilities

- details of forward foreign exchange contracts, and exchange management policies.

All this information will be useful in planning the financial absorption of the business into the acquiring group, and will in particular reveal any 'hidden assets' (e.g. low coupon loans) and 'hidden liabilities' (guarantees liable to be called, or hedged foreign exchange positions).

KAPLAN PUBLISHING

| 7 **Tax information** | 8 **Other commercial/financial information** |
|---|---|
| Special requirements, e.g. | Special requirements, e.g. |
| • historic tax computations, agreed, submitted and unsubmitted by company<br><br>• significant disputes with revenue<br><br>• trading losses brought forward<br><br>• potential tax liabilities, including deferred tax and sales tax<br><br>• understanding of tax position of vendors, especially with respect to capital gains tax liability as a result of sale. | • details of ordinary and preference shareholders, with amounts held by each class, and voting restrictions if appropriate, together with share options held and partly paid shares<br><br>• contingent liabilities, including litigation, forward purchase or sales contracts, including capital commitments and loss-making contracts not otherwise provided for<br><br>• actuarial assessment of current pension funding, with assumptions. |
| This can identify any potential tax assets (e.g. utilisable losses) and liabilities (e.g. likely payments of tax not provided), and assist in pricing and structuring the transaction having regard to the vendor's tax position. | This relates primarily to a better understanding of the capital structure and shareholdings to be acquired, and any potential financial liabilities overhanging the acquired company, of which the most significant may well be under funded pension schemes. |

## 4 Synergy

As in other areas of the syllabus the ultimate justification of any policy is that it leads to an increase in value, i.e. it increases shareholder wealth. As in capital budgeting where projects should be accepted if they have a positive NPV, in a similar way combinations should be pursued if they increase the wealth of shareholders.

### Illustration 1 - Synergy

Suppose firm A has a market value of £2m and it combines with firm B, market value £2m, with considerations at current market prices.

If the resultant new firm AB has a market value in excess of £4m then the combination can be counted as a success, if less it will be a failure.

Essentially, for a successful combination we should be looking for a situation where:

Market value of combined companies (AB) > Market value of A + Market value of B

If this situation occurs we have experienced synergy, that is, the whole is worth more than the sum of the parts. This is often expressed as 'the 2 + 2 = 5 effect'.

### Expandable Text - Types of synergy

#### Revenue synergy

Sources of revenue synergy include:

#### Market power/eliminate competition

Firms may merge to increase market power in order to be able to exercise some control over the price of the product. Horizontal mergers may enable the firm to obtain a degree of monopoly power, which could increase its profitability by pushing up the price of goods because customers have few alternatives.

#### Economies of vertical integration

Some acquisitions involve buying out other companies in the same production chain, e.g. a manufacturer buying out a raw material supplier or a retailer. This can increase profits by 'cutting out the middle man', improved control of raw materials needed for production, or by avoiding disputes with what were previously suppliers or customers.

#### Complementary resources

It is sometimes argued that by combining the strengths of two companies a synergistic result can be obtained. For example, combining a company specialising in research and development with a company strong in the marketing area could lead to gains.

## Cost synergy

Sources of cost synergy are:

### Economies of scale

Horizontal combinations (of companies in a similar line of business) are often claimed to reduce costs and therefore increase profits due to economies of scale. These can occur in the production, marketing or finance areas. Economies of scale occur through such factors as:

- fixed operating and administrative costs being spread over a larger production volume

- consolidation of manufacturing capacity on fewer and larger sites

- use of space capacity

- increased buyer power, i.e. bulk discounts

- savings on duplicated central services and accounting staff costs.

These benefits are sometimes also claimed for conglomerate combinations (of companies in unrelated areas of business) in financial and marketing costs.

### Economies of scope

May occur in marketing as a result of joint advertising and common distribution.

## Financial synergy

Sources of financial synergy include:

### Elimination of inefficiency

If the 'victim' company in a takeover is badly managed its performance and hence its value can be improved by the elimination of inefficiencies. Improvements could be obtained in the areas of production, marketing and finance.

### Elimination of inefficiency – bargain buying

If the 'victim' company in a merger is badly managed its performance and hence its value can be improved by the elimination of inefficiencies.

### Tax shields/accumulated tax losses

Another possible financial synergy exists when one company in an acquisition or merger is able to use tax shields or accumulated tax losses, which would have been unavailable to the other company.

### Surplus cash

Companies with large amounts of surplus cash may see the acquisition of other companies as the only possible application for these funds. Of course, increased dividends could cure the problem of surplus cash, but this may be rejected for reasons of tax or dividend stability.

### Corporate risk diversification

One of the primary reasons put forward for all mergers but especially conglomerate mergers is that the income of the combined entity will be less volatile (less risky) as its cash flows come from a wide variety of products and markets. This is a reduction in total risk, but has little or no affect on the systematic risk.

### Diversification and financing

If the future cash flow streams of the two companies are not perfectly positively correlated then by combining the two companies the variability of their operating cash flow may be reduced. A more stable cash flow is more attractive to creditors and this could lead to cheaper financing.

### Others

Other sources of synergy are:

### Surplus managerial talent

Companies with highly skilled managers can make use of this resource only if they have problems to solve. The acquisition of inefficient companies is sometimes the only way of fully utilising skilled managers.

### Speed

Acquisitions may be far faster than organic growth in obtaining a presence in a new and growing market.

These gains are not automatic and for example diseconomies of scale may also be experienced. In an efficient stock market A and B will be correctly valued before the combination and we need to ask how synergy will be achieved, i.e. why any increase in value should occur.

### Test your understanding 3 - Synergy

**Explain why synergy might exist when one company merges with or takes over another company.**

### Test your understanding 4 - Williams and GSL

Williams Inc is the manufacturer of cosmetics, soaps and shower gels. It also markets its products using its own highly successful sales and marketing department. It is seen as an employer of choice and as such has a talented and loyal work-force with a history of developing new and exciting products which have sold well. It is now considering extending its range, however it has currently a build-up of unfulfilled orders due to a lack of capacity.

GSL is a well-known herbal remedy for skin problems. GSL Co was founded by three brothers in the 1950s and until the death of the remaining brother in 2004 has performed well – however the new Chairman has limited experience and the company has not performed well over recent years. GSL has a dedicated team of herbalists who have developed products, which would find a ready market – however, there is insufficient funds and expertise to correctly market these products and market share is low.

Williams' products and GSL's products are made using similar production technologies and their financial and administrative systems are similar and it is hoped savings can be made here.

**Identify any potential synergy gains that would emerge from a merger of Williams and GSL.**

## 5 Why is there a high failure rate of acquisitions?
### Research conclusions

Research in this area has two major conclusions:

- Value or synergistic gains are in practice quite small.

- Bidding companies usually pay a substantial premium over the market value of the 'victim' company prior to the bid.

### Illustration 2 - Acquisition of Company D by Company C

Both companies having a market value of $2m each in isolation.

- Assume that when these are combined a small amount of synergy is obtained and their combined value rises to $4.5m.

- Assume that to acquire D's shares C has had to pay a premium of $1 m, i.e. total cost of D is $3 m.

- The benefit/(cost) of the takeover to C's shareholders is as follows:

|  | $ |
|---|---|
| Market value of CD | 4.5 m |
| Original value of C | (2.0 m) |
| Price paid for D | (3.0 m) |
| Loss | (0.5 m) |

- This loss will be to the cost of the acquiring company shareholders but to the benefit of the victim company shareholders (as they received the $1 m premium).

This in fact reflects the overall conclusion of research in this area: the consistent winners in mergers and takeovers are victim company shareholders; the consistent losers are acquiring company shareholders.

## Expandable Text - More detail on causes of failure

### Causes of failure

Reasons advanced for the high failure rate of combinations are:

- Over-optimistic assessment of economies of scale. Such economies can be achieved at a relatively small size; expansion beyond the optimum results in disproportionate cost disadvantages.

- Once a company has been bought, management move on to identify the next target rather than ensuring that predicted synergy is realized. The post-acquisition management phase is often critical.

- Inadequate preliminary investigation combined with an inability to implement the amalgamation efficiently.

- Insufficient appreciation of the personnel problems which will arise.

- Dominance of subjective factors such as the status of the respective boards of directors.

- Difficulty of valuation.

- Arguments given as justification for merger or acquisition are suspect.

- Laziness of management in looking for alternatives.

- Winners curse – where two or more predators bid to buy a target the winner has often had to pay an excessive premium to secure the deal.

For example,

- Racal's original £65 million bid for Decca was approved by the Decca chairman and by 30% of the voting shares.

- After the intervention of GEC, Racal eventually took control with a bid in excess of £100 million.

- Such a large gap between the original and final valuation indicates the kind of variation in measures of value that can exist.

## 6 The regulation of takeovers

The regulation of takeovers varies from country to country but focuses primarily on controlling the directors. Typical factors include the following:

- At the most important time in the company's life – when it is subject to a takeover bid – its directors should act in the best interest of their shareholders, and should disregard their personal interests.

- All shareholders must be treated equally.

- Shareholders must be given all the relevant information to make an informed judgement.

- The board must not take action without the approval of shareholders, which could result in the offer being defeated.

- All information supplied to shareholders must be prepared to the highest with standards of care and accuracy.

- The assumptions on which profit forecasts are based and the accounting polices used should be examined and reported on by accountants.

- An independent valuer should support valuations of assets.

### Expandable Text - The UK position

The acquisition of quoted companies is circumscribed by the City Code on Takeovers and Mergers ('the City Code'), which is the responsibility of the Panel on Takeovers and Mergers.

- This code does not have the force of law.

- It is enforced by the various City regulatory authorities, including the Stock Exchange, and specifically by the Panel on Takeovers and Mergers (the 'Takeover Panel').

- Its basic principle is that of equity between one shareholder and another.

- It sets out rules for the conduct of such acquisitions.

The Stock Exchange Yellow Book also has certain points to make in these circumstances:

- Details of documents to be issued during bids for quoted companies.
- Such documents to be cleared by the Stock Exchange.
- Timely announcement of all price sensitive information.

The Office of Fair Trading (OFT) regulates the monopoly aspects of bids. Many bids, because of their size, will require review by the OFT, and a limited number will subsequently be referred to the Competition Commission under the Fair Trading Act if the OFT thinks that a merger might be against the public interest (i.e. constraining of competition).

As a rule of thumb the Competition Commission may investigate an acquisition if it will result in the combined entity acquiring 25% or more of market share.

Their investigations may take several months to complete during which time the merger is put on hold. Thus giving the target company valuable time to organise its defence. The acquirer may abandon its bid as it may not wish to become involved in a time consuming Competition Commission investigation.

The Commission may simply accept or reject the proposals or accept them subject to certain conditions, e.g. on price. There has been a recent surge in the level of merger activity within Europe due to reduction of barriers to overseas ownership and a desire by multinational companies to enter the European market. These are subject to regulation by the European Commission in Brussels.

In addition, if the offer gives rises to a concentration (i.e. a potential monopoly) within the EC, the European Commission may initiate proceedings. This can result in considerable delay, and constitutes grounds for abandoning a bid.

**Expandable Text - Shareholder/stakeholder models of regulation**

In the UK and US the market-based 'shareholder model' of regulation is used:

- Shareholder model – to protect rights of shareholders.
- Wide shareholder base.

In contrast, the European model looks at regulation from a wider stakeholder perspective:

- Stakeholder perspective to protect all stakeholders in a company.

- Stakeholders include:
  - employees
  - creditors
  - government
  - suppliers
  - general public.

## Which model is better?

There is a wide ranging debate as to whether the shareholder or stakeholder model is better from an economic and a more general public interest viewpoint.

- Stakeholder model appears to be more successful at dealing with the agency problem and managerial abuse of their power.

- Shareholder model appears to be more economically efficient.

- In practice the shareholder model is becoming more dominant:
  - Due to strength of UK/US economies.
  - Power of US/UK capital markets.
  - The move is reflected in legislation.

- Synergy is often gained through redundancies in an acquired firm. Many are concerned with what they see as an unethical practise. A stakeholder model is more likely to give emphasis to employee protection.

### Test your understanding 5 - Hi TV and Gino Media

Gino Media has substantial business interests in all areas of the media in the UK.

Gino Media is considering merging with Hi TV plc – a major television company with control of a large proportion of the UK domestic commercial TV terrestrial market.

There are currently concerns about the standard of programmes produced by Hi TV.

**If the proposed merger was to be referred to the regulatory authorities (e.g. Competition Commission in the UK) what issues are likely to arise?**

### Test your understanding 6 - International gold GmbH

Builder Group plc, a UK company, currently subject to a takeover bid by International Gold GmbH – the German arm of the South African owned Kugel gold mining operation which also owns a significant proportion of the European building industry. Kugel wishes to expand into the European markets to offset a downturn in its main markets of Africa and Latin America and is also attempting to alter its 'dodgy' image.

**What needs to be considered when determining whether the offer is likely to be in the shareholders' best interests?**

## 7 Defence against hostile takeovers

- Every group is potentially subject to takeover.

- There will be a price at which the owners (shareholders) may be induced to sell their shares.

- If a bid is received, then the directors should consider it from the shareholders' perspective – if it will increase shareholder wealth, then the directors should recommend accepting the offer.

- A problem arises where a publicly quoted group, with a widely spread shareholding, receives an unwelcome ('predatory') bid, with the clear objective of buying the group at a price below the value that management put on it.

- Shareholders need to determine the management's motives in defending the bid.

- The purpose of corporate defence is either to obtain a full and satisfactory price from an unwelcome bidder, or to ward off the bid, and remain independent.

### Expandable Text - Agency issues

It is important to emphasise that this is a management, as opposed to shareholders', view, since presumably the latter, if they are induced to sell, will be happy with the transaction, on the 'willing buyer, willing seller' assumption.

It is also important to determine management's motives in defending a bid strongly. The intention may genuinely be to obtain the best price for the shares, and prevent them being sold below their intrinsic value. However, the intention may merely be to maintain the group's independence at any price – which may not be the best solution for shareholders.

## Reasons for predatory bids

The circumstances under which a predator may seek to buy a group at less than full value are usually as follows:

- The share price is depressed. This can usually be identified by:
    - the group's market value being below the net value of its shareholders' funds; or
    - the group's price/earnings ratio being below, or its yield being above that for its sector.

In this case, however, the predator may believe that under its management the group can recover and perform much better financially than under existing management.

- The group's prospects are better than the share price would indicate. A period of fluctuating profits may be about to be followed by a good recovery. A predator might recognise this before it became apparent to the stock market as a whole, and seek to capitalise on the opportunity.

- The group occupies a strong position in one or more markets. The predator may see the acquisition of the group as a unique opportunity to purchase a major market share, and wish to do so without paying the market premium which should, in theory, attach to such a one-off situation.

## Non-financial considerations

There are two non-financial reasons for strong resistance that arise from time to time, regardless of the financial benefits to shareholders:

- Monopoly – generally defined by reference to laws regulating market shares but can also involve any transaction above a defined size and reviewed in terms of national economic interest.

- Employee interest – employment may be more secure if the group remains independent than it would be under a new employer whose objectives may be major rationalisation/divestment.

- The emphasis of current political attitudes to corporate law is increasingly on the rights of employees as well as shareholders.

## Expandable Text - Examples of defences

### Strategic defences

The principal aim of strategic defence is to try to eliminate, as far as possible, the attractions of the group to a would-be predator.

Defences can be split into pre- and post-bid defences.

### Pre-bid defences

- Eternal vigilance

  Maintain a high share price by being an effective management team and educate shareholders.

- Communicate

  Investors may be told of any good research ideas within the company and of the management potential or merely be made more aware of the company's achievements.

- Clearly defined strategy

  Communicate the strategy effectively to ensure that it is well understood, this will reassure shareholders and tend to maintain the share price.

- Cross shareholdings

  Your company buys a substantial proportion of the shares in a friendly company, and it has a substantial holding of your shares.

- Strong dividend policy

  The level of cash dividend is often held to influence share price.

### Post-bid defences

- Attack the logic of the bid.
- A White Knight Strategy – Find a friendlier bidder instead.
- Improve the image of the company.

This can be done through revaluation, profit projections, dividend promises and public relation consultants.

- Refer to regulatory authorities (e.g. Competition Commission).
- Encourage unions, the local community, politicians, customers and suppliers to lobby on your behalf.

### Other potential defences

The following tactics are likely to be frowned upon by the Takeover Panel in the UK but are used in the USA:

(1) **PacMan defence – (Reverse takeovers)**

The bidding company is itself the subject of a take-over bid by the targeted company, it has seldom been used successfully.

(2) **Poison Pill Strategy**

Make yourself unpalatable to the bidder by ensuring additional costs will be incurred should it win. The most common method is to give existing shareholders the right to buy future loan stock or preference shares. If a bid is made before the date of exercise of the rights then the rights will automatically be converted into full ordinary shares. Others are:

(a) **Flip-in pills** involve the granting of rights to shareholders, other than the potential acquirer, to purchase shares of the targeted company at a deep discount. This type of plan will dilute the ownership interest of the potential acquirer.

(b) **Back-end rights** are usually in the form of a cash dividend allowing shareholders other than the potential acquirer to exchange their shares for cash or senior debt securities at a price determined by the Board of Directors. The price set by the Board is usually well in excess of the market price or the price likely to be offered by a potential acquirer. Because the price that the target shareholder would receive is likely to be higher than that offered by the potential acquirer, shares will not be tendered.

(3) **Crown Jewels**

This is the tactic of selling off certain highly valued assets of the company subject to the bid, those that are of greatest interest to the raider.

(4) **Scorched Earth**

In practical terms, this means that the targeted company liquidates all or substantially all of its assets leaving nothing to the raider, thereby eliminating the raider's motive for acquiring the target.

**(5)  Golden Parachutes**

Managers get pay-offs that may be substantial if the company is taken over. Although a golden parachute for one chief executive officer involved in a takeover battle in the USA was reportedly US $35 m, they usually are a low multiple of the most recent year's salary.

**(6)  Fatman**

The targeted company acquires a large and/or under performing company in order to decrease its attractiveness to the raider.

### Test your understanding 7 - Development of bids

**Follow the developments of bids in progress every day by reading a good financial newspaper. Can you see examples of where the above anti-takeover mechanisms have been used successfully?**

## Acceptable offers

Any board recognises that there is a point at which an offer becomes irresistible:

- Offer strong and logical resistance right up to this point.
- Decision based primarily on price.
- Other important considerations being the interests of employees and customers.
- Directors recommending acceptance of a bid clearly have a duty to make sure that the price is the best available in the circumstances and that independence is still not a better course, bearing in mind longer term considerations.

### Test your understanding 8 - Downcrest plc

Downcrest Inc is a medium-sized quoted company whose 1 m shares in issue are currently traded at 18 cents each. Its shareholders' funds are $250,000, and its post-tax earnings are 3.25 cents per share. It has maintained steady earnings, and has been able to reduce its debt to $50,000; market interest rates are approximately 12% pa.

Rawhide Inc, also quoted, has quietly built up a 2.9% stake in Downcrest and makes a market raid at 25 cents per share, acquiring 14.9% as a result. Rawhide has been a persistent predator, although it is basically in the same markets as Downcrest, and it has 10 m shares in issue currently trading at 80 cents. Shareholders' funds are $8 m. Its latest earnings are 11.7 cents per share and its acquisition activities have driven up its debt to $7 m. Both companies are paying tax at 35%.

(a) **What defences could Downcrest mount against a full bid?**

(b) **How might Downcrest have avoided the raid in the first instance?**

## 8 Methods of financing mergers

- In general a purchaser and a vendor will need to agree on three basic issues in regard to an acquisition:
    - Whether shares or assets are to be purchased.
    - Type of consideration.
    - Financial value.

- Although determination of value is likely to take place prior to the decision on the type of consideration, they are considered here in reverse order (see later chapter) as the complexity of valuation necessitates its own chapter.

### Type of consideration

The means of transferring the financial value of the shares or assets of the business, the consideration, can be satisfied in a combination of several alternatives:

- Cash.
- Debt.
- Preference shares.
- Ordinary shares.
- Debt and preference share consideration that can be convertible into ordinary shares.
- Share and loan stock used as consideration are known as 'paper issues'.
- If a share exchange is used – the target company's shares are purchased using shares of the predator.

**Cash** – most popular method especially after stock market declines in 73–74 and October 1987.

**For the acquirer**

| Advantages | Disadvantages |
|---|---|
| When the bidder has sufficient cash the merger can be achieved quickly. | Cash flow strain – usually either must borrow (increased gearing) or issue new shares in order to raise the cash. |
| Cheaper: the consideration is likely to be less than a share exchange, as there is less risk to the shareholders. | |
| Retains control of their company. | |

**For the target shareholders**

| Advantages | Disadvantages |
|---|---|
| Certainty about bids value | Liable to CGT |
| Freedom to invest in a wide ranging portfolio. | Do not participate in new group. |

- The cash to fund the purchase may have been raised by a rights issue before the takeover bid.

**Shares** – second most popular method.

**For the acquirer**

| Advantages | Disadvantages |
|---|---|
| No cash outflow | Dilution of control |
| Bootstrapping – P/E ratio game can be played | |

**For the target shareholders**

| Advantages | Disadvantages |
|---|---|
| Postponement of CGT liability | Uncertain value |
| Participate in new group | |

- Many bids are mixed – cash or shares – to appeal to the widest range of potential sellers.

## Expandable Text - More detail on shares, cash and mixed bids

### Shares

- Shares can be issued by one company in order to pay for the acquisition of another company.

- The value of ordinary shares issued is, generally speaking, based on their market value at the time of issue

- Shares may be issued in exchange for the target's shares - the target company's shareholders becoming shareholders of the predator.

- Paper offers (shares) are often accompanied by an alternative cash offer.

- Paper offers lead to an increase in the issued share capital of the predator.

In principle the issue of shares is no more expensive to the purchaser than cash or debt consideration, despite the implicit difference in the cost of equity and debt. The reason for this is that, in general, projects, whether internal or external (i.e. acquisitions) should be considered to be financed from a 'pool' of financial resources based on the optimum relationship between debt and equity, and basing the appropriate hurdle on the 'blended' cost of such a pool. If equity is issued as consideration for a project, the change in the debt/equity ratio resulting is usually considered to be temporary, and the group will subsequently make appropriate adjustments in the level of debt in order to optimise the ratio. Adjustments would equally have to be made where debt rather than equity is issued.

- However, certain complicating factors need to be borne in mind and may go against the use of such shares:
    - Temporary depression of share price.
    - Dilution of existing shareholders' interests.
    - Difficulty in valuing shares.
    - Maintenance of debt/equity ratio.

### Temporary depression of share price

The acquirer may feel that the current share price might rise in the future, either because the share market as a whole is depressed, or because the value of the acquiring company's shares are temporarily depressed. Thus, the vendor may be getting the shares 'cheap'.

### Dilution of existing shareholders' interests

This will be a problem where the acquirer has a limited number of major shareholders who may not, for control or other reasons, wish to see their interests diluted.

### Difficulty in valuing shares

Unquoted companies may have difficulty in establishing an appropriate price.

### Maintenance of debt/equity ratio

If the change in the equity base is large in relation to the pre-acquisition level of equity, it may be difficult to get back to an optimum debt/equity ratio. Under these circumstances, the ordinary shares issue may indeed have a higher cost, closer to the cost of equity rather than to the 'blended cost of capital'.

- The type, cost and term/redemption arrangement of debt or preference shares to be issued is a matter for negotiation.
- However, the vendor's capital gains tax may be deferred by the issue of either debt or shares of any type, the deferral being until repayment date/redemption date/date of sale of ordinary shares.
- Where debt or preference shares are concerned, there is often a quid pro quo exacted by the acquirer in the form of a lower interest and dividend rate than the going market, in return for the tax advantage conveyed.

### Cash purchases

When the purchase consideration is cash, the shares of the target company are purchased in exchange for cash. Hence the target shareholders are "bought out".

### Cash bid example

Easter Co and Pomerettes Co have net assets at book value of $3,000,000 and $100,000 respectively, and their respective expected earnings are $450,000 and $75,000. The shareholders of Pommerettes have recently accepted a takeover bid of $200,000 in cash.

Immediately after takeover Easter Ltd will have net assets of $3,000,000 + $100,000 - $200,000 (cash payment) = $2,900,000.

Its number of shares will remain unchanged.

Its expected earnings will be $450,000 + $75,000 = $525,000 less any interest lost on the cash used to purchase pommerettes, plus any synergy gains.

## Choice of payment type

Sometimes investors are given a choice in the method of payment, with the logic that different forms of payment might be attractive to different types of investor.

- Could influence the success or failure of a bid.

- Problematic for the bidder in that the cash needs and the number of shares to be issued are not known.

- Capital structure may alter in an unplanned manner.

- Ideally a bidder would like to tailor the form of the bid to that favoured by major investors in the targeted company.

### Factors used to decide payment type

| Predator and its shareholders | Target company shareholders |
|---|---|
| • Control – if a large number of shares are issued then control of the company may alter | • Share price – shareholders want shares that will at least retain their value |
| • Increases in authorised capital may be needed | • Future investments – some shareholders may prefer shares to maintain an investment in the company |
| • Increases in borrowing limits may be required | |
| • The cost to the company will vary with debt, equity and convertible loan stocks | • Taxation – liability may be deferred if the consideration was in shares |
| • There may be a dilution of earnings per share | • Income – shareholders will want a minimum income stream. |
| • The level of gearing resultant on an issue of debt to finance a cash acquisition may be unacceptable. | |

**Test your understanding 9 - Shareholder choice**

Assume you are a shareholder in a target company that is subject to a take-over bid. Payment is to be by means of a share for share exchange.

**What factors are you particularly interested in?**

## Expandable Text - Financing available: cash-based acq'ns

The main options for raising finance to fund cash purchases are:

**Retained earnings**
- May be the cheapest option
- Generally restricted to smaller acquisitions
- Need liquidity as well as retained earnings.

**Debt**
- Larger companies may use bond market – likely impact on share price
- Bridging loan to reduce impact on share price followed by bond issue could be used
- Bank loan are an option for small companies – terms depend on how much, what for, credit risk
- Loans normally medium-term and secured
- Loan from other financial institutions are available – similar issues to bank loans
- May use mezzanine finance.

**Sale of existing assets**
- Dependent on matching sale and purchase
- May result in better fit for group.

**Share issue**
- Dilution of control
- Funding may match projected income better than debt.

Predator companies often raise loans to pay for a cash takeover which are:

- Unsecured and with a relatively high interest rate.
- Give the lender the option, after the takeover, to swap the loan for shares.
- Short-to-medium term.

(i.e. Mezzanine finance)

## Expandable Text - Merger and acquisition accounting

- There are two different methods of consolidation designed to reflect the substance of two different types of business combination.

- Acquisition accounting is used for the purchase of one company by another with the purchaser controlling the net assets of the subsidiary.

  - Net assets acquired are included at their fair values.

  - Only post-acquisition profits of the subsidiary included in consolidated reserves.

- Merger accounting is when there is a pooling of interests of two or more roughly equal partners. Effectively adds the two sets of accounts together.

- The investment in a new subsidiary will be shown as a fixed asset investment in the parent company's own accounts.

- The amount at which this investment will be stated will depend upon whether merger accounting or acquisition accounting is used.

- Under acquisition accounting the investment will be recorded at cost (generally the fair value of the consideration given).

- If merger accounting is used the investment is recorded at the nominal value of the shares issued as purchase consideration plus the fair value of any additional consideration.

## Comparison of merger and acquisition accounting - illustration

Fred makes an offer to all the shareholders of Ginger to acquire their shares on the basis of one new $1 share (market value $3) plus 25 c for every two $1 shares (market value $1.10 each) in Ginger. The holders of 95,000 shares in Ginger (representing 95% of the total shares) accept this offer.

The investment in Ginger will be recorded in the books of Fred as follows:

If acquisition accounting is to be used on consolidation:

|  | $ | $ |
|---|---|---|
| Dr: Investment in Ginger plc | 154,375 | |
| Cr: $1 ordinary shares | | 47,500 |
| Cr: Share premium | | 95,000 |
| Cr: Cash | | 11,875 |
| | 154,375 | 154,375 |

If merger accounting is to be used on consolidation:

|  | $ | $ |
|---|---|---|
| Dr: Investment in Ginger plc | 59,375 | |
| Cr: $1 ordinary shares | | 47,500 |
| Cr: Cash | | 11,875 |
| | 59,375 | 59,375 |

## 9 Chapter summary

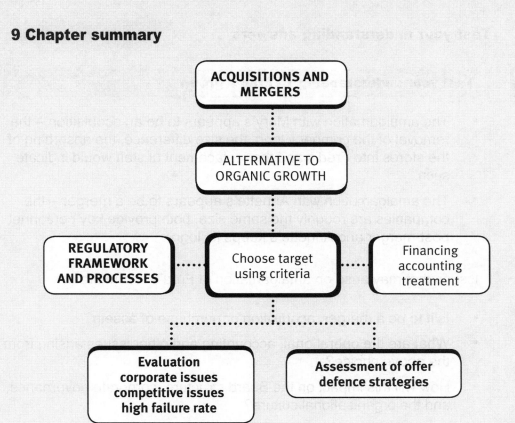

## Test your understanding answers

### Test your understanding 1 - Fred's group

- The amalgamation with Mary's appears to be an acquisition – the removal of the company logo, the size difference, the absorbing of the stores into Fred's and the replacement of staff would indicate such.

- The amalgamation with Annette's appears to be a merger – the companies are roughly the same size, both provide key personnel post-merger and Annette's keeps its logo.

Issues that may arise on amalgamation of Fred's and Moira's:

- Is it to be a merger, acquisition or purchase of assets?

- What are the operational, accounting and other issues arising from the above choice?

- How will this impact on the Board structure, corporate governance, and the organisational culture?

- Will there be hostility to such a move and from what level?

- Should there by a transfer of assets or a transfer of shares?

- What price should be paid?

- Is there potential for synergy (see later)?

- What are the competitive issues surrounding this (see later)?

### Test your understanding 2 - Premier foods

In areas where a food label owned by premier foods competes with one owned by RHM, e.g. cook-in sauces or gravy products then there will be a reduction in competition.

There may be a referral to the Competition Commission if any product's market share is deemed to be greater than 25% – this may depend on how tightly products are defined, e.g. is the market for Oxo stock cubes and Bisto gravy granules the same?

## Test your understanding 3 - Synergy

Synergy might exist for many reasons including:

### Economic efficiency gains

Gains might relate to economies of scale or scope. Economies of scale occur through such factors as fixed operating costs being spread over a larger production volume, equipment being used more efficiently with higher volumes of production, or bulk purchasing reducing costs. Economies of scope may arise from reduced advertising and distribution costs when companies have complementary resources. Economies of scale and scope relate mainly to horizontal acquisitions and mergers. Economic efficiency gains may also occur with backward or forward vertical integration which might reduce production costs as the 'middle man' is eliminated, improve control of essential raw materials or other resources that are needed for production, or avoid disputes with what were previously suppliers or customers.

Economic efficiency gains might also result from replacing inefficient management as the result of a merger/takeover.

### Financial synergy

Financial synergy might involve a reduction in the cost of capital and risk. The variability (standard deviation) of returns of a combined entity is usually less than the weighted average of the risk of the individual companies. This is a reduction in total risk, but does not affect systematic risk, and hence might not be regarded as a form of synergy by shareholders. However, reduced variability of returns might improve a company's credit rating making it easier and/or cheaper to obtain a loan. Another possible financial synergy exists when one company in an acquisition or merger is able to use tax shield, or accumulated tax losses, which would otherwise have been unavailable to the other company.

### Market power

A large organisation, particularly one which has acquired competitors, might have sufficient market power to increase its profits through price leadership or other monopolistic or oligopolistic means.

**Test your understanding 4 - Williams and GSL**

- Operating efficiencies – the unused capacity at GSL can be used to produce William's products without adding to costs and capacity.

- Marketing synergies.

- If the cash flow streams of Williams and GSL are not perfectly positively correlated then by acquiring GSL – Williams may reduce the variability of their operating cash flow. This being more attractive to investors may lead to cheaper financing.

- The 'dedicated' herbalists of GSL and the R+D staff of William's may be a complementary resource.

- Fixed operating and administrative costs savings.

- Consolidation of manufacturing capacity on fewer and larger sites.

- There may be bulk buying discounts.

- Possibility of joint advertising and distribution.

- GSL is badly managed – thus the elimination of inefficiency could allow for financial synergy.

## Test your understanding 5 - Hi TV and Gino Media

Issues likely to be considered include:

- What is the definition of the market or markets being considered:
  - For advertising revenue how wide is the definition of market – all media – just TV advertising – or just a sub-section of channels?
  - For television viewing – which sections of the market (free-to-air, pay-TV) are to be considered – or are all areas to be included in the definition of market.

- Would the merged company have control or a large influence over a section of the TV media and if so would this be beneficial or detrimental to the viewing public?

- Would the merger reduce competition for TV advertising revenues?

- What would be the impact on other television and media companies?

- What would be the impact on advertisers?

- How might the pricing structure for advertising be altered by such a merger?

- How the parties involved intend to comply with legislation specific to the industry and how have they complied in the past?

- What would the impact be on the quality and pricing of programming?

- Would the merger be in the public interest?

## Test your understanding 6 - International gold GmbH

- Need to assess potential offer from the point of view of both the target shareholders and that of the predators shareholders.

- The cost of preparing information to defend any potential breach of European market share regulations would reduce the profits of the 'merged' firm and potentially the wealth of shareholders.

- If the bid fails due to a breach of regulation then the money spent on the bid would reduce the predator's profit and may lead to a reduction in share price.

- Similarly the costs of defending any case as to whether the merger was not in the country's interest would reduce profits.

- Despite an initial increase in shareholder wealth should the merger occur there may be a reduction in post-acquisition share prices if Kugel maintains its poor image.

### Test your understanding 7 - Development of bids

There is no feedback to this activity.

### Test your understanding 8 - Downcrest plc

- Downcrest's defence is likely to have three prongs:

    - In view of Rawhide's position in the same market, it would certainly seem, prima facie, as if the regulatory authorities should be consulted to see whether they would consider blocking the bid on competition grounds.

    - Downcrest would also argue that the price of 25 c proposed was too cheap, being exactly equal to its book shareholders' funds and with no regard for its business prospects. It would in the first instance revalue its property assets, if appropriate, and emphasise its future earnings and cash generation capacity, with forecasts as appropriate, including a dividend forecast.

    - Downcrest would argue that Rawhide's actual performance in the same industry was in reality worse than its own, as follows:

|   |   | Downcrest | Rawhide |
|---|---|---|---|
|   |   | $000 | $000 |
| 1 | Debt | 50 | 7,000 |
| 2 | Shareholders' funds | 250 | 8,000 |
| 3 | Total value (1 + 2) | 300 | 15,000 |
| 4 | Post-tax profit | 32.5 | 1,170 |
| 5 | Pre-tax profit | 50 | 1,800 |
| 6 | Interest paid | 6 | 840 |
| 7 | Trading profit (5 + 6) | 56 | 2,640 |
| 8 | Return on capital (7 ÷ 3) | 18.7% | 17.6% |

It would therefore argue that it, Downcrest, was a better custodian of its assets by making a higher return on its capital; that it therefore had a higher quality management, and Rawhide certainly could not expect to improve on management performance, given its track record; and that there was therefore no commercial logic in the bid: Downcrest's shareholders, if they accepted Rawhide's shares as consideration, would become investors in a lower quality group.

- It allowed Rawhide to buy nearly 3% without noting the build-up in shares. This could have been avoided by watching the level of new shareholdings, and any unaccounted-for nominee accumulations in the shareholders' register.

- The fact that it was, before the raid, selling at a sizeable (25 - 18) / 25 = 28% discount to net asset value, despite a better underlying trading performance than Rawhide, indicated that its financial communication programme could be much improved.

- It appeared to have given no thought to a possible 'white knight' in the event of an unfriendly bid. Given Rawhide's low level of attraction such an alternative bidder should at least bring some enhanced commercial value to Downcrest.

- It should give thought to increasing its gearing through good quality investment and acquisition in order to increase the return on shareholders' funds.

### Test your understanding 9 - Shareholder choice

- Synergy.

- Acquisition premium.

- Dividends.

- Gearing.

- Intrinsic value.

- Future prospects.

- Control.

# 10

# Business valuation

## Chapter learning objectives

Upon completion of this chapter you will be able to:

- Explain the issue of overvaluation and outline the problems it can cause

- Estimate the potential near-term and continuing growth levels of a firm's earnings using internal measures such as the earnings retention model

- Estimate the potential near-term and continuing growth levels of a firm's earnings using external measures such as extrapolation from past dividend patterns

- Describe the potential risks of an acquisition or merger on the acquirer, distinguishing between business, financial and other risks

- In a scenario question, identify and analyse the impact on the risk profile of the acquirer in a Type 1, Type 2 and Type 3 acquisition

- Calculate and discuss the value of an acquisition of both quoted and unquoted entities using asset based approaches:
    - Without considering intangibles
    - Including the valuation of intangibles using the calculated intangible value method
    - Including the valuation of intangibles using Lev's knowledge earnings method.

- Calculate and discuss the value of an acquisition of both quoted and unquoted entities using market relative models:
    - PE ratio model
    - Earnings yield model
    - Market to book ratios.

- Calculate and discuss the value of an acquisition of both quoted and unquoted entities using cash flow approaches:
  - Dividend valuation model
  - FCF and FCFE models
  - Economic value added

- Discuss the value of a Type 2 and 3 acquisitions of both quoted and unquoted entities using:
  - The adjusted net present value approach
  - Iterative revaluation procedures.

- Describe the procedure for valuing high growth start-ups.

*Earning Based Model* (handwritten)

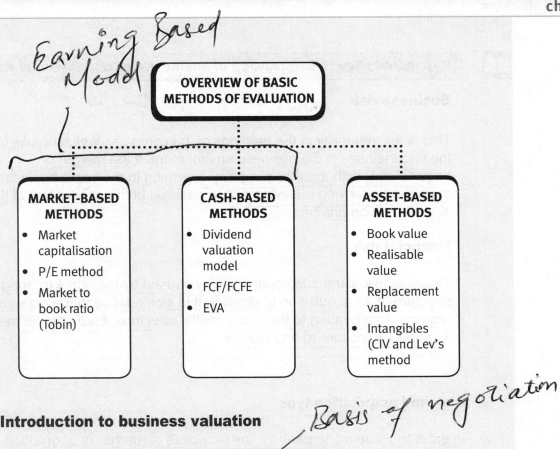

**OVERVIEW OF BASIC METHODS OF EVALUATION**

**MARKET-BASED METHODS**
- Market capitalisation
- P/E method
- Market to book ratio (Tobin)

**CASH-BASED METHODS**
- Dividend valuation model
- FCF/FCFE
- EVA

**ASSET-BASED METHODS**
- Book value
- Realisable value
- Replacement value
- Intangibles (CIV and Lev's method

# 1 Introduction to business valuation

*Basis of negotiation* (handwritten)

This chapter covers several different methods of business valuation. You should view the different methods as complementary which enable you to suggest a possible value region. It is essential that you are able to comment on the suitability of each approach in a particular scenario.

Do not put yourself under pressure in the exam to come up with a precise valuation, as business valuation is not an exact science. In reality the final price paid will depend on the bargaining skills and the economic pressures on the parties involved.

# 2 Risk in acquisitions and mergers

An acquisition may expose an acquiring company to risk. It is important to distinguish between:

- business risk
- financial risk.

---

**Expandable Text - Explanation of business risk and financial risk**

**Business risk**  *variability in the earnings*

This is the variability in the earnings of the company, which results from the uncertainties in the business environment. If the merger or acquisition is with another company operating in the same business area, the underlying business risk (measured bt the asset beta) of the acquirer will be unaffected.

**Financial risk**

Financial risk is the additional volatility caused by the firm's gearing structure. If an acquisition is significant in size relative to the acquirer or requires an alteration to the firm's capital structure, it will change the acquirer's exposure to finance risk.

---

### Risk and acquisition type

In order to value a company for the purposes of merger or acquisition, the value added to the acquirer must be identified. For this purpose, acquisitions can be categorised into three types:

- Type 1 – Those that do not disturb the acquirer's exposure to business or financial risk.

- Type 2 – Those that do not disturb the acquirer's exposure to business risk but impact their exposure to finance risk.

- Type 3 – Those that alter the acquirer's exposure to business risk and possibly its financial risk.

### Test your understanding 1

**Separate the following acquisitions into Types 1, 2 and 3 based on the data provided below:**

| | Acquiring company business | Target company business | Impact on acquirer's capital structure | |
|---|---|---|---|---|
| a | Asset beta 0.8 | Asset beta 0.95 | Financed by new debenture issue | *Type 3* |
| b | Electrical wholesaler | Electrical wholesaler | Finance raised in long term gearing ratio | *Type 1* |
| c | Paper mill | Paper mill | Finance raised by issue of new equity | *Type 2* |
| d | Travel consultancy | Cottage rental | Finance raised in long term gearing ratio | *Type 3* |

## Valuation and acquisition type

It is a key principle that the most an acquirer should ever pay for a target company is the increase in the value of the acquiring firm arising from the acquisition.

However, it is rarely a simple matter of valuing the target and assuming that will be the level of increase experienced. This ignores the impact of:

- potential synergy gains – although there is an argument that they are so rarely achieved in practice that they should be very conservatively estimated, and only then if they are arising because of the target itself (that is they wouldn't arise from any merger)

- the change in potential risk profile of the combined entity as discussed above

The valuation techniques available must therefore depend on which type of acquisition is being considered.

For example, if an NPV based approach is being used, a risk adjusted cost of capital may need to be calculated and used for discounting.

## 3 Overview of the different valuation methods

### Three basic valuation methods

There are three basic ways of valuing a business

- market based methods – where we assume that the market is efficient, so use market information (such as share prices and P/E ratios) for the target company and other companies. The assumption is that the market values businesses consistently so, if necessary, the value of one company can be used to find the value of another.

- cash based methods – the theoretical premise here is that the value of the company should be equal to the discounted value of future cash flows.

- asset based methods – the firm's assets form the basis for the company's valuation. Asset based methods are difficult to apply to companies with high levels of intangible assets, but we shall look at methods of trying to value intangible as well as tangible assets.

We shall cover these methods in detail in the rest of this chapter.

## 4 Market based methods

### Stock market value (market capitalisation)

For a listed company, the stock market value of the shares (or "market capitalisation") is the starting point for the valuation process.

In a perfectly efficient market, the market price of the shares would be fair at all times, and would accurately reflect all information about a company. In reality, share prices tend to reflect publicly available information.

The market share price is suitable when purchasing a minority stake. However, a premium usually has to be paid above the current market price in order to acquire a controlling interest.

### The price-earnings ratio (P/E) method

The P/E method is a very simple method of valuation. It is the most commonly used method in practice.

Value of equity = PAT × Suitable industry PE ratio.

Value of a share = EPS × Suitable industry PE ratio.

## PE ratio

The PE ratio applied should be that of a company (or average of several companies), that are similar with respect to:

- business risk – i.e. in the same industry
- finance risk – i.e. have approximately the same level of gearing
- growth – are growing at about the same rate.

In practice this may be difficult to find, and the parties involved in the acquisition will then negotiate the applied PE ratio up or down depending on the specific company circumstances.

In particular, if using a quoted company's PE to value an unquoted business, a substantial discount is often applied to reflect the lower marketability of unquoted shares (around 25% in practice).

### Profit figure

The PAT must be:

- maintainable earnings going forward – some adjustment will be needed for changes anticipated as a result of the acquisition or future trading conditions (e.g. forecast synergies)

### Weaknesses of the model

- It is applied to accounting earnings which are more subjective than cash flows.
- It assumes that the market is actually valuing earnings rather than some other aspect of the company's output – dividends, earnings growth, risk etc.
- It assumes that the market does accurately value shares

### Earnings yield approach

The earnings yield is simply the inverse of the PE ratio:

Earnings yield = EPS/Price per share

It can therefore be used to value the shares or market capitalisation of a company in exactly the same way as the PE ratio:

Value of company = Total earnings × 1 / Earnings yield

Value per share = EPS × 1 / Earnings yield

### Test your understanding 2

Company A has earnings of $300,000. A similar listed company has an earnings yield of 12.5%.

Company B has earnings of $420,500. A similar listed company has a PE ratio of 7.

**Find the market capitalisation of each company.**

### Test your understanding 3

ABC Co is considering making a bid for the entire equity capital of XYZ Co, a firm which has a PE ratio of 9 and earnings of $390m.

ABC Co has a PE of 13 and earnings of $693m, and it is thought that $125m of synergistic savings will be made as a consequence of the takeover. The PE of the combined company is expected to be 12.

**Calculate the minimum value acceptable to XYZ's shareholders, and the maximum amout which ABC should consider paying.**

### Market to book ratio (based on Tobin's Q)

Market value of target company = Market to book ratio × book value of target company's assets

where market to book ratio = (Market capitalisation/Book value of assets) for a comparator company (or take industry average)

This method assumes a constant relationship between market value of the equity and the book value of the firm.

Problems with the model

- Choosing an appropriate comparator – should we use industry average, or an average of similar firms only?

- The ratio the market applies is not constant throughout its business cycle, so strictly the comparator should be taken only from other companies at the same stage.

### Expandable Text - Illustration of Tobin's Q

The industry sector average Market to Book ratio for the industry of X plc is 4.024.

The book value of X plc is \$3,706m and it has 1,500m shares in issue.

Find the predicted share price.

### Solution

Predicted value of X plc = \$3,706m × 4.024 = \$14,912.94m.

Predicted share price = \$14,912.94m / 1,500m = 994.2¢.

### Test your understanding 4

The industry sector average Market to Book ratio for B's industry is 2.033

The book value of B plc is \$1,572m and it has 768m shares in issue.

Find the predicted share price.

## 5 Cash based methods

### The dividend valuation model (DVM)

**Theory:** The value of the company/share is the present value of the expected future dividends discounted at the shareholders' required rate of return.

Assuming a constant growth rate in dividends, g:

$$P_0 = D_0(1 + g) / (K_e - g)$$

Note that:

If $D_0$ = Total dividends $P_0$ = Value of company.

If $D_0$ = Dividends per share $P_0$ = Value per share.

If the growth pattern of dividends is not expected to be stable, but will vary over time, the formula can be adapted.

### Expandable Text - Explanation of terms in DVM formula

Ke = cost of equity.

g = constant rate of growth in dividends, expressed as a decimal.

$D_0(1 + g)$ = dividend just paid adjusted for one year's growth.

### Expandable Text - DVM calculations

**Basic application of DVM formula**

A company has just paid a dividend of 20¢. The company expects dividends to grow at 7% in the future. The company's current cost of equity is 12%.

**Calculate the market value of the share.**

**Solution**

$P_0$ = 20(1 + 0.07)/(0.12 - 0.07) = 428¢ = $4.28

**More advanced application of the DVM formula**

C plc has just paid a dividend of 25¢ per share. The return on equities in this risk class is 20%.

**Find the value of the shares assuming:**

(i) **no growth in dividends**

(ii) **constant growth of 5% pa**

(iii) **constant dividends for 5 years and then growth of 5% pa to perpetuity.**

**Solution**

(i)   $P_0 = 0.25/0.2 = \$1.25$

(ii)  $P_0 = 0.25(1.05)/(0.2 - 0.05) = \$1.75$

| | | |
|---|---|---|
| (iii) Present value of first 5 years' dividends | = 0.25 × 5 yr 20% AF | 0.748 |
| | = 0.25 × 2.991 | |
| Present value of growing dividend | = Value at T5 × 5 yr DF | |
| | = [0.25(1.05)/(0.2 - 0.05)] × 0.402 | 0.704 |
| | | ———— |
| Share value | | $1.452 |
| | | ———— |

**Test your understanding 5**

C plc has just paid a dividend of 32¢ per share. The return on equities in this risk class is 16%. Find the value of the shares assuming constant dividends for 3 years and then growth of 4% pa to perpetuity.

The model is highly sensitive to changes in assumptions:

- Where growth is high relative to the shareholders required return, the share price is very volatile.

- Even a minor change in investors expectations of growth rates can cause a major change in share price contributing to the share price crashes seen in recent years.

iii) P.V of first 3 years

= 0.32 × 3 year 16% annuity fact

= 0.32 × 2.246

0.7187

P.V of growing div = $\left(\dfrac{0.32(1.04)}{0.16-0.04}\right)$ 0.692

1.127

2.848

### Expandable Text - Illustration of sensitivity of DVM

Consider the impact of a change in growth predictions of 0.5% in two cases – the first where growth is low compared to the firms required return, the other where it is high.

A firm's $k_e$ is 7% and $D_0$ is 10p

The change in share price as a result of changing growth predictions is shown:

Assuming:

(i)   a growth rate of 2% dropping to 1.5%

(ii)  a growth rate of 5% dropping to 4.5%

Assumption (i)

Share price at g = 2%   10 × 1.02 / (0.07 - 0.02) = 204

Share price at g = 1.5%   10 × 1.015 / (0.07 - 0.015) = 184.55

Fall in share price is (204 - 184.55) / 204 = 9.5%

Assumption (ii)

Share price at g = 5%   10 × 1.05 / (0.07 - 0.05) = 525

Share price at g = 4.5% 10 × 1.045 / (0.07 - 0.045) = 418

Fall in share price is (525 - 418) / 525 = 20.4%

The share price shows far greater volatility where growth is high relative to required return.

DVM is more suitable for valuing minority stakes, since it only considers dividends. In practice the model does tend to accurately match actual stock market share prices.

KAPLAN PUBLISHING

## The free cash flow method

Free cash flows can used to find the value of a firm. This value can be used:

- to determine the price in a merger or acquisition
- to identify a share price for the sale of a block of shares
- to calculate the 'shareholder value added' (SVA) by management from one period to another.

## Calculating the value

Technically, in order for the value of the business to be accurately determined, free cash flow for all future years should be estimated. However rather than attempting to predict the free cash flows for every year, in practice a short cut method is applied. Future cash flows are divided into two time periods:

- Those that occur during the 'planning horizon'.
- Those that occur after the planning horizon.

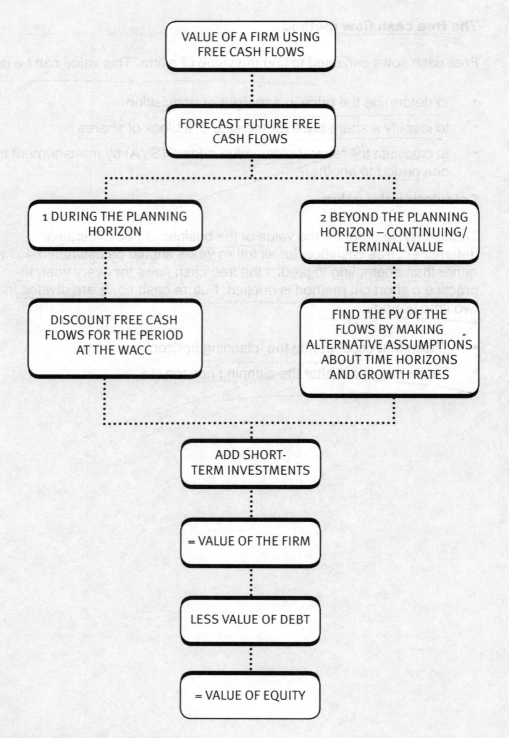

The planning horizon

The planning horizon is the period where:

- the firm can earn above average returns
- cash flows are assumed to grow over time.

Beyond the planning horizon, returns are expected to reach a steady state.

## Expandable Text - The planning horizon

In competitive industries, a business may have a period of 'competitive advantage' where it can earn excess returns on capital by maintaining a commercial advantage over the competition. However this period is unlikely to last indefinitely. Returns are likely to reach a steady state where the business earns on average its cost of capital but no more.

The planning horizon (which may last up to ten years or more) is the period during which the returns are expected to be higher than the cost of finance.

In period beyond the planning horizon it is usually assumed that the returns earned will continue at their current rate for the remainder of the investors' time horizon. This may be a given number of years or in perpetuity. Alternatively the value of the cash flows may be expressed as a lump sum using a PE ratio.

## Illustration 1

A company prepares a forecast of future free cash flow at the end of each year. A period of 15 years is used as this is thought to represent the typical time horizon of investors in this industry.

It is assumed that the planning horizon is three years – i.e. returns are likely to grow each year for the first three years after which they will reach a steady state.

The following data is available:

Free cash flows are expected to be $2.5 million in the first year, $4.5 million in the second year and $6.5 million in year 3. The stock market value of debt is $5m and the company's cost of capital is 10%.

**Find the current value of the firm and the value of the equity.**

## Solution

|  | Year 1 | Year 2 | Year 3 | Years 4–15 |
|---|---|---|---|---|
| Free cash flow | 2.5 | 4.5 | 6.5 | 6.5 |
| PV factor @10% | 0.909 | 0.826 | 0.751 | 6.814 × 0.751* |
| PV | 2.273 | 3.717 | 4.882 | 33.263 |

| | |
|---|---|
| **Total PV = value of firm** | 44.135 ←——Continuing/ |
| Less value of debt | (5.000)    terminal |
| **Value of equity** | 39.135    value |

*12 year AF (gives $T_3$ value of CF years 4–15) × 3 year DF (to discount to $T_0$).

### Expandable Text - The valuation of debt

The value of debt was given in the previous illustration.

If you are not told the value in a question, the best way of estimating the value is by using the formula:

Value of debt = Present value of receipts to the lender (i.e. interest and redemption payment) discounted at the lender's required rate of return

### Illustration 2

The company in the previous illustration now believes that earnings after the planning horizon will:

(a)  continue at the year 3 level into perpetuity or

(b)  grow at 0.9% pa into perpetuity.

**Recalculate the current value of the firm and the value of the equity.**

## Solution

### Part (a)

|  | Year 1 | Year 2 | Year 3 | Year 4 onwards |
|---|---|---|---|---|
| Free cash flow | 2.5 | 4.5 | 6.5 | 6.5 |
| PV factor @10% | 0.909 | 0.826 | 0.751 | $1/0.1 \times 0.751$* |
| PV | 2.273 | 3.717 | 4.882 | 48.815 |

| | | |
|---|---|---|
| **Total PV = value of firm** | 59.687 | Continuing/ |
| Less value of debt | (5.000) | terminal |
| **Value equity** | 54.687 | value |

*$1/i$ (gives $T_3$ value of CF from year 4 onwards) $\times$ 3 year DF (to discount to $T_0$).

Note the higher value that results when the time horizon is altered.

### Part (b)

|  | Year 1 | Year 2 | Year 3 | Years 4–infinity |
|---|---|---|---|---|
| Free cash flow | 2.5 | 4.5 | 6.5 | 6.5 (infl 0.9%) |
| PV factor @10% | 0.909 | 0.826 | 0.751 | See working |
| PV | 2.273 | 3.717 | 4.882 | 54.126 |

**Value of equity is 54.126 + 2.273 + 3.717 + 4.882 - (debt value) 5 = $59.998m**

### Working:

The value of the growing perpetuity from Year 4 onwards can be calculated as:

$$[(6.5 \times 1.009) / (0.10 - 0.009)] \times 0.751 = 54.126$$

### Test your understanding 6

A company is preparing a free cash flow forecast in order to calculate the value of equity.

The following information is available:

Sales: Current sales are $500m. Growth is expected to be 8% in year 1, falling by 2% pa (e.g. to 6% in year 2) until sales level out in year 5 where they are expected to remain constant in perpetuity.

The operating profit margin will be 10% for the first two years and 12% thereafter.

Depreciation in the current year will be $7m increasing by $1m pa over the planning horizon before levelling off and replacement asset investment is assumed to equal depreciation. Incremental investment in assets is expected to be 8% of the increase in sales in year 1, 6% of the increase in sales in each of the following two years, and 4% of the increase in year 4.

Tax will be charged at 30% pa.

The WACC is 15%.

The market value of short-term investments is $4m and the market value of debt is $48m.

**Calculate the value of equity.**

### Use of free cash flow to equity (FCFE) in valuation

The previous calculations have found equity value by:

- discounting free cash flow to present value using the WACC, and then deducting debt value.

Alternatively, the value of equity can be found directly by:

- discounting free cash flow TO EQUITY at the cost of equity.

In the simplest case (if FCFE is assumed to be growing at a constant rate into perpetuity), the following formula can be applied:

$$FCFE_0(1 + g) / (k_e - g)$$

The formula is based on the dividend valuation model theory.

## Economic value added (EVA®)

The economic value added EVA® valuation model was developed by a firm called Stern Stewart. It combines:

- the logic of the NPV model  *( logic of NPV model )*

- the use of accounting data produced by a firm.

EVA® is an estimate of 'economic' profit – the amount by which earnings exceed the required minimum rate of return that investors could get from other securities of comparable risk.

It follows the same principles as residual income by deducting from profits a charge for the opportunity cost of the capital invested.

EVA® is defined as:

NOPAT – rC

where:

NOPAT = Net operating profit after tax

r = WACC

C = firm's invested capital

The EVA® is then "capitalised". Assuming the earnings will continue in perpetuity, the capitalised value is EVA®/WACC

Then, the value of the firm = C + capitalised EVA®, and the value of equity = value of the firm less value of the total debt outstanding.

### Expandable Text - EVA adjustments and numerical illustration

The NOPAT and C figures are not simply taken from the company's financial statements. There are over 160 different adjustments that may be required to bring the figures into closer alignment with the true underlying profitability and level of capital invested – i.e. to remove the distortions caused by conforming to the governing GAAP – although in practice only between 5 and 15 of them are usually needed to achieve a meaningful result.

### Numerical illustration of the EVA® valuation method

FD plc has a NOPAT as adjusted for EVA® purposes of $562.98 million. It currently has invested capital of $5,609.48 million and a WACC of 7.25%. The company has total debt of $1,500 million.

Find the EVA® for FD plc, the value of the firm and the value of the firm's equity.

**Solution**

EVA® = NOPAT – rC

EVA® = 562.98 – (0.0725 × 5,609.48) = $156.30 million.

Firm value = C + EVA®/WACC

Firm value = 5,609.48 + 156.30/0.0725 = $7,765.34 million

Equity = Firm value – value of debt

Equity = $7,765.34 – 1,500 = $6,265.34 million

### Test your understanding 7

FD plc has a NOPAT as adjusted for EVA® purposes of $798.75 million. It currently has invested capital of $3,987.26 million and a WACC of 12.56%. Total debt is valued at $954.23 million and the company currently has 506,609,497 shares in issue.

**Find the EVA® for FD plc, the value of the firm and the equity value per share.**

## 6 Asset based methods

### The basic model

The traditional asset based valuation method is to take as a starting point the value of all the firm's balance sheet assets less any liabilities. Asset values used can be:

- book value - the book value of assets can easily be found from the financial statements. However, it is unlikely that book values (which are based on historic cost accounting principles) will be a reliable indicator of current market values.

- replacement cost - the buyer of a business will be interested in the replacement cost, since this represents the alternative cost of setting up a similar business from scratch (organic growth versus acquisition).

- net realisable value - the seller of a business will usually see the realisable value of assets as the minimum acceptable price in negotiations.

However:

- replacement cost is not easy to identify in practice, and
- the business is more than just the sum of its constituent parts. In fact the value of the tangible assets in many businesses is minimal since much of the value comes from the intangible assets and goodwill (e.g. compare a firm of accountants with a mining company).

## 7 Intangible asset valuation methods

### Definition of intangible assets

Intangible assets are those assets that cannot be touched, weighed or physically measured. They include:

- assets such as patents with legal rights attached
- intangibles such as goodwill, purchased and valued as part of a previous acquisition
- relationships, networks and skills built up by the business over time.

A major flaw with the basic asset valuation model is that it does not take account of the true value of intangibles.

### Basic intangible valuation method

The simplest way of incorporating intangible value into the process is by the following basic formula:

Firm value = [book or replacement cost of the real assets] + [multiplier × annual profit or turnover]

The multiplier is negotiated between the parties to compensate for goodwill.

Effectively, some attempt is being made to estimate the extra value generated by the intangible assets, above the value of the firm's tangible assets.

This simple formula provides the basis for the two main intangible valuation methods: CIV (Calculated Intangible Value) and Lev's method.

### Expandable Text - More detail on intangible assets

Often intangible assets, making up a significant part of the real worth of the company, are formed by the staff of a company – their skills, knowledge and creativity. Such assets are created by spending on areas such as R&D, advertising and marketing, training and staff development. This type of expenditure serves to enhance the underlying value of the firm rather than assisting directly in earning this year's profits.

A significant problem with the basic asset valuation model is that the assets to be valued are taken to be those identified on the balance sheet. Where a firm has significant levels of intangible assets, accounting conventions mean they will be either not be included at all, or included at amounts well below their real commercial value.

If the asset based model is to be of use, a way of valuing these intangibles must be found.

## Calculated intangible value (CIV)

This method is based on comparing (benchmarking) the return on assets earned by the company with:

- a similar company in the same industry or
- the industry average.

The method is similar to the residual income technique you may remember from your earlier studies. It calculates the company's **valuespread** – the profit it earns over the return on assets that would be expected for a firm in that business.

### Method

(1) A suitable competitor (similar in size, structure etc.) is identified and their return on assets calculated:

Operating profit/Assets employed

(2) If no suitable similar competitor can be identified, the industry average return may be used.

(3) The company's value spread is then calculated.

|                                        | $     |
|----------------------------------------|-------|
| Company operating profit               | X     |
| Less:                                  |       |
| Appropriate ROA × Company asset base   | (X)   |
| Value spread                           | X     |

(4) Assuming that the value spread would be earned in perpetuity, the Calculated Intangible Value (CIV) is found as follows:

- Find the post-tax value spread.

- Use the likely short-term growth rate to find the expected post-tax value spread at $T_1$.

- Find the CIV by capitalising the post-tax value spread – the PV of the $T_1$ value spread (assuming it will grow at the same rate in perpetuity).

(5) The CIV is added to the net asset value to give an overall value of the firm.

### Expandable Text - CIV calculation

CXM plc operates in the advertising industry. The directors are keen to value the company for the purposes of negotiating with a potential purchaser and plan to use the CIV method to value the intangible element.

In the past year CXM plc made an operating profit of $137.4 million on an asset base of $307 million. Earnings are predicted to grow at 3.4% over the next few years, and the company WACC is 6.5%.

A suitable competitor for benchmarking has been identified as R plc. R plc made an operating profit of $315 million on assets employed in the business of $1,583 million.

Corporation tax is 30%.

**What value should be placed on CXM?**

## Solution

(1)  R plc is currently earning a return of 315/1,583 = 19.9%

(2)  The value spread for CXM is:

|  | $m |
|---|---|
| Company operating profit | 137.40 |
| Less | |
| Appropriate ROA × Company asset base | 61.09 |
| (19.9% × 307) | |
| Value spread | 76.31 |

(3)  Calculate the CIV:

- Find the post-tax value spread

  $76.31 × (1 - 0.3) = 53.42$

- Find the predicted post-tax value spread at $T_1$

  $53.42 × (1 + 0.034) = $55.24$

- Find the CIV by calculating the PV of the $T_1$ earnings (assuming they will continue to grow at the same rate in perpetuity)

  Since we are valuing a NOPAT earnings stream our formula is

  $E_1 / WACC$

  $CIV = 55.24 / 0.065 = $850m$

(4)  The overall value of the firm = CIV + asset base

  Firm value = $850m + $307m = $1,157m.

## Test your understanding 8

DCH plc operates in a specialised sector of the telecommunications industry. A company value is needed as part of merger talks and the CIV method has been chosen to value the intangible element of the business.

In the past year DCH plc made an operating profit of $256.8 million on an asset base of $522 million. Earnings are predicted to grow at 5% over the next few years, and the company WACC is 9%.

The average return on assets for the industry sector in which DCH plc operates is 16%

Corporation tax is 30%

**What value should be placed on the company?**

Problems with the CIV model:

- Finding a similar company in terms of industry, similar asset portfolio, similar cost gearing etc.

- Since the competitor firm presumably also has intangibles, CIV actually measures the surplus intangible value our company has over that of the competitor rather than over its own asset value.

### Lev's knowledge earnings method

An alternative method of valuing intangible assets involves isolating the earnings deemed to be related to intangible assets, and capitalising them. However it is more complex than the CIV model in how it determines the return to intangibles and the future growth assumptions made.

In practice, this model does produce results that are close to the actual traded share price, suggesting that is a good valuation technique.

However, it is often criticised as over complex given that valuations are in the end dependent on negotiation between the parties.

### Method

### (1) Calculate normalised earnings.

These are taken as a weighted average of:

- 3–5 years of past earnings (adjusted for any one-off items)

- 3–5 years of forecast earnings (based on analyst predictions or sales patterns)

  with the forecast **earnings** being given heavier weight.

**Note:** In the exam you may simply have to use current earnings as an approximation.

### (2)  Isolate the earnings driven by intangible assets.

|  | $ |
|---|---|
| Normalised earnings | X |
| Less | |
| Return on financial/monetary assets | (X) |
| ($R_f$ × monetary assets employed) | |
| Less | |
| Return on physical/tangible assets | (X) |
| (Av industry return on tangibles × tangible assets employed) | |
| | |
| **Earnings driven by intangible assets** | X |

Lev identified the expected returns on assets as the:

- financial / monetary assets – risk free rate

- tangible assets – average market return in industries primarily driven by their investment in tangible assets

- intangible assets – 6% premium on the risk free rate.

**Note:** Financial assets are cash and other assets that convert directly into *known amounts* of cash. The three basic categories are cash, marketable securities, and receivables. They are essentially current assets.

### (3)  Capitalise the intangible earnings

Rather than simply assume these earnings will grow in perpetuity as under the CIV model, Lev's model is more sophisticated. He assumes they will grow as follows:

(i)   Five years at the current rate of growth

(ii)   Declining growth year on year for the next five years

(iii)   Year eleven onwards – growing at the long term predicted growth rate.

## Expandable Text - Illustration of Lev's method

### Example:

D plc is a technology company with a high level of spending on research and development. The normalised earnings for the company have been calculated as $65 million.

D plc has $4.5 million of monetary assets and $176 million of tangible assets. It has an 8% cost of capital and a current forecast growth rate of 10%, which is expected to fall to a long run rate of 4%. The current risk free rate is 4% and the current industry average return on firms trading primarily on the basis of their tangible assets is 7%.

**Calculate the value of intangible assets using Lev's knowledge earnings method.**

### Solution

**Step 1: Calculate normalised earnings** - given as $65m

**Step 2: Isolate the earnings driven by intangible assets**

|  | $m |
|---|---|
| Normalised earnings | 65.00 |
| Less | |
| Return on financial/monetary assets | (0.18) |
| (0.04 × 4.5) | |
| Less | |
| Return on physical/tangible assets | (12.32) |
| (0.07 × 176) | |
| | ——— |
| Earnings driven by intangible assets | 52.5 |
| | ——— |

### Step 3: Capitalise the intangible earnings:

Earnings now are $52.5 million. To capitalise them we will need to first work out the growth rate to apply each year:

Year 1–Year 5 – growth 10%

Year 6–Year 10 – growth rate declines each year by a factor we will call D

Year 11 onwards – growth 4%

Therefore growth rate falls from 10% to 4% over 6 years (Year 5 to Year 11)

4% = 10% with 6 years decline

$4\% = 10\% \ (D)^6$

$$D = \sqrt[6]{\frac{4}{10}} = 0.8584 = 85.84\%$$

| | Growth rate for the year | Earnings $m | DF@ 10% (rf + 6%) | PV $m |
|---|---|---|---|---|
| Now | | 52.5 | | |
| Year 1 | 10% | 57.75 | 0.909 | 52.49 |
| Year 2 | 10% | 63.53 | 0.826 | 52.48 |
| Year 3 | 10% | 69.88 | 0.751 | 52.48 |
| Year 4 | 10% | 76.89 | 0.683 | 52.52 |
| Year 5 | 10% | 84.58 | 0.621 | 52.52 |
| Year 6 | 10% × .8584 = 8.58% | 91.84 | 0.564 | 51.80 |
| Year 7 | 8.58% × 0.8584 = 7.36% | 98.60 | 0.513 | 50.58 |
| Year 8 | 7.36% × 0.8584 = 6.32% | 104.83 | 0.467 | 48.96 |
| Year 9 | 6.32% × .8584 = 5.43% | 110.52 | 0.424 | 46.86 |
| Year 10 | 5.43% × .8584 = 4.66% | 115.67 | 0.386 | 44.65 |
| Year 11 onwards | 4.66% × 0.8584 = 4% (as we knew) | 120.30 | (1/.01) × 0.386* | 464.36 |

**Capitalised value of the intangible earnings =** **969.70**

*To find the present value of the earnings starting at $T_{11}$ we need to:

- Use the formula for earnings growing in perpetuity shown above $E_1/k$
- This will give the value of the earnings from $Y_{11}$ onwards as at $T_{10}$.
- We must then discount this value back 10 years to $T_0$ to find the present value.

The value for intangible assets is then added to the net asset value to provide an overall company valuation.

## Expandable Text - Additional example of Lev's method

F plc is a training organisation and a significant level of its value comes from the skills and knowledge of its staff. The normalised earnings for the company have been calculated as $124 million.

F plc has $7 million of monetary assets and $234 million of tangible assets. It has an 12% cost of capital. It has a current forecast growth rate of 12%, which is expected to fall to a long run rate of 6%. The current risk free rate is 5% and the current industry average return on firms trading primarily on the basis of their tangible assets is 8%.

**Calculate the value of intangible assets using Lev's knowledge earnings method.**

|  | $m |
|---|---|
| Normalised earnings | 124.00 |
| Less | |
| Return on financial/monetary assets | (0.35) |
| (0.05 × 7) | |
| Less | |
| Return on physical/tangible assets | (18.72) |
| (0.08 × 234) | |
| | ——— |
| Earnings driven by intangible assets | 104.93 |

Capitalised earnings:

Earnings now = $104.93 m. To capitalise them we will need to first work out the growth rate to apply each year:

Year 1–Year 5 – growth 12%

Year 6–Year 10 – growth rate declines each year by a factor we will call D

Year 11 onwards – growth 6%

Therefore growth rate falls from 12% to 6% over 6 years (Year 5 to Year 11)

6% = 12% with 6 years decline

$$D = \sqrt[6]{\frac{6}{12}} = 0.8909 = 89.09\%$$

| | Growth rate for the year | Earnings $m | DF @11% (rf + 6%) | PV $m |
|---|---|---|---|---|
| Now | | 104.93 | | |
| Year 1 | 12% | 117.52 | 0.901 | 105.89 |
| Year 2 | 12% | 131.62 | 0.812 | 106.88 |
| Year 3 | 12% | 147.41 | 0.731 | 107.76 |
| Year 4 | 12% | 165.10 | 0.659 | 108.80 |
| Year 5 | 12% | 184.91 | 0.593 | 109.65 |
| Year 6 | 12% × 0.8909 = 10.69% | 204.68 | 0.535 | 109.50 |
| Year 7 | 10.69% × 0.8909 = 9.52% | 224.17 | 0.482 | 108.05 |
| Year 8 | 9.52% × 0.8909 = 8.48% | 243.18 | 0.434 | 105.54 |
| Year 9 | 8.48% × 0.8909 = 7.55% | 261.54 | 0.391 | 102.26 |
| Year 10 | 7.55% × 0.8909 = 6.73% | 279.14 | 0.352 | 98.26 |
| Year 11 | 6.73% × 0.8909 = | 295.89 | (1/0.11) × 0.352* | 946.85 |
| onwards | 6% (as we knew) | | | |
| **Capitalised value of the intangible earnings =** | | | | 2,009.44 |

### Intangible asset value

*To find the present value of the earnings starting at $T_{11}$ we need to:

- Use the formula for earnings growing in perpetuity shown above $E_1$ / k.

- This will give the value of the earnings from $Y_{11}$ onwards as at $T_{10}$.

- We must then discount this value back 10 years to $T_0$ to find the present value.

The value for intangible assets is then added to the net asset value to provide an overall company valuation.

## 8 Type 2 and Type 3 acquisitions - the impact of changing risk on valuation

Valuations can be more complex in the situation where the business and/or financial risk of the acquirer will be affected by the acquisition. For example, when discounting cash flows (in the DVM approach, or FCF method) it is important to use an appropriate discount rate. Alternatively, the adjusted present value approach can be used to deal with changes in finance risk.

### Iterative approach (recursion)

An alternative method involves separating the post-acquisition cash flows into three streams depending on their level of business risk (acquirer's cashflows, target's cashflows and synergies). Then, the cashflows are discounted using an appropriate "combined firm" WACC.

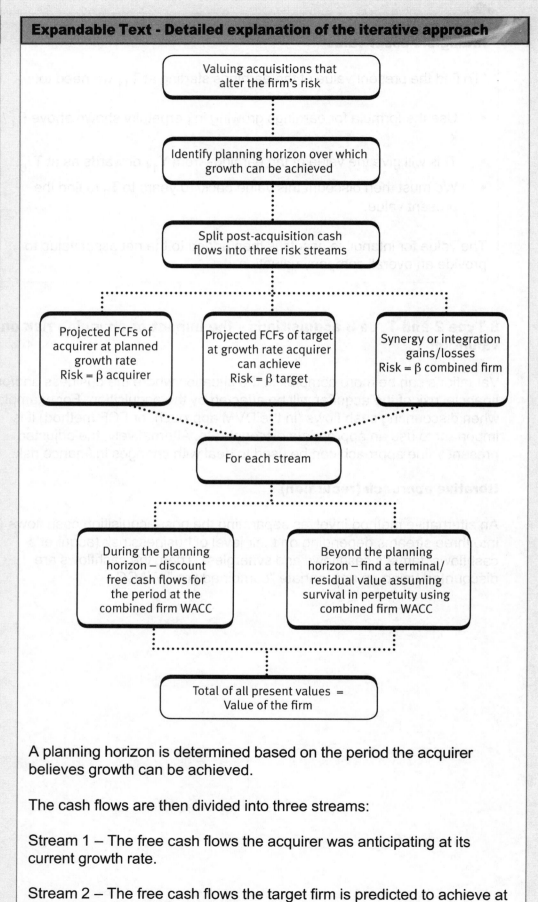

**Expandable Text - Detailed explanation of the iterative approach**

A planning horizon is determined based on the period the acquirer believes growth can be achieved.

The cash flows are then divided into three streams:

Stream 1 – The free cash flows the acquirer was anticipating at its current growth rate.

Stream 2 – The free cash flows the target firm is predicted to achieve at the post-acquisition growth rate.

Stream 3 – Any increase or decrease expected in the acquiring firms cash flows due to synergy effects or integration costs.

The risks for each stream can be represented by the asset beta for that type of business. The beta of Stream 3 presents a challenge as this will be based on the combined beta of the new firm and so a problem of circularity arises:

(1) To find a combined firm beta, the betas of each stream must be weighted using market values - i.e. the present values of that stream of cash flows

(2) To discount the stream 3 cash flows, we need the WACC of the new combined entity

(3) The WACC can only be calculated using the new combined beta

This circularity can be dealt with by using the iteration function of an Excel spreadsheet.

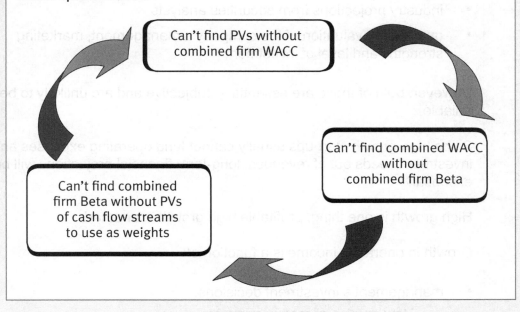

## 9 High growth start-ups

A start-up business that wishes to attract equity investment will need to put a value on the business.

Valuing start-up businesses presents a different challenge from valuing an existing business, because unlike well-established firms many start-ups have:

- little or no track record
- ongoing losses

- few concrete revenues
- unknown or untested products
- little market presence.

In addition, they are often staffed by inexperienced managers with unrealistic expectations of future profitability and the lack of past data makes prediction of future cash flows extremely difficult.

Any mathematical valuation will inevitably be only an early starting point in the negotiations.

### Expandable Text - More detail on valuation of start up businesses

**Estimating growth**

Growth for a start-up can be estimated based on:

- industry projections from securities analysts
- qualitative evaluation of the company's management, marketing strengths and level of investment.

However, both of these are essentially subjective and are unlikely to be reliable.

Since high-growth start-ups usually cannot fund operating expenses and investment needs out of revenues, long-term financial projections will be essential.

High growth is one thing, profitable high growth is another!

Growth in operating income is a function of:

- management's investment decisions:
  - How much a company reinvests.
  - The effectiveness of the investment in achieving results.
- the markets acceptance of the product and the action of competitors
- managements' skills
- the riskiness of the industry.

## Valuation methods

Since the estimate of growth is so unpredictable and initial high growth can so easily stagnate or decline, valuation methods that rely on growth estimates are of little value:

- Cash is key indicator of start-up success and asset models are therefore an important starting point.

However, they cannot provide an accurate value, since value rests more on potential than on the assets in place:

- DCF models are problematic because of the non-linear and unpredictable performance often exhibited in the early years, rendering the estimates highly speculative.

- Market based models are difficult to apply because of the problem of finding similar companies to provide a basis for comparison.

## Valuing the firm as an option

A procedure developed in 2000, attempted to value high-growth start-ups using options pricing and simulation methods.

In order to value equity as an option, the volatility of future cash flows is needed as an input to the model.

A stochastic model is created which builds in:

- expected revenue growth
- uncertainty levels
- expenditure plans
- tax impacts
- the potential for bankruptcy.

Potential cash flow patterns are then generated over a predetermined time horizon, and the volatility of the company's future cash flows predicted, to allow for the valuation of the option component of the company.

Detailed knowledge of this method is outside the syllabus.

## 10 Problems of overvaluation

A share is overvalued if it is trading at a price that is higher than its underlying value.

In an efficient market this can still occur if:

- the market doesn't properly understand the business (as with internet businesses in the late 1990s) and overestimates the expected returns

- the managers running the company do not convey full company information honestly and accurately.

### Management responses to overvaluation

Managers may be reluctant to correct the markets' mistaken perceptions. This can lead to:

- the use of creative accounting to produce the results the city is expecting

- poor business decisions aimed at giving the impression of success

- 'poor' acquisitions made using inflated equity to finance the purchase.

### The impact of overvaluation on reported earnings

Since managers may manipulate reported earnings to produce more favourable results, the financial data they supply should be treated with caution. When valuing a company the financial statements should first be analysed and adjusted as necessary.

| Expandable Text - Why firms may be overvalued |
| --- |

Empirical evidence suggests that stock markets are semi-strong efficient – i.e. equity prices reflect all publicly available information. However, this does not necessarily mean that the shares will be fairly valued:

- If the market doesn't fully understand the information available – as was the case in the late 1990s and early 2000s with some high-tech, telecommunications, and internet ventures – it tends to overestimate the potential returns and so overvalue the equity.

- The price of overvalued equity may not be corrected by the market if:

    - the data provided by managers is deliberately misleading; a particular problem where the agency relationships within companies breaks down

    - there is collusion by gatekeepers including investment and commercial banks, and audit and law firms (many of whom have been accused of knowingly contributing to the misinformation and manipulation that fed the overvaluation of stocks such as Enron and Worldcom amongst others).

## The response of management

When a firm produces earnings that beat analysts' forecasts, the share price rises by 5.5% on average. For unexpected negative earnings, the share price falls on average by 5.05%. Even where shares are fairly priced shares, managers may hide the inherent uncertainty in the business by smoothing earnings figures – delaying expenses and bringing forward revenue recognition, for example to ensure they consistently meet investor expectations.

If equity remains overpriced, the company will not be able to deliver—except by pure luck—the performance to justify its value. Where the management of an overvalued company is unwilling to accept the pain of a stock market correction, earnings smoothing can escalate into false accounting and outright lying. In addition, projects that give the appearance of potential earnings may be adopted even where the true likely outcome is a negative NPV, in order to forestall city concerns.

Research has also shown that companies are more likely to make acquisitions when their shares are overvalued. This is because they can use the shares to buy assets (which have true worth). However, these mergers often do not make good business sense and can destroy the core value of the firm.

## Case study

At the time of Enron's peak market value of $70 billion, the company was worth about $30 billion. The company was a major innovator, and the business had a viable future. However, senior managers were unwilling to see the excess valuation diminished. Rather than communicate honestly with the market to reduce its expectations, they tried to hide the overvaluation by manipulating the financial statements and over-exaggerating the value of new ventures. By the time the market had realised the extent of the problem, the core value of the company had been destroyed.

## Implications for valuations

In valuing a company, reported results form an essential core of data. Since reported earnings may be manipulated to produce more favourable results (aggressive accounting) the financial statements should be scrutinised and restated as necessary before being used as the basis for any valuation .

The detailed techniques are outside the syllabus but would include:

- Calculating the Cash to Operating Profit (COP) ratio. This involves comparing EBITDA (Earnings before Interest, Tax, Depreciation and Amortisation) with operating cash flow – they should be about equal. A figure above one is an indicator of aggressive accounting.

- Adjusting for changes in:
  - depreciation/amortisation policy
  - bad debt provisions.

- Considering whether the amortisation of intangibles and R&D is appropriate and adjusting if necessary.

- Making changes if necessary to the way operating leases and hire purchase agreements have been accounted for:
  - Removing any exceptional items.
  - Removing any exceptional payments such as directors severence payments.

## 11 Chapter overview

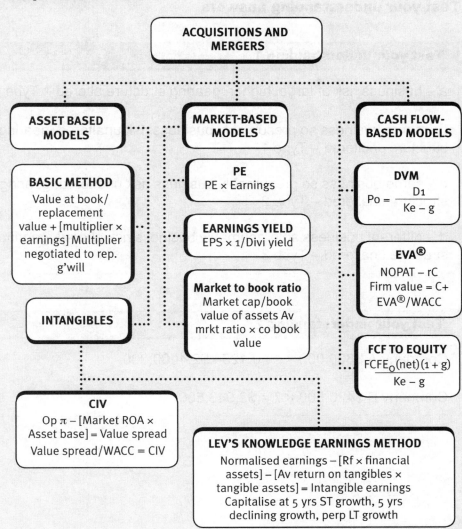

**ACQUISITIONS AND MERGERS**

**ASSET BASED MODELS**

**MARKET-BASED MODELS**

**CASH FLOW-BASED MODELS**

**BASIC METHOD**
Value at book/ replacement value + [multiplier × earnings] Multiplier negotiated to rep. g'will

**PE**
PE × Earnings

**EARNINGS YIELD**
EPS × 1/Divi yield

**Market to book ratio**
Market cap/book value of assets Av mrkt ratio × co book value

**DVM**
$$Po = \frac{D_1}{Ke - g}$$

**EVA®**
NOPAT – rC
Firm value = C+ EVA®/WACC

**INTANGIBLES**

**FCF TO EQUITY**
$$\frac{FCFE_0(net)(1 + g)}{Ke - g}$$

**CIV**
Op $\pi$ – [Market ROA × Asset base] = Value spread
Value spread/WACC = CIV

**LEV'S KNOWLEDGE EARNINGS METHOD**
Normalised earnings – [Rf × financial assets] – [Av return on tangibles × tangible assets] = Intangible earnings
Capitalise at 5 yrs ST growth, 5 yrs declining growth, perp LT growth

## Test your understanding answers

### Test your understanding 1

a – business risk of target higher, gearing structure altered – Type 3

b – same business so presumably business risk unaltered, gearing structure unaltered – Type 1

c – same business so presumably business risk unaltered, gearing structure unaltered – Type 2

d – different business so presumably business risk altered, gearing structure unaltered – Type 3

### Test your understanding 2

Company A $300,000 × 1 / 0.125= $2,4000,000

Company B $420,500 × 7 = $2,943,500

## Test your understanding 3

The minimum acceptable value to XYZ's shareholders will be the current value of the equity, i.e.

9 × $390m = **$3,510m**

However, from ABC's perspective, it is important to estimate the value created by the likely synergies as well as the basic value of XYZ. Hence:

Value of XYZ to ABC = Value of the combination − Value of ABC at the moment

This measures the likely increase in value to ABC if XYZ is acquired, so will indicate the maximum amount payable.

Therefore,

Value of XYZ to ABC =
(New PE × Total forecast earnings) − (13 × $693m)

$$= (12 × (\$693m + \$390m + \$125m)) \ − \$9,009m$$

$$= \$14,496m \ − \$9,009m = \textbf{\$5,487m}$$

In reality, following negotiations between ABC and XYZ, the final value is likely to be somewhere between these two figures.

## Test your understanding 4

Predicted value of B plc = $1,572m × 2.033 = $3,195.88m

Predicted share price = $3,195.88m/768m = 416.13¢

## Test your understanding 5

| | |
|---|---:|
| Present value of first 3 years' dividends | 0.719 |
| = 0.32 × 3 yr 16% AF = 0.32 × 2.246 | |
| Present value of growing dividend | 1.778 |
| = Value at $T_3$ × 3 yr DF = [0.32(1.04) / (0.16 - 0.04)]× 0.641 | |
| | ——— |
| Share value | $2.497 |
| | ——— |

## Test your understanding 6

| Free cash flows ($m) | Planning horizon | | | | Beyond |
|---|---|---|---|---|---|
| Year | 1 | 2 | 3 | 4 | 5 onwards |
| Sales | 540 | 572.4 | 595.3 | 607.2 | 607.2 |
| | | | | | |
| Operating profit | 54 | 57 | 71.4 | 72.9 | 72.9 |
| Tax | (16.2) | (17.1) | (21.4) | (21.9) | (21.9) |
| Depreciation | 7.0 | 8.0 | 9.0 | 10.0 | 10.0 |
| | | | | | |
| Operating cash flow | 44.8 | 47.9 | 59 | 61 | 61 |
| Replacement assets | (7.0) | (8.0) | (9.0) | (10.0) | (10.0) |
| Incremental assets (W1) | (3.2) | (1.9) | (1.4) | (0.5) | (0.0) |
| | | | | | |
| Free cash flows | 34.6 | 38 | 48.6 | 50.5 | 51 |
| PV factor | 0.870 | 0.756 | 0.658 | 0.572 | 1/0.15 × 0.572 |
| | | | | | |
| PV | 30.1 | 28.7 | 32.0 | 28.9 | 194.5 |
| Total PV | | | 314.2 | | |
| Short-term investments | | | 4.0 | | |
| | | | ___ | | |
| Value of firm | | | 318.2 | | |
| Market value of debt | | | (48.0) | | |
| | | | ___ | | |
| Value of equity | | | 270.2 | | |

W1

$8\% \times (540 - 500) = 40 \times 0.08$

$6\% \times (572.4 - 540) = 32.4 \times 0.06$

$6\% \times (595.3 - 572.4) = 22.9 \times 0.06$

$4\% \times (607.2 - 595.3) = 11.9 \times 0.04$

**Test your understanding 7**

EVA = NOPAT - rC

EVA = 798.75 - (0.1256 × 3,987.26) = $297.95 million

Firm value = C + EVA / WACC

Firm value = 3,987.26 + 297.95 / 0.1256 = $6,359.47 million

Equity = Firm value - value of debt

Equity = $6,359.47 - 954.23 = $5,405.24 million

Equity per share = 5,405,240,000 / 506,907,497= $10.66 per share.

### Test your understanding 8

(1)  The value spread for CXM is:

|  | $m |
|---|---:|
| Company operating profit | 256.80 |
| Less | |
| Appropriate ROA × Company asset base (16% × 522) | 83.52 |
| Value spread | 173.28 |

(2)  Calculate the CIV

- Find the post-tax value spread

  $173.28 × (1 - 0.3) = $121.30

- Find the predicted post-tax value spread at $T_1$

  $121.3 × (1 + 0.05) = $127.37

- Find the CIV by calculating the PV of the $T_1$ earnings (assuming they will continue to grow at the same rate in perpetuity)

  Since we are valuing a NOPAT earnings stream our formula is $E_1$ / WACC

  CIV = 127.37 / 0.09 = $1,415 million

(3)  The overall value of the firm = CIV + asset base

  Firm value = $1,415m + $522m = $1,937m

# Corporate failure and reconstruction

## Chapter learning objectives

Upon completion of this chapter you will be able to:

- describe the main indicators of financial distress

- use supplied data to calculate a Z score using Altman's model

- apply Altman's Z score model to an entity in a scenario and assess the risk of corporate failure within the short to medium term

- discuss the application of financial distress models such as the Z score to firms in emerging markets given local regulatory and financial market conditions

- discuss the limitations of corporate failure prediction models such as the Z score and explain other factors which need to be considered

- assess a company situation and assess the risk of corporate failure within the short to medium term using a range of appropriate financial evaluation methods.

- list and explain the factors which would suggest a financial reconstruction is the most appropriate strategy for dealing with the problem as presented

- assess a company situation and determine whether a financial reconstruction is the most appropriate strategy for dealing with the problem as presented

- explain the likely response of the capital market and/or individual suppliers of capital to any reconstruction scheme and the impact their response could have upon the value of a firm

- recommend a reconstruction scheme from a given business situation, justifying the proposal in terms of its impact upon the reported performance and financial position of the firm

- list, explain and evaluate the various strategies for unbundling (demerging) parts of a quoted company

- explain how the benefits of the concentration of growth and the maximisation of shareholder value may result from the unbundling of parts of a quoted company

- explain how benefits of the reduction of complexity and increased managerial efficiency may result from the unbundling of parts of a quoted company

- explain how the benefit of the release of financial resources for new investment may result from the unbundling of parts of a quoted company

- define and explain the reasons for a management buyout

- explain the issues to consider when evaluating a management buyout proposal

- explain the sources of finance available for a management buyout

- evaluate and advise on a management buyout proposal in a scenario question.

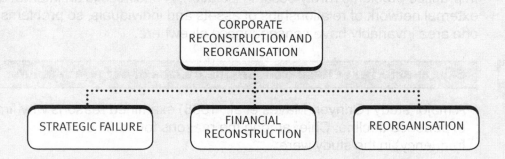

## 1 Indicators of financial distress

### What is corporate failure?

Corporate failure occurs when a company cannot achieve a satisfactory return on capital over the longer term. If unchecked, the situation is likely to lead to an inability of the company to pay its obligations as they become due.

If a company is in financial distress, corporate failure will follow unless the company's problems can be identified and corrected.

Therefore, it is important that we can recognise the main causes of financial distress.

## 2 The five core causes of financial distress

The five core causes of financial distress in a business are:

- **Revenue failure**, caused by either internal or external factors. Revenue failure may be through a loss of orders (market failure) or through the acceptance of business which does not contribute to the growth of shareholder value.

- **Cost failure**, caused by weak cost control, changes in technology, inappropriate accounting policies, inadvertent or exceptional cost burdens, poor financial management or failure of effective governance.

- **Failure in asset management,** through failure to invest in appropriate technology, poor working capital management, inappropriate write off and reinvestment or poor organisation of the available assets.

- **Failure in liability management**, through failure to manage the company's relationship with the money markets, weak control of interest rate risk and currency risk or unsustainable credit policies.

- **Failure of capital management,** through either over or under-capitalisation or poor management of the company's relationship with the capital markets and in particular the company's debt portfolio and the optimisation of its cost of capital.

In practice problems rarely occur in isolation. A business is an internal and external network of relationships of assets and individuals, so problems in one area invariably have consequences elsewhere.

### Expandable Text - Research into the causes of corporate failure

A major study (Grinyer, Mayes et al., 1988) examined reasons why firms experience decline. Chief among the reasons found (in order of frequency) in the study were:

- adverse changes in total market demand

- intensification of competition

- high cost structure

- poor financial controls

- weak management

- failure of a large project

- poor marketing effort

- poor acquisitions

- poor quality.

Clearly, some of these are not, in themselves, strategic issues. Much can be done, by strong management accounting, to reduce costs, improve financial information and controls, improve project management and quality control systems, without changing strategy. It is always worth repeating the adage that strategic management builds on good operations management. No strategy can compensate for operational inefficiency in the long run.

However, many of the items listed involve changes in the market place, and the way that competition is carried out. Strategy is chiefly about adapting the firm to such changes, and strategic failure results when the organisation does not change as quickly as the market.

KAPLAN PUBLISHING

## Expandable Text - An illustration of financial distress

### Norman English

Norman English was a mechanical engineer, who founded his own company in the early 1970s, producing automotive parts. His early successes enabled him to diversify into a wide range of component manufacturing, and eventually into assembly of unbranded products. Many households are entirely unaware that the product they identify by an expensive, foreign brand was actually made locally.

In the mid 1980s, the company was floated and attracted favourable City opinion. New investment was used to launch into several new projects, and exporting. The latter was particularly well received and, with his forthright views, made Norman English a minor spokesperson for industry. Public speaking and committee work took a great part of his time. During the 1980s, company size increased by more than five times.

By 1998, Norman was ageing, unwell, and thinking about retirement. For several years, his involvement as CEO had been somewhat peripheral, and he was aware that his middle managers spent some time fighting each other. In the past, he had seen off such problems with his forceful personality and understanding of the business. The geographical spread of the company, and the proliferation of information made it extremely hard for him to keep the issues clear in his mind.

Further, the company's financial performance was not good and dividends were low. Manufacturing plant was old, and needed replacement. Product design was also looking dated; the firm had been slow to incorporate microchip technology into its products and was increasingly forced into producing budget models with little margin.

A widely-circulated report suggested that the export initiative had never been profitable, but had consumed a great deal of capital. Nonetheless, investors and lenders wanted to feel that Norman English was still in control.

**Is this corporate failure? Give reasons for your answer. How has this arisen?**

> ### Solution
>
> Although the company has not yet failed, it would seem to be only a question of time. When we look back at the purpose of a strategy, we see that the company is under-performing in most respects. The firm has failed to adapt to the environment – it is no longer producing goods that top firms wish to be associated with. It has failed to develop its resource base, both in terms of plant and learning about the capabilities of recent technologies. It no longer has a sense of purpose about the future, rather it seems that middle and senior managers cannot even agree on how to manage the business in its present state. Finally, it has confused a strategy – exporting – with the purpose of the strategy, to produce a return on investment.
>
> The problem may have arisen in several ways, but it is likely that a formerly dramatic leader has lost his touch, leaving an absence of strategic thinking and energy. There is the added problem that the obvious solution, succession planning, leading to replacement of the CEO, would not be well received by the City. Consequently, this situation has been allowed to continue for longer than usual.

## Identifying financial distress

It is possible to identify a business in financial distress by analysing its financial statements.

Trends in profitability ratios (such as return on capital employed) and liquidity ratios (such as receivables collection period) can be used to identify the first signs of distress.

Also, declining levels of cash. or reducing Economic Value Added (EVA®) can be a sign of distress.

(read the October 2007 Student Accountant magazine article by Johnson/Bamber for more information on EVA®)

This basic understanding of financial distress has been used by Altman in his Z score model.

## The Z score – a financial technique for predicting failure

The Z score model was first developed by Altman in 1968 based on research in the USA into bankrupt manufacturing companies:

- The Z score attempts to identify financial distress and anticipate strategic and financial failure by examining company financial statements.

- The Z score is calculated using the formula:

$$\text{Z score} = 1.2X_1 + 1.4X_2 + 3.3X_3 + 0.6X_4 + 1.0X_5$$

where::

| | Ratio | Included to measure |
|---|---|---|
| $X_1$ | Working capital to total assets | Liquidity |
| $X_2$ | Retained earnings to total assets | Gearing |
| $X_3$ | Earnings before interest and tax to total assets | Productivity of the company's assets |
| $X_4$ | Market value of equity (including preference shares) to total liabilities | The extent to which the equity can decline before the liabilities exceed the assets and the company becomes insolvent |
| $X_5$ | Sales to total assets | The ability of the company's assets to generate revenue |

## Assessing the risk of failure

Once the model had been developed, further research was carried out to determine:

- The accuracy of prediction of the model. The Z score model was found to be an accurate predictor of failure for up to two years prior to bankruptcy, but that the accuracy decreases over longer periods.

- What level of Z score indicates different levels of likelihood of failure? It was found that:
  - Z score <1.81 indicates that the company is in danger and possibly heading towards bankruptcy.
  - Z score of 3 or above indicates financially sound.
  - Companies with scores between 1.81 and 2.99 need further investigation.

### Test your understanding 1 - Calculating a Z score

The following shows the balance sheet (statement of financial position) and income statement for Zed Manufacturing for the year ended 31 December 20X7:

**Summarised income statement for year ended 31 December 20X7**

|  | $m |
|---|---|
| Sales revenue | 840 |
| Cost of sales | 554 |
|  | —— |
| Gross profit | 286 |
| Selling, distribution and administration expenses | 186 |
|  | —— |
| Profit before interest | 100 |
| Interest | 6 |
|  | —— |
| Profit before tax | 94 |
| Tax | 45 |
|  | —— |
| Profit for the year | 49 |
|  | —— |

## Summarised statement of financial position (balance sheet) at 31 December 20X7

|  | $m | $m |
|---|---|---|
| **Non-current assets :** | | |
| Intangible assets | | 36 |
| Tangible assets at net book value | | 176 |
| | | 212 |
| **Current assets:** | | |
| Inventory | 237 | |
| Receivables | 105 | |
| Bank | 52 | |
| | | 394 |
| **Total assets** | | 606 |
| | | |
| **Equity** | | |
| Share capital(ordinary 50c shares) | | 100 |
| Retained earnings | | 299 |
| | | 399 |
| **Non-current liabilities:** | | |
| Long-term loans | | 74 |
| | | 473 |
| **Current liabilities:** | | |
| Payables | | 133 |
| **Total equity and liabilities** | | 606 |

The current share price is $0.80.

**Calculate the Z score and comment on the likelihood of corporate failure.**

## Expandable Text - Limitations of the Z score model

The Z score was originally developed and applied to manufacturing companies. However it was subsequently modified for use with private companies and non-manufacturing companies.

(1)  The Z score for private companies.

The most obvious reason for changing the Z score model to allow it to be used in private companies is that the original model uses stock market price data and is therefore only valid for publicly-traded companies. The revised model is based on the use of the book value of equity instead of the market value in variable $X_4$. The weightings for all five variables have then been re-estimated to give the revised calculation of the Z' score for use with private companies. The cut-off scores which indicate a problem also change (see the next section for the discussion of the assessment of risk of corporate failure).

Z' score = $0.717X_1 + 0.847X_2 + 3.107X_3 + 0.420X_4 + 0.998X_5$

(2)  Non-manufacturing companies.

Modifications were also made to estimate a score for non-manufacturing companies without the use of the sales to total assets ratio. This was done because this ratio was seen to be too industry-sensitive. This results in a Z'' score for non-manufacturing companies based on only four variables:

Z'' score = $6.56X_1 + 3.26X_2 + 6.72X_3 + 1.05X_4$

### The Z score model in emerging markets

### Investing in emerging markets

Emerging markets can be attractive to investors as there is potential for high returns. However:

- there can be significant risks in emerging markets such as lack of liquidity and transparency

- it can be difficult to compare companies across markets as there are variations in financial reporting and accounting standards

- indicators such as price/earnings ratios can be unreliable for international comparisons

- investments are susceptible to local inflation rates and exchange rate fluctuations

- the political environment can be very volatile.

### The application of the Z score model

The standard Z score can be adapted In order to provide a means of making comparisons between the value and risk of debt issues of companies in emerging markets.

- This has been done by modifying the Z score for non-manufacturing companies to remove the need to use the market value of equity and so that a negative score indicates a company which is likely to default on the debt, and then adjusting for:

  - differences in accounting treatment – the Z score is based on accounting standards in the USA

  - the likely impact of exchange rates on the individual company's ability to service its foreign currency debts

  - specific industry risk

  - the competitive position of the company in its industry

  - any specific characteristics of the debt instrument.

- The assessment then needs to take account of any characteristics of the market as a whole which will affect the risk level of the investment such as government interventions and the local financial environment, for example the local banking system.

## 3 Assessing the risk of corporate failure – other considerations

### Limitations of corporate failure prediction models

There are a number of limitations of the Z score and other similar failure prediction models:

- The score estimated is a snapshot – it gives an indication of the situation at a given point in time but does not determine whether the situation is improving or deteriorating.

- Further analysis is needed to fully understand the situation.

- Scores are only good predictors in the short term.

- Some scoring systems tend to rate companies low – that is they are likely to classify distressed firms as actually failing.

- The Z score was estimated based on manufacturing companies. Care needs to be taken when applying it to other types of companies. Modified models exist which can be used for companies in different industries.

## Test your understanding 2

A researcher has developed a model for predicting corporate failure in a service industry. The output from the model is the "F score" which is an indicator of whether the company is failing. The model is:

F score = $6.56F_1 + 1.26F_2 + 6.72F_3 + 1.05F_4$

where:

$F_1$ = earnings before interest and tax/market value of equity

$F_2$ = working capital/capital employed

$F_3$ = market value of equity/market value of debt

$F_4$ = present value to infinity of current operating free cash flow/long term debt

**Suggest reasons why these ratios have been chosen.**

## Expandable Text - Other corporate failure prediction models

### The development of other corporate failure prediction methods

A large amount of research has been carried out into corporate failure with the aim of developing an accurate model, using a range of statistical and modelling techniques. These have taken a number of different approaches and considered a range of possible variables:

- Some have attempted to estimate the probability of companies of entering a number of possible states, rather than the actual state at a point in time.

- Models have incorporated trend analysis.

- Research has also attempted to take account of variations by industry.

- Other models have included a range of different variables, such as:
  - macroeconomic variables
  - the quality of management of the company
  - the growth phase of the firm
  - the quality of the company's assets.

However it is not clear from the research that the more complicated models predict failure more accurately, and the Z score remains in common use as a predictor.

## The development of the ZETA® score

In order to address the limitations of the Z score Altman and others carried out further research and developed the ZETA® score. This is a proprietary method and only available to subscribers to the company which owns the model – therefore it is not possible to give details of the formula here. The approach taken is similar to the Z score, but the ZETA® score is based on seven variables, with the addition of an assessment of the stability of the company's earnings over a period of five to ten years, and the size of the company based on its total assets. Further research showed that the most important factors are the stability of earnings and the cumulative profitability, that is the ratio of retained earnings to total assets, also included in the Z score.

## Argenti's failure model

From historical data on a wide range of actual cases, Argenti developed a model, which is intended to predict the likelihood of company failure. The model is based on calculating scores for a company based on:

- defects of the company e.g. autocratic chief executive, passive board and lack of budgetary control .

- management mistakes e.g. overtrading (expanding faster than cash funding), gearing – high bank overdrafts/loans, failure of large project jeopardises the company.

- the symptoms of failure – deteriorating ratios, creative accounting – signs of windowdressing, declining morale and declining quality.

## Beaver

Beaver's work in 1966 demonstrated the predictive ability of the operating cash flow to total debt ratio. Beaver's key indicator of a firm's short term survival was its ability to meet its immediate interest payments.

For each of the scores there is a 'danger mark'.

## Practical indicators of financial distress

You should not think that ratio analysis of published accounts and score analysis are the only ways of spotting that a company might be running into financial distress. There are other possible indicators too. Some of this information might be given to you in an exam case study.

- Information in the published accounts, for example:
  - a worsening cash and cash equivalents position shown by the cash flow statement
  - very large contingent liabilities
  - important post balance sheet events.

- Information in the chairman's report and the directors' report (including warnings, evasions, changes in the composition of the board since last year).

- Information in the press (about the industry and the company or its competitors).

- Information about environmental or external matter. You should have a good idea as to the type of environmental or competitive factors that affect firms.

### Student Accountant article

Read Michael Pogue's July 2008 article "Business Failure" in the Student Accountant magazine for more details on the failure prediction models.

### Expandable Text - More practical indicators

### Going concern evaluation

A useful source of guidance on the troubled company is the International Standard on Auditing (ISA) 570. Of particular practical assistance is paragraph 8, which identifies possible symptoms of going concern problems. Examples are outlined below. Again, if you come across any of these features in a case study the warning bells should start to sound.

### Financial issues

- Net liability or net current liability position.

- Necessary borrowing facilities have not been agreed.

- Fixed-term borrowings approaching maturity without realistic prospects of renewal or repayment; or excessive reliance on short-term borrowings to finance long-term assets.

- Major debt repayment falling due where refinancing is necessary to the entity's continued existence.
  Major restructuring of debt.

- Indications of withdrawal of financial support by debtors and other creditors.

- Negative operating cash flows indicated by historical or prospective financial statements.

- Adverse key financial ratios.

- Substantial operating losses or significant deterioration in the value of assets used to generate cash flows.

- Arrears or discontinuance of dividends.

- Inability to pay creditors on due dates.

- Inability to comply with the terms of loan agreements.

- Change from credit to cash-on-delivery transactions with suppliers.

- Inability to obtain financing for essential new product development or other essential investments.

## Operating issues

- Loss of key management without replacement.

- Loss of key staff without replacement.

- Loss of a major market, franchise, licence, or principal supplier.

- Labour difficulties or shortages of important supplies.

- Fundamental changes in the market or technology to which the entity is unable to adapt adequately.

- Excessive dependence on a few product lines where the market is depressed.

- Technical developments which render a key product obsolete.

## Other issues

- Non-compliance with capital or other statutory requirements.

- Pending legal or regulatory proceedings against the entity that may, if successful, result in claims that are unlikely to be satisfied.

- Changes in legislation or government policy expected to adversely affect the entity.

### Test your understanding 3

**You have been asked to determine whether a company is failing. What areas would your analysis cover?**

# 4 Corporate reconstruction

## Corporate reconstruction of a failing company

Companies in financial distress often undergo corporate reconstructions to enable them to remain in business rather than go into liquidation. Corporate reconstruction in a failing company often involves raising some new capital and persuading creditors / lenders to accept some alternative to the repayment of their debts. This will ensure that the business continues in the short term.

Longer term, the management need to consider whether the reconstruction will help the company develop a sustainable competitive advantage, and provide opportunities for raising further finance.

## Options open to failing companies

Options open to failing companies not wishing to go into liquidation, and which allow space for the development of recovery plans, usually include:

- a Company Voluntary Arrangement (CVA)
- an administration order.

### Expandable Text - Reconstruction of failing companies

(1)  A Company Voluntary Arrangement (CVA)

This is a legally binding arrangement between a company and its creditors. It may involve writing off debit balances on the profit and loss account against shareholders' capital and creditors' capital and therefore affects creditors' rights. However it is designed to ensure that the return to creditors is maximised. It is useful in companies under pressure from cash flow problems.

The procedure is as follows:

- An application is made to the court, asking it to call a meeting between the company and its creditors or a class of creditor, e.g. debenture holders.

- The scheme of reconstruction is put to the meeting and a vote taken.

- If there is 75% in value and including proxies vote in favour the court will be asked to sanction it.

- If the court sanctions it, the scheme is then binding on all the creditors.

**(2) Administration orders**

Administration orders were introduced to allow space for a recovery plan to be put in place. The company, its Directors or one of the creditors can apply for an order. The company continues to trade whilst plans are put in place to rescue the company or achieve a better return for the creditors than if the company were liquidated immediately.

## The use of an administration order

Consider the case of a manufacturing company which has become insolvent. There are also indications of poor credit control, and production problems including long lead times, high defect rates and high levels of stock. However there is a growing market for the company's products which are well-designed.

The company was put into administration to allow for a recovery plan to be developed. Its debts were written down and creditors and the bank given equity in the business. New management was brought in which improved the production and financial management and turned round the company which is now profitable.

**Test your understanding 4**

**Why might the decision be made to liquidate a failing company rather than attempt to carry out a reconstruction?**

## Corporate reconstruction of a solvent company

Corporate reconstructions can also be undertaken by successful companies. The specific objectives of the reorganisation / reconstruction may be one or more of the following:

- To reduce net of tax cost of borrowing.
- To repay borrowing sooner or later.
- To improve security of finance.
- To make security in the company more attractive.
- To improve the image of the company to third parties.
- To tidy up the balance sheet.

## Options for solvent companies

There are four main types of reorganisation used by solvent companies, depending on the individual situation. These are:

- conversion of debt to equity
- conversion of equity to debt
- conversion of equity from one form to another
- conversion of debt from one form to another.

### Expandable Text - Reconstruction of solvent companies

#### 1 Conversion of debt to equity

The most likely reasons for converting debt to equity are:

- Automatically by holders of convertible debentures exercising their rights.
- In order to improve the equity base of a company. This situation is particularly likely to arise when a company has financed expansion by short-term borrowings. Sooner or later, it will run into working capital problems, and if long-term loan funds are not available (because, for example, they would make the gearing excessively high) the only solution is to issue new shares, possibly by way of a rights issue.

#### 2 Conversion of equity to debt

Conversion of equity to debt usually involves the conversion of preference shares to some form of debenture. Although through the eyes of both companies and investors there is little to choose between debentures or preference shares bearing a fixed rate of return, in the eyes of both tax and company law they are very different:

- From the tax point of view, payments to preference shareholders are dividends, and are not, therefore, an allowable charge in computing taxable profits.
- From the legal point of view, conversion of preference shares into debentures constitutes a reduction of capital. Company law provisions relating to redemption of shares must therefore be followed. In accounting terms the broad effect of these provisions is to reduce distributable profits by the nominal value of the preference shares redeemed (by transferring amounts from distributable profit to capital redemption reserve).

## 3 Conversion of equity from one form to another

This includes:

- Simplifying the capital structure. It was once common to have a variety of types of share capital, designed to appeal to a variety of investors. This has now become less favoured, and the tendency is to have only one, or at most two, classes of share capital. Conversion of shares from one type to another can only be carried out in accordance with the procedures in the articles, normally approved by a prescribed majority of the class affected, subject to rights of appeal to the court.

- Making shares more attractive to investors, for example by sub-division into smaller units, or conversion into stock.

- Eliminating reserves by issuing fully paid bonus shares. This is very much a tidying up operation, and may be especially useful to remove share premium accounts and capital redemption reserves. Additionally, in a period of inflation, it may be recognising the fact that a substantial part of the revenue reserves could never be paid out as dividends.

## 4 Conversion of debt from one form to another

This procedure might be undertaken to improve security, flexibility or cost of borrowing. For example:

- Security – Consider the example of a company financing itself out of creditors and overdraft facilities, neither of which give any security. Rather than a rights issue, converting the creditors to long-term loans, e.g. debentures, would be equally satisfactory in that it would give security as to the source of funds.

- Flexibility – Again, a company financing itself out of short-term borrowings has little room to manoeuvre. Flexibility could be improved by arranging more permanent financing. Alternatively, a company already borrowing to the limits of its ability could reduce its borrowings and improve flexibility by using other sources of finance – leasing for example.

- Cost – Some loan finance is cheaper than others for example secured loans compared with unsecured loans. An opportunity may arise to shift from a relatively high cost to a relatively low cost source of funds.

### Expandable Text - The legal aspects of corporate reconstruction

Reconstruction schemes may be undertaken in companies which are healthy or those in financial difficulties.

The boundary line between these two types of scheme is not clear cut. Some provisions of company law can be used by both types of company.

For example the capital reduction provisions of S135 in the UK Companies Act 1985 can be used by a company to tidy up its balance sheet reserves or to write off debit balances arising from trading losses so that further finance can be obtained.

## 5 Devising a corporate reconstruction scheme

### General principles in devising a scheme

In most cases the company is ailing:

- Losses have been incurred with the result that capital and long-term liabilities are out of line with the current value of the company's assets and their earning potential.

- New capital is normally desperately required to regenerate the business, but this will not be forthcoming without a restructuring of the existing capital and liabilities.

The general procedure to follow would be:

(1) Write off fictitious assets and the debit balance on profit and loss account. Revalue assets to determine their current value to the business.

(2) Determine whether the company can continue to trade without further finance or, if further finance is required, determine the amount required, in what form (shares, loan stock) and from which persons it is obtainable (typically existing shareholders and financial institutions).

(3) Given the size of the write-off required and the amount of further finance required, determine a reasonable manner in spreading the write off (the capital loss) between the various parties that have financed the company (shareholders and creditors).

(4) Agree the scheme with the various parties involved.

## The impact on stakeholders

The interests of a number of different stakeholder groups must be taken into account in a reconstruction. A reconstruction will only be successful if it manages to balance the different objectives (risk and ptential return) of:

- ordinary shareholders
- preference shareholders
- creditors, including trade payables, bankers and debenture holders

In a failing company, the reconstruction should be organised so that the main burden of any loss falls on the ordinary shareholders.

### Test your understanding 5

**Why is it important to consider the interests of shareholders in developing a reconstruction scheme?**

### Expandable Text - Different stakeholder requirements

- Solvent companies often enter reconstruction schemes to improve their ability to raise finance in the future by making security in the company more attractive or to improve the image of the company to third parties. The view taken of the scheme by banks and investors is therefore vital in ensuring that this aim is achieved.

- Banks have been criticised in the past for being too quick to close down failing companies in order to protect their investment at the expense of others – it is important that they are initially supportive and allow time for decisions about the company's future to be made with the full co-operation of all stakeholders.

- The design of a reconstruction scheme for a failing company needs to take into account the interests of:
    - ordinary shareholders
    - preference shareholders
    - creditors.

- In a failing company the main burden of the losses should be borne primarily by the ordinary shareholders, as they are last in line in repayment of capital on a winding up. In many cases, the capital loss is so great that they would receive nothing upon a liquidation of the company. They must, however, be left with some remaining stake in the company if further finance is required from them.

- Preference shares normally give holders a preferential right to repayment of capital on a winding up. Their loss should be less than that borne by ordinary shareholders. They may agree to forgo arrears of dividends in anticipation that the scheme will lead to a resumption of their dividends.

- If preference shareholders are expected to suffer some reduction in the nominal value of their capital, they may require an increase in the rate of their dividend or a share in the equity, which will give them a stake in any future profits.

- Creditors, including debenture and loan stock-holders may agree to a reduction in their claims against the company if they anticipate that full repayment would not be received on liquidation. Like preference shareholders, an incentive may be given in the form of an equity stake.

- In addition trade creditors may also agree to a reduction if they wish to protect a company which will continue to be a customer to them.

## Case study – Wire Construction plc

Wire Construction plc has suffered from losses in the last three years. Its statement of financial position (balance sheet) as at 31 December 20X1 shows:

| | £ | £ |
|---|---|---|
| **Non-current assets** | | |
| Land and buildings | | 193,246 |
| Equipment | | 60,754 |
| Investment | | 27,000 |
| | | 281,000 |
| **Current assets** | | |
| Inventory | 120,247 | |
| Receivables | 70,692 | |
| | | 190,939 |
| **Total assets** | | 471,939 |
| | | |
| **Equity and liabilities** | | |
| Ordinary shares – £1 | | 200,000 |
| 5% Cumulative preference shares – £1 | | 70,000 |
| Profit and loss | | (39,821) |
| | | 230,179 |
| **Non-current liabilities** | | |
| 8% Debenture 20X4 | | 80,000 |
| **Current liabilities** | | |
| Trade payables | 112,247 | |
| Interest payable | 12,800 | |
| Overdraft | 36,713 | |
| | | 161,760 |
| | | 471,939 |

Sales have been particularly difficult to achieve in the current year and inventory levels are very high. Interest has not been paid for two years. The debenture holders have demanded a scheme of reconstruction or the liquidation of the company.

**Required:**

Show the likely position of the key stakeholders (ordinary shareholders, preference shareholders and debenture holders) if the firm goes into liquidation. Assume that

(1)  The investment is to be sold at the current market price of £60,000.

(2)  10% of the receivables are to be written off.

(3)  The remaining assets were professionally valued as follows:

|  | £ |
| --- | --- |
| Land | 80,000 |
| Building | 80,000 |
| Equipment | 30,000 |
| Inventory and work-in-progress | 50,000 |

### Illustration 1 - Wire Construction Part 2

Continuing with the information on Wire Construction from the previous Test Your Understanding:

During a meeting of shareholders and directors, it was decided to carry out a scheme of internal reconstruction. The following scheme has been proposed:

(1)  Each ordinary share is to be re-designated as a share of 25p.

(2)  The existing 70,000 preference shares are to be exchanged for a new issue of 35,000 8% cumulative preference shares of £1 each and 140,000 ordinary shares of 25p each.

(3)  The ordinary shareholders are to accept a reduction in the nominal value of their shares from £1 to 25p, and subscribe for a new issue on the basis of 1 for 1 at a price of 30p per share.

(4)  The debenture holders are to accept 20,000 ordinary shares of 25p each in lieu of the interest payable. It is agreed that the value of the interest liability is equivalent to the nominal value of the shares issued. The interest rate is to be increased to 9½% and the repayment date deferred for three years. A further £9,000 of this 9½% debenture is to be issued and taken up by the existing holders at £90 per £100.

(5)  The profit and loss account balance is to be written off.

(6) The bank overdraft is to be repaid.

(7) It is expected that, due to the refinancing, operating profits will be earned at the rate of £50,000 pa. after depreciation but before interest and tax.

(8) Corporation tax is 21%.

**Required:**

**Prepare the statement of financial position (balance sheet) of the company, assuming that the proposed reconstruction has just been undertaken.**

**Solution**

**Tutorial note:** in a question like this, do not waste time producing a statement of financial position unless it is specifically asked for by the examiner.

Statement of financial position at 1 January 20X2 (after reconstruction)

|  | £ | £ |
|---|---|---|
| Non-current assets |  |  |
| Land at valuation |  | 80,000 |
| Building at valuation |  | 80,000 |
| Equipment at valuation |  | 30,000 |
|  |  | 190,000 |
| Current assets |  |  |
| Inventory | 50,000 |  |
| Receivables (70,692 × 90%) | 63,623 |  |
| Cash (W1) | 91,387 |  |
|  |  | 205,010 |
|  |  | 395,010 |

| | £ | £ |
|---|---|---|
| Called up share capital | | |
| Issued ordinary shares of 25p each (W2) | | 140,000 |
| Issued 8% cumulative preference shares of £1 each (W2) | | 35,000 |
| Share premium account (W2) | | 16,900 |
| Capital reconstruction account (balancing figure) | | 1,863 |
| | | ——— |
| | | 193,763 |
| Non-current liabilities: 9½% Debenture 20X7 | | 89,000 |
| Current liabilities: Trade payables | | 112,247 |
| | | ——— |
| Total equity and liabilities | | 395,010 |
| | | ——— |

**Workings**

**(W1) Cash**

| | | £ |
|---|---|---|
| | New share issue – Ords 200,000 × 30p | 60,000 |
| | New debentures - 9,000 × 90% | 8,100 |
| | Sale of investment | 60,000 |
| | | ——— |
| | | 128,100 |
| | Less: Overdraft | 36,713 |
| | | ——— |
| | | 91,387 |
| | | ——— |

### (W2) Shareholdings

|  | Ords | | Prefs | | Share premium |
|---|---|---|---|---|---|
|  | No. | £ | No. | £ | £ |
| Per balance sheet | 200,000 | 200,000 | 70,000 | 70,000 | |
| Redesignation | | 50,000 | | | |
| Exchange | 140,000 | 35,000 | (35,000) | (35,000) | |
| New issue | 200,000 | 50,000 | | | 10,000 |
| Debenture interest | 20,000 | 5,000 | | | 7,800 |
| (12,800 – 5,000) | | | | | |
| | 560,000 | 140,000 | 35,000 | 35,000 | 17,800 |
| Discount on debentures issued (10% × 9,000) | | | | | (900) |
| | | | | | 16,900 |

**Tutorial note:** as £12,800 of debenture interest is to be cancelled for £5,000 nominal of ordinary shares the excess is share premium (i.e. the consideration for the shares is deemed to be the liability removed.

### Test your understanding 7 - Wire Construction Part 3

**Advise the shareholders and debenture-holders as to whether they should support the Wire Construction plc reconstruction.**

## Expandable Text - More detail on the Wire Construction Case

### Reconstruction account, relating to the second part of the case study

**Note:** The capital reconstruction account can be proved as follows:

| | £ | | £ |
|---|---|---|---|
| Book value: | | Revised values: | |
| Non-current assets | 281,000 | Land and buildings | 160,000 |
| Inventory | 120,247 | Equipment | 30,000 |
| Receivables written off | 7,069 | Investment | 60,000 |
| | | Inventory | 50,000 |
| 10% × 70,692 | | | |
| Profit and loss balance | 39,821 | Share capital reduced | 150,000 |
| | | 200,000 × 75p | |
| Balance – Capital reserve | 1,863 | | |
| | 450,000 | | 450,000 |

### Detailed advice to shareholders and debenture holders, relating to the third part of the case study

It follows that the scheme must be favourable to the debenture-holders if it is to have success. The holders are being offered an increased rate of interest but an extended repayment date.

The expected interest cover is reasonable:

| | £ |
|---|---|
| Expected profits | 50,000 |
| Interest | |
| 9.5% × 89,000 | 8,455 |
| Interest cover = 5.9 | |

In financial terms it is a matter of comparing the prospective rate of interest with interest rates currently available elsewhere.

The preference shareholders are having half of their investment turned into equity. This is very reasonable as about half their capital would be lost on a liquidation. They will have 140,000/560,000 × 100 = 25% of the ordinary share capital. In addition they will have an increased dividend rate and are not required to contribute any further capital.

The ordinary shareholders retain part of their stake in the company if they participate 200,000/560,000 = 36% without any further cash investment. The further cash investment required of £50,000 leaves them with the majority holding.

The expected available earnings will be:

|  | £ |
|---|---|
| Profit | 50,000 |
| Interest | (8,455) |
|  | 41,545 |
| Tax at 21% | (8,724) |
|  | 32,821 |
| Preference dividend 35,000 × 8% | (2,800) |
| Available to equity | 30,021 |
| EPS 30,021/560,000 × 100 = | 5.4p |

However, as the shareholders would receive nothing on a liquidation, the additional expected return to them is twice 5.4p per share i.e.:

On old shareholding

200,000 × 5.4p

On new shareholding

200,000 × 5.4p

This therefore seems a reasonable proposition to the ordinary shareholders.

## 6 Business reorgaisation methods

### Unbundling companies

Unbundling is the process of selling off incidental non-core businesses to release funds, reduce gearing and allow management to concentrate on their chosen core businesses. The main aim is to improve shareholder wealth. Unbundling can take a number of forms:

- Spin-offs, or demergers, in which the ownership of the business does not change, but a new company is formed with shares in the new company owned by the shareholders of the original business. This results in two or more companies instead of the original one.

- Sell-offs, which involves the sale of part of the original company to a third party, usually in return for cash.

- Management buyouts, in which the management of the business acquires a substantial stake in and control of the business which they managed.

- Liquidation, when the entire business is closed down, the assets sold and the proceeds distributed to shareholders. This is done when the owners of the business no longer want it or the business is not seen as viable

The rest of this chapter explains these unbundling options in detail..

### Test your understanding 8

**Why might shareholders support the unbundling of a diversified organisation?**

### Expandable Text - Spin-offs or demergers

#### Demergers

The aim of a demerger is to create separate businesses which together have a higher value than the original company. Following a demerger:

- shareholders own the same proportion of shares in the new business or businesses as they did in the previous one

- each company owns a share of the assets of the original company

- the new company or companies generally have new management who can take the individual companies in diverging directions; and each company could eventually be sold separately

- the original company may no longer exist, with all its assets distributed to the new business.

## Expandable Text - Sell-offs

### Sell-offs

A company may sell-off parts of the business for a number of reasons, such as:

- to raise cash
- to prevent a loss-making part of the business from lowering the overall performance business
- to concentrate on the core areas of the business
- to dispose of a desirable part of the business to protect the rest from the threat of a takeover.

## Expandable Text - Management buy-outs

### What is a management buy-out?

Overall the distinguishing feature of an MBO is that a group of managers acquires effective control and substantial ownership and forms an independent business. Several variants of an MBO may be identified and are explained below:

- **Management buy-out** – where the executive managers of a business join with financing institutions to buy the business from the entity which currently owns it. The managers may put up the bulk of the finance required for the purchase.
- **Leveraged buyout** – where the purchase price is beyond the financial resources of the managers and the bulk of the acquisition is financed by loan capital provided by other investors.
- **Employee buyout** – which is similar to the above categories but all employees are offered a stake in the new business.
- **Management buy-in** – where a group of managers from outside the business make the acquisition.
- **Spin-out** – this is similar to a buyout but the parent company maintains a stake in the business.

### Example of a MBO (Springfield ReManufacturing Corporation)

One of the most well-known examples of a management buy-out is the Springfield ReManufacturing Corporation (SRC) in 1982. Prior to the buy-out the company was the Springfield, Missouri unit of International Harvester, a manufacturer of agricultural and construction equipment in the USA. The unit remanufactured components for the company's construction division.

In 1981 although the unit was profitable, International Harvester was in significant difficulties and decided it no longer needed the Springfield unit. However a group of managers led by Jack Stack, now CEO of SRC Holdings Corporation, kept the plant running and eventually bought the unit.

SRC Holdings now owns more companies, all extremely successful.

### Reasons for a management buy-out

Opportunities for MBOs may arise for several reasons:

- The existing parent company of the 'victim' firm may be in financial difficulties and therefore require cash.

- The subsidiary might not 'fit' with the parent's overall strategy, or might be too small to warrant the current management time being devoted to it.

- In the case of a loss-making part of the business, selling the subsidiary to its managers may be a cheaper alternative than putting it into liquidation, particularly when redundancy and other wind-up costs are considered.

- The victim company could be an independent firm whose private shareholders wish to sell out. This could be due to liquidity and tax factors or the lack of a family successor to fill the owner-manager role.

### Advantages of buy-outs to the disposing company

There are a number of advantages to the parent company:

- If the subsidiary is loss-making, sale to the management will often be better financially than liquidation and closure costs.

- There is a known buyer.

- Better publicity can be earned by preserving employee's jobs rather than closing the business down.

- It is better for the existing management to acquire the company rather than it possibly falling into the hands of competitors.

## Advantages to the acquiring management

The advantages to the acquiring management are that:

- it preserves their jobs

- it offers them the prospect of significant equity participation in their company

- it is quicker than starting a similar business from scratch

- they can carry out their own strategies, no longer having to seek approval from head office.

## Issues to be addressed when preparing a buy-out proposal

MBOs are not dissimilar to other acquisitions and many of the factors to be considered will be the same:

- Do the current owners wish to sell? The whole process will be much easier (and cheaper) if the current owners wish to sell. However, some buy-outs have been concluded despite initial resistance from the current owners, or in situations of bids for the victim from other would-be purchasers.

- Will the new business be profitable? Research shows that MBOs are less likely to fail than other types of new ventures, but several have collapsed. As the new owners the management team must ensure that the business will be a long-run profit generator. This will involve analysing the performance of the business and drawing up a business plan for future operations.

- If loss-making, can the new managers return it to profitability? Many loss-making firms have been returned to profitability via management buyouts. Managers of a subsidiary are in a unique position to appreciate the potential of a business and to know where cost savings can be made by cutting out 'slack'.

- What will be the impact of loss of head office support? On becoming an independent firm many of the support services may be lost. Provision will have to be made for support in areas such as finance, computing, and research and development. Although head office fees might be saved after the buyout these support services can involve considerable expense when purchased in the outside market.

- What is the quality of the management team? The success of any MBO will be greatly influenced by the quality of the management team. It is important to ensure that all functional areas are represented and that all managers are prepared to take the required risks. A united approach is important in all negotiations and a clear responsibility structure should be established within the team.

- What is the price? The price paid will be crucial in determining the long-term success of the acquisition. Care must be taken to ensure that all relevant aspects of the business are included in the package. For example, trademarks and patents may be as important as the physical assets of the firm. In a similar way responsibilities for costs such as redundancy costs must be clearly defined.

- Is the deal in the best interests of shareholders? Managers known to the existing owners may be able to secure the buyout at a favourable price, and the final price paid will be a matter for negotiation. However, the current directors of the firm have a responsibility to shareholders to obtain the best deal possible, which may mean a full 'commercial' price being paid for the victim company.

### Sources of finance for buy-outs

For small buy-outs the MBO, the price may be within the capabilities of the management team, but the acquiring group usually lack the financial resources to fund the acquisition. Several institutions specialise in providing funds for MBOs. These include:

- the clearing banks

- pension funds and insurance companies

- merchant banks

- specialist institutions such as the 3i group and Equity Capital for Industry

- government agencies and local authorities, for example regional development agencies.

### Different types of finance

The types of finance and the conditions attached vary between the institutions. Points to be considered include:

- The form of finance – Some institutions will provide equity funds. However, more commonly loan finance will be advanced. Equity funds will dilute the management team's ownership but on the other hand high gearing could put substantial strain on the firm's cash flow. Leveraged buyouts, with gearing levels up to 20:1, have been known.

- Duration of finance – Some investors will require early redemption of loans and will provide funds in the form of redeemable loan stock or preference shares. Others may accept longer-term involvement and look to an eventual public flotation as an exit from the business.

- The involvement of the institution – Some institutions may require board representation as a condition of providing funds.

- Ongoing support – The management team should also consider the institution's willingness to provide funds for later expansion plans. Some investors also offer other services such as management consultancy to their clients.

- Syndication – In large buyouts it is possible that a syndicate of institutions may be required to provide the necessary funds.

- The need for financial input from the management team – All institutions will look for a 'significant' input of finance from the management team relative to their personal wealth as a demonstration of their commitment. Managers can expect to have to plough in their redundancy payments, take second mortgages on their homes and often provide personal guarantees on loans.

- The need for a business plan – Institutional investors will also expect to see a well-prepared business plan and usually an investigating accountant and a technical advisor will be employed to investigate the proposal.

- Other sources of finance – The management team can also look for other sources of finance to assist in the MBO. Hire purchase or leasing of specific assets may ease initial cash flow problems. Government grants might be available for certain firms, and the managers' and employees' pension scheme may be available to provide some of the required finance.

## MBO terminology

The management buy-out industry has developed a range of colourful jargon terms over its period of existence, such as:

- **BIMBO** - A deal involving both a buy-in by outside managers and a buy-out by current managers has been coined a bimbo by Investors in Industry (the 3i group) and unfortunately the name has stuck. Around 50% of recent deals take this form.

- **Caps, floors and collars** are limits to which the interest rate charged in a leveraged buy-out can respectively rise, fall and range between.

- **Junk bonds** are trade-able high yielding unsecured debt certificates issued by companies in US leveraged buy-outs. Their equivalent in the UK is mezzanine finance, though this is less easily traded than junk bonds since it is not usually issued in certificate form.

- **Lemons** are deals that go wrong.

- **Plums** are successful deals.

- **The living dead** are companies which just earn enough cash to pay the interest on their borrowings, but no more. They can continue indefinitely, but are never expected to flourish.

- **A ratchet arrangement** permits managers to be allocated a larger share of the company's equity if the venture performs well. It is intended as an incentive arrangement to encourage managers to be committed to the success of the company.

## Assessing the viability of buy-outs

Both the management buy-out team and the financial backers will wish to be convinced that their proposed MBO will succeed. It is important to ask the following questions:

- Why do the current owners wish to sell? If the owners are trying to rid themselves of a loss-making subsidiary, are the new management being over-confident in believing that they can turn it round into profitability?

- Does the proposed management team cover all key functions? If not, new appointments should be made as soon as possible.

- Has a reliable business plan been drawn up, including cash flow projections, and examined by an investigating accountant?

- Is the proposed purchase price too high?

- Is the financing method viable? The trend is now away from highly geared buy-outs.

### Test your understanding 9

**Identify some advantages and disadvantages of management buy-outs.**

### Expandable Text - Numerical example of a management buy-out

Example question – Management buy-out

(a) The following information relates to the proposed financing scheme for a management buy-out of a manufacturing company.

| | % | €000 |
|---|---|---|
| Share capital held by | | |
| Management | 40 | 100 |
| Institutions | 60 | 150 |
| | | 250 |
| 10% redeemable preference shares (redeemable in ten years' time) | | 1,200 |
| | | 1,450 |
| Loans | | 700 |
| Overdraft facilities | | 700 |
| | | 2,850 |

Loans are repayable over the next five years in equal instalments. They are secured on various specific assets, including properties. Interest is 12% pa.

The manufacturing company to be acquired is at present part of a much larger organisation, which considers this segment to be no longer compatible with its main line of business. This is despite the fact that the company in question has been experiencing a turnover growth in excess of 10% pa.

The assets to be acquired have a book value of €2,250,000, but the agreed price was €2,500,000.

You are required to write a report to the buy-out team, appraising the financing scheme.

(b) What problems are likely to be encountered in assembling a financing package in a management buy-out of a service company as opposed to a manufacturing company?

## Solution

(a) **Report**

**To:** Buy-out team

**From:** Consulting accountant

**Date:** X-X-20XX

**Subject: MBO Financing Scheme**

### Overview

The financing scheme involves the purchase of assets with a net book value of €2,250,000 for an agreed price of €2,500,000. The finance that will be raised will provide funds of €2,850,000 in the form of:

|  | €000 |
|---|---|
| Equity | 250 |
| Preference shares | 1,200 |
| Loan | 700 |
| Overdraft | 700 |
|  | ——— |
|  | 2,850 |
|  | ——— |

Of the funds raised only €350,000 will be available to the business after the purchase price has been paid. This will be in the form of unused overdraft facilities.

### Gearing

As is common to MBOs the gearing level will be very high. There is only €250,000 of equity compared to €2,250,000 of debt finance (including the preference shares and excluding the unused element of the overdraft). The gearing level will mean that the returns to equity will be risky, but the buyout team own 40% of a €2.5 million company for an investment of only €100,000. The rewards are potentially very high.

One consequence of the level of gearing is that it will be difficult to raise any additional finance. There are unlikely to be any assets that are not secured, and in any case the level of interest and loan repayments would probably prohibit further borrowing.

## Cash commitments

The annual cash commitments from the financing structure are summarised below:

(i)  Loan repayments

Annual payments will have to be made in the repayment of capital and interest on the €700,000 loan. The annual amount will be:

£700,000/3.605* = €194,175

\* The cumulative discount factor for 5 years at 12%.

(ii)  Redeemable preference shares

The redeemable preference shares will be either cumulative or non-cumulative. Assuming that they are cumulative €120,000 will, on average, have to be paid every year. There is a little flexibility in that if the dividend cannot be met it can be postponed (but not avoided).

The redeemable preference shares will have to be repaid after 10 years. This can either be provided for over the 10 years, or an alternative source of finance found to replace the funds. Assuming that they will be required to be provided for according to the terms of the financing package this will require a commitment of €120,000 pa.

(iii)  Overdraft

The element of the overdraft used to finance the purchase price is effectively a source of long term finance. The rate of interest is not known but if we make the (unrealistic) assumption that it is also at 12%, then the €350,000 drawn down will cost €42,000 pa. In total there will be a commitment to pay approximately €476,000 pa.

This will be the first priority of the new company. The management team will need to generate sufficient funds from the only available source, operations, in order to meet this commitment.

### Other cash requirements

Apart from the need to generate cash to satisfy the requirements of the financing scheme the company will also need to generate funds to invest in working capital and fixed assets as required. At the moment these capital requirements are unknown. In the context of 10% annual growth in turnover, however, they might exceed the unused element of the overdraft facility.

### Institutional involvement

By virtue of their stake in the company of 60% of the equity the financial institutions hold the controlling stake. This will be enhanced by their position as the providers of the remainder of the finance. Consequently the institutions will able to determine many aspects of the company's management, including the appointment of directors. The institutions are likely to have two overriding objectives:

(i) The security of loan and interest repayments. Any breach of the loan arrangements might trigger the appointment of administrators or receivers, and the institutions' investment would almost certainly be lost.

(ii) Realising their equity investment. The institutional investors will probably expect to realise their investment in a relatively short time frame. This is commonly set at between 5 and 7 years.

### Profit growth

Apart from the requirement to generate cash as noted above the company must also generate steady profit growth. The institutional investors will require a history of profit growth in order to enable the sale of their stake through either flotation or a trade sale.

### Conclusion

The financing scheme will place a heavy cash burden on the company, particularly in the early years. The involvement of the institutions will perhaps prove unwelcome, but the MBO would be impossible without accepting it.

(b) There are three main problems particular to arranging a finance package for a service company.

(i) The lack of tangible assets

Because MBOs normally have to be highly geared there is a requirement to provide security for the loans in a package. Service companies commonly have a very low level of tangible assets. It will therefore be difficult to attract much debt finance.

(ii) 'People' businesses

The success of service companies depends on their staff. Institutions tend to view such success with suspicion because people, unlike plant and machinery, can resign. Unless the people in question are tied into the company within the MBO financing package by, for example, insisting on their investing in equity there is little guarantee that they will stay with the company.

(iii) Working capital

The nature of most service businesses is that they have unusually high working capital requirements. The main expense for a service company is staff costs. It is almost impossible to take extended credit from staff without losing their services. The supplies of service companies often involve a long period of work before customers can be billed. Consequently, a finance package would have to provide for the working capital, and working capital finance is particularly risky because it is difficult to secure and so may be equally difficult to raise.

### Expandable Text - Evaluating the benefits of reorganisations

## Concentration of growth and maximisation of shareholder value

Following the unbundling of a company the resulting value of the new businesses can exceed that of the original business. This suggests that the shares in the original business were selling for less than their potential value and can be for a number of reasons:

- The splitting-off of non-core activities from the rest of the business may increase the visibility of an under-valued asset which is then valued more highly by the market.

- Businesses may be valued more highly in the hands of the new managers than under the previous management.

- The sale of less profitable parts of the business may be viewed favourably by the market, result in an increased valuation for the remainder.

- The performance of the individual businesses may improve, also resulting in a higher valuation.

## Reduction in complexity and improved managerial efficiency

Since the 1980s, increasing numbers of demergers and sell-offs have taken place in order to reduce the complexity of the organisation:

- Diversified businesses are complex to manage. As the pace of change and uncertainty facing organisations has increased, the complexity of large businesses becomes more difficult to cope with and absorbs management time and energy which is diverted from the business itself.

- Smaller companies tend to be more flexible and respond more easily to change.

- Following a demerger, the new companies have a clearer, more focused management structure.

- Improved managerial effectiveness also results from the splitting off of non-core businesses as managers are free to concentrate on what they do best.

- Changes in the market can also mean that benefits of synergy no longer exist, and there is no longer any business reason for the organisation to retain unrelated businesses.

### The release of financial resources for new investment

Unbundling parts of the company can also release financial resources:

- selling a loss-making part of the business which is absorbing funds can release cash to invest in the core businesses or new activities

- a reduction in the size and complexity of the organisation can reduce the central management costs, freeing up resources

- unbundling generates a lump sum in proceeds which can be invested in a specific project

### Illustration

In October 2006 GUS plc, a major UK retail and business services conglomerate, completed the process of demerger into three separate businesses. Burberry, a luxury brand, was demerged first, and the remaining company was demerged in October 2006 into Experian, a provider of analysis and information services, and Home Retail Group, a major home and general retailer.

This demerger was the culmination of a strategy to maximise shareholder wealth by focusing on a small number of high-growth businesses. Other parts of the business were sold off to raise funds for reinvestment. Among the reasons given for the demerger were:

- the lack of synergy between the businesses

- separate opportunities for investment for shareholders

- allowing the independent businesses to pursue individual strategies and benefit from a better management focus.

## 7 Chapter summary

```
                    ┌─────────────────────┐
                    │     CORPORATE       │
                    │ RECONSTRUCTION AND  │
                    │   REORGANISATION    │
                    └─────────────────────┘
```

### STRATEGIC FAILURE

- Causes
- Predicting failure
- Responses

### FINANCIAL RECONSTRUCTION

- Appropriate situations
- Impact on suppliers of capital
- Development of schemes

### REORGANISATION

- Demergers
- MBOs

## Test your understanding answers

### Test your understanding 1 - Calculating a Z score

- Working capital = 394 - 133 = $261 million
- Total assets = $606 million
- Retained earnings = $299 million
- Earnings before interest and tax = $100 million
- Market value of equity = $0.80 × 200 million shares = $160 million
- Total liabilities = 133 + 74 = $207
- Sales revenue = $840 million

Z score is:

1.2 × (261/606) + 1.4 × (299/606) + 3.3 × (100/606) + 0.6 × (160/207) + 1.0 × (840/606)

= 0.52 + 0.69 + 0.54 + 0.46 + 1.38

= 3.59.

This score is above 3, indicating that the company is financially sound. However it is still a relatively low score, and should be monitored carefully.

### Test your understanding 2

$F_1$ is a measure of the return on equity as an indicator of profitability. The continued existence of the business is dependent on the earning power of its assets.

$F_2$ is a measure of liquidity. A decrease in liquidity is characteristic of a failing company.

$F_3$ is a measure of the gearing of the company. High levels of debt will result in a low value for this ratio.

$F_4$ will indicate the company's ability to service its debt.

## Test your understanding 3

The analysis is likely to include:

- The calculation of score based on a corporate failure prediction model such as the Z score, with a trend over several years.

- An analysis of key ratios, including trends.

- Changes in the cash flow of the business.

- An analysis of the company report to identify any significant changes over the year.

- An assessment of the environment facing the company and any opportunities and threats.

- An assessment of the strengths and weaknesses of the company.

## Test your understanding 4

Possible reasons include:

- The main reason for the company's failure is that there is no longer a market for its products.

- The level of assets is so low that there is no chance of covering any of the company's debts.

- The management of the company and the creditors are not prepared to co-operate with one another, making it impossible to agree a way forward.

## Test your understanding 5

The shareholders are important for the future financing of the business. If they are not happy with the scheme or don't retain a stake in the business they will not invest in the company in the future.

However, the ordinary shareholders have the most to gain if the company performs well, so it is only fair that if the company is failing, they should bear the greatest loss.

Balancing these two factors is key to the success of the reconstruction.

## Test your understanding 6 - Wire Construction Case Study Part 1

### Position of interested parties in a liquidation (assuming assets can be sold at going concern value)

|  | £ | £ |
|---|---|---|
| Value of non-current assets |  | 190,000 |
| Inventory |  | 50,000 |
| Receivables |  | 63,623 |
| Assets available |  | 303,623 |
| Secured debts |  |  |
| Debentures |  | (80,000) |
|  |  | 223,623 |
| Other payables |  |  |
| Overdraft | 36,713 |  |
| Interest | 12,800 |  |
| Trade payables | 112,247 |  |
|  |  | 161,760 |
| Available to preference shareholders |  | 61,863 |

The above statement of assets reflects the position of the three interested parties with no reconstruction scheme. The debenture holders would be sure of their capital repayment on a liquidation and most probably the arrears of interest. The preference shareholders would get part (how much depends on the difference between going concern and break up values of the assets). Ordinary shareholders would get nothing.

## Test your understanding 7 - Wire Construction Part 3

### Ordinary shareholders

Before the reconstruction, the ordinary shareholders own 100% of the control and voting rights in the company. After the reconstruction, their control will be diluted to 71.4% (400,000 shares out of a total of 560,000) assuming they take up their rights.

These shareholders may be unwilling to take up their rights given that the company is failing, but clearly if the company cannot raise any new finance it will slide into liquidation and the shareholders will receive no return (shown in the first part of this case).

This should be the key consideration of the ordinary shareholders: if they don't accept the reconstruction, they may well end up with nothing. Accepting the reconstruction will mean that they keep control of the company and will benefit in the future if the company's performance improves.

On balance it appears that the scheme is acceptable to the shareholders.

### Preference shareholders

Before the reconstruction, the preference shareholders are guaranteed a return of £3,500 per year (5% x 70,000 £1 shares).

Initially they may well be unhappy about exchanging this income stream for a new proposal of 8% on 35,000 £1 shares (i.e. £2,800), but there are two other factors which make the scheme more appealing on further examination:

- the preference shareholders will also own some ordinary shares, so that if the company's performance improves, they will receive more dividends (and capital growth) from these shares in the future.

- as mentioned above with the ordinary shareholders, the risk is that if the company goes into liquidation, the shareholders will receive a lower than hoped for return. (Admittedly the preference shareholders' position is slightly less risky than the ordinary shareholders' position, but some risk remains).

Again, on balance, it seems that the scheme is acceptable to the preference shareholders.

## Debenture holders

The debenture holders' patience is wearing thin: no interest has been paid for two years, so the debenture holders could apply to the courts to liquidate the company, in which case (according to part one of this case study) they would receive a full settlement of all that is owed to them.. However, in a liquidation there is no guarantee that the debenture holders would get back all that is owed to them (assets may not be worth as much as was first thought), so a reconstruction may well be more appealing.

The terms of this reconstruction seem quite favourable to the debenture holders. Despite having to forgo interest in the short term , the debenture holders are being offered:

- ordinary shares - i.e. the chance of capital growth and dividends in the longer term if the company's performance improves.

- higher longer term interest rates (9.5% per annum will be paid until 20X7 rather than 8% until 20X4 as at present)

- extra debentures offered at a discount, so redemption will bring a capital gain here.

Providing the debenture holders are not struggling for cash in the short term, the scheme should be appealing to them in the long term. If the debenture holders do have a preference for short term income, a liquidation may be abetter option, since we have forecast that they will receive all their money back.

### Test your understanding 8

- There is potential for improved performance leading to increased shareholder value.

- There may be an increase in the total value of the investment.

- Selling off unrelated or loss-making businesses may improve financial performance.

- There is an opportunity to choose how much to invest in particular parts of the business.

**Test your understanding 9**

Advantages:

- Although the risks are high so are the potential rewards. In the situation of leveraged buyouts, where the bulk of the equity is in the hands of the management team, the returns to shareholders once the loans have been covered can be very large.

- They are usually considered to be less risky than starting a new business from scratch.

- Firms that have been subject to MBOs tend to operate at a higher level of efficiency. The traditional divorce between ownership and control is effectively ended and managers (and shareholding employees) have great incentive to improve the efficiency of the firm.

Disadvantages:

- They are risky (approximately one in ten fail) and can involve managers losing their personal wealth as well as their jobs.

- Problems will be encountered when the new company becomes independent. For example, head office support services will be lost, and existing customers may go elsewhere if they see the new firm being too risky.

# Risk management

## Chapter learning objectives

Upon completion of this chapter you will be able to:

- describe capital investment monitoring and risk management systems and analyse the factors which would influence the extent to which they could be established in a firm

- suggest appropriate capital investment monitoring and risk management systems in a scenario question

- define and distinguish between risk mitigation, hedging and diversification strategies

- discuss the factors which would influence the choice of risk mitigation, hedging and diversification strategies in the development of a framework for risk management

- suggest an appropriate framework for risk management in a scenario question

- describe political risk, explain how it can be measured and evaluate the strategies available to mitigate it

- describe and evaluate economic risk and describe the strategies available to mitigate it

- describe regulatory risk and describe the strategies available to mitigate it

- describe fiscal risk and describe the strategies available to mitigate it

- assess the exposure of a given firm to political, economic, regulatory and fiscal risk and suggest strategies for its mitigation

- describe the operation of the derivatives market

- explain the relative advantages and disadvantages of exchange traded versus OTC agreements

- in the context of the derivatives market explain the characteristics and relevance of standard contracts, tick sizes, margin requirements and margin trading

- explain the methods of incorporating risk in an investment appraisal, such as expected values, simulation, sensitivity analysis, and CAPM
- explain the concept of Value at Risk (VaR) and calculate the VaR at a given confidence level.

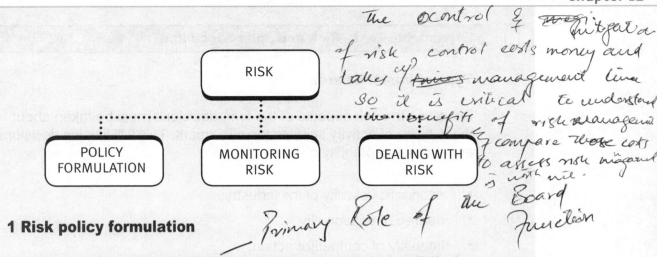

*The control & mitigation of risk control costs money and takes up management time so it is critical to understand the benefits of risk management & compare those costs to assess risk management is worthwhile.*

*Board Function*

# 1 Risk policy formulation

*Primary Role of the*

An important part of the financial manager's role and responsibility is considering how risk is to be managed.

Paper P1 covered managing and controlling risk in some detail. This section initially introduces an overview of risk management in relation to capital investment projects, then explains some specific examples of risks. More detailed techniques for risk management, such as the use of derivatives and Value at Risk (VaR), are covered later in the chapter.

## Risk and stakeholder conflict

- Shareholders will invest in companies with a risk profile that matches that required for their portfolio.

- Management should thus be wary of altering the risk profile of the business without shareholder support.

- An increase in risk will bring about an increase in the required return and may lead to current shareholders selling their shares and so depressing the share price.

- Inevitably management will have their own attitude to risk. Unlike the well-diversified shareholders, the directors are likely to be heavily dependent on the success of the company for their own financial stability and be more risk averse as a consequence.

## Risk and policy decisions

The financial manager will need to make policy decisions in the following areas:

- Type of business area
- Operating gearing
- Financial gearing
- Accuracy of forecasts

## Expandable Text - Risk and policy decisions

### Type of business area

Based on the risk appetite of the firm, decisions must be taken about those types of activity suitable for investment. This will involve decisions about the acceptability of:

- economic volatility of the industry
- degree of seasonality
- intensity of competitor action.

### Operating gearing

The level of operating gearing of the firm is the proportion of fixed costs to variable in the cost structure. Whilst some industries are destined to have higher levels of operating gearing than others (compare the travel industry with manufacturing for example), policy decisions about what level is acceptable will drive choices about factors such as:

- outsourcing v. providing internally
- leasing v. buying
- full-time staff v. freelance providers.

### Financial gearing

More fully discussed elsewhere, increasing debt levels can reduce the cost of finance but increases the risks of bankruptcy as the same time. Directors must decide what level of gearing they are prepared to accept.

### Accuracy of forecasts

The success of any planned investment programme will rely heavily on the accuracy of forecasts of future cash flows (in and out) and an NPV assessment also relies on an accurate calculation of the discount rate. The sensitivity of these forecasts can be calculated, and the probability of the variation assessed, but in the end the directors must decide what level of risk they are willing to accept in order to accept or reject the project.

## 2 The risk framework

All projects are risky. When a capital investment programme commences, a framework for dealing with this risk must be in place.

This framework must cover:

- risk awareness
- risk assessment and monitoring
- risk management (i.e.strategies for dealing with risk and planned responses should unprotected risks materialise)

### Risk awareness

In appraising most investment projects, reliance will be placed on a large number of estimates. For all material estimates, a formal risk assessment should be carried out to identify:

- potential risks that could affect the forecast
- the probability that such a risk would occur.

Risks may be:

- strategic
- tactical
- operational.

Once the potential risks have been identified, a monitoring process will be needed to alert management if they arise.

| Expandable Text - Different types of risk |
| --- |

Strategic risks are those affecting the overall direction and outcome of the project, such as changes in macroeconomic factors or changes in corporate policies.

Tactical risks affect the way the various parts of the project are interlinked, the way resources are acquired or the way in which the business functions involved in the project are run.

Operational risks are those affecting the day to day running of the project.

> ### Test your understanding 1
>
> **Suggest strategic, tactical and operational risks that would affect the estimates on a typical investment project.**

## Risk assessment and monitoring

A useful way to manage risk is to identify potential risks (usually done in either brainstorming meetings or by using external consultants) and then categorise them according to the likelihood of occurrence and the significance of their potential impact.

Decisions about how to manage the risk are then based on the assessment made.

These assessments may be time consuming and the executive will need to decide:

- how they should be carried out
- what criteria to apply to the categorisation process and
- how often the assessments should be updated.

The essence of risk is that the returns are uncertain. As time passes, so the various uncertain events on which the forecasts are based will occur. Management must monitor the events as they unfold, reforecast predicted results and take action as necessary. The degree and frequency of the monitoring process will depend on the significance of the risk to the project's outcome.

> ### Expandable Text - Specific risk assmt & monitoring methods
>
> #### Internal audit
>
> Many companies set up internal audit departments to assist them in their responsibility to monitor and manage risk.
>
> It is not the job of the internal audit department to monitor results and perform risk assessments, but they can provide valuable support in the creation and successful running of such monitoring systems.

## Information systems

Information systems play a key part in effective risk monitoring. Once risk factors have been identified, information systems must be put in place to ensure that any changes affecting project estimates are:

- recorded
- brought to the attention of the responsible manager
- dealt with in an appropriate way.

This will usually include:

- management information systems (MIS)
- executive information systems (EIS).

These systems are expensive to set up and the executive team must decide on the extent to which they wish to use them and the scope required.

The difference between them is:

- Management information systems – feeding back operational data to allow for action to prevent or mitigate risk.
- Executive information systems – bringing senior executives up-to-date with external information such as competitor action, currency fluctuations and economic forecasts as well as providing summarised operational data.

## 3 Risk management

### Strategies for dealing with risk

Risk can be either accepted or dealt with. Possible solutions for dealing with risk include:

- mitigating the risk – reducing it by setting in place control procedures
- hedging the risk – taking action to ensure a certain outcome
- diversification – reducing the impact of one outcome by having a portfolio of different ongoing projects.

## Expandable Text - More on mitigation, hedging and diversification

### Mitigation

- All companies should have in place a comprehensive system of controls. These controls play an essential role in good corporate governance and mitigate risk by working to prevent, or detect and correct potential risks before they become a problem.

- Management would be expected to implement controls over most material risks subject to the following:
  - The cost of the control should not be disproportionate to the potential loss.
  - For non-routine events it may be more practical to devise a specific strategy for dealing with the risk should it arise.

Controls are covered extensively in Papers F8 and P1.

### Hedging the risk

- Hedging is a strategy, usually some form of transaction, designed to minimise exposure to an unwanted business risk, commonly arising from fluctuations in exchange rates, commodity prices, interest rates etc.

- It will often involve the purchase or sale of a derivative security (such as options or futures) in order to reduce or neutralise all or some portion of the risk of holding another security. This is dealt with in detail later in this chapter.

- A perfect hedge will eliminate the prospects of any future gains or losses and put the company into a risk-free position in respect of the hedged risk.

- This strategy may be chosen where the downside risk would have serious negative consequences for the firm, and the costs of hedging (including the chance to participate in any upside) are outweighed by the benefits of certainty.

### Diversification

- This involves reducing the impact of one outcome by having a portfolio of different ongoing projects.

- Within the context of a single project, this may take the form of selling to a number of different customers to reduce reliance on a single one or sourcing from a number of different suppliers.

- For businesses operating internationally, it may involve locating key parts of the business in different countries.

- Diversification would be chosen wherever reliance on a single source of resource has been identified as a potential risk.

## Expandable Text - The 4T approach to risk management

A company can adopt four possible approaches to a risk, known as the **4T** approach:

- Tolerate it.
- Transfer it.
- Terminate it.
- Treat it (i.e. by mitigating it, hedging or diversifying).

Potential risks are often categorised according to the likelihood of occurrence and the significance of their potential impact. An appropriate response can then be adopted. This method was covered in Paper P1 and is summarised here:

|  |  | Impact/consequence | |
|---|---|---|---|
|  |  | Low | High |
| Likelihood | High | Treat | Terminate |
| Likelihood | Low | Tolerate | Transfer |

Appropriate responses would be matched to the risk as shown above.

### Tolerate

Accept that the risk might occur but do not put in place any systems to manage it. For example, a power failure may cause a serious production stoppage but few firms would consider acquiring a back-up generator. However a call centre, heavily reliant on its computer system, may decide that it would be worthwhile.

## Transfer

The risk is passed on elsewhere. This can be achieved by activities such as:

- insuring against the risk (for example against the risk of fire)
- taking out fixed price contracts (such as with construction companies or suppliers)
- outsourcing production (buying in from a range of providers rather than relying on own production.

## Terminate

This can mean deciding against the activity altogether, but in the context of a project, would mean identifying at what point it would be better to 'bail out' rather than proceed with the project – i.e. when the NPV of the revised future cash flows is negative.

## Treat

A risk is treated when controls are in place to reduce either:

- the likelihood or
- the consequences

of the event occurring.

### Illustration of the 4T approach

A leisure company has just approved a large-scale investment project for the development of a new sports centre and grounds in a major city. The forecast NPV is approximately $6m, assuming a time horizon of five years steady growth in business and constant returns in perpetuity thereafter.

(a) What would the company need to do, to ensure that the risks associated with the project were properly managed?

(b) A number of specific risks have been identified:

   (1) **A potential lawsuit may be brought for death or injury of a member of the public using the equipment. No such event has ever occurred in the company's other centres.**

   (2) **The loss of several weeks' revenue from pool closure for repairs following the appearance of cracks in the infrastructure. This has occurred in several of the other centres in the past few years.**

   (3) **Income fraud as a result of high levels of cash receipts.**

   (4) **Loss of playing field revenue from schools and colleges because of poor weather.**

**Suggest how these risks could be best managed.**

**Solution**

(a)

   (i) Risk awareness – The potential risks associated with the project at strategic, tactical and operational levels should be identified. The fact that the company has carried out such projects before should make this task relatively straightforward.

   (ii) Risk monitoring – Information systems should be put into place to ensure that all material risk factors are continuously monitored. The impact of any changes likely to the affect the success of the project can then be identified and action taken as necessary. The forecast growth and return figures are undoubtedly critical to the success of the project and the underlying assumptions such as economic predictions, local demographics, competitor activity and recreational trends should be carefully monitored and assessed.

   (iii) Risk management – Risks identified can be categorised according to the likelihood of occurrence and the significance of the impact, in order to decide how best to manage them.

(b) The identified risks could be mapped as shown below:

| | Impact/consequence | |
|---|---|---|
| | **Low** | **High** |
| **High** (Likelihood) | **3** Fraud – Treat | **2** Pool closure – Can't terminate so have to prevent |
| **Low** (Likelihood) | **4** Weather – Tolerate | **1** Lawsuit – Transfer |

(1) The risk of a lawsuit should be dealt with my taking out indemnity insurance. The risk is then transferred to the insurance company.

(2) The risk of pool closure is serious and since a provision of a pool is clearly essential for the sports centre, the risk must be treated instead. This would mean putting in place a series of controls over the building process to prevent later cracks from occurring.

(3) The risk of fraud is exactly the type of risk that a good internal control system would be designed to prevent.

(4) Bad weather will always be a risk when dealing with outdoor activities and is probably best accepted and the lost revenues factored into the initial forecasts.

## 4 Specific types of risk

### Political risk

Political risk is the risk that a company will suffer a loss as a result of the actions taken by the government or people of a country. It arises from the potential conflict between corporate goals and the national aspirations of the host country.

This is obviously a particular problem for companies operating internationally, as they face political risk in several countries at the same time.

## Expandable Text - Sources, measurement & mgmnt: political risk

### Sources of political risk

Whilst governments want to encourage development and growth there are also anxious to prevent the exploitation of their countries by multinationals.

Whilst at one extreme, assets might be destroyed as the result of war or expropriation, the most likely problems concern changes to the rules on the remittance of cash out of the host country to the holding company.

**Exchange control regulations,** which are generally more restrictive in less developed countries for example:

- rationing the supply of foreign currencies which restricts residents from buying goods abroad
- banning the payment of dividends to foreign shareholders such as holding companies in multinationals, who will then have the problem of blocked funds.

**Import quotas** to limit the quantity of goods that subsidiaries can buy from its holding company to sell in its domestic market.

**Import tariffs** could make imports (from the holding company) more expensive than domestically produced goods.

**Insist on a minimum shareholding,** i.e. that some equity in the company is offered to resident investors.

**Company structure** may be dictated by the host government – requiring, for example, all investments to be in the form of joint ventures with host country companies.

### Discriminatory actions

**Super-taxes** imposed on foreign firms, set higher than those imposed on local businesses with the aim of giving local firms an advantage. They may even be deliberately set at such a high level as to prevent the business from being profitable.

**Restricted access to local borrowings** by restricting or even barring foreign-owned enterprises from the cheapest forms of finance from local banks and development funds. Some countries ration all access for foreign investments to local sources of funds, to force the company to import foreign currency into the country.

**Expropriating assets** whereby the host country government seizes foreign property in the national interest. It is recognised in international law as the right of sovereign states provided that **prompt consideration at fair market value in a convertible currency** is given. Problems arise over the exact meaning of the terms prompt and fair, the choice of currency, and the action available to a company not happy with the compensation offered.

## Measurement of political risk

When considering measurement, distinctions are sometimes made between macro and micro political risk.

Micro political risks are ones that are specific to an industry, company or project within a host country. For example, the tobacco industry has faced increasing global opposition since the 1970s, nowhere more so than in the USA. There are increasing threats that tobacco will be classified as a drug and that companies supplying tobacco may face continuing litigation. This has been a consequence of a change in the social and political climate in the USA and elsewhere.

By contrast Iraq at the moment presents political risks for almost any organisation who may wish to operate there in terms of the threat of loss of assets or personnel. This therefore represents macro political risk.

Different methods may be appropriate to measuring different types of risk. Traditional methods for assessing political risk range from comparative techniques such as rating and mapping systems to the analytical techniques of special reports, expert systems and probability determination, through to use of econometric techniques of model building. More recently, option-pricing techniques (using real options) have been applied to the evaluation of political risk associated with foreign direct investment.

Some examples of methods used to measure political risk are indicated below:

- 'Old hands' – Experts on the country provide advice upon the risk of investment in a specific country. Experts may include those with existing businesses, academics, diplomats or journalists. The value of the advice depends on how directly it can be applied to the investment under consideration.

- 'Grand tours' – The home firm may send a selection of employees to the potential investment country to act as an inspection team. The employees meet government officials, business people and local leaders to gain an understanding of the country first hand. However, this technique is generally considered inferior to the use of advice from well established experts as outlined above.

- Surveys – Commercially produced country political risk indices are available. These are produced by groups of experts using Delphi techniques via the ranking of key risk variables. The experts individually answer a comprehensive questionnaire. Their answers are then collected, aggregated and returned to the experts, who have the chance to change their minds having seen the answers of their peers.

- Quantitative measures – Measures such as GNP and ethnic fractionalisation are combined to give countries an overall score.

Commercially produced indices are available such as the business environment risk index (BERI). This index gives each country a score out of 100, anything below 41 indicating unacceptable business conditions.

The economist political risk Service (PRS) also allocates 100 points with 33 going to economic factors such as falling per capita GDP, high inflation, capital flight, decline in productivity and raw materials as a percentage of exports. Fifty points go to political factors such as bad neighbours, authoritarianism, staleness, illegitimacy, generals in power, war/armed insurrection. Finally 17 points relate to social factors such as urbanisation, corruption and ethnic tension.

Often some form of sensitivity or simulation analysis is incorporated to examine the effect of different possible scenarios.

A general risk index offers a cost effective overview of potential investment climates but cannot take account of the variations in risk on individual projects. It should also be borne in mind that the scoring systems are essentially subjective.

## Management of political risk

There are a number of ways of managing the political risk associated with an investment.

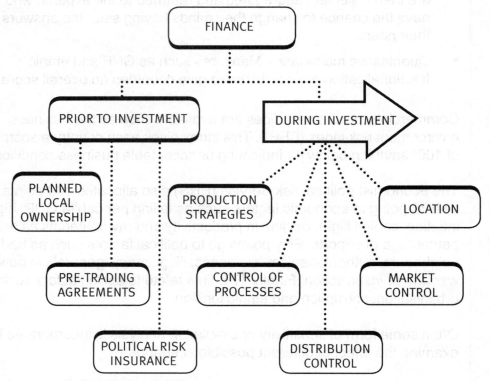

- **Planned local ownership**

  Target dates can be set on which proportions of company ownership will pass to the local nationals. These should be spread into the long term so that local authorities can see the eventual benefits that will be gained through allowing successful foreign investments.

- **Pre-trading/concession agreements**

  Prior to making the investments, agreements should be secured with the local government or other authority regarding rights, responsibilities, remittance of funds and local equity investments. This attempts to solve anticipated problems and prevent misunderstandings at some later date.

  The biggest problem with this policy is that host governments in developing countries are very volatile; consequently, agreements made with previous administrations can be repudiated by the new government.

Wells (1977) argues that the terms of concession agreements will normally change even with the same host government as:

The terms and conditions required to entice a company to invest in a particular country are different from the terms and conditions required to a company remain, once it has committed and developed its investment. (Remember sunk costs)

If the multinational is more successful than both parties anticipated in the beginning of the investment, thus the government may want their share of the windfall.

The agreement will cover transfer of capital, transfer of remittances, transfer of products, access to local capital markets, transfer pricing, taxation and social and economic obligations.

- **Political risk insurance**

  It may be possible to transfer the risk by taking out insurance. In the UK, the export credits guarantee department (ECGD) provides protection against various threats including expropriation and nationalisation, currency inconvertibility, war and revolution.

### During investment

Political risk can be managed on a continuous basis through consideration of the following areas:

- **Production strategies**

  The decision here is to find the balance between:

  - contracting out to local sources (local sourcing) and losing control
  - producing directly in the host country (increasing investment in host country)
  - importing from outside the host country (foreign sourcing).

  By using local materials and labour it becomes in the interest of the country for the company to succeed. However, following success the locals may then have the knowledge to continue operations alone. Chrysler in Peru imported 50% of components from abroad and thus avoided expropriation of its plant because the plant was worthless without the foreign sourced Chrysler parts.

- **Control of patents and processes**

  Coca Cola is a prime example of how control of patents reduces political risk. The secret ingredient in Coca Cola has never been divulged. Therefore, Coca Cola can quite happily set up bottling plants worldwide, as the plants are worthless to any host government as they would not be able to create 'the taste of Coca Cola'. Patents can be enforced internationally.

- **Distribution control**

  Control and development of such items as pipelines and shipping facilities will deter expropriation of assets.

- **Market control**

  Securing markets through copywriting, patents and trademarks deters political intervention as the local markets come to depend on 'protected' goods.

- **Location**

  Oil companies frequently mine oil in a politically unstable area but refine it in western Europe. Expropriation of assets would not therefore benefit the less stable countries.

### Financing decisions

Political risk may be mitigated by choosing the right location for raising funds:

- **Local finance**

  As the foreign investment grows, further finance can be raised locally to maintain the authorities' interest in the success of the business – any damaging intervention would also damage the local institutions. Also the wealthier locals who provide this finance often have considerable power. As a result there is less likelihood of others expropriating the assets. However, the cost of such funds may be relatively more expensive and many governments restrict the ability of multinational to borrow from local money and capital markets.

- **Borrow worldwide**

  A multinational also has the option of financing worldwide, using institutions from several countries. This discourages expropriation because if the host government intervenes in the company's operations, default on the loans may cause a diplomatic backlash from a number of countries, not just the multinational's own parent country. However, it is important to take account of the new risks associated with, for example, foreign exchange and tax, that may be introduced where funds are borrowed overseas.

## Economic risk

Economic risk is the variations in the value of the business (i.e. the present value of future cash flows) due to unexpected changes in exchange rates. It is the long-term version of transaction risk which is covered in detail in the hedging chapters.

In a broader sense, economic risk can also be defined as the risk facing organisations from changes in economic conditions, such as economic growth or recession, government spending policy and taxation policy, unemployment levels and international trading conditions.

It affects:

- the affordability of exports and therefore competitiveness
- the affordability of imports and therefore profitability
- the value of repatriated profits.

### Expandable Text - Examples and management of economic risk

Economic risk is the possibility that the value of the company (the present value of all future post-tax cash flows) will change due to unexpected changes in future exchange rates. The size of the risk is difficult to measure as exchange rates can change significantly and unexpectedly. Such changes can affect firms in many ways:

- Consider the example of a US firm, which operates a subsidiary in a country that unexpectedly devalues its currency. This could be 'bad news' in that every local currency unit of profit earned would now be worth less when repatriated to the US. On the other hand it could be 'good news' as the subsidiary might now find it far easier to export to the rest of the world and hence significantly increase its contribution to parent company cash flow. The news could, alternatively, be neutral if the subsidiary intended to retain its profits to reinvest in the same country abroad.

- An exporter may suffer different forms of economic risk:

**Direct:** If the firm's home currency strengthens, foreign competitors are able to gain sales at their expense because their products become more expensive (unless the firm reduces margins) in the eyes of customers both abroad and at home.

**Indirect:** Even if the home currency does not move vis-à-vis the customers' currency the firm may lose competitive position. For example, suppose a South African firm is selling into Hong Kong and its main competitor is a New Zealand firm. If the New Zealand dollar weakens against the Hong Kong dollar, the South African firm has lost some competitive position.

Although economic exposure is difficult to measure it is of vital importance to firms as it concerns their long-run viability. Economic exposure is really the long-run equivalent of transaction exposure, and ignoring it could lead to reductions in the firm's future cash flows or an increase in the systematic risk of the firm, resulting in a fall in shareholder wealth.

## Managing economic risk

Note that the recommended methods of mitigating economic exposure, are also suggested as ways of mitigating political exposure:

- Diversification of production and supply.
- Diversification of financing.

If a firm manufactures all its products in one country and that country's exchange rate strengthens, then the firm will find it increasingly difficult to export to the rest of the world. Its future cash flows and therefore its present value would diminish.

However, if it had established production plants worldwide and bought its components worldwide (a policy which is practised by many multinationals, e.g. Ford) it is unlikely that the currencies of all its operations would revalue at the same time. It would therefore find that, although it was losing exports from some of its manufacturing locations, this would not be the case in all of them. Also if it had arranged to buy its raw materials worldwide it would find that a strengthening home currency would result in a fall in its input costs and this would compensate for lost sales.

**Diversification of financing**

When borrowing internationally, firms must be aware of foreign exchange risk. When, for example, a firm borrows in Swiss francs it must pay back in the same currency. If the Swiss franc then strengthens against the home currency this can make interest and principal repayments far more expensive. However, if borrowing is spread across many currencies it is unlikely they will all strengthen at the same time and therefore risks can be reduced. Borrowing in foreign currency is only truly justified if returns will then be earned in that currency to finance repayment and interest.

International borrowing can also be used to hedge off the adverse economic effects of local currency devaluations. If a firm expects to lose from devaluations of the currencies in which its subsidiaries operate it can hedge off this exposure by arranging to borrow in the weakening currency. Any losses on operations will then be offset by cheaper financing costs.

## Regulatory risk

Regulatory risk is the potential for laws related to a given industry, country, or type of security to change and affect:

- how the business as a whole can operate
- the viability of planned or ongoing investments.

Regulations might apply to:

- businesses generally (for example, competition laws and anti-monopoly regulations)
- specific industries (for example, catering and health and safety regulations, publishing and copyright laws).

**Expandable Text - Managing regulatory risk**

Managing regulatory risk

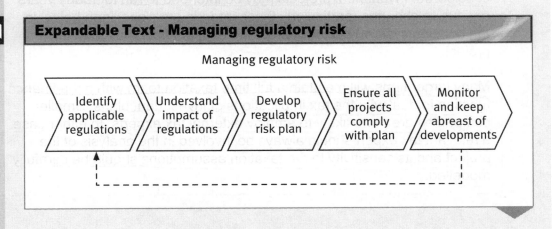

Whilst larger companies may have the resources to set up a permanent regulatory team, smaller firms may:

- incorporate the role within the internal audit department
- consult a firm specialising in regulatory risk.

In practice, research suggests that many firms do not commit sufficient resources to this area and are exposed to a high degree of regulatory risk.

Associated with regulatory risk is compliance risk.

Compliance risk is the risk of losses, such as fines or even temporary closure, resulting from non-compliance with laws or regulations.

Measures to ensure compliance with rules and regulations should be an integral part of an organisation's internal control system.

## Fiscal risk

Fiscal risk from a corporate perspective is the risk that the government will have an increased need to raise revenues and will increase taxes, or alter taxation policy accordingly. Changes in taxation will affect the present value of investment projects and thereby the value of the company.

### Expandable Text - Managing fiscal risk

The primary requirement of a fiscal risk management strategy is an awareness of the huge impact tax can make to the viability of a project. Tax should be factored in to the calculations for all significant investment appraisal projects.

It is important not only to ensure that the tax rules being applied are up-to-date, but that any potential changes in the tax rules are also considered. Investment projects may be intended to run for many years and future changes (particularly those intended to close 'loop holes' in the taxation system) could wipe out the expected benefits from the project.

Many larger firms will maintain a full time taxation team within the finance function to deal with the tax implications of investment plans. Smaller companies are more likely to employ external tax experts. In either case, a relevant tax expert should always be involved in the analysis of the project and its sensitivity to the taxation assumptions should be carefully modelled.

### Test your understanding 2

M plc is a mineral extraction company based in the UK but with plants based in many countries worldwide. Following recent discovery of mineral reserves in Mahastan in Central Asia, M plc has acquired a licence to extract the minerals from the recently elected Mahastani government and plans to commence work on the plant there within the next six months.

In the past ten years, Mahastan has seen significant unrest, following the deposing of the previous dictator in a military coup. However, the recent election of the newly fledged democracy is hoped to be the beginning of a new era of stability in the region. The currency of Mahastan is the puto. It is not traded internationally and the preferred currency for international business is the US dollar. There are currently no double tax treaties between Mahastan and the rest of the world, but the prime minister has signalled his intention to develop them within his first term of office to encourage inward investment.

**Assess the exposure of M plc to political, economic, regulatory and fiscal risk and suggest how these risks may be mitigated.**

## Other types of risk

It is important to read the financial press to keep abreast of recent developments in risk management.

Risk management is a constantly evolving process. Financial managers need to understand the threats from emerging risks such as:

- global terrorist risk

- computer virus risks

- spreadsheet risk - for example, Fannie Mae's $1 billion-plus underestimate of total stockholder equity in 2003 was the result of errors in a spreadsheet used in the implementation of a new accounting standard.

Policies will need to be kept up to date, so that these newer risks are managed properly.

## 5 Incorporating risk into investment appraisal

### Overview of methods

The input variables in an investment appraisal are all estimates of likely future outcomes. There are several methods of incorporating risk into an investment appraisal, for example:

- expected values
- use of the CAPM model to derive a discount rate
- sensitivity analysis, and simulation

These methods have all been covered in detail in paper F9.

## 6 Value at Risk (VaR)

### The meaning of VaR

**Value at risk (VaR)** is a measure of how the market value of an asset or of a portfolio of assets is likely to decrease over a certain time, the **holding period** (usually one to ten days), under 'normal' market conditions.

VaR is measured by using normal distribution theory.

It is typically used by security houses or investment banks to measure the market risk of their asset portfolios.

VaR = amount at risk to be lost from an investment under usual conditions over a given holding period, at a particular "confidence level".

Confidence levels are usually set at 95% or 99%,

i.e. for a 95% confidence level, the VaR will give the amount that has a 5% chance of being lost.

**Illustration 1**

A bank has estimated that the expected value of its portfolio in two weeks' time will be $50 million, with a standard deviation of $4.85 million.

**Using a 95% confidence level, identify the value at risk.**

**Solution**

A 95% confidence level will identify the reduced value of the portfolio that has a 5% chance of occurring.

From the normal distribution tables, 1.65 is the normal distribution value for a one-tailed 5% probability level. Since the value is below the mean, −1.65 will be needed.

$z = (x - \mu)/\sigma$

$(x - 50)/4.85 = -1.65$

$x = (-1.65 \times 4.85) + 50 = 42$

There is thus a 5% probability that the portfolio value will fall to $42 million or below.

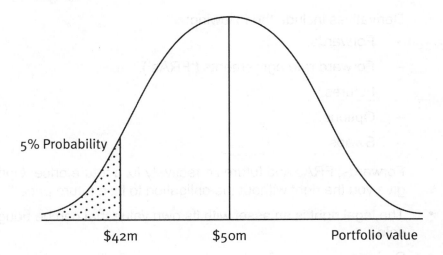

5% Probability

$42m        $50m        Portfolio value

A bank can try to control the risk in its asset portfolio by setting target maximum limits for value at risk over different time periods (one day, one week, one month, three months, and so on).

**Test your understanding 3**

A bank has estimated that the expected value of its portfolio in 10 days' time will be $30 million, with a standard deviation of $3.29 million.

**Using a 99% confidence level, identify the value at risk.**

## 7 Introduction to hedging methods

### The use of derivative products

Hedging methods relating to currency risk and interest rate risk are covered in separate later chapters. Many of the hedging methods use "derivatives" (e.g. futures contracts) to reduce the firm's exposure to risk.

This section introduces some basic terms relating to derivatives.

### Expandable Text - The operation of the derivatives market

- A derivative is an asset whose performance (and hence value) is derived from the behaviour of the value of an underlying asset (the 'underlying').

- The most common underlyings are commodities (e.g. tea, pork bellies), shares, bonds, share indices, currencies and interest rates.

- Derivatives are contracts that give the right and sometimes the obligation, to buy or sell a quantity of the underlying or benefit in some other way from a rise or fall in the value of the underlying.

- Derivatives include the following:
    - Forwards.
    - Forward rate agreements ('FRAs').
    - Futures.
    - Options.
    - Swaps.

- Forwards, FRAs and futures effectively fix a future price. Options give you the right without the obligation to fix a future price.

- The legal right is an asset with its own value that can be bought or sold.

- Derivatives are not fixed in volume of supply like normal equity or bond markets. Their existence and creation depends on the existence of counter-parties, market participants willing to take alternative views on the outcome of the same event.

- Some derivatives (esp. futures and options) are traded on exchanges where contracts are standardised and completion guaranteed by the exchange. Such contracts will have values and prices quoted. Exchange-traded instruments are of a standard size thus ensuring that they are marketable.

- Other transactions are over the counter ('OTC'), where a financial intermediary puts together a product tailored precisely to the needs of the client. It is here where valuation issues and credit risk may arise.

## Futures contracts

### Introduction

- A futures contract is an exchange traded forward agreement to buy or sell an underlying asset at some future date for an agreed price.

- There are two ways of closing a position:
  - Deliver the underlying on the maturity date – RARE.

  - If futures contracts have been bought, then equivalent contracts can be sold before maturity, resulting in the company having a net profit or loss (and no obligation to deliver).

- Hedging is achieved by combining a futures transaction with a market transaction at the prevailing spot rate.

### Illustration 2 - TAL

TAL Inc is a sugar grower looking to **sell** 3,000 tonnes of white sugar in August and wants to fix the price via futures.

Suppose that the quoted futures price today on LIFFE for white sugar for August delivery is $221.20 per tonne and that each contract is for 50 tonnes.

TAL would agree to **sell** 60 futures contracts at a price of $221.20.

Suppose the market price in August (on the final day of the contract) has risen to $230. The futures price would also equal $230.

TAL thus has two transactions:

- TAL would sell their sugar in the open market (i.e. not via the futures contract) for $230/tonne.
- Separately TAL would buy 60 futures contracts for August delivery for $230 per tonne, making a loss on the futures of $8.8 per tonne.

This gives an overall (fixed) net receipt of $221.2 per tonne.

**Note:** Futures do not always give a perfect hedge because of

(1) Basis risk – see below.
(2) The size of contracts not matching the commercial transaction.

### Tick sizes

- A 'tick' is the standardised minimum price movement of a futures or options contract.

- Ticks are useful for calculating the profit or loss on a contract.

**Illustration 3 - TAL continued**

For the sugar futures contract in the above example, a tick is $0.01 per tonne. Given that a contract is for 50 tonnes, each tick is worth $0.50 per contract.

The overall movement of $8.80 per tonne would be expressed as 880 ticks.

The total loss on the contracts would thus be:

60 contracts × 880 ticks × $0.50 per tick = $26,400

As detailed below, this amount would not be collected in one amount when the position is closed but instead daily 'marking to market' occurs.

### Margins

A potential problem of dealing in futures is that having made a profit, the other party 'to the contract' has therefore made a loss and defaults on paying you your profit. This is termed 'counter party credit risk'.

- However the buyer and seller of a contract do not transact with each other directly but via members of the market.

- Therefore the markets Clearing House is the formal counter party to every transaction.

- This effectively reduces counter party default risk for those dealing in futures.

- As the Clearing House is acting as guarantor for all deals it needs to protect itself against this enormous potential credit risk. It does so by operating a margining system, i.e. an initial margin and the daily variation margins.

### The initial margin

- When a futures position is opened the Clearing House requires that an initial margin be placed on deposit in a margin account to act as a security against possible default.

- The objective of the initial margin is to cover any possible losses made from the first days trading.

chapter 12

*   The size of the initial margin depends on the future market, the level of volatility of the interest rates and the risk of default.

*   For example, the initial margin on a £500,000 '3 month sterling contract' traded on LIFFE is £750, i.e. £750/£500,000 = .0015%.

*   Some investors use futures for speculation rather than hedging. The margin system allows for highly leveraged 'bets'.

**The variation margin**

*   At the end of each day the Clearing House calculates the daily profit or loss on the futures position. This is known as 'marking to market'.

*   The daily profit or loss is added or subtracted to the margin account balance. The margin account balance is usually maintained at the initial margin.

*   Therefore if a loss is made on the first day the losing party must deposit funds the following morning in the margin account to cover the loss.

*   An inability to pay a daily loss causes default and the contract is closed, thus protecting the Clearing House from the possibility that the party might accumulate further losses without providing cash to cover them.

*   A profit is added to the margin account balance and may be withdrawn the next day.

**Test your understanding 4**

Peter Ng is a wealthy speculator who believes that oil prices will fall over the next three months. Oil futures are quoted with the following details:

*   Futures price for 3 month delivery = $68.20.
*   Contract size = 1,000 barrels.
*   Tick size = 1 cent per barrel.
*   Initial margin = 10% of contract.

Peter decides to set his level of speculation at 10 contracts.

(a) **Compute Peter's initial margin.**
(b) **Calculate the cash flow the next day if the futures price moves to $68.35.**

KAPLAN PUBLISHING                                                                              431

## 8 Chapter summary

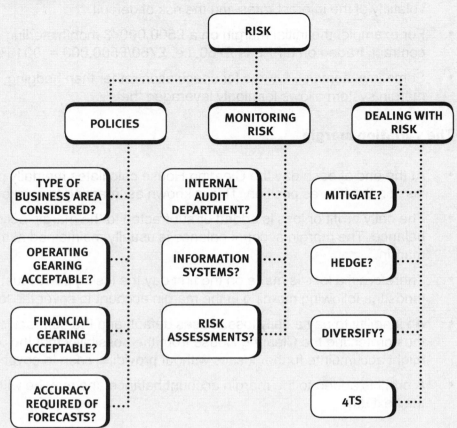

# Test your understanding answers

## Test your understanding 1

Strategic:

- brand awareness in the new sector
- risk of recession
- political changes

Tactical – changes to forecasts based on:

- supply chain changes
- major payment timings
- intended sales of machinery
- contractor overruns on time or amounts spent.

Operational – changes occurring because:

- production breakdown
- breakdown of the supply chain
- failure of the distribution network
- failure to recruit staff with the necessary skills.

### Test your understanding 2

**Political risks**

Possible ramifications would include:

- revocation of the licence

- significant increase in the licence fee

- company subject to regulations designed to prevent the company taking profits earned from the country:
  - imposition of punitive taxes
  - restrictive exchange controls.

- seizure of control of the plant

- expropriation of the extracted minerals

- total disruption to operations from further coup attempts.

**Economic risks**

In terms of exchange risk, the primary risk will be caused by changes in value between UK sterling and the US dollar. Although some payments (such as employee wages) will presumably be made in putos and M plc will therefore be subject to some risk associated with fluctuations between the puto and the dollar, it is unlikely to have any significant impact on the long term viability of the project.

**Regulatory risk**

As M plc are based in the UK, which can be expected to have a fairly stringent set of regulations covering mineral extraction, it is not anticipated that the Mahastan project will present any significant specific regulatory risk.

However, new regulations imposed on all foreign companies operating in Mahastan may come into force once the new government finds its feet. This could affect the ability of the company to operate effectively.

**Fiscal risk**

The uncertainty over the double tax position is an obvious risk for M plc. In addition, the country's tax legislation may not be well established and may be changed as the prime minister looks to encourage investment.

**Risk mitigation**

The recent political instability in Mahastan and the newness of the government, make this investment a very high-risk project.

*Political risk*

M plc already have a licence for the extraction of the minerals. They could attempt to negotiate further terms surrounding matters as diverse as levels of price increases, transfer of capital, transfer of remittances, transfer of products, access to local capital markets, transfer pricing, taxation and social and economic obligations.

However no matter what is negotiated the risk that the agreement will be not be honoured by this government (or subsequent ones should it fail) remains high.

The political risks can be best mitigated by gaining the goodwill of the community and ensuring that the wealth generated by the mineral extraction is not perceived to be entirely the preserve of M plc. Solutions may include:

- employing local workers where possible
- paying fair wages
- considering joint ventures with local companies over some parts of the construction or extraction processes
- investing some part of the profits in local opportunities.

It may be worth considering political risk insurance. However where the risk is so high the premiums may be prohibitive.

*Economic risk*

Since M plc has an international presence, the economic risk of the project will already be mitigated by their diversification. However, if many of the areas in which it operates also trade in dollars then the benefits are reduced. Consideration should also be given to financing using dollar-based loans.

*Regulatory risk*

The risk that onerous regulations may be imposed on M plc cannot be easily avoided. The methods of mitigating political risk mentioned above, would also apply here, although they are unlikely to help with regulations aimed at all organisations.

M plc must ensure that they consistently monitor the changing regulatory environment and consider the impact on their firm. As the government is keen to encourage inward investment, it would be worth attempting to identify key ministers and open up lines of communication with them. Being viewed as an important stakeholder may mean that M plc is consulted on major regulatory changes before they are implemented.

*Fiscal risk*

Given the considerable uncertainty, fiscal risk may be best managed by assuming worst case tax treatment (based on current information) and only accepting the project if the NPV is still positive. Again constant monitoring of the situation and reforecasting as necessary will also be required.

**Test your understanding 3**

A 99% confidence level will identify the reduced value of the portfolio that has a 1% chance of occurring.

From the normal distribution tables, 2.33 is the normal distribution value for a one-tailed 1% probability level. Since the value is below the mean – 2.33 will be needed.

$z = (x - \mu)/\sigma$

$(x - 30)/3.29 = -2.33$

$x = (-2.33 \times 3.29) + 30 = 22.3$

There is thus a 1% probability that the portfolio value will fall to $22.3 million or below.

**Test your understanding 4**

(a)  Initial margin = 10% × 10 contracts × 1,000 barrels × $68.20 = $68,200.

(b)  Price has increased so Peter will make a loss of $0.15 per barrel or 15 ticks. This equates to a total loss (which will need to be paid into the exchange) of

Loss = 10 contracts × 15 ticks × $10 per tick = $1,500.

# Hedging foreign exchange risk

## Chapter learning objectives

Upon completion of this chapter you will be able to:

* explain the characteristics of the following and calculate the financial position after their use as hedging tools:
  - forward contracts
  - money market hedges
  - exchange-traded currency futures contracts
  - FOREX swaps
  - currency swaps
  - currency options

* explain the characteristics of synthetic foreign exchange agreements (SAFE's)

* explain how bilateral and multilateral netting and matching tools work to minimise FOREX transactions costs and manage the market barriers to the free movement of capital and other remittances

* calculate the required payments for a party to a bilateral or multilateral net settlement system.

Many aspects of forex risk management were met in F9. These are recapped briefly for completeness. In P4 the range of techniques considered is extended.

```
┌─────────────────────┐
│   HEDGING FOREIGN   │
│   EXCHANGE RISK     │
└─────────────────────┘
```

**Techniques/instruments**

- Forward contracts, including synthetic foreign exchange agreements (SAFEs)
- Money market hedges
- Futures
- Forex swaps
- Currency swaps
- Currency options
- Netting and matching agreements

## 1 Introduction
### Types of forex risk

Firms may be exposed to three types of foreign exchange risk:

### Transaction risk

- The risk of an exchange rate changing between the transaction date and the subsequent settlement date on an individual transaction.

- i.e. it is the gain or loss arising on conversion.

- Associated with exports/imports.

- Hedge using a variety of financial products/methods – see below.

### Economic risk

- Includes the longer-term effects of changes in exchange rates on the market value of a company (PV of future cash flows).

- Looks at how changes in exchange rates affect competitiveness, directly or indirectly.

- Reduce by geographic diversification.

## Translation risk

- How changes in exchange rates affect the translated value of foreign assets and liabilities (e.g. foreign subsidiaries).
- Can hedge by borrowing in local currency to fund investment.
- Gains/losses usually unrealised so many firms do not hedge.

### Expandable Text - Types of foreign exchange risk

**Transaction risk**

Is the risk of an exchange rate changing between the transaction date and the subsequent settlement date, i.e. it is the gain or loss arising on conversion.

This type of risk is primarily associated with imports and exports.  If a company exports goods on credit then it has a figure for  debtors in its accounts. The amount it will finally receive depends  on the foreign exchange movement from the transaction date  to the settlement date.

As transaction risk has a potential impact on the cash flows of a company, most companies choose to hedge against such exposure. Measuring and monitoring transaction risk is normally an important component of treasury management.

The degree of exposure involved, which is dependent on:

(a) The size of the transaction, is it material?

(b) The hedge period, the time period before the expected cash flows occurs.

(c) The anticipated volatility of the exchange rates during the hedge period.

The corporate risk management policy should state what degree of exposure is acceptable. This will probably be dependent on whether the Treasury Department is been established as a cost or profit centre.

**Economic risk**

Transaction exposure focuses on relatively short-term cash flows effects; economic exposure encompasses these plus the longer-term affects of changes in exchange rates on the market value of a company. Basically this means a change in the present value of the future after tax cash flows due to changes in exchange rates.

There are two ways in which a company is exposed to economic risk.

*Directly:* If your firm's home currency strengthens then foreign competitors are able to gain sales at your expense because your products have become more expensive (or you have reduced your margins) in the eyes of customers both abroad and at home.

*Indirectly:* Even if your home currency does not move vis-à-vis your customer's currency you may lose competitive position. For example suppose a South African firm is selling into Hong Kong and its main competitor is a New Zealand firm. If the New Zealand dollar weakens against the Hong Kong dollar the South African firm has lost some competitive position.

Economic risk is difficult to quantify but a favoured strategy is to diversify internationally, in terms of sales, location of production facilities, raw materials and financing. Such diversification is likely to significantly reduce the impact of economic exposure relative to a purely domestic company, and provide much greater flexibility to react to real exchange rate changes.

---

**Tutorial note: Borrowing in a foreign currency**

In addition, when companies borrow in a foreign currency, committing themselves to regular interest payments and principal repayments they are exposing themselves to forex risk. This is a problem that beset a number of Far Eastern companies in the late 1990s. They had borrowed in US dollars or sterling. This became a serious problem when their currency depreciated and the loan repayments became much more expensive. Of course if your firm takes out a loan in dollars and your home currency appreciates against the dollar the loan repayments become cheaper.

---

## Translation risk

The financial statements of overseas subsidiaries are usually translated into the home currency in order that they can be consolidated into the group's financial statements. Note that this is purely a paper-based exercise – it is the translation not the conversion of real money from one currency to another.

The reported performance of an overseas subsidiary in home-based currency terms can be severely distorted if there has been a significant foreign exchange movement.

If initially the exchange rate is given by $/£1.00 and an American subsidiary is worth $500,000, then the UK parent company will anticipate a balance sheet value of £500,000 for the subsidiary. A depreciation of the US dollar to $/£2.00 would result in only £250,000 being translated.'

Unless managers believe that the company's share price will fall as a result of showing a translation exposure loss in the company's accounts, translation exposure will not normally be hedged. The company's share price, in an efficient market, should only react to exposure that is likely to have an impact on cash flows.

## Hedging transaction risk – the internal techniques

Internal techniques to manage/reduce forex exposure should always be considered before external methods on cost grounds. Internal techniques include the following:

### Invoice in home currency

- One easy way is to insist that all foreign customers pay in your home currency and that your company pays for all imports in your home currency.

- However the exchange-rate risk has not gone away, it has just been passed onto the customer. Your customer may not be too happy with your strategy and simply look for an alternative supplier.

- Achievable if you are in a monopoly position, however in a competitive environment this is an unrealistic approach.

### Leading and lagging

- If an importer (payment) expects that the currency it is due to pay will depreciate, it may attempt to delay payment. This may be achieved by agreement or by exceeding credit terms.

- If an exporter (receipt) expects that the currency it is due to receive will depreciate over the next three months it may try to obtain payment immediately. This may be achieved by offering a discount for immediate payment.

- The problem lies in guessing which way the exchange rate will move.

## Matching

- When a company has receipts and payments in the same foreign currency due at the same time, it can simply match them against each other.

- It is then only necessary to deal on the forex markets for the unmatched portion of the total transactions.

- An extension of the matching idea is setting up a foreign currency bank account.

- Bilateral and multilateral netting and matching tools are discussed in more detail later in the chapter.

## Decide to do nothing?

- The company would 'win some, lose some'.

- Theory suggests that, in the long run, gains and losses net off to leave a similar result to that if hedged.

- In the short run, however, losses may be significant.

- One additional advantage of this policy is the savings in transaction costs.

## 2 Forward contracts

### Characteristics

- The forward market is where you can buy and sell a currency, at a fixed future date for a predetermined rate, i.e. the forward rate of exchange.

### Test your understanding 1

An Australian firm has just bought some machinery from a US supplier for US$250,000 with payment due in 3 months time. Exchange rates are quoted as follows:

| Spot (US$ /A$) | 0.7785 – 0.7891 |
|---|---|
| Three months forward | 0.21 – 0.18 cents premium |

**Determine the amount payable if a forward contract is used.**

KAPLAN PUBLISHING

## Availability and use

- Although other forms of hedging are available, forward cover represents the most frequently employed method of hedging.

- However, the existence and depth of forward markets depends on the level of demand for each particular currency.

- In the exam you need to consider; does the forward market exist and would it extend far enough into the future before you recommend it.

- For major trading currency like the $, £, Yen or Euro it can be up to 10 years forward. Normally forward markets extend six months into the future. Forward markets do not exist for the so-called exotic currencies.

## Advantages and disadvantages

| Advantages | Disadvantages |
|---|---|
| • OTC, so can be matched exactly to the future sums involved. <br><br> • Simple and easy to understand. | • Availability – see above. <br><br> • Binding contract for delivery, even if commercial circumstances change – e.g. a customer is late paying. <br><br> • Eliminates exposure to upside as well as down-side movements. |

### Expandable Text - Synthetic foreign exchange agreements

### Synthetic foreign exchange agreements (SAFE's)

- Some governments have banned forward FX trading – usually as a means to reduce exchange rate volatility.

- For example:
  - Brazilian Reals.
  - Philippine Peso.
  - Indian Rupee.
  - Taiwan Dollars.
  - Korean Won.
  - Russian Ruble.
  - Chinese Renminbi (or Yuan)

- In such markets the use of non-deliverable forwards (NDFs) has developed.

- These are like forward contracts, except no currency is delivered. Instead the profit or loss (i.e. the difference between actual and NDF rates) on a notional amount of currency (the face value of the NDF) is settled between the two counter parties.

- Combined with an actual currency exchange at the prevailing spot rate, this effectively fixes the future rate in a similar manner to futures.

- One other feature is that the settlement is in US dollars.

## SAFE illustration

Let the spot rate between the US$ and the Brazilian Real be 1.6983 Reals to $1 and suppose we agree a 3 month NDF to buy $1 million worth of Reals at 1.7000.

If the spot rate moves to 1.6800 in 3 months, then the counter-party will have to pay us 1million x 0.02 = 20,000 Reals.

This will be settled in US$, so the actual receipt will be 20,000/1.6800 = $11,905

## 3 Money market hedges

### Characteristics

- The basic idea is to avoid future exchange rate uncertainty by making the exchange at today's spot rate instead.

- This is achieved by depositing/borrowing the foreign currency until the actual commercial transaction cash flows occur:

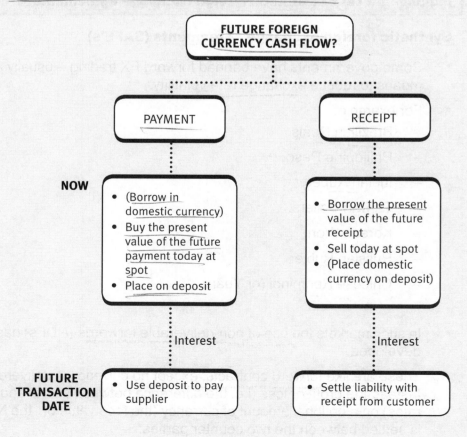

- In effect a foreign currency asset is set up to match against a future liability (and vice-versa).

### Test your understanding 2

Marcus is based in France has recently imported raw materials from the USA and has been invoiced for US$240,000, payable in three months' time.

In addition, it has also exported finished goods to Japan and Australia.

The Japanese customer has been invoiced for US$69,000, payable in three months' time, and the Australian customer has been invoiced for A$295,000, payable in four months' time.

**Current spot and forward rates are as follows:**

**US$/Euro**

| | |
|---|---|
| Spot: | 0.9830 – 0.9850 |
| 3 months forward: | 0.9520 – 0.9545 |

**Euro/A$**

| | |
|---|---|
| Spot: | 1.8890 – 1.8920 |
| 4 months forward: | 1.9510 – 1.9540 |

**Current money market rates (pa) are as follows:**

| | |
|---|---|
| US$: | 10.0% – 12.0% |
| A$: | 14.0% – 16.0% |
| Euro: | 11.5% – 13.0% |

**Show how the company can hedge its exposure to FX risk using:**

**(a)  The forward markets**

**(b)  The money markets**

**and in each case, determine which is the best hedging technique.**

### Further comments

- Interest rate parity implies that a money market hedge should give the same result as a forward contract.

- Money market hedges may be feasible as a way of hedging for currencies where forward contracts are not available.

- This approach has obvious cash flow implications which may prevent a company from using this method, e.g. if a company has a considerable overdraft it may be impossible for it to borrow funds now.

## 4 Futures contracts

### Characteristics

- Futures contracts are standard sized, traded hedging instruments. The aim of a currency futures contract is to fix an exchange rate at some future date.

- A key issue with currency futures is to establish the 'currency of the contract' or CC. For example if the CC is $ and your transaction involves buying $, you should buy futures now to set up the hedge.

In exam questions the contract size will always be given to you, quoted in terms of the CC. For example,

| Future | Contract size | Price quotation | Tick size | Value of one tick |
|--------|---------------|-----------------|-----------|-------------------|
| £/US dollar | £62,500 | US$ per £1 | $0.0001 | $6.25 |
| €/US dollar | €200,000 | US$ per €1 | $0.0001 | $20.00 |
| Swiss franc/ US dollar | SFr 125,000 | US$ per SFR1 | $0.0001 | $12.50 |
| Yen/US dollar | 12.5 million yen | US$ per 1 yen | $0.000001 | $12.50 |
| €/sterling | €100,000 | £ per €1 | £0.0001 | £10 |

- The CC is the currency in which the contract size is quoted.

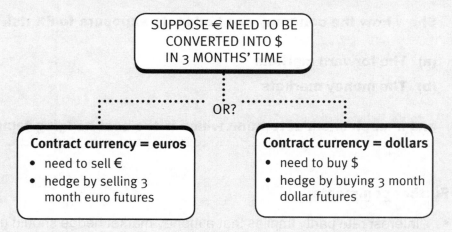

- We assume that the contracts mature or expire at the end of March, June, September and December. It is normal to choose the first contract to expiry after the conversion date.

- The range of available futures is limited and includes: $/£, $/Y, $/SFR, $/A$, $/C$ and $/€. Therefore if you are asked to give a hedge strategy for a 'minor' currency you should not recommend a futures contract.

## Futures hedging calculations

Step 1: Set up the hedge by addressing 3 key questions:

- Do we initially buy or sell futures?
- How many contracts?
- Which expiry date should be chosen?

Step 2: Contact the exchange. Pay the initial margin. Then wait until the transaction / settlement date.

Step 3: Calculate profit or loss in the futures market by closing out the futures contracts, and calculate the value of the transaction using the spot rate on the transaction date.

### Expandable Text - Futures calculation

It is 15 October and a treasurer has identified the need to convert euros into dollars to pay a US supplier $12 million on 20 November. The treasurer has decided to use December Euro futures contracts to hedge with the following details:

- Contract size €200,000.
- Prices given in US$ per Euro (i.e. €1 = ...).
- Tick size $0.0001 or $20 per contract.

He opens a position on 15 October and closes it on 20 November. Spot and relevant futures prices are as follows:

| Date | Spot | Futures price |
|------|------|---------------|
| 15 October | 1.3300 | 1.3350 |
| 20 November | 1.3190 | 1.3240 |

**Calculate the financial position using the hedge described.**

**Solution**

| Step 1 | 1. Buy or sell initially?<br><br>2. How many contracts?<br><br>3. Which expiry date? | 1. CC is €, and we need to sell € (to buy $), so sell futures now.<br><br>2. Cover $12m/1.3300 = €9.02 million, using €200,000 contracts, hence €9.02m / €0.2m =45.1 - round to 45 contracts.<br><br>3. Transaction date is 20 November, so choose December futures (the first to expire after the transaction date). |
|---|---|---|
| Step 2 | Contact the exchange - state the hedge | Sell 45 December futures (at a futures price of $1.3350/€1) |
| Step 3 | Calculate profit/loss in futures market by closing out the position. | Initially: Sell at 1.3350<br><br>Close out: Buy at 1.3240<br><br>Difference is $0.011 per €1 profit<br><br>45 × €200,000 covered, so total profit is 0.011 × 45 × 200,000 = $99,000 |
| Step 3 continued | Transaction at spot rate on 20 November:<br><br>Buy $11.901m extra needed at spot rate of $1.3190/€1 | Cost in € is €9,022,745 |

## Test your understanding 3

It is 4 May and the treasurer of a Swiss company has identified a net receipt of US$2 million on 10 June. These dollars will need to be converted into Swiss Francs (CHF). The treasurer has decided to use June US dollar – Swiss Franc futures contracts to hedge with the following details:

- New York Board of Trade (NYBOT) options and futures exchange.

- Contract size $200,000.

- Prices given in Swiss francs per US dollar (i.e. $1 = …).

- Tick size CHF 0.0001 or CHF20 per contract.

She opens a position on 4 May and closes it on 10 June. Spot and relevant futures prices are as follows:

| Date | Spot | Futures price |
|---|---|---|
| 4 May | 1.2160 | 1.2200 |
| 10 June | 1.2750 | 1.2760 |

**Calculate the financial position using the hedge described.**

## 5 Currency options

### Characteristics

- A currency option is a right, but not an obligation, to buy or sell a currency at an exercise price on a future date. If there is a favourable movement in rates the company will allow the option to lapse, to take advantage of the favourable movement. The right will only be exercised to protect against an adverse movement, i.e. the worst-case scenario.
  - A call option gives the holder the right to buy the underlying currency.
  - A put option gives the holder the right to sell the underlying currency.

- Options are more expensive than the forward contracts and futures.

- A European option can only be exercised on the expiry date whilst an American option can be exercised at any time up to the expiry date.

## OTC options

- Currency options can be bought OTC or on major exchanges.

- Like forward contracts, the OTC options are tailor made to fit a company's precise requirements. Branches of foreign banks in major financial centres are generally willing to write options against their home currency.

  - e.g. Australian banks in Chicago will write options on the Australian dollar.

- Option sizes are much larger on the OTC market, with most options being in excess of $1 million.

## Exchange traded options

- Exchange traded options are also available but the OTC market is the larger.

  - e.g. Euronext.liffe (formerly LIFFE) offers European style dollar:euro option contracts.

- Two types of currency option are available:

  - Cash options contracting for delivery of the underlying currency.

  - Options on currency futures.

| Illustration 1 - Currency options |

A typical pricing schedule for the US$/€ currency option on the Philadelphia exchange is as follows.

| Strike price | CALLS | | | PUTS | | |
|---|---|---|---|---|---|---|
| | Jun | Sept | Dec | Jun | Sept | Dec |
| 115.00 | 1.99 | 2.25 | 2.47 | 0.64 | 1.32 | 2.12 |
| 116.00 | 1.39 | 2.03 | 2.28 | 1.00 | 1.56 | - |
| 117.00 | 0.87 | 1.55 | 1.81 | 1.43 | 2.22 | - |
| 118.00 | 0.54 | 1.08 | 1.30 | - | - | - |

- Here, the options are for a contract size of €125,000 and prices (both strike price and premia) are quoted in US$ (cents) per €1.

- So to buy a call option on €125,000 with an expiry date of September and at a strike price of €1 = $1.17 would cost 1.55 cents per euro, or $1,937.50.

- Similarly, the premium on a June put at a strike price of 115.00 (€1 = $1.15) would cost 0.64 cents per euro, or $800.

- The decision as to which exercise price to choose will depend on cost, risk exposure and expectations. If you have to choose in the exam then one approach is to consider the cost implications only for calculation purposes: The best exercise price is then the one which (incorporating the premium cost) is most financially advantageous.

### Expandable Text - Choosing an exercise price

#### Call option

Using the above schedule, determine which June call option would give the lowest net cost of **acquiring euros**.

| Strike price | Premium | Total cost per € |
|---|---|---|
| 115.00 | 1.99 | 116.99 |
| 116.00 | 1.39 | 117.39 |
| 117.00 | 0.87 | 117.87 |
| 118.00 | 0.54 | 118.54 |

The lowest cost would involve using call options with a strike price of 115.

#### Put option

Using the above schedule, determine which September put option would give the highest net receipt from **selling euros.**

| Strike Price | Premium | Net receipt from €1 |
|---|---|---|
| 115.00 | 1.32 | 113.68 |
| 116.00 | 1.56 | 114.44 |
| 117.00 | 2.22 | 114.78 |
| 118.00 | - | - |

The highest receipt would involve using put options with a strike price of 117.

### Options hedging calculations

Step 1: Set up the hedge by addressing 4 key questions:

- Do we need call or put options?
- How many contracts?
- Which expiry date should be chosen?
- Which strike price / exercise price should be used?

Step 2: Contact the exchange. Pay the upfront premium. Then wait until the transaction / settlement date.

Step 3: On the transaction date, compare the option price with the prevailing spot rate to determine whether the option should be exercised or allowed to lapse.

Step 4: Calculate the net cash flows - beware that if the number of contracts needed rounding, there will be some exchange at the prevailing spot rate even if the option is exercised.

### Test your understanding 4 - Pongo

Pongo plc is a UK-based import-export company. It has an invoice, which it is due to pay on 30 June, in respect of $350,000.

The company wishes to hedge its exposure to FX risk using FX options with an exercise price of $1.50.

The current $/£ spot rate is 1.5190 – 1.5230.

On Euronext.liffe, contract size is £25,000.

| Exercise price ($/£) | June contracts | |
| --- | --- | --- |
| | Calls | Puts |
| 1.50 | 6.80 | 12.40 |

Option premiums are given in cents per £.

Assume that it is now the 31 March and that UK £ interest rates are 12%.

**Calculate the cash flows in respect to the payment if the spot rate is: 1.4810 – 1.4850 on the 30 June**

**Test your understanding 5 - Pongo (continued)**

Using the circumstances described in the previous example above, suppose Pongo plc is also due to receive $275,000 from a US customer on 30 September. Euronext.liffe quotes for September option contracts are as follows:

| Exercise price ($/£) | September contracts | |
| --- | --- | --- |
| | Calls | Puts |
| 1.50 | 8.00 | 13.40 |

**Calculate the cash flows in respect to the receipt if the spot rate is 1.5250 – 1.5285 on the 30 September.**

## 6 Forex swaps

### Characteristics

- In a forex swap, the parties agree to swap equivalent amounts of currency for a period and then re-swap them at the end of the period at an agreed swap rate. The swap rate and amount of currency is agreed between the parties in advance. Thus it is called a 'fixed rate/fixed rate' swap.

- The main objectives of a forex swap are:
    - To hedge against forex risk, possibly for a longer period than is possible on the forward market.
    - Access to capital markets, in which it may be impossible to borrow directly.

- Forex swaps are especially useful when dealing with countries that have exchange controls and/or volatile exchange rates.

**Illustration 2**

Suppose that A plc, a UK construction company, wins a contract to construct a bridge in Argentina. The bridge will require an initial investment now, and will be sold to the Argentinean Government in one year's time. The Government will pay in pesos.

The problem is the company's exposure to currency risk. They know how much will be received in one year's time in pesos but not in sterling as the exchange rate changes daily.

**Various possible hedging strategies:**

(1)  **Decide to do nothing,** i.e. accept the risk – win some, lose some.

(2)  Lock into **a forward contract** for converting the amount receivable in one year's time into sterling, if a forward market exists.

(3)  Undertake **a money market hedge:** take out a loan in pesos to cover the initial cost, and repay the loan from the disposal proceeds in a year's time. We would then only be exposed on the profit we make (if we make any).

(4)  Enter into **a forex swap**. Instead of taking out a loan in pesos we

   (a)  Swap sterling today for the pesos required to cover the initial investment, at an agreed swap rate.

   (b)  Take out a loan in sterling today to buy the pesos.

   (c)  In one year's time (in this example) arrange to swap back the pesos obtained in (a) for pounds at the same swap rate.

   (d)  Just like taking out a loan in pesos we are therefore only exposed on the profit that we make. We could of course use another hedging technique to hedge the profit element.

## Calculations

### Illustration 3

Say the bridge will require an initial investment of 100m pesos and is will be sold for 200m pesos in one year's time.

The currency spot rate is 20 pesos/£, and the government has offered a forex swap at 20 pesos/£. A plc cannot borrow pesos directly and there is no forward market available.

The estimated spot rate in one year is 40 pesos/£. The current UK borrowing rate is 10%.

Determine whether A plc should do nothing or hedge its exposure using the forex swap.

## Solution

| £m | 0 | 1 |
|---|---|---|
| **Without swap** | | |
| Buy 100m pesos @20 | (5.0) | |
| Sell 200m pesos @40 | | 5.0 |
| Interest on sterling loan (5 x 10%) | | (0.5) |
| | _____ | _____ |
| | (5.0) | 4.5 |
| | _____ | _____ |
| | | |
| **With forex swap** | | |
| Buy 100m pesos @20 | (5.0) | |
| Swap 100m pesos back @20 | | 5.0 |
| Sell 100m pesos @40 | | 2.5 |
| Interest on Sterling loan (5 × 10%) | | (0.5) |
| | _____ | _____ |
| Net receipt of (£2.0 million) | (5.0) | 7.0 |
| | _____ | _____ |

A plc should use a forex swap.

(Key idea: The forex swap is used to hedge foreign exchange risk. We can see that in this basic exercise that the swap amount of 100m pesos is protected from any deprecation, as it is swapped at both the start and end of the year at the swap rate of 20, whilst in the spot market pesos have depreciated from a rate of 20 to 40 pesos per pound.)

## Test your understanding 6

Goldsmith Co, a mining company based in the fictitious country of Krownland, wishes to hedge 1 year foreign exchange risk, which will arise on an investment in Chile. The investment is for 800m escudos and is expected to yield an amount of 1000m escudos in 1 year's time.

Goldsmith cannot borrow escudos directly and is therefore considering two possible hedging techniques:

(a) Entering into a forward contract for the full 1000m escudos receivable.

(b) Entering into a forex swap for the 800m escudos initial investment, and then a forward contract for the 200m escudos profit element.

The currency spot rate is 28 escudos to the krown, and the bank has offered a forex swap at 22 escudos/krown with Goldsmith making a net interest payment to the bank of 1% in krowns (assume at $T_1$).

| Interest rates | Borrowing | Lending |
|---|---|---|
| Krownland | 15% | 12% |
| Chile | N/A | 25% |

A forward contract is available at a rate of 30 escudos per krown.

**Determine whether Goldsmith should hedge its exposure using a forward contract or a forex swap.**

## 7 Currency swaps

### Characteristics

- A currency swap allows the two counterparties to swap interest rate commitments on borrowings in different currencies.

- In effect a currency swap has two elements:
    - An exchange of principal in different currencies, which are swapped back at the original spot rate – just like a forex swap.

    - An exchange of interest rates – the timing of these depends on the individual contract.

- The swap of interest rates could be 'fixed for fixed' or 'fixed for variable'.

### Illustration 4

Warne Co is an Australian firm looking to expand in Germany and is thus looking to raise €24 million. It can borrow at the following fixed rates:

A$ 7.0%

€ 5.6%

Euroports Inc is a French company looking to acquire an Australian firm and is looking to borrow A$40 million. It can borrow at the following rates:

A$ 7.2%

€ 5.5%

The current spot rate is A$1 = €0.6.

Show how a 'fixed for fixed' currency swap would work in the circumstances described, assuming the swap is only for one year and that interest is paid at the end of the year concerned.

## Solution

| Timing | | Warne Co | Euroports Inc |
|---|---|---|---|
| Now | Borrow from banks | A$40m at 7.0% | €24m at 5.5% |
| | Exchange principals | Pay A$40m to Euroports receive €24m | Pay €24m to Warne receive A$40m |
| End of year | Pay interest to banks | Pay A$2.8m interest | Pay €1.32m interest |
| | Exchange interest | Pay €1.32m to Euroports receive A$2.8m | Receive €1.32m Pay A$2.8m to Warne |
| | Swap back principals | Pay €24m to Warne receive A$40m | Pay A$40m to Euroports receive €24m |

Net result:

| Interest costs | Warne Co | Euroports Inc |
|---|---|---|
| Without swap (24 × 5.6%) (40×7.2%) | €1.344m | A$2.88m |
| With swap | €1.320m | A$2.80m |
| Saving | €24,000 | A$80,000 |

### Test your understanding 7

Wa Inc is a Japanese firm looking to expand in the USA and is looking to raise $20 million at a variable interest rate. It has been quoted the following rates:

$ LIBOR+60 points

¥ 1.2%

McGregor Inc is an American company looking to refinance a ¥2,400m loan at a fixed rate. It can borrow at the following rates:

$ LIBOR + 50 points
¥ 1.5%

The current spot rate is $1 = ¥120.

**Show how the 'fixed for variable' currency swap would work in the circumstances described, assuming the swap is only for one year and that interest is paid at the end of the year concerned.**

## 8 Bilateral and multilateral netting and matching agreements

### Introduction

**Netting and matching**

- Where two or more entities have mutual indebtedness
- Look at the net forex exposures before considering external hedging techniques

**Netting**

- Involves two or more entities within a single group

**Matching**

- Involves two or more companies with a formal agreement to net off

**Expandable Text - Netting and matching**

Netting and matching are carried out to reduce the scale of external hedging required.

For example, Group X is expecting to receive $10 million in one subsidiary and pay $6 million at the same time in another subsidiary. Clearly the group only has a net exposure of a receipt of $4 million.

The terms 'netting' and 'matching' are often used interchangeably but strictly speaking they are different:

- Netting refers to netting off group receipts and payments, as in the example above.

- Matching extends this concept to include third parties such as external suppliers and customers.

## Calculations

Step 1: Convert all currency flows to a common ('base') currency using spot rates (NOT forward or future rates).

Step 2: Clear the overlap of any bi-lateral indebtedness.

E.g.

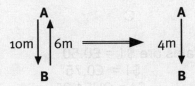

Step 3: Clear the smallest leg of any 3 way circuits.

E.g.

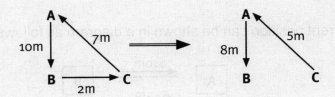

Step 4: Clear the smallest leg of any 4 way circuits (then 5, etc).

E.g.

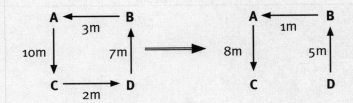

Step 5: Convert back into original currencies.

Step 6: Use the simplified figures for:

A   Settlement

B   Setting up appropriate hedging tools.

### Expandable Text - Numerical example of netting and matching

A, B, and C are three companies within the same US group. D is a company outside of the group. The following liabilities have been identified for the forthcoming year:

| Owed by | Owed to | Amount (millions) |
|---------|---------|-------------------|
| A | B | €45 |
| B | A | $10 |
| B | C | CHF20 |
| C | A | $20 |
| C | D | £10 |
| D | B | €15 |
| D | C | CHF10 |

Mid-market spot rates are $1 = £0.50
$1 = €0.75
$1 = CHF1.25

Establish the net external indebtedness that would require external hedging and the net intra-group settlement required.

### Solution

The current position can be shown in a diagram as follows:

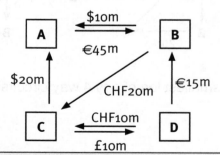

Step 1: Convert to base – here dollars.

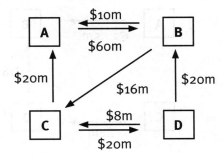

Step 2: Clear bilateral indebtedness.

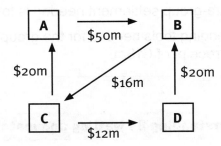

Step 3: Clear 3 way indebtedness – e.g. ABC.

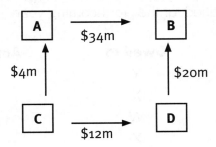

Step 4: Clear 4 way indebtedness.

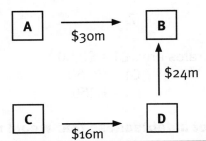

Step 5: Convert back to original currencies.

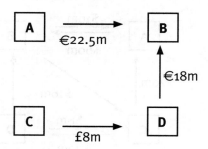

Step 6:

- The only intra-group settlement needed is for A to pay B €22.5m.
- The final hedging tools needed for the group are for a payment of £8m and a receipt of €18m.

## Test your understanding 8 - Netting and matching

X, Y, and Z are three companies within the same UK based international group. W is a company outside of the group. The following liabilities have been identified for the forthcoming year:

| Owed by | Owed to | Amount (millions) |
|---------|---------|-------------------|
| X | Y | €39 |
| Y | X | £10 |
| Y | W | $20 |
| Z | X | ¥200 |
| Z | Y | €15 |
| W | X | $15 |
| W | Z | ¥100 |

Mid-market spot rates are: £1 = $2.00
£1 = €1.50
£1 = ¥250

**Establish the net indebtedness that would require external hedging.**

## 9 Chapter summary

**HEDGING FOREIGN EXCHANGE RISK**

**Techniques/instruments**

- Forward contracts, including synthetic foreign exchange agreements (SAFEs)
- Money market hedges
- Futures
- Forex swaps
- Currency swaps
- Currency options
- Netting and matching agreements

## Test your understanding answers

### Test your understanding 1

Step 1: Get the appropriate spot rate from the spread (remember the bank always wins): 0.7785.

Step 2: Adjust to get the forward rate (remember to add discounts and deduct premiums) 0.7785 - 0.0021 = 0.7764.

Step 3: Use the rate: cost = 250,000/0.7764 = **A$ 322,000 CERTAIN SUM**.

### Test your understanding 2

**1 US$ exposure**

As Porto plc has a US$ receipt (US$69,000) and payment (US$240,000), maturing at the same time (3 months), they can match them against each other to leave a net liability of US$ 171,000 to be hedged.

**Forward market hedge**

Buy US$171,000 3 months forward at a cost of:

US$171,000/0.9520 = **(€179,622)** payable in 3 months time.

**Money market hedge**

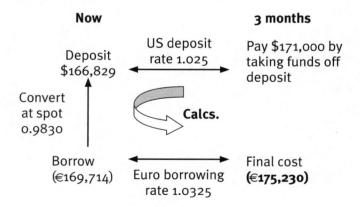

This is cheaper than the forward market hedge.

**Note:** Interest rates can simply be time-apportioned.

## 2 A$ exposure

### Forward market hedge

Sell A$295,000 4 months forward to produce a receipt of:

A$295,000 × 1.9510 = **€575,545** receivable in 4 months time.

### Money market hedge

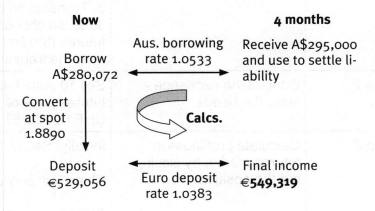

| Now | | 4 months |
|---|---|---|
| Borrow A$280,072 | Aus. borrowing rate 1.0533 | Receive A$295,000 and use to settle liability |
| Convert at spot 1.8890 | **Calcs.** | |
| Deposit €529,056 | Euro deposit rate 1.0383 | Final income **€549,319** |

As this is smaller amount than received from the forward market hedge, we can conclude that the forward market hedge gives the better outcome.

**Test your understanding 3**

| Step 1 | 1. Buy or sell initially? | 1. CC is $, and we need to sell $ (to buy CHF), so sell futures now. |
| | 2. How many contracts? | 2. Cover $2m using $200,000 contracts, hence 10 contracts. |
| | 3. Which expiry date? | 3. Transaction date is 10 June, so choose June futures (the first to expire after the transaction date). |
| Step 2 | Contact the exchange - state the hedge | Sell 10 June futures (at a futures price of CHF1.2200/$1 |
| Step 3 | Calculate profit/loss in futures market by closing out the position. | Initially: Sell at 1.2200<br><br>Close out: Buy at 1.2760<br><br>Difference is CHF0.056 per $1 loss<br><br>10 × $200,000 covered, so total loss is 0.056 × 10 × 200,000 = CHF112,000 |
| Step 3 continued | Transaction at spot rate on 10 June<br><br>Sell $2m at spot rate of CHF1.2750/$1 | CHF received is CHF2,550,000, hence net receipt is 2,550,000 - 112,000 = CHF2,438,000 |

**Test your understanding 4 - Pongo**

Step 1:    4 key questions:

Call or put options? – CC is £, we
need to sell £ to get $ so buy put options on £.

How many contracts? Cover $350,000 / 1.5190 =
£230,415 using £25,000 contracts, so 230,415 / 25,000
= 9.22 - round to 9 contracts

Which expiry date? Only June quoted here, but that
matches the transaction date exactly, so choose June
contracts.

Which exercise price? Only $1.50 / £1 quoted.

Step 2:    Contact the exchange. We need to buy 9 June Put
options at an exercise price of $1.50/£1.

Premium payable is 12.40c per £1 covered i.e. $0.1240
× (9 × £25,000) = $27,900, which has to be purchaesd
at spot (1.5190) so costs $27,900 / 1.5190 = £18,367.

If this has to be borrowed for 3 months until the
transaction date, the eventual cost will be 18,367 × 1.03
= £18,918

Step 3:    On the settlement date compare the option price ($1.50)
with the prevailing spot ($1.4810) to determine whether
the option would be exercised or allowed to
lapse.Exercise ('sell the big number').
Sell 9 × 25 = £225,000.
Buy 225,000 × 1.5 = $337,500.

Step 4:    Determine net cash flows.

|  | $ | £ |
|---|---|---|
| Payments in real world | (350,000) | |
| Buy $s and sell £s using options | 337,500 | (225,000) |
| Shorfall | (12,500) | |
| Buy at spot (12,500 ÷1.4810) | | (8,440) |
| Cost of option | | (18,918) |
|  | 12,500 | |
| Net payments in £s | | (252,358) |

**Test your understanding 5 - Pongo (continued)**

Step 1    4 key questions:

Call or put options? CC is £, we need to sell $ to get £ so buy call options on £.

How many contracts? Cover $275,000 / 1.5230 = £180,565 using £25,000 contracts, so 180,565 / 25,000 = 7.22 - round to 7 contracts

Which expiry date? Only September quoted

Which exercise price? Only $1.50 / £1 quoted.

Step 2    Contact the exchange: We need to buy  7 September Call Options at an exercise price of $1.50.

Determine option premium – usually payable upfront.

Option premium = $0.08 × (£25,000 × 7) = $14,000.

Assume the option premium is payable upfront $14,000/1.5190 = £9,217.

If this has to be borrowed until the transaction date, the eventual cost in 6 months will be  = £9,217 × 1.06 = £9,770.

Step 3    On the settlement date compare the option price ($1.50) with the prevailing spot ($1.5285) to determine whether the option would be exercised or allowed to lapse.

Exercise ('buy the low number').

Buy 7 × 25 = £175,000.

Sell 175,000 × 1.5 = $262,500.

Step 4    Determine net cash flows.

|  | $ | £ |
|---|---|---|
| Receipts in real world | 275,000 |  |
| Buy £s and sell $s using options | (262,500) | 175,000 |
| Surplus | 12,500 |  |
| Sell at spot (12,500 ÷ 1.5285) | (12,500) | 8,178 |
| Cost of options |  | (9,770) |
| Net receipt in £s |  | 173,408 |

KAPLAN PUBLISHING

### Test your understanding 6

| Krowns (millions) | 0 | 1 |
|---|---|---|
| **Forward hedge** | | |
| Buy 800m escudos @28 | (28.57) | |
| Sell 1,000m escudos @30 | | 33.33 |
| Interest on krown loan (28.57 × 15%) | | (4.29) |
| | (28.57) | 29.04 |

Net receipt of **0.47** million krowns.

**With forex swap and forward**

| | 0 | 1 |
|---|---|---|
| Buy 800m escudos @22 | (36.36) | |
| Swap 800m escudos back @22 | | 36.36 |
| Sell 200m escudos @30 | | 6.67 |
| Interest on krown loan (36.36 × 15%) | | (5.45) |
| Swap fee (36.36 × 1%) | | (0.36) |
| | (36.36) | 37.22 |

Net receipt of **0.86** million krowns.

Goldsmith should use a forex swap.

### Test your understanding 7

| Timing | | Wa Inc | McGregor Inc |
|---|---|---|---|
| Now | Borrow from banks | ¥2,400m at 1.2% | $20m at L+0.5% |
| | Exchange principals | Pay ¥2,400m to McGregor receive $20m | Pay $20m to Wa receive ¥2,400m |
| End of year | Pay interest to banks | Pay ¥28.8m interest | Pay $20 × (L + 0.5%) interest |
| | Exchange interest based on swap terms | Pay McGregor $20 × (L + 0.5%) receive ¥28.8m | Receive $20 × (L + 0.5%) Pay ¥28.8m to Wa |
| | Swap back principals | Pay $20m to Wa receive ¥2,400m | Pay ¥2,400m to McGregor receive $20m |

Net result:

| Interest costs | Wa | McGregor |
|---|---|---|
| Without swap | $20m × (L + 0.6%) | 2,400 × 1.5% = ¥36m |
| With swap | $20m × (L + 0.5%) | ¥28.8m |
| Saving | $20m × 0.1% = $20,000 | ¥7.2m |

## Test your understanding 8 - Netting and matching

The current position can be shown in a diagram as follows:

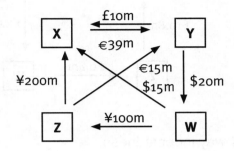

Step 1: Convert to base – here GB pounds.

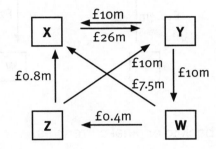

Step 2: Clear bilateral indebtedness.

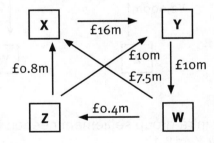

Step 3: Identify and clear 3 way circutis

(a) XYW

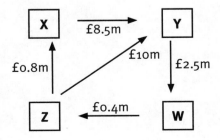

(b) ZXY

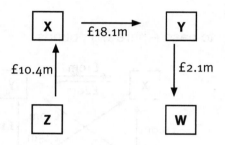

**Step 4: Clear 4 way indebtedness.**

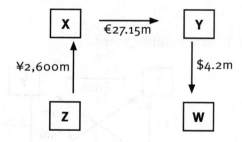

**Step 5: Convert back to original currencies.**

X — €27.15m → Y

¥2,600m (Z → X)    $4.2m (Y → W)

Z                  W

**Step 6:** The only intra-group settlement needed is for Z to pay X 2,600m Yen and X to pay Y £18.1m..

The final hedging tools needed for the group are for a payment of $4.2m.

# Hedging interest rate risk

## Chapter learning objectives

Upon completion of this chapter you will be able to:

- explain the characteristics of forward rate agreements and calculate the financial position after their use as a hedging tool

- explain the characteristics of interest rate futures and calculate the financial position after their use as a hedging tool

- explain the characteristics of interest rate swaps and calculate the financial position after their use as a hedging tool

- explain the characteristics and use of options on FRA's (caps and collars), Interest rate futures and interest rate swaps.

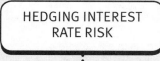

HEDGING INTEREST
RATE RISK

**Techniques/instruments**
- Forward rate agreements
- Interest rate futures
- Interest rate swaps
- Options on FRAs
- Options on futures
- Swaptions

## 1 Introduction

Firms are exposed to interest rate movements in two ways:

- The cost of existing borrowings (or the yield on deposits) may be linked to interest rates in the economy. This risk exposure can be eliminated by using fixed rate products.

- Cash flow forecasts may indicate the need for future borrowings/deposits. Interest rates may change before these are needed and thus affect the ultimate cost/yield.

- The second type of risk is the focus of this chapter.

### Expandable Text - More explanation of interest rate risk

#### Interest rate risk exposure

Interest rate risk is the risk of incurring losses due to adverse movements in interest rates. An exposure to interest rate risk arises in the following situations.

- An organisation is expecting some income in the future, and the amount of income received will depend on the interest rate at that time.

- An organisation is expecting to make some payment in the future, and the amount of the payment will depend on the interest rate at the time.

- The organisation has an asset whose market value changes whenever market interest rates change.

The greatest exposures to interest rate risk are faced by banks and investment institutions. However, non-bank companies can also have substantial exposures to interest rate risk.

- Many companies borrow at a floating rate of interest (or variable rate of interest).

- For example, a company might borrow at a variable rate of interest, with interest payable every six months and the amount of the interest charged each time varying according to whether short-term interest rates have risen or fallen since the previous payment.

- Some companies also budget to receive large amounts of cash, and so budget large temporary cash surpluses that can be invested short-term. Income from those temporary investments will depend on what the interest rate happens to be when the money is available for depositing. Some investments earn interest at a variable rate of interest (for example money in bank deposit accounts) and some short-term investments go up or down in value with changes in interest rates (for example, Treasury bills and other bills).

- Some companies hold investments in marketable bonds, either government bonds or corporate bonds. These change in value with movements in long-term interest rates.

- Some companies borrow by issuing bonds. If a company foresees a future requirement to borrow by issuing bonds, it will have an exposure to interest rate risk until the bonds are eventually issued.

- Many companies borrow, and if they do they have to choose between borrowing at a fixed rate of interest (usually by issuing bonds) or borrow at a floating rate (possibly through bank loans). There is some risk in deciding the balance or mix between floating rate and fixed rate debt. Too much fixed rate debt creates an exposure to falling long-term interest rates and too much floating rate debt creates an exposure to a rise in short-term interest rates.

Interest rate risk can be significant. For example, suppose that a company wants to borrow $10 million for one year, but does not need the money for another three weeks. It would be expensive to borrow money before it is needed, because there will be an interest cost. On the other hand, a rise in interest rates in the time before the money is actually borrowed could also add to interest costs. For example, a rise of just 0.25% (25 basis points) in the interest rate on a one-year loan of $10 million would cost an extra $25,000 in interest.

## 2 Forward rate agreements (FRAs)

### Introduction

- An FRA is an agreement on interest rates relating to a notional loan or deposit. The loan or deposit is for a stated period, such as two months, three months, six months and so on, starting at a specified time in the future.

- In the terminology of the markets, an FRA on a notional three-month loan/deposit starting in five months time is called a '5–8 FRA' (or '5v8 FRA').

- When an FRA reaches its settlement date (usually the start of the notional loan or deposit period), the buyer and seller must settle the contract:

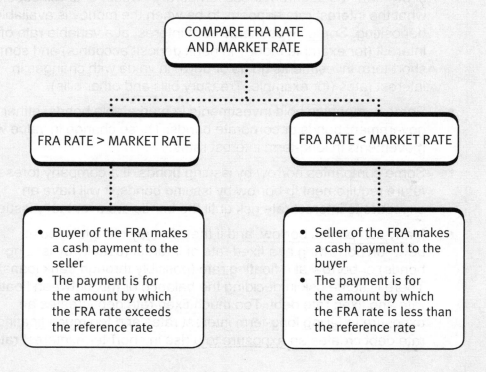

### Hedging using FRAs

Hedging is achieved by a combination of an FRA with the 'normal' loan or deposit.

### Borrowing (hence concerned about interest rate rises)

- The firm will borrow the required sum on the target date and will thus contract at the market interest rate on that date.

- Separately the firm will buy a matching FRA from a bank or other market maker and thus receive compensation if rates rise.

**Depositing (hence concerned about a fall in interest rates)**

- The firm will deposit the required sum on the target date and will thus contract at the market interest rate on that date.

- Separately the firm will sell a matching FRA to a bank or other market maker and thus receive compensation if rates fall.

In each case this combination effectively fixes the rate.

### Illustration 1 - FRA

Enfield Inc's financial projections show an expected cash deficit in two months time of $8m, which will last for approximately three months.

It is now the 1st November 20X6. The treasurer is concerned that interest rates may rise before the 1st January 20X7. Protection is thus required for two months.

| Now | | Rate agreed |
| --- | --- | --- |
| 1 Nov | | 1 Jan |

Risk of adverse movement
i.e. that interest rates will increase in this period

The treasurer can lock into an interest rate today for a future loan.

- The company takes out a loan as normal, i.e. the rate it pays is the going market rate at the date the loan is taken out.

- It will then receive or pay compensation under the separate forward rate agreement to return to the locked-in rate.

Suppose a 2 – 5 FRA at 5.00 – 4.70 is agreed.

- The agreement starts in 2 months time and ends in 5 months time.

- The FRA is quoted as interest rates for borrowing and lending – the borrowing rate is always the highest.

Calculate the interest payable if in two months' time the market rate is: (a) 7% or (b) 4%.

## Solution

| | | | 7% | 4% |
|---|---|---|---|---|
| Loan payments | | | | |
| Interest payable on loan: | 8m×0.07×3/12 | = | (140,000) | |
| | 8m×0.04×3/12 | = | | (80,000) |
| FRA payments Compensation: | | | | |
| Receivable | 8m×(0.07-0.05) ×3/12 | = | 40,000 | |
| Payable | 8m×(0.04-0.05) ×3/12 | = | | (20,000) |
| **Combination gives an effective interest rate of 5%.** | | | **(100,000)** | **(100,000)** |

- In this case the company is protected from a rise in interest rates but is not able to benefit from a fall in interest rates – a FRA hedges the company against both an adverse movement and a favourable movement.

- The FRA is a totally separate contractual agreement from the loan itself and could be arranged with a completely different bank.

- FRAs are usually on amounts > $1m and enable you to hedge for a period of one month up to two years. However, as an 'over the counter' instrument, they can be tailor-made to the company's precise requirements.

### Expandable Text - Settlement payment on an FRA

Because the settlement payment is made at the **start** of the loan/deposit period, the actual payment made is the **present value** of the interest differential at that date, discounted using the **market** reference interest rate.

### Illustration

Using the details for the Enfield Inc example above with a 7% market rate:

- The difference in interest rates gave rise to a potential receipt of $40,000 from the bank.

- The actual amount received will be 40,000/(1 + 0.07 × 3/12) = $39,312.

- One approach is to use this to reduce the loan from $8 million to $7,960,688. If this sum is then borrowed at 7% for 3 months, then the final repayment will be:

  7,960,688 × (1 + 0.07×3/12) = 8,100,000

This gives an effective interest rate of $100,000 on $8m, or 5%.

## 3 Options on FRAs

### Interest rate guarantees (options on FRAs)

- An interest rate guarantee (IRG) is an option on an FRA and, like all options, protects the company from adverse movements and allows it take advantage of favourable movements.

- If borrowing money, a firm would buy an FRA (explained above), so a **call** option over FRAs would be used. Similarly a **put** option over FRAs would be used to cover a deposit.

- IRGs are usually written by banks and other financial houses (i.e. the same organisations that may offer FRAs).

### Decision rules

| **If there is an adverse movement** | **If there is a favourable movement** |
|:---:|:---:|
| ↓ | ↓ |
| **Exercise the option to protect** | **Allow the option to lapse** |

- IRGs are more expensive than the FRAs as one has to pay for the flexibility to be able to take advantage of a favourable movement.

### Illustration 2 - IRG

Harry Inc wishes to borrow $8m in two months' time for a period of three months.

An IRG is available at 5% for a premium of 0.1% of the size of the loan.

Calculate the interest payable if in two months time the market rate is:
(a) 7% or (b) 4%.

## Solution

| | | 7% – exercise | 4% – allow to lapse |
|---|---|---|---|
| Interest | 8m × 3/12 × 5% | (100,000) | |
| | 8m × 3/12 × 4% | | (80,000) |
| Premium = | Cost of option | (8,000) | (8,000) |
| **Total payment** | | **(108,000)** | **(88,000)** |

**Note:** There is no need to time apportion the premium percentage.

### Test your understanding 1

RGI Co wishes to invest $12 million in 6 months time for two months and considering the following hedging strategies.

(1)  A 6–8 FRA quoted at 4%.

(2)  An IRG at 4% for a premium of 0.1%.

**Determine the costs if in six months time the market rate is: (a) 5% (b) 3% and comment.**

### When to hedge using FRAs or IRGs

- If the company treasurer believes that interest rates will rise, will he use an FRA or an IRG? He will use an FRA, as it is the cheaper way to hedge against the potential adverse movement.

- If the treasurer is unsure which way interest rates will move he may be willing to use the more expensive IRG to be able to benefit from a potential fall in interest rates.

## 4 Interest rate futures (IRFs)

### Introduction

### Types of IRFs

There are two broad types of interest rate futures:

- Short-term interest rate futures (STIRs). These are standardised exchange-traded forward contracts on a notional deposit (usually a three-month deposit) of a standard amount of principal, starting on the contract's final settlement date.

- Bond futures. These are contracts on a standard quantity of notional government bonds. If they reach final settlement date, and a buyer or seller does not close his position before then, the contracts must be settled by physical delivery.

### Underlying assets

To understand whether you need to buy or sell contracts, interest rate futures are best understood as involving the sale or purchase of bonds.

- borrowing money equates to issuing (selling) bonds, so sell futures to set up the hedge.

- depositing funds equates to buying bonds, so buy futures to set up the hedge

### Futures hedging calculations

Step 1: Set up the hedge by addressing 3 key questions:

- Do we initially buy or sell futures?

- How many contracts?

- Which expiry date should be chosen?

Step 2: Contact the exchange. Pay the initial margin. Then wait until the transaction / settlement date.

Step 3: Calculate profit or loss in the futures market by closing out the futures contracts, and calculate the value of the transaction using the market rate of interest rate on the transaction date.

## Calculations – particular characteristics of IRFs

### Ticks and tick values

- For STIRs, the minimum price movement is usually 0.01% or one basis point. The value of a tick is calculated as follows:
  - Tick value = unit of trading (i.e amount of principal) × one basis point × fraction of year.
  - For three-month sterling ('short sterling') futures, the underlying deposit for one contract is £500,000, so the value of one tick is £500,000 × 0.0001 × 3/12 = £12.50.

### Futures prices

- Interest rate futures prices are stated as (100 – the expected market reference rate), so a price of 95.5 would imply an interest rate of 4.5%.

- Open and settlement prices - in an exam question, when setting up the hedge, you may be quoted "Open" and "Settlement" futures prices. When setting up the hedge, the "Settlement" price should be used - the "Open" price is not relevant in our calculations.

### Calculating the number of contracts needed

$$\text{Number of contracts} = \frac{\text{Loan or deposit amount}}{\text{Contract size}} \times \frac{\text{Loan or deposit period in months}}{\text{Contract duration}}$$

---

### Expandable Text - More practical information on IRFs

### Contract specifications

Short-term interest rate futures are traded on a number of futures exchanges. For example:

- STIRs for sterling (three-month LIBOR) and the euro (three-month euribor) are traded on Euronext.liffe (formerly LIFFE), the London futures exchange.

- A STIR contract for the US dollar (eurodollar) is traded on the Chicago Mercantile Exchange (CME).

---

KAPLAN PUBLISHING

Here are just a few STIR contract specifications.

**Short-term interest rate futures**

| Reference rate | Futures exchange | Notional deposit |
|---|---|---|
| 3-month sterling | LIFFE | £500,000 |
| 3-month euribor | LIFFE/Eurex | €1 million |
| 3-month eurodollar | CME | $1 million |
| 3-month euroyen | TFE/LIFFE | ¥100 million |

**Tick values**

- For three-month sterling ('short sterling' futures), the underlying deposit is £500,000, so the value of one tick is £500,000 × 3/12 × 0.0001 = £12.50.

- For three-month euribor futures, the underlying deposit is €1,000,000, so the value of one tick is €1,000,000 × 3/12 × 0.0001 = €25.

- For three-month eurodollar futures, the underlying deposit is $1,000,000, so the value of one tick is $1,000,000 × 3/12 × 0.0001 = $25.

**Note:** For three-month euroyen futures, the underlying deposit is ¥100 m but the tick size is 0.005%, so the value of one tick is ¥100 million × 3/12 × 0.00005 = ¥1250.

**Illustration 3 - IRF**

Global Inc wishes to borrow €9,000,000 for one month starting in 5 weeks' time. Euribor is currently 3% and the treasurer of Global decides to fix the rate by selling IRFs at 96.90. The market rate subsequently rises by 25 basis points to 3.25%. As soon as the loan is agreed, the treasurer closes out Global's position by buying a matching number of contracts at 96.65.

(a) Calculate the number of contracts required (Note: one 3-month contract is for €1,000,000)

(b) Demonstrate that, in this case, the gain on the futures contracts exactly matches the extra interest on the loan.

## Solution

(a)  Number of contracts = (9,000,000/1,000,000 ) × 1/3 = 3

(b)  Extra interest cost on loan = 0.25% × 9,000,000 × 1/12 = €1,875

Gain on futures = 3 contracts × 25 ticks per contract × €25 per tick (W) = €1,875

(W: value of tick = €1,000,000 × 3/12 × 0.0001 = €25)

### Test your understanding 2

A company is going to borrow £2,000,000 in two month's time for a period of three months. It fears that the current interest rate will rise from its current level of 5%. It is decided to use £500,000 3-month interest rate futures to hedge the position. The current price is 94.90. In two months time the interest rates have risen to 7% and the futures price is 92.90.

**Calculate the cash flow that results from the profit or loss on the futures.**

## Imperfect hedges

The futures hedge is imperfect due to:

- If you are not dealing in whole contracts and have to round to whole contracts.

- Basis risk – the future rate (as defined by the future prices) moves approximately but not precisely in line with the cash market rate. An understanding of basis risk can help to predict the closing futures price if you are not given the necessary information in a question.

### Illustration 4 - Basis calculation

Sopoph Co is using June interest rate futures to cover the interest rate risk on a borrowing starting on 31 May.

At the time the futures contracts were set up on 1 January, the LIBOR rate was 5.00% and the futures price was 95.48.

LIBOR on 31 May is predicted to be 4.00%.

**Estimate the closing futures price on 31 May, assuming that basis risk reduces in a linear manner.**

**Solution**

|  | **1 January** | **31 May** | **30 June** |
|---|---|---|---|
| LIBOR | 5.00% | 4.00% | |
| Futures price | 95.48 | 96.08 **(W3)** | |
| | 100 − 95.48 (i.e. 4.52%) | 100 − 96 = 96 + 0.08 → | |
| Basis | 0.48% | 0.08% **(W2)** | 0 **(W1)** |

*(handwritten)* $0.48\% \times \dfrac{1}{6} = 0.08$

**(W1)** Basis will reduce to zero by the expiry date of the contract, because on that date, the futures price will equal 100 - the (known) LIBOR rate.

**(W2)** Assuming basis reduces in a linear manner, the basis at 31 May should be 1/6 of the original 0.48% i.e. 0.08%.

**(W3)** Basis is the difference between LIBOR and the implied futures price interest rate, so implied interest rate is 4.00% - 0.08% = 3.92% and futures price is 96.08.

*(handwritten)* → 100 − 3.92 %

## 5 Options on interest rate futures

### Options on futures

*(handwritten)* Call = right To buy
Put = to Sell

- These are options to buy or sell futures. Therefore all the futures information is still valid, for example:
  - The standard size of the contracts, i.e. £500,000, $1,000,000 etc.
  - The duration of the contract, i.e. 3 month contracts.
  - The appropriate tick value, i.e. £12.50, $25.00.
  - Maturity dates end of March, June, September and December.
- A call option gives the holder the right to buy the futures contract.
- A put option gives the holder the right to sell the futures contract.
- You always buy the option – buy the right to buy or buy the right to sell.

| Cash market | Deposits | Loan |
|---|---|---|
| Futures market | Buy futures contracts | Self futures contracts |
| Options market | Buy calls | Buy puts |

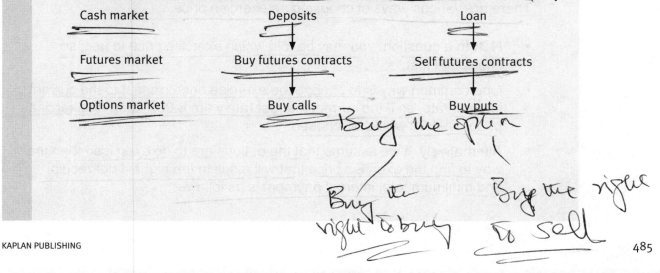

*(handwritten)* Buy the option

*(handwritten)* Buy the right to buy     Buy the right to sell

### Exercise prices and premium costs

- When you are setting up the hedge position for an option you have a number of prices (exercise prices) from which to choose (as opposed to the futures position where you buy or sell at the current price).

### Illustration 5 - Option prices

Euronext.liffe option price on three-month Sterling December futures

| Exercise price | Premium | |
|---|---|---|
| | Calls | Puts |
| 93.50 | 2.20 | 1.25 |
| 94.00 | 1.74 | 1.84 |
| 94.50 | 1.32 | 2.90 |
| 95.00 | 0.87 | 3.46 |

- If a company had a deposit of £500,000 and the treasurer wanted to hedge the position using traded options, he would buy a call option. If he purchased it at an exercise price of 95.00 he would be buying the right to interest receipts at 5% this would cost him a premium 0.87% (i.e. 0.87% × 100) 87 ticks (i.e. 87 × £12.50) = £1,088 per contract.

- If he purchased it at 93.50 he would be buying the right to interest receipts at 6.50% this would cost him a premium 2.20% (i.e. 2.20% × 100) 220 ticks (i.e. 220 × £12.50) = £2,750 per contract.

- The premium cost of the option will obviously depend on the exercise price chosen. Buying a call option at 93.50 should be more expensive than buying at 95.00, as the company has a greater chance of a profit when it comes to closing out its futures position.

### Choosing an exercise price

There are various ways of choosing an exercise price.

- **NB:** In a question, you may be told which exercise price to use, so check that first.

- One common way is to choose the exercise price closest to the current interest rate, so if the current interest rate were 6.00% then an exercise price of 94.00 would be chosen.

- Alternatively, if we assume that the options are to be exercised then the way to find the exercise price that will result in the highest net receipt and minimum total interest payment is as follows:

### Illustration 6 - Option prices (continued)

CALL OPTIONS – deposit – highest net receipt.

| Exercise price | Deposit interest | Cost | Net Receipt |
|---|---|---|---|
| | % | % | % |
| 93.50 | 6.50 | (2.20) | 4.30 |
| 94.00 | 6.00 | (1.74) | 4.26 |
| 94.50 | 5.50 | (1.32) | 4.18 |
| 95.00 | 5.00 | (0.87) | 4.13 |

PUT OPTIONS – loan – lowest total payment

| Exercise price | Loan interest | Cost | Total Payment |
|---|---|---|---|
| | % | % | % |
| 93.50 | 6.50 | 1.25 | 7.75 |
| 94.00 | 6.00 | 1.84 | 7.84 |
| 94.50 | 5.50 | 2.90 | 8.40 |
| 95.00 | 5.00 | 3.46 | 8.46 |

## Options hedging calculations

Step 1: Set up the hedge by addressing 4 key questions:

- Do we need call or put options?
- How many contracts?
- Which expiry date should be chosen?
- Which strike price / exercise price should be used?

Step 2: Contact the exchange. Pay the upfront premium. Then wait until the transaction / settlement date.

Step 3: On the transaction date, compare the option price with the prevailing market interest rate to determine whether the option should be exercised or allowed to lapse.

Step 4: Calculate the net cash flows - beware that if the number of contracts needed rounding, there will be some borrowing or deposit at the prevailing market interest rate even if the option is exercised.

### Decision point – exercise the option or allow it to lapse

General rule:

| If there is an adverse movement | If there is a favourable movement |
| --- | --- |
| ↓ | ↓ |
| Exercise the option to protect | Allow the option to lapse |

Double check:

- Would you ever exercise an option that results in a loss?
- Therefore you must always have a profit on the futures when exercising and a potential loss if you allow the option to lapse.

## Caps and floors

### Caps (buying call options)

- A cap is a call option.
- The bank as writer of the option agrees to cap the interest rate charged on a loan.
- If interest rates rise above the cap, then the bank pays the difference in rates to the holder.
- If the interest rate stays below the cap, then there is no need to pay the bank, as is the case with an FRA.

### Floors (buying put options)

- A minimum interest rate is set on a deposit.

## Collars

- A company buys an option to protect against an adverse movement whilst allowing it to take advantage of a favourable movement in interest rates. The option will be more expensive than a futures hedge. The company must pay for the flexibility to take advantage of a favourable movement.

- A collar is a way of achieving some flexibility at a lower cost than a straight option.

- Under a collar arrangement the company limits its ability to take advantage of a favourable movement. It buys a cap (a put option) as normal but also sells a floor (a call option) on the same futures contract, but with a different exercise price.

- The floor sets a minimum cost for the company. The counterparty is willing to pay the company for this guarantee of a minimum income. Thus the company gets paid for limiting its ability to take advance of a favourable movement if the interest rate falls below the floor rate the company does not benefit therefore the counterparty does.

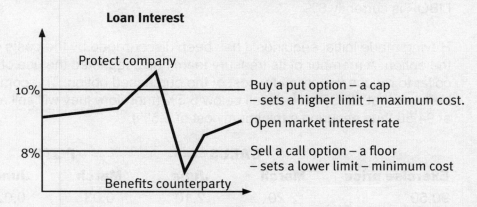

- It involves a company arranging both a minimum and a maximum limit on its interest rates payments or receipts. It enables a company to convert a floating rate of interest into a semi-fixed rate of interest.

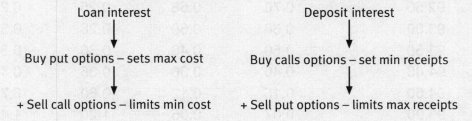

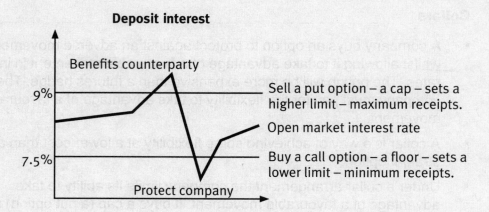

**Deposit interest**

Benefits counterparty

9%

Sell a put option – a cap – sets a higher limit – maximum receipts.

Open market interest rate

7.5%

Buy a call option – a floor – sets a lower limit – minimum receipts.

Protect company

## Test your understanding 3

A company wishes to borrow £10m on the 1st of January for three months. The company does not wish to pay above its current rate of 10% the company borrows at LIBOR + a fixed margin of 2% (therefore they will buy a put at 92.00 to ensure a maximum company cost of 10%). LIBOR is currently 8%.

Having made initial enquiries it has been discouraged by the costs of the option. A member of its treasury team has suggested the use of a collar to reduce the premium cost of the purchased option. The company believes that LIBOR will not fall below 5.5% (therefore they will sell a call at 94.50 thus ensuring a minimum cost of 5.5%).

| Exercise price | CALLS | | PUTS | |
|---|---|---|---|---|
| | March | June | March | June |
| 90.50 | 2.20 | 2.10 | 0.03 | 0.02 |
| 91.00 | 1.80 | 1.70 | 0.05 | 0.07 |
| 91.50 | 0.95 | 0.91 | 0.18 | 0.20 |
| 92.00 | 0.80 | 0.77 | 0.20 | 0.22 |
| 92.50 | 0.70 | 0.68 | 0.25 | 0.28 |
| 93.00 | 0.66 | 0.60 | 0.28 | 0.30 |
| 93.50 | 0.50 | 0.48 | 0.30 | 0.32 |
| 94.00 | 0.40 | 0.36 | 0.35 | 0.40 |
| 94.50 | 0.15 | 0.12 | 0.60 | 0.70 |
| 95.00 | 0.07 | 0.05 | 1.20 | 1.40 |
| 95.50 | 0.02 | 0.01 | 2.10 | 2.50 |

**Calculate the effective interest rate the company will pay using a collar if:**

(a) **LIBOR rise to 9.5% and future prices move to 90.20.**

(b) **LIBOR fall to 4.5% and future prices move to 96.10.**

# 6 Interest rate swaps

## Introduction

An interest rate swap is an agreement whereby the parties agree to swap a floating stream of interest payments for a fixed stream of interest payments and via versa. There is no exchange of principal:

- The companies involved are termed 'counter-parties'.

- Swaps can run for up to 30 years.

- Swaps can be used to hedge against an adverse movement in interest rates. Say a company has a $200m floating loan and the treasurer believes that interest rates are likely to rise over the next five years. He could enter into a five-year swap with a counter party to swap into a fixed rate of interest for the next five years. From year six onwards, the company will once again pay a floating rate of interest.

- A swap can be used to obtain cheaper finance. A swap should result in a company being able to borrow what they want at a better rate under a swap arrangement, than borrowing it directly themselves.

## Calculations based on splitting gains

- The precise details of the swap arrangement will depend on how the potential gains are split between the two counter-parties.

### Illustration 7 – Interest rate swap

Company A wishes to raise $10m and to pay interest at a floating rate, as it would like to be able to take advantage of any fall in interest rates. It can borrow for one year at a fixed rate of 10% or at a floating rate of 1% above LIBOR.

Company B also wishes to raise $10m. They would prefer to issue fixed rate debt because they want certainty about their future interest payments, but can only borrow for one year at 13% fixed or LIBOR + 2% floating, as it has a lower credit rating than company A.

Calculate the effective swap rate for each company – assume savings are split equally.

### Solution

**Step 1:** Identify the type of loan with the biggest difference in rates.

- *Answer:* Fixed

**Step 2:** Identify the party that can borrow this type of loan the cheapest.

- *Answer:* Company A

- Thus Company A should borrow fixed, company B variable, reflecting their comparative advantages.

**Step 3:**

- Company A has cheaper borrowing in both fixed and variable. Interest rate differentials are 3% for fixed and 1% for variable. The difference between these (2%) is the potential gain from the swap.

- Splitting this equally between the two counter parties, each should gain by 1%.

One way (there are many!) of achieving this is for A to pay B LIBOR (variable) and for B to pay A 10%.

**Summary**

|                              | A            | B            |
|------------------------------|--------------|--------------|
| Actual borrowing             | (10%)        | (LIBOR + 2%) |
| A to B                       | (LIBOR)      | LIBOR        |
| B to A                       | 10%          | (10%)        |
| **Interest rates after swap**| **(LIBOR)**  | **(12%)**    |
| Open market cost – no swap   | (LIBOR + 1%) | (13%)        |
| Saving                       | 1%           | 1%           |

**Test your understanding 4**

Company X also wishes to raise $50m. They would prefer to issue fixed rate debt and can borrow for one year at 6% fixed or LIBOR + 80 points.

Company Y also wishes to raise $50m and to pay interest at a floating rate. It can borrow for one year at a fixed rate of 5% or at LIBOR + 50 points.

**Calculate the effective swap rate for each company – assume savings are split equally.**

## Calculations involving quoted rates from intermediaries

In practice a bank normally arranges the swap and will quote the following:

- The 'ask rate' at which the bank is willing to receive a fixed interest cash flow stream in exchange for paying LIBOR.

- The 'bid rate' that they are willing to pay in exchange for receiving LIBOR.

- The difference between these gives the bank's profit margin and is usually at least 2 basis points.

**Note:** LIBOR is the most widely used benchmark or reference rate for short-term interest rates worldwide, although the swap could relate to Euribor, say.

### Illustration 8 - Interest rate swap via an intermediary

Co A currently has a 12-month loan at a fixed rate of 5% but would like to swap to variable. It can currently borrow at a variable rate of LIBOR + 12 basis points.

The bank is currently quoting 12-month swap rates of 4.90 (bid) and 4.95 (ask).

**Show Co A's financial position if it enters the swap.**

**Solution**

|  | Co A |
|---|---|
| Actual borrowing | (5.00%) |
| Payment to bank | (LIBOR) |
| Receipt from bank (bid) | 4.90% |
| **Net interest rate after swap** | **(LIBOR + 0.10%)** |
| Open market cost – no swap | (LIBOR + 0.12%) |
| Saving | 2 basis points |

## Test your understanding 5

Co B has a 12-month loan at a variable rate of LIBOR + 15 basis points but, due to fears over interest rate rises, would like to swap to a fixed rate. It can currently borrow at 5.12% fixed.

The bank is currently quoting 12-month swap rates of 4.90 (bid) and 4.95 (ask). Assume this is the same bank as in the previous illustration.

**Show Co B's financial position if it enters the swap. Comment on the bank's position, bearing in mind the positions of Co A (in the previous Illustration) and Co B.**

## Expandable Text - Further swap example

Company A has a 12 month loan at a variable rate of LIBOR + 50 basis points but, due to fears over interest rate rises, would like to swap to a fixed rate. It can currently borrow at 5.40% fixed.

Company B currently has a 12 month loan at a fixed rate of 4.85% but would like to swap to variable. It can currently borrow at a variable rate of LIBOR + 65 basis points.

The bank is currently quoting 12 month swap rates of 4.50 (bid) and 4.52 (ask).

**Show how the swap via the intermediary would work.**

**Solution**

- Co A already has a variable outflow so must receive LIBOR from the bank to convert this to fixed. It will pay the bank the ask rate.

- Similarly Co B must pay the bank variable and receive fixed at the bid rate.

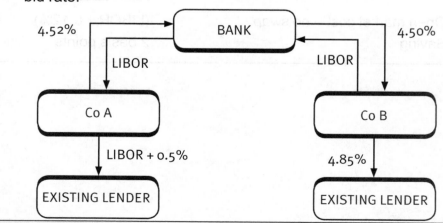

| | A | B |
|---|---|---|
| Actual borrowing | (LIBOR + 0.5%) | (4.85%) |
| Payment to bank | (4.52%) | (LIBOR) |
| Receipt from bank | LIBOR | 4.50% |
| **Net interest rates after swap** | **(5.02%)** | **(LIBOR + 0.35%)** |
| Open market cost – no swap | (5.40%) | (LIBOR + 0.65%) |
| Saving | 38 basis points | 30 basis points |

**Note:** In this case A can borrow variable cheaper but B can get the best fixed rates. In this case the total potential saving = D fixed + D variable = 55 + 15 = 70 basis points.

Of this, 2 basis points have gone to the bank via the spread in quoted prices, leaving 68 to be shared between the two companies.

## 7 Swaptions

### Options on swaps

- Swaptions are hybrid derivative products that integrate the benefits of swaps and options. They are options on swaps.

- The purchaser of an interest rate swaption has the right, but not the obligation, to enter into an interest rate swap at some future date on terms agreed today. An up front premium is payable.

**Expandable Text - Interest rate swaption example**

Shun Inc has a $10m loan, repayable in 5 years, at LIBOR + 2%. LIBOR is currently at 5.75%. The company is thus exposed to the risk of fluctuating interest rates.

The treasurer believes that LIBOR will stay low for the next two years, after which period, however, the outlook is at best uncertain. She would like to hedge this risk but is not sure if the current swap rate is the best available. The treasurer wants to lock in the swap rate in two years time for the following three years and have the flexibility to benefit from a lower swap rate should swap rates fall.

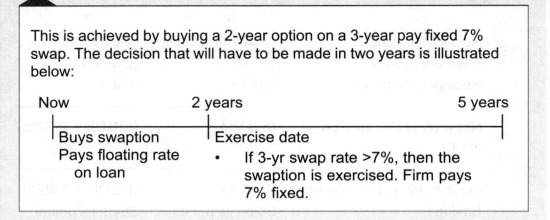

This is achieved by buying a 2-year option on a 3-year pay fixed 7% swap. The decision that will have to be made in two years is illustrated below:

Now          2 years               5 years

Buys swaption
Pays floating rate
on loan

Exercise date

• If 3-yr swap rate >7%, then the swaption is exercised. Firm pays 7% fixed.

## 8 Chapter summary

### Summary of terminology

|  | **Borrowing** | **Depositing** |
|---|---|---|
| FRA | Buy an FRA | Sell an FRA |
| IRG | Call option | Put option |
| Futures | Sell IR futures | Buy IR futures |
| Options | Buy put options | Buy call options |

**HEDGING INTEREST RATE RISK**

**FRAs**
- OTC
- Effectively fix rate

**STIRFs**
- Exchange
- Effectively fix rate

**Swaps**
- OTC
- Swap fixed for variable flows
- Splitting gains

**Options**
- Options on FRAs – Interest rate guarantees, caps floors
- Options on futures – collars
- Swaptions

## Test your understanding answers

### Test your understanding 1

|  | IRG at 4% | | FRA at 4% | |
| --- | --- | --- | --- | --- |
| Market rate | 5% – lapse | 3% – exercise | 5% | 3% |
| Interest | 100,000 | 80,000 | 80,000 | 80,000 |
| Premium | (12,000) | (12,000) | – | – |
| Net receipt | 88,000 | 68,000 | 80,000 | 80,000 |

Comment: the choice between FRA and IRG will depend on expectations and the desired risk exposure of the firm.

### Test your understanding 2

- Number of contracts = (2,000,000/500,000) × 3/3 = 4
- Number of ticks movement per contract = (94.90 - 92.90) × 100 = 200
- Value of a tick = £500,000 × 3/12 × 0.0001 = £12.50
- Profit on futures = ticks per contract × tick value × numbers of contracts = 200 × 12.50 × 4 = £10,000

**Test your understanding 3**

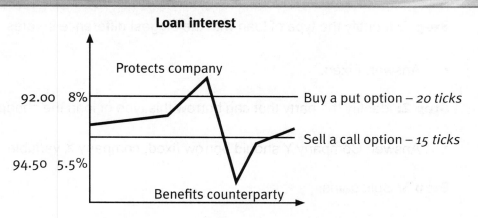

(a) Interest rates exceed the cap so the company will exercise its put option: (9.5%) + (2%) + (-0.20 + 0.15) + 92.00 − 90.20 = (9.75%).

(b) Interest rates have fallen below the floor so the bank will exercise its call option: (4.5%) + (2%) + (-0.20 + 0.15) − 96.10 + 94.50 = (8.15%).

## Test your understanding 4

**Step 1:** Identify the type of loan with the biggest difference in rates.

- Answer: Fixed.

**Step 2:** Identify the party that can borrow this type of loan the cheapest.

- Answer: Company Y should borrow fixed, company X variable.

**Step 3:** Split gains.

- Company Y has cheaper borrowing in both fixed and variable. Interest rate differentials are 1% for fixed and 0.3% for variable. The difference between these (70 basis points) is the potential gain from the swap.
- Splitting this equally between the two counter parties, each should gain by 35 basis points.
- One way of achieving this is for X to pay Y 4.85% and for Y to pay X LIBOR (variable).

**Summary**

|  | X | Y |
|---|---|---|
| Actual borrowing | (LIBOR + 0.8%) | (5%) |
| X to Y | (4.85%) | 4.85% |
| Y to X | LIBOR | (LIBOR) |
|  | —————— | —————— |
| Interest rates after swap | (5.65%) | (LIBOR + 0.15%) |
|  | —————— | —————— |
| Open market cost – no swap | (6%) | (LIBOR + 0.5%) |
| Saving | 35 points | 35 points |

## Test your understanding 5

| | **B** |
| --- | --- |
| Actual borrowing | (LIBOR + 0.15%) |
| Payment to bank (ask) | (4.95%) |
| Receipt from bank | LIBOR |
| | ———————— |
| **Net interest rates after swap** | **(5.10%)** |
| | ———————— |
| Open market cost – no swap | (5.12%) |
| Saving | 2 basis points |

Both Co A and Co B have saved 2 basis points by entering their swaps.

The bank has made a profit of 5 basis points - the difference between the bid and ask rates:

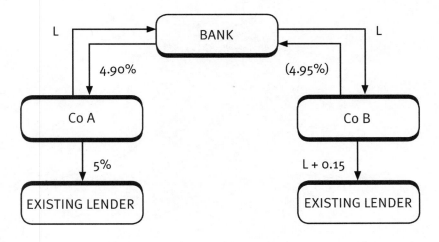

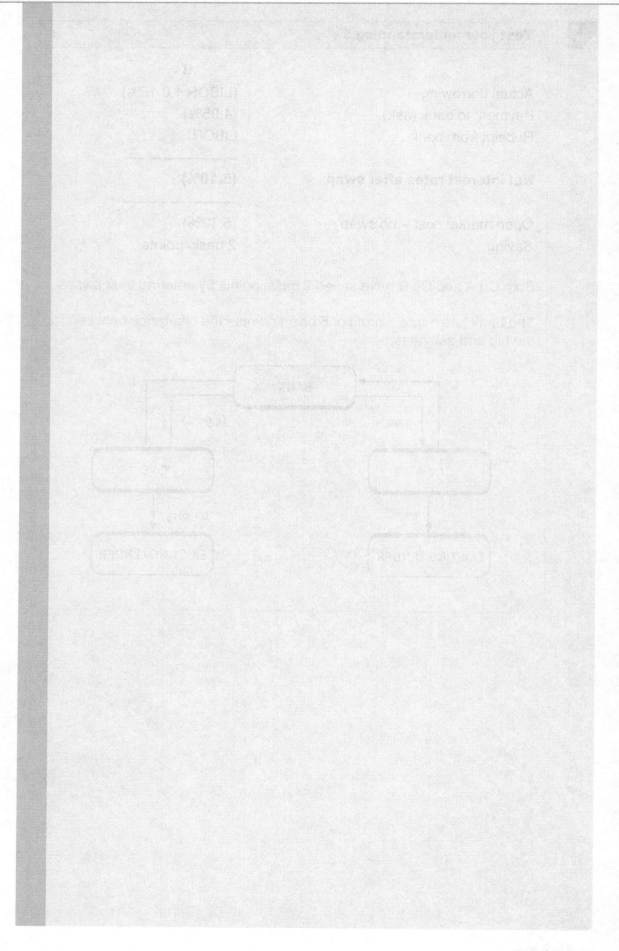

# The economic environment for multinationals

## Chapter learning objectives

Upon completion of this chapter you will be able to:

- explain the theory of comparative advantage

- explain the theory of free trade and the development of barriers to trade

- list and explain the major trade agreements and common markets currently in operation

- for a given business, on the basis of contemporary circumstances, advise on the policy and strategic implications of explain the major trade agreements and common markets currently in operation

- list and explain the objectives of the World Trade Organisation

- explain the objectives and function of the main international financial institutions, within the context of a globalised economy:
    - International Monetary Fund.
    - The Bank of International Settlements.
    - The World Bank.
    - The principal Central Banks (The Fed, ECB and Bank of Japan):

- explain the role of the international financial markets with respect to the management of global debt, the financial development of the emerging economies and the maintenance of global financial stability

- explain the implications for financial planning of the level of mobility of capital across borders and national limitations on remittances and transfer pricing

- explain the implications for financial planning of the pattern of economic and other risk exposures in the different national markets
- explain the implications for financial planning of agency issues in the central coordination of overseas operations and the balancing of local financial autonomy with effective central control.

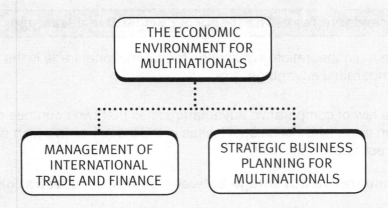

# 1 Free trade and the development of barriers to trade

## Free trade

### Practical reasons for overseas trade

- Choice – The diversity of goods available in a domestic economy is increased through the import of goods that could be uneconomic or impossible to produce at home.

- Competition – International trade will increase competition in domestic markets, which is likely to lead to both a reduction in price, together with increasing pressure for new products and innovation.

- Economies of scale – By producing both for the home and international markets companies can produce at a larger scale and therefore take advantage of economies of scale.

- Specialisation – If a country specialises in producing the goods and services at which it is most efficient, it can maximise its economic output.

**Illustration 1**

Imagine the impact on a country's consumers if international trade did not take place. No bananas, no tropical fruits at any time of the year, vegetables only when they are in season. Less obviously, some countries would be chronically short of many basic metals and materials. Many countries are also increasingly dependent on energy imports. Overall, world economic output would be far lower as countries would be forced to allocate resources to inefficient methods of production.

## Expandable Text - The theory of comparitive advantage

The main theoretical justification for international trade is the law of comparative advantage.

The law of comparative advantage states that two countries can gain from trade when each specialises in the industries in which each has the lowest opportunity cost.

### Comparative advantage between countries - illustration

Imagine a global economy with two countries and two products. Each country needs both products and at present all needs are met by domestic production. Each country has the same resources available to it and they are split equally between the two products.

Suppose the current situation with regard to production is as follows:

|  | Units of X per day | Units of Y per day |
| --- | --- | --- |
| Country A | 1,200 | 720 |
| Country B | 960 | 240 |
| Total daily production | 2,160 | 960 |

As the situation currently stands, country A has an absolute advantage in production of both X and Y.

Given this what are the benefits of A trading with B?

To answer this question we need to consider the opportunity costs incurred by producing X and Y.

- If country A were to focus on making X only, it would give up 720 units of Y to produce an extra 1,200 units of X, i.e. the opportunity cost of 1 unit of X is 720/1,200 = 0.6 units of Y.

- If country B were to focus on making X only, it would give up 240 units of Y to produce an extra 960 units of X, i.e. the opportunity cost of 1 unit of X is 240/960 = 0.25 units of Y.

- The opportunity cost of producing X is lower for country B than it is for country A. It follows that B has a comparative advantage in production of X and should specialise in this product.

If country B is to make product X, it follows that country A should make product Y. An analysis of opportunity costs supports this conclusion.

- If country A were to focus on making Y only, it would give up 1,200 units of X to make 720 units of Y, i.e. the opportunity cost of 1 unit of Y is 1,200/720 = 1.67 units of X.

- If country B were to focus on making Y only, it would give up 960 units of X to make 240 units of Y, i.e. the opportunity cost of 1 unit of Y is 960/240 = 4 units of X.

- Since country A has the lowest opportunity cost for production of Y, it should specialise in production of this product.

The impact of this decision by each country to specialise in production of the good for which they have the lowest opportunity cost on world output is shown below:

**Specialisation based on lowest opportunity cost**

|  | Units of X per day | Units of Y per day |
| --- | --- | --- |
| Country A | 0 | 1,440 |
| Country B | 1,920 | 0 |
| Total daily production | 1,920 | 1,440 |

## Trade barriers

There are a number of ways that a country can seek to restrict imports. Trade barriers include:

- Quotas – imposition of a maximum number of units that can be imported e.g. quotas on the number of cars manufactured outside of Europe that can be imported into the EU.

- Tariffs – imposition of an import tax on goods being imported into the country to make them uncompetitive on price.

- Exchange controls – domestic companies wishing to buy foreign goods will have to pay in the currency of the exporter's country. To do this they will need to buy the currency involved by selling sterling. If the government controls the sale of sterling it can control the level of imports purchased.

- Administrative controls – a domestic government can subject imports to excessive levels of administration, paperwork and red tape to slow down and increase the cost of importing goods into the home economy.

- Embargoes – the prohibition of commerce and trade with a certain country.

## 2 Trade agreements and common markets

In many parts of the world, governments have created trade agreements and common markets to encourage free trade. However, the World Trade Organisation (WTO) is opposed to these trading blocs and customs unions (e.g. the European Union) because they encourage trade between members but often have high trade barriers for non-members.

## Expandable Text - E.g. of trade agreements & common markets

### Bi-lateral trade agreements

These are agreements between two countries to eliminate quotas and tariffs on the trade of most (if not all) goods between them.

e.g. The Closer Economic Relations (CER) agreement between Australia and New Zealand.

### Multi-lateral trade agreements

These are similar to bi-lateral agreements except more than two countries are involved.

e.g. The North American Free Trade Agreement (NAFTA) between Canada, the United States, and Mexico.

### Free trade areas

If the members of a multi-lateral free trade agreement are all in the same geographical area then it is sometimes described as a free trade area.

e.g. The ASEAN Free Trade Area (AFTA) is an agreement by the Association of Southeast Asian Nations (Brunei, Indonesia, Malaysia, Philippines, Singapore, Thailand, Vietnam, Laos, Myanmar and Cambodia).

### Customs unions

A customs union is a free trade area with a common external tariff. The participant countries set up common external trade policy, but in some cases they use different import quotas.

e.g. Mercosur is a customs union between Brazil, Argentina, Uruguay, Paraguay and Venezuela in South America.

### Single markets (economic communities)

A single market is a customs union with common policies on product regulation, and freedom of movement of all the four factors of production (goods, services, capital and labour).

e.g. The Economic Community of West African States (ECOWAS).

### Economic unions

An economic and monetary union is a single market with a common currency.

e.g. The largest economic and monetary union at present is the Eurozone. The Eurozone consists of the European Union member states that have adopted the Euro.

### Expandable Text - The World Trade Organistaion (WTO)

In 1995 the World Trade Organisation based in Geneva replaced GATT.

### Objectives

*   To ensure compliance of member countries with previous GATT agreements.
*   To negotiate future trade liberalisation agreements.
*   To resolve trading disputes between nations.

For example, there is growing tension between the developed and the developing world. The developing world regards the heavy subsidy of EU and American farmers as a huge barrier to trade for their domestic farmers. At the same time, the developed world complains about exports of low cost manufactured goods from the developing world that are not subject to the same health, safety and environmental regulations that they face.

## 3 Specific strategic issues for multinational organisations – national governance requirements

A multinational company (MNC) is defined as one which generates at least 25% of its sales from activities in countries other than its own. This rules out returns from portfolio investment and eliminates unit and investment trusts.

Different countries have different governance requirements. These national governance requirements will impact on the behaviour of multinational organisations.

### Test your understanding 1

**Explain the difficulties faced by national governments when placing restrictions upon multinational organisations.**

## 4 Specific strategic issues for multinational organisations – the mobility of capital across borders

### The mobility of capital

One of the drivers of globalisation has been the increased level of mobility of capital across borders.

### Implications of an increased mobility of capital:

- Lower costs of capital.
- Ability of MNCs to switch activities between countries.
- Ability of MNCs to circumnavigate national restrictions.
- Potentially increased exposure to foreign currency risk.

## 5 Specific strategic issues for multinational organisations – local risk

Local risk for multinationals includes the following:

- Economic risk is the possibility of loss arising to a firm from changes in the economy of a country.
- Political risk is the possibility of loss arising to a firm from actions taken by the government or people of a country.

### Political risk

Examples of political risk:

### Confiscation political risk

- This is the risk of loss of control over the foreign entity through intervention of the local government or other force.

**Illustration 2**

- Countries vulnerable to changes of regime – Chile.
- Invasion by powerful neighbours – Lebanon.
- Transition to local ownership – India.
- Confiscation is a very real possibility – Zimbabwe.

## Commercial political risk

**Illustration 3**

The Portuguese revolution of 1974 was followed by several years of left-wing military rule in which wages were compulsorily raised and prices controlled at unrealistic falling real levels. Subsidiaries of foreign parents found their margins squeezed and little sympathy from the authorities. Those that which happened to be suppliers to the government were hit hardest and also had to face serious attempts by the unions to take control of the management. Many such subsidiaries were either abandoned by their shareholders or sold at knockdown prices to local interests. It was interference with the commercial processes of supply and demand that drove their parents out, not confiscation. What drove their parents out was not confiscation but interference with the commercial processes of supply and demand.

## Financial political risk

This risk takes many forms:

- Restricted access to local borrowings.

- Restrictions on repatriating capital, dividends or other remittances. These can take the form of prohibition or penal taxation.

- Financial penalties on imports from the rest of the group such as heavy interest-free import deposits.

## Exchange control risk

One form of exchange control risk is that the group may accumulate surplus cash in the country where the subsidiary operates, either as profits or as amounts owed for imports to the subsidiary, which cannot be remitted out of the country. This can be mitigated by using FOREX hedging.

**Illustration 4**

A good example is the French regulation under which intra-group trade debts of a French subsidiary to its associated companies, if not made within 12 months of import, become unremittable as 'capital invested in the subsidiary'. Often the French subsidiary delays payment by more than 12 months because of a shortage of cash created by other French official actions or policies.

## 6 Specific strategic issues for multinational organisations – control

Within the hierarchy of firms (in a group) goal incongruence may arise when divisional managers in overseas operations promote their own self-interest over those of other divisions and of the organisation generally.

### Test your understanding 2

Consider a multinational organisation setting up a new overseas subsidiary. List the issues arising from decentralising control to local management.

### Expandable Text - International Financial Institutions

#### International Monetary Fund (IMF)

The IMF was founded in 1944 at an international conference at Bretton Woods in the USA but did not really begin to fully function until the 1950s. The so called Bretton Woods System that the IMF was to supervise was to have two main characteristics: stable exchange rates and a multilateral system of international payments and credit.

IMF objectives and functions:

- Promoting international financial cooperation and establishing a system of stable exchange rates and freely convertible currencies.
- Providing a source of credit for members with balance of payments deficits while corrective policies were adopted.
- Managing the growth of international liquidity.

#### The Bank for International Settlements

**The Bank for International Settlements** (BIS) is an intergovernmental organisation (IGO) whose membership consists of central banks and national monetary authorities.

Objectives:

- to foster international monetary and
- to foster financial cooperation and
- to serve as a bank for central banks.

## World Bank

The International Bank for Reconstruction and Development (IBRD), also known as the World Bank, was the second institution created at the Bretton Woods meeting in 1944. Its membership and decision making processes are similar to those of the IMF. The original purpose of the IBRD was to help finance the reconstruction of economies damaged by the war. However, it soon shifted the focus of its lending to countries of the developing world. The bank now comprises three principal constituent elements:

- The IBRD proper whose function is to lend long-term funds for capital projects in developing economies at a commercial rate of interest. The main source of these funds is borrowing by the IBRD itself.

- The International Development Association (IDA) which was established in 1960 to provide 'soft' loans to the poorest of the developing countries. The IDA:
    - (a) is mainly financed by 20 donor countries providing funds every three years; funding therefore depends on the generosity or otherwise of these countries
    - (b) provides loans on concessionary terms, normally interest free loans repayable over 50 years.

- The International Finance Corporation which promotes the private sector in developing countries by lending or by taking equity.

The World Bank is clearly an important source of capital funds for the developing countries. However, it has been criticised in recent years over the nature of its lending conditions. For example criticisms have been levelled about conditions that tie farmers into growing cash crops (e.g. oil seed rape) in countries that have a historical propensity for famine (e.g. parts of Eastern Africa).

## Principal Central Banks

### The Fed

The Federal Reserve System, also known as 'The Fed,' is the central bank of the United States.

Functions and objectives:

- In its role as a central bank, the Fed is a bank for other banks and a bank for the federal government.

- It was created to provide the US with a safer, more flexible, and more stable monetary and financial system.

- Over the years, its role in banking and the economy has expanded. The Federal Reserve System is a network of 12 Federal Reserve Banks and a number of branches under the general oversight of the Board of Governors. The Reserve Banks are the operating arms of the central bank.

## ECB

The **European Central Bank (ECB)** is one of the world's most important central banks, responsible for monetary policy covering the 13 member countries of the Eurozone.

The ECB was established on June 1, 1998 and its headquarters are located in Frankfurt, Germany.

Objectives of the ECB:

- The primary objective of the ECB, and the wider ESCB, is 'to maintain price stability' within the euro area, i.e. to keep inflation low.

- In addition, and without prejudice to the objective of price stability, the bank has to support the economic policies of the European Union. These are designed to foster a high level of employment and sustainable and non-inflationary economic growth under Article 2 of the Treaty of the European Union (otherwise known as the Maastricht Treaty).

## Bank of Japan

The Bank of Japan is headquartered in Nihonbashi, Tokyo.

Objectives and functions.

According to its charter, the missions of the Bank of Japan are:

- issuance and management of banknotes

- implementation of monetary policy

- providing settlement services and ensuring the stability of the financial system

- treasury and government securities-related operations

- international activities

- compilation of data, economic analyses and research activities.

KAPLAN PUBLISHING

## The Bank of England

The Bank of England's Monetary Policy Committee sets interest rates in the UK.

Another of the Bank's main roles is to act as "lender of last resort" to other UK banks.

## 7 Chapter summary

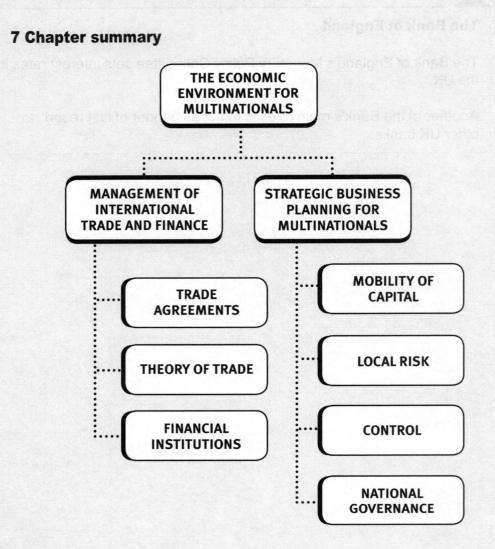

## Test your understanding answers

### Test your understanding 1

Individual countries have imposed their own restrictions from time to time by, for example, reserving certain shareholdings for their own nationals or by limiting the transference of profits or royalties. But even governments have to tread carefully lest the subject of their attentions abandons the market altogether.

### Test your understanding 2

**Pro centralisation**

- Decisions are made at one point and so are easier to coordinate (congruence).
- Senior managers can take a wider view.
- Policies and procedures can be standardised.
- Possibly cheaper.

**Pro decentralisation**

- Improved motivation.
- Better local knowledge.
- Quicker decision making.
- Greater speed of decision making.

# 16

# Money markets and complex financial instruments

## Chapter learning objectives

Upon completion of this chapter you will be able to:

- explain the role of the money markets in providing short-term liquidity to industry and the public sector

- explain the role of the money markets in providing short-term trade finance

- explain the role of the money markets in allowing a multinational firm to manage its exposure to FOREX and interest rate risk

- explain the role of the banks and other financial institutions in the operation of the money markets

- explain the role of the treasury management function in the short-term management of the firm's financial resources

- explain the role of the treasury management function in the longer term maximisation of shareholder value

- explain the role of the treasury management function in the management of risk exposure

- describe the characteristics of coupon bearing instruments and their use in the money markets

- describe the characteristics of discount instruments and their use in the money markets

- describe the characteristics of derivatives and their use in the money markets

- explain and evaluate the role of money market instruments (coupon bearing, discount and derivatives) for the short term financing of a multinational business

INTERNATIONAL MONEY MARKETS AND
COMPLEX FINANCIAL INSTRUMENTS

FINANCIAL
INSTRUMENTS

THE ROLE OF
MONEY MARKETS

THE ROLE OF THE
TREASURY FUNCTION

# 1 Introduction – the financial system

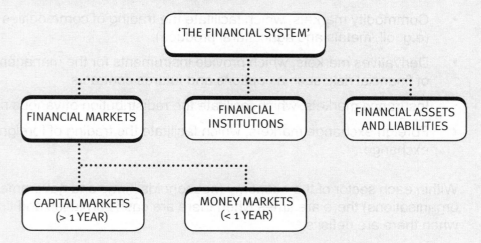

Collectively the financial system does the following:

(1) Channels funds from lenders to borrowers.

(2) Provides a mechanism for payments – e.g. direct debits, cheque clearing system.

(3) Creates liquidity and money – e.g. banks create money through increasing their lending.

(4) Provides financial services such as insurance and pensions.

(5) Offers facilities to manage investment portfolios – e.g. to hedge risk.

## Expandable Text - Details of the financial system

### The financial system

'The financial system' is an umbrella term covering the following:

• Financial markets – e.g. stock exchanges, money markets.

• Financial institutions – e.g. banks, building societies, insurance companies and pension funds.

• Financial assets and liabilities – e.g. mortgages, bonds, bills and equity shares.

### Financial markets

The financial markets can be divided into different types, depending on the products being issued/bought/sold:

• Capital markets which consist of stock-markets for shares and bond markets.

- Money markets, which provide short-term (< 1 year) debt financing and investment.

- Commodity markets, which facilitate the trading of commodities (e.g. oil, metals and agricultural produce).

- Derivatives markets, which provide instruments for the management of financial risk, such as options and futures contracts.

- Insurance markets, which facilitate the redistribution of various risks.

- Foreign exchange markets, which facilitate the trading of foreign exchange.

Within each sector of the economy (households, firms and governmental organisations) there are times when there are cash surpluses and times when there are deficits.

- In the case of surpluses the party concerned will seek to invest/deposit/lend funds to earn an economic return.

- In the case of deficits the party will seek to borrow funds to manage their liquidity position.

## 2 Money market instruments

A financial manager needs to understand the characteristics of the following money market instruments:

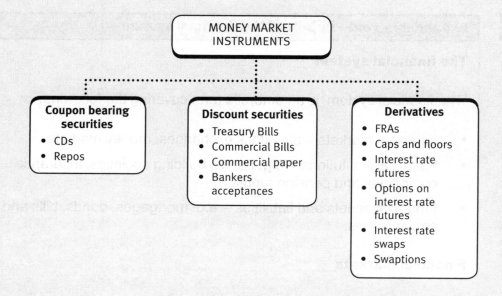

## Expandable Text - Explanation of money market instruments

### Coupon bearing instruments

Coupon bearing securities have a fixed maturity and a specified rate of interest.

### Certificates of deposit (CDs)

- CDs are evidence of a deposit with an issuing bank (or building society).

- They are fully negotiable and hence attractive to the depositor since they ensure instant liquidity if required.

- They provide the bank with a deposit for a fixed period at a fixed rate of interest.

### Sale and repurchase agreements ('repos')

- In a repo transaction, X sells certain securities (treasury bills, bank bills etc) to Y and simultaneously agrees to buy them back at a later date at a higher price.

- This could be arranged through the repo desk of a major bank, for example.

- In effect, a repo is a secured short-term loan and the higher repurchase price reflects the interest on the loan.

- Central banks often fix the short-term repo interest rate, which in turn affects all other short-term interest rates (e.g. base rates, LIBOR).

### Illustration of repos

Reaper Co enters a repo agreement as follows:

(1) Sell £4 million (nominal) UK Treasury Bills for £3.94 million.

(2) Buy them back 45 days later for £3.96 million.

Determine the effective interest rate.

### Solution

Interest rate = $((3.96 - 3.94)/(3.94)) \times 365/45 = 0.0411$, or 4.11%

This could be compared with the borrowing rate offered by banks, for example.

**Note:** In some areas, notably the USA, a 360 day count is used instead of 365.

## Discount instruments

In the discount market, funds are raised by issuing bills at a discount to their eventual redemption or maturity value.

Bills have the following characteristics:

- Issued in large denominations.
- Highly liquid – due to short maturity and highly organised market for buying/selling.
- Reward for the lender comes as a capital gain.
- Effectively fixed-interest as redemption value fixed.

### Treasury bills

- Issued mainly by governments via central banks.
- Usually one or three month maturity.

### Commercial bills

- Similar to treasury bills except issued by large corporations.

### Commercial paper

- Initial maturity usually between seven and forty-five days.
- May be unsecured so credit ratings important.
- High issue costs so only suitable for larger amounts.

### Banker's acceptances

- These are discussed in more detail below under trade finance.

### Illustration of commercial paper

CP Co wishes to issue £10 million of commercial paper for 90 days at an implicit interest rate of 5% pa.

(**Note:** this could be expressed as stating that the paper will be issued 'at a discount of 5%'.)

Determine the issue price.

## Solution

Issue price = present value of future redemption

= £10m × 1/(1 + 0.05 × 90/365) = £9,878,213

## Derivatives

Derivatives are so called because their value derives from the value of other assets.

- Instruments bought on the 'over the counter' market – OTC are purchased from the major banks and are usually 'tailor-made' to suit the precise requirements of the company.

- Exchange-traded instruments are of a standard size thus ensuring that they are marketable.

There are essentially two types of derivative:

- Instruments that fix a future price (e.g. FRAs, futures).

- Instruments that give the owner the right but not the obligation to fix a future price (e.g. options).

Money market instruments include the following:

- Forward rate agreements (FRAs).
- Caps and floors (options on FRAs).
- Interest rate futures.
- Options on interest rate futures.
- Interest rate swaps.
- Swaptions.

Specific details of individual instruments are discussed in more detail elsewhere in this Text.

### The role of money market instruments for short term financing

While some firms encounter a mixture of short-term cash surpluses and deficits, many can be classified as either cash generators or cash consumers.

- Cash generators (e.g. many retailers) will look to lay off cash on short-term markets or return surplus funds to investors (e.g. via a dividend).

- Cash consumers (e.g. young, fast growing firms) will look to borrow short-term.

### Test your understanding 1

**By considering the product lifecycle, comment as to whether a major drugs company is likely to be a cash generator or a cash consumer?**

## 3 The role of the money markets in international business
### Managing short-term liquidity
### Companies

- For many companies bank borrowing is the simplest method of short-term finance.
    - Loans are usually fixed term, may be for variable or fixed rates and are normally secured, overdrafts variable rate and unsecured.
    - Rates will depend on perceived credit risk.

- Factoring can be useful where sales are made to low risk customers.

- Companies with high credit ratings often take advantage of commercial paper markets, where they may be able to borrow at lower rates than those offered by banks.

### Banks

- Banks participate in 'inter-bank markets', either lending to other banks, or borrowing from them. Recently they have been joined by the larger building societies.

- This is a very important source of funds to banks. For example, the London Inter-Bank Offered Rate (or LIBOR) is now used instead of base rate to determine the interest payable on some types of company borrowing.

## Local authorities

Local authorities obtain their borrowing requirements from:

- central government,and money markets

- stock exchanges, and

- from advertising for loans from the general public.

### Test your understanding 2

**What do you consider to be the key factors to consider when choosing which instruments to use?**

## Inter-relationships

All the markets in a money market closely inter-mesh with each other and in that way the market may be regarded as an entity. The players are the same and they pass the ball between each other.

However, since the global "credit crunch" of 2008, the liquidity in the money markets has reduced as the different players have begun to view each other with suspicion. The credit crunch is covered in more detail in the later chapter on topical issues.

### Illustration 1

- A large company might deposit $500,000 with Bull's Bank, which issues it with a CD.

- Bull's Bank then looks at the local authority market, decides that rates there are rather low, and instead lends the money for a week on the inter-bank market to another bank that is short of funds.

- A week later local authority rates have improved and Bull's Bank lends the $500,000 to a big city council.

- Meanwhile, the large company has decided to bring forward an investment project and wants its $500,000 quickly to help pay for some sophisticated new electronic equipment. It sells the CD to a bank, which might either carry it to maturity or sell it to any of the banks – except Bull's Bank.

All these transactions, with the possible exception of the CD deals, will have taken place through a broker who sits at the end of a telephone switching the funds from one market to another as rates move and potential borrowers and lenders acquaint the broker with information about their requirements.

### Short-term trade finance

As well as having routine cash surpluses /deficits that need managing, firms often need short-term finance for individual (usually large) trade deals. A supplier faces two problems in such cases:

- Default risk from the customer.

- The time delay between cash outflows to make the product and receipt of payment.

The most common way of managing these is by using banker's acceptances by creating a 'letter of credit'.

---

**Expandable Text - Letter of credit illustration**

Step 1 **Initial trade deal**

- Company A agrees to buy goods from Company B for $10 million (say), payable in 30 days' time.

Step 2 **Create letter of credit (LOC)**

- Co. A agrees payment terms with their bank (Bank A).

- Bank A issues Co. B's bank (Bank B) with a letter of credit, stating that it will pay the $10m in 30 days.

- Bank B informs Company B of the receipt.

Step 3 **Supply of goods**

- Co. B then ships the goods to Co. A.

- Co. B passes shipping and other necessary documents to Bank B.

Step 4 **Create banker's acceptance**

- Bank B passes the letter of credit and supporting documentation back to Bank A.

- If all is in order, Bank A 'accepts' the letter of credit, accepting responsibility for payment. This creates the 'banker's acceptance', which is passed back to Bank B.

---

Step 5 **Options for using the banker's acceptance.**

Bank B could:

- wait until payment in 30 days

- request immediate payment (of the discounted value) from Bank A – effectively selling it back to Bank A

- sell the acceptance (at its discounted value) to the money markets.

Step 6 **Banker's acceptance redeemed**

- After 30 days Bank A redeems the acceptance, paying the then holder.

## Short-term risk management

Money markets are particularly useful for hedging interest rate and exchange rate risks. These are discussed in detail in the hedging chapters.

## The role of banks and other financial institutions

Faced with a desire to lend or borrow, there are three choices open to the end-users of the financial system:

(1) Lenders and borrowers contact each other directly.

This is rare due to the high costs involved, the risks of default and the inherent inefficiencies of this approach.

(2) Lenders and borrowers use an organised financial market.

For example, an individual may purchase corporate bonds from a recognised bond market. If this is a new issue of bonds by a company looking to raise funds, then the individual has effectively lent money to the company.

If the individual wishes to recover their funds before the redemption date on the bond, then they can sell the bond to another investor.

(3) Lenders and borrowers use intermediaries.

In this case the lender obtains an asset which cannot usually be traded but only returned to the intermediary. Such assets could include a bank deposit account, pension fund rights, etc.

The borrower will typically have a loan provided by an intermediary.

Financial intermediaries thus have a number of important roles.

- Risk reduction
- Aggregation
- Maturity transformation
- Financial intermediation

### Expandable Text - The important roles of financial intermediaries

#### Risk reduction

By lending to a wide variety of individuals and businesses financial intermediaries reduce the risk of a single default resulting in total loss of assets.

#### Aggregation

By pooling many small deposits, financial intermediaries are able to make much larger advances than would be possible for most individuals.

#### Maturity transformation

Most borrowers wish to borrow in the long term whilst most savers are unwilling to lock up their money for the long term. Financial intermediaries, by developing a floating pool of deposits, are able to satisfy both the needs of lenders and borrowers.

#### Financial intermediation

Financial intermediaries bring together lenders and borrowers through a process known as financial intermediation.

## 4 The role of the treasury department

### The role of the treasury function

The treasury function of a firm usually has the following roles:

### Short-term management of resources

- Short-term cash management – lending/borrowing funds as required.
- Currency management.

### Long-term maximisation of shareholder wealth

- Raising long-term finance, including equity strategy, management of debt capacity and debt and equity structure.
- Investment decisions, including investment appraisal, the review of acquisitions and divestments and defence from takeover.
- Dividend policy.

### Risk management

- Assessing risk exposure.
- Interest rate risk management.
- Hedging of foreign exchange risk.

### Expandable Text - Treasury: cost centre or profit centre?

As a cost centre the aggregate treasury function costs would simply be charged throughout the group on a fair basis. If no such fair basis can be agreed, the costs can remain as central head office unallocated costs in any group segmental analysis.

However it is also possible to identify revenues arising from treasury departments and thus to establish the treasury as a profit centre. Revenues could be realised as follows:

- Each division can be charged the market value for the services provided by the treasury. The total value charged throughout the group should exceed the treasury's costs enabling it to report a profit.
- By deciding not to hedge all currency and interest rate risks. Experts in the treasury could decide which risks not to hedge, hoping to profit from unhedged favourable exchange rate and interest rate movements.

- Hedging using currency and interest rate options leaves an upside potential which could be realised if the rate moves in the company's favour.

- Taking on additional exchange rate or other risks purely as a speculative activity, e.g. writing options on currencies or on shares held.

The trend in recent years has been for large companies to turn their treasuries from cost centres into profit centres and to expect the treasury to pay its way and generate regular profits each year. However the following points should be noted:

- A treasury engaged in speculation must be properly controlled by the company's board of directors. Millions of dollars can be committed in one telephone call by a treasurer, so it is crucial that limits are set on traders' risk exposures and that these limits are monitored scrupulously. The temptation has been for directors to let treasurers 'get on with whatever they do' as long as regular profits are being earned. Such a policy is no longer acceptable; the finance director in particular must control the treasury on a day-to-day basis.

- For example, in 1993 the German oils and metals company Metallgesellschaft managed to lose $1 billion after becoming over-exposed to oil derivative contracts.

- Treasury staff must be well trained and probably well paid, so that staff of the right calibre can be secured.

- The low volume of foreign currency transactions undertaken by a small company would probably make a profit centre approach unviable. A regular flow of large foreign transactions is needed before the cost centre approach is abandoned.

## The international treasury function

The corporate treasurer in an international group of companies will be faced with problems relating specifically to the international spread of investments.

- Setting transfer prices to reduce the overall tax bill.
- Deciding currency exposure policies and procedures.
- Transferring of cash across international borders.
- Devising investment strategies for short-term funds from the range of international money markets and international marketable securities.
- Netting and matching currency obligations.

KAPLAN PUBLISHING

## Expandable Text - The centralisation of treasury activities

The question arises in a large international group of whether treasury activities should be centralised or decentralised.

- If centralised, then each operating company holds only the minimum cash balance required for day to day operations, remitting the surplus to the centre for overall management. This process is sometimes known as cash pooling, the pool usually being held in a major financial centre or a tax haven country.

- If decentralised, each operating company must appoint an officer responsible for that company's own treasury operations.

### Advantages of centralisation

- No need for treasury skills to be duplicated throughout the group. One highly trained central department can assemble a highly skilled team, offering skills that could not be available if every company had their own treasury.

- Necessary borrowings can be arranged in bulk, at keener interest rates than for smaller amounts. Similarly bulk deposits of surplus funds will attract higher rates of interest than smaller amounts.

- The group's foreign currency risk can be managed much more effectively from a centralised treasury since only they can appreciate the total exposure situation. A total hedging policy is more efficiently carried out by head office rather than each company doing their own hedging.

- One company does not borrow at high rates while another has idle cash.

- Bank charges should be lower since a situation of carrying both balances and overdraft in the same currency should be eliminated.

- A centralised treasury can be run as a profit centre to raise additional profits for the group.

- Transfer prices can be established to minimise the overall group tax bill.

- Funds can be quickly returned to companies requiring cash via direct transfers.

### Advantages of decentralisation

- Greater autonomy leads to greater motivation. Individual companies will manage their cash balances more attentively if they are responsible for them rather than simply remitting them up to head office.

- Local operating units should have a better feel for local conditions than head office and can respond more quickly to local developments.

### Test your understanding 3

**Compare and contrast the roles of the treasury and finance departments with respect to a proposed investment.**

# 5 Chapter summary

```
┌─────────────────────────────────────┐
│  INTERNATIONAL MONEY MARKETS AND     │
│  COMPLEX FINANCIAL INSTRUMENTS       │
└─────────────────────────────────────┘
```

**Financial instruments**
- Coupon bearing
- Discount
- Derivatives
  - standard contracts
  - tick size
  - margins
  - basis risk

**The role of money markets**
- Short-term liquidity
- Trade finance
- Risk management
- Role of intermediaries

**The role of the treasury function**
- Short-term
- Long-term
- Risk management

## Test your understanding answers

### Test your understanding 1

In the drug development stage of the product lifecycle, the firm will be a cash consumer due to the huge sums that need to be spent on research and development.

If patent protection can be established, then high prices should ensure that the company is a cash generator until the patent expires.

### Test your understanding 2

- Effective interest rate – linked to default risk.
- Risk – especially with regard to investing surplus cash.
- Amounts.
- Marketability/liquidity.
- Timescales/maturity.
- Availability.

## Test your understanding 3

Treasury is the function concerned with the provision and use of finance and thus handles the acquisition and custody of funds whereas the Finance Department has responsibility for accounting, reporting and control. The roles of the two departments in the proposed investment are as follows:

### Evaluation

- Treasury will quantify the cost of capital to be used in assessing the investment.

- The finance department will estimate the project cash flows.

### Implementation

- Treasury will establish corporate financial objectives, such as wanting to restrict gearing to 40%, and will identify sources and types of finance.

- Treasury will also deal with currency management – dealing in foreign currencies and hedging currency risks – and taxation.

- The finance department will be involved with the preparation of budgets and budgetary control, the preparation of periodic financial statements and the management and administration of activities such as payroll and internal audit.

### Interaction

- The Treasury Department has main responsibility for setting corporate objectives and policy and Financial Control has the responsibility for implementing policy and ensuring the achievement of corporate objectives. This distinction is probably far too simplistic and, in reality, both departments will make contributions to both determination and achievement of objectives.

- There is a circular relationship in that Treasurers quantify the cost of capital, which the Financial Controllers use as the criterion for the deployment of funds; Financial Controllers quantify projected cash flows which in turn trigger Treasurers' decisions to employ capital.

# Topical issues in financial management

## Chapter learning objectives

Upon completion of this chapter you will be able to:

- describe and discuss the significance to the firm, of the latest developments in the world financial markets with reference to the removal of barriers to the free movement of capital and the international regulations on money laundering

- identify the latest emerging derivative products, explain the risks of derivative trading, and describe how tools such as value at risk, scenario analysis and stress testing can help a firm to manage the process

- identify the latest developments in the macroeconomic environment (regarding international trade and finance) - such as the credit crunch - and explain the impact on a firm.

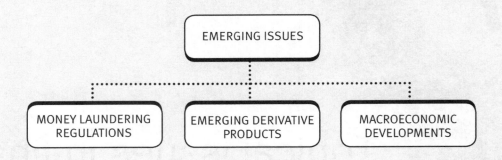

EMERGING ISSUES

MONEY LAUNDERING REGULATIONS

EMERGING DERIVATIVE PRODUCTS

MACROECONOMIC DEVELOPMENTS

## 1 Introduction to topical issues

### Note on further reading

The Advanced Financial Management examiner has stated that he wants the paper to be a contemporary, "Masters Level" paper. Therefore it is very important to read widely around the subject to develop an awareness of emerging, topical issues and techniques.

The starting point for further reading is the Student Accountant magazine, and the ACCA website, where the examiner and other experts regularly post articles on key topical financial management topics.

However, you should also subscribe to a quality newspaper, and use the internet to develop a broader awareness of topical issues.

### Introduction to this chapter

This chapter introduces a few of the main topical issues in financial management at the moment, such as the "credit crunch", financial engineering and international regulations on money laundering.

## 2 Regulation of world financial markets

The free movement of goods, services and capital across national barriers has long been considered a key factor in establishing stable and independent world economies.

However, removing barriers to the free movement of capital, also increases the opportunities for international money laundering and terrorist financing.

**Money laundering** is a process in which assets obtained or generated by criminal activity are moved or concealed to obscure their link with the crime.

## Expandable Text - The International Monetary Fund (IMF)

Ever since the second world war, organisations such as the international monetary fund (IMF) have been working to establish a multilateral framework for trade and finance. The free movement of goods, services and capital has been seen as a vitally important part of the increasing economic and financial stability and independence of the world's economies.

The IMF is an international organisation of 184 member countries. It was established, amongst other things, to promote international monetary cooperation, exchange stability, and orderly exchange arrangements and to foster economic growth and high levels of employment.

However, terrorist activities are sometimes funded from the proceeds of illegal activities, and perpetrators must find ways to launder the funds in order to use them without drawing the attention of authorities.

The international community has made the fight against money laundering and terrorist financing a priority. Among the goals of this effort are:

- protecting the integrity of the international financial system

- cutting off the resources available to terrorists

- making it harder for criminals to profit from their crimes.

The IMF is especially concerned about the possible consequences of money laundering on its members' economies, which could include risks to the soundness and stability of financial institutions and financial systems and increased volatility of international capital flows.

International efforts to combat such activities have resulted in:

- the establishment of an international task force on money laundering

- the issue of specific recommendations to be adopted by nation states

- the enactment of legislation by many countries on matters covering:
    - the criminal justice system and law enforcement

    - the financial system and its regulation

    - international co-operation.

## Expandable Text - The international financial action task force

In order to combat activities such as money laundering and terrorist financing the international financial action task force on money laundering (FATF) was established to determine what measures should be taken by the international community.

FATF is a 33-member organisation established by the G-7 summit in Paris in 1989 with primary responsibility for developing a worldwide standard for anti-money laundering and combating the financing of terrorism. It works in close cooperation with other key international organisations, including the IMF, the World Bank, the United Nations, and FATF-style regional bodies (FSRBs), most of which participate in its meetings as observers.

Within a year, FATF had issued forty recommendations to provide a comprehensive plan of action needed to fight against money laundering. These were supplemented by another nine recommendations specifically focused on the financing of terrorism in the wake of the events of 9/11. They have been recognised, endorsed, or adopted by many international bodies and though not a binding international convention, many countries in the world have made a political commitment to combat money laundering by implementing them.

In the UK, the third money laundering directive was adopted in October 2005. It represents Europe's response to the global standards produced by the financial action task force (FATF) in 2003. The UK government has to implement the directive into UK law by December 2007. It lays down in detail the roles and responsibilities of individuals and firms in the drive to combat money laundering and terrorist financing.

One of the results of this activity is to create a wide definition of the offence to include:

- possessing, dealing with, or concealing the proceeds of a crime

- attempting or conspiring to commit such an offence

- failing to inform the national financial intelligence unit (FIU) of knowledge or suspicion of such an offence.

## Expandable Text - Details on framework introduced by task force

### Money laundering regulations and the financial system

The regulatory framework recommended by the taskforce and implemented in countries throughout the world, place significant responsibilities on accountants and other professional advisors.

The rules are designed to ensure:

- all customers are properly identified as legitimate and no anonymous accounts are permitted

- any suspect financial activities are immediately reported to the appropriate authorities

- records of all due diligence investigations and financial transactions are kept for the proscribed number of years

- adequate and appropriate policies and procedures are established to forestall and prevent operations related to money laundering or terrorist financing including staff training

- sanctions for non-compliance are in place.

The laws implemented by most countries have had a significant impact on professional accountants who are obliged to:

- undertake customer due diligence (CDD) procedures before acting for a client

- keep records of transactions undertaken and of the verification procedures carried out on clients

- report suspicions to the relevant financial intelligence unit (FIU) e.g. the national criminal intelligence service (NCIS) in the UK.

Professional accountants are not in breach of their professional duty of confidence if, in good faith, they report any knowledge or suspicions of money laundering to the appropriate authorities.

Penalties for non-compliance can be imposed by the regulator (such as the financial services authority in the UK) on any firm or individual. In addition, the ACCA may take its own disciplinary action against its members. It is therefore essential for all accountants to:

- monitor developments in legislation

- stay abreast of the requirements

- implement all recommended protocols.

## 3 Financial engineering and emerging derivative products

Derivatives are financial instruments that have no intrinsic value, but derive their value from something else, such as equity securities, fixed-income securities, foreign currencies, or commodities.

They fall into three main categories:

- Options.
- Forwards.
- Swaps.

Some simple derivatives were covered earlier in this text.

However, there is a vast and diverse range of potential underlying assets and payoff alternatives, and consequently a huge range of derivatives contracts available to be traded in the market, beyond the basic varieties of derivatives covered in this paper.

### Derivatives and risk

Derivatives can be used to hedge risk or to speculate. Most derivatives are sold as a way to hedge the risk of a portfolio. However, even as a hedging tool, as derivatives become more complex, so they become more difficult to measure, manage, and understand.

Use of complex derivatives requires:

- a firm understanding of the trade-off of risks and rewards

- a guiding set of principles to provide a framework for effectively managing and controlling financial derivative activities, covering matters such as:
    - the role of senior management
    - valuation and market risk management
    - credit risk measurement and management
    - operating systems and controls
    - accounting and disclosure of risk-management positions.

# Financial engineering and the management of derivative risk

Today dealers manage portfolios of derivatives and oversee the net, or residual, risk of their overall position.

**Financial engineering** refers to the development of pricing methodologies and hedging techniques that underpin the use of financial derivative products. Black, Scholes and Merton were the first financial engineers when they used mathematics to model the price of a plain (vanilla) option.

Financial engineering techniques can also be used to measure and therefore manage the risk of a portfolio of derivatives.

Examples of financial engineering techniques are Value at Risk (VaR), scenario analysis and stress testing.

## Expandable Text - Details of financial engineering techniques

### Value at risk

The concept of value at risk (VaR) was covered in detail earlier in this text.

VaR measures the maximum expected loss for a given portfolio, under normal market conditions, attributable to changes in the market price of financial instruments:

- for a given time horizon
- for a given confidence interval.

### Scenario analysis

In addition to understanding the expected maximum loss under normal market conditions, a portfolio manager must also understand the implications for the portfolio of abnormal market conditions.

Using the Monte Carlo simulation method, particular market conditions and the effects of hypothetical events can be simulated to determine their effect on the value of the portfolio.

For each iteration:

- the scenario of random market moves is generated based on a model of the particular conditions under analysis
- the portfolio is then revalued assuming the simulated scenario occurred as before.

After a large number of iterations have been performed, a distribution is computed. This may be a distribution of:

- the potential range of values of the portfolio under these specific conditions, or
- the potential range of profits or losses on the portfolio under these conditions.

## Stress testing

Stress testing is a simplified version of scenario analysis. It assesses the impact of a specific set of circumstances on a portfolio:

- Particular high risk events are identified.
- The value of the portfolio is calculated assuming the occurrence of this specific set of possible risk factors.
- The size of the potential loss is calculated.

Note that stress testing does not assign probabilities to the likelihood of these events occurring. It is used to:

- understand the weak spots is in a portfolio
- reconfigure a portfolio to reduce risk to a manageable level, or
- help a portfolio manager act decisively if the worst-case scenario should unexpectedly unfold.

This kind of stress testing prevents portfolio managers from having to react at speed in a moving market, a situation that can exacerbate the losses. In a complex derivatives portfolio, stress-testing that reveals excessively risky exposures either to movements in the underlying cash rate or shifts in volatility or interest rates (or combinations of these factors) is said to identify 'risk holes.' These are particular combinations of circumstances that would make the portfolio very difficult to manage and the profitability of the portfolio too volatile for the company's risk appetite.

### Test your understanding 1

**Distinguish between:**

- **Value at risk.**
- **Scenario analysis.**
- **Stress testing.**

## 4 The global credit crunch and toxic assets

Over the last few months, since the "Credit Crunch" began, the phrase "toxic assets" has been used by the international media to describe the range of financial products traded by banks and other financial institutions in order to earn income and lay off risk.

To understand the problem of toxic assets it is first necessary to understand how banks have traditionally moved to lay off risk through a process of securitisation using "Collateralised Debt Obligations" (CDOs).

### Securitisation through CDOs

When banks lend money to borrowers (for mortgages, car loans etc), they invariably try to lay off their risk by a process of securitisation. This involves selling the asset from the bank's balance sheet to a company called a "Special Purpose Vehicle" (SPV). This sale generates cash for the bank in the short term which can then be lent again, in an expanding cycle of credit formation.

CDOs are "packages" of many securitised loans which are put together by an SPV and sold to investors. The investors decide what level of risk they are prepared to tolerate and invest in an appropriate grade of CDO accordingly. The CDOs are then traded between investors (usually banks).

### The Credit Crunch

During the last few months, it has become apparent that the banks had pursued borrowers so aggressively that many of the loans sold to SPVs in the securitisation process were likely not to be repaid (so called "sub-prime" loans). This in turn means that it has become very difficult to trace which CDOs represent loans which are sound, and which are likely to be defaulted. Even some CDOs which were sold as AAA grade investments have been found to be unexpectedly risky.

Consequently, suspicion has grown in the financial markets that some bank balance sheets are carrying large amounts of CDOs which are not worth what they appear to be.

This has meant that inter-bank lending has reduced dramatically, as banks view each other with suspicion.These CDOs are known as toxic assets.

The main problem is the uncertainty about which loans (and CDOs) are sound and which aren't. In practice, until time passes and some of the loans are repaid, it will be impossible to tell which banks' balance sheets are most badly affected.

### The impact on business in general

As a consequence of the credit crunch, the banks have been more reluctant to lend and have set more stringent lending criteria. This has meant that many businesses have struggled to refinance their debts.

It is hoped that the financial stimulus packages introduced by governments in early 2009 will encourage banks to lend, and will have a positive impact on businesses in general.

### Student Accountant article

The examiner's January 2009 article in Student Accountant magazine provides further details on toxic assets.

## 5 Developments in the macroeconomic environment

Part of your responsibility as a member of the ACCA is to keep yourself up-to-date with developments that will impact the advice you give and the decisions you take as an accountant.

Developments in the macroeconomic environment, may be global or national, but are likely to be the result of:

- political factors
- legal factors
- economic factors.

### Test your understanding 2

**Suggest specific areas, under each of the three headings above, which financial accountants should monitor in order to keep abreast of potentially significant developments affecting the company.**

As you pursue your studies, ensure that you keep up to date with economic developments both nationally and internationally and consider how the changes would impact specific firms and decisions.

Many of the topics covered in this paper are of particular relevance in assessing the effect of such factors on a firm, both internally and externally.

**Test your understanding 3**

**For each of the factors listed below consider how they might impact the financial decisions made by a firm.**

- Increases in the capital allowances given on investment.
- Reduction in planned government spending.
- Significant strengthening of the home currency.

## 6 Chapter summary

**MACROECONOMIC DEVELOPMENTS**
**Keep up to date on:**

- Political
- Legal
- Economic
- Developments nationally and globally and consider the impact on company finance decisions

**EMERGING ISSUES**

**EMERGING DERIVATIVE PRODUCTS**
**Complex products more difficult to measure and manage. Tools include:**

- Value at risk
- Scenario analysis
- Stress testing

**MONEY LAUNDERING REGULATIONS**

- Undertake due diligence on all clients
- Keep full records
- Report suspicions to the FIU

## Test your understanding answers

### Test your understanding 1

Value at risk measures the maximum expected loss for a given portfolio, under normal market conditions, attributable to changes in the market price of financial instruments.

Scenario analysis, using Monte Carlo simulation techniques, gives a probability distribution of the potential range of values of a portfolio under a particular set of abnormal market conditions.

Stress testing values a portfolio under a given set of high-risk assumptions.

### Test your understanding 2

- Political factors:
    - taxation policy
    - government spending policies
    - regional and national economic groupings
    - foreign trade regulations
    - price controls
    - government stability.

- Legal factors:
    - monopolies legislation
    - corporate governance regulations
    - international harmonisation of accounting standards
    - national implementation of international regulations such as those on money laundering
    - national regulation of companies such as the Companies Acts in the UK.

- Economic factors:
    - business cycles
    - interest rates
    - inflation rates
    - exchange rates.

### Test your understanding 3

Increases in the capital allowances given on investment:

- The acceleration of capital allowances may improve the present value of the returns on some projects such that they become worth taking on.

- The increases may however reduce the tax payable such that the tax shield on debt is lost and the advantages of gearing are lost alongside.

Reduction in planned government spending:

- May result in lower wage settlements & higher unemployment.

- This could mean a reduction in labour costs but also in ready income and therefore consumer spending on luxury items.

- Would impact on cashflow and revenue forecasts.

- Need for accurate market research and sensitivity analysis on the estimates.

Significant strengthening of the home currency:

- If long-term would affect competitive position overseas – potential problems for exporters as goods become more expensive.

- In the short-term may impact on contract settlements if risk not previously hedged.

- May lead to changes in borrowing plans if balance sheet hedge deemed appropriate to offset translation exposure.

- Could impact the value of derivatives portfolios.

# Questions & Answers

## 1 The role and responsibility of the financial manager

### Influence on objectives

#### Question

Discuss, and provide examples of, the types of non-financial, ethical and environmental issues that might influence the objectives of companies. Consider the impact of these non-financial, ethical and environmental issues on the achievement of primary financial objectives such as the maximisation of shareholder wealth.

**(15 marks)**

## 2 Investment appraisal

### Breckhall

#### Question

Assume that you have been appointed finance director of Breckhall Inc. The company is considering investing in the production of an electronic security device, with an expected market life of five years.

The previous finance director has undertaken an analysis of the proposed project; the main features of his analysis are shown below.

Proposed electronic security device project

| | Year 0 $000 | Year 1 $000 | Year 2 $000 | Year 3 $000 | Year 4 $000 | Year 5 $000 |
|---|---|---|---|---|---|---|
| Investment in depreciable non-current assets | 4,500 | | | | | |
| Cumulative investment in working capital | 300 | 400 | 500 | 600 | 700 | 700 |
| Sales | | 3,500 | 4,900 | 5,320 | 5,740 | 5,320 |
| Materials | | 535 | 750 | 900 | 1,050 | 900 |
| Labour | | 1,070 | 1,500 | 1,800 | 2,100 | 1,800 |
| Overhead | | 50 | 100 | 100 | 100 | 100 |
| Interest | | 576 | 576 | 576 | 576 | 576 |
| Depreciation | | 900 | 900 | 900 | 900 | 900 |
| | | 3,131 | 3,826 | 4,276 | 4,726 | 4,276 |
| Taxable profit | | 369 | 1,074 | 1,044 | 1,014 | 1,044 |
| Taxation | | 129 | 376 | 365 | 355 | 365 |
| Profit after tax | | 240 | 698 | 679 | 659 | 679 |

All of the above cash flow and profit estimates have been prepared in terms of present day costs and prices as the previous finance director assumed that the sales price could be increased to compensate for any increase in costs.

You have available the following additional information:

(1) Selling prices, working capital requirements and overhead expenses are expected to increase by 5% per year.

(2) Material costs and labour costs are expected to increase by 10% per year.

(3) Capital allowances (tax deduction) are allowable for taxation purposes against profits at 25% per year on a reducing balance basis.

(4) Taxation of profits is at a rate of 35% payable one year in arrears.

(5) The non-current assets have no expected salvage value at the end of five years.

(6) The company's real after-tax discount rate (or weighted average cost of capital) is estimated to be 8% per year and nominal after-tax discount rate 15% per year.

(7) Assume that all receipts and payments arose at the end of the year to which they relate except those in year 0 which occur immediately.

**Required**

(a) Estimate the net present value of the proposed project. State clearly any assumptions that you make.

**(16 marks)**

(b) Calculate by how much the discount rate would have to change to result in a net present value of approximately zero.

**(4 marks)**

**(Total: 20 marks)**

## 3 The weighted average cost of capital

There are no additional questions on this chapter.

# 4 Risk adjusted WACC and APV

## Goddard Inc

### Question

Goddard Inc a company in the educational sector is evaluating two new projects. One is in the leisure industry and the other is in the publishing industry. Goddard's summarised balance sheets (statements of financial position), and those of Cottons Inc and Blackwell Inc, quoted companies in the leisure and publication industry respectively, are shown below:

|  | Goddard Inc | Cottons Inc | Blackwell Inc |
|---|---|---|---|
|  | $m | $m | $m |
| Non-current assets | 96 | 42 | 102 |
| Current assets | 95 | 82 | 65 |
| Total assets | 191 | 124 | 167 |
| Ordinary shares[1] | 15 | 10 | 30 |
| Reserves | 50 | 27 | 20 |
| Medium and long-term loans[2] | 56 | 15 | 69 |
| Current liabilities | 70 | 72 | 48 |
| Total equity and liabilities | 191 | 124 | 167 |
| Ordinary share price (cents) | 380 | 180 | 230 |
| Debenture price ($) | 104 | 112 | – |
| Equity beta | 1.1 | 1.3 | 1.2 |

(1) Goddard and Blackwell 50 cents par value, Cottons 25 cents par value.

(2) Goddard 12% debentures 2008-2010, Cotton 14% debentures 2012, Blackwell medium-term bank loan.

Goddard's capital structure will remain unchanged if both or either of the projects are undertaken. Goddard's investors currently require a return on debt of 11%. The risk free rate of interest is estimated to be 6% per year and the market return 14% per year. Corporate tax is at a rate of 30% per year.

**Required**

(a) Calculate the appropriate discount rate to use for each of these projects. Explain your answer and state clearly any assumptions that you make.

**(10 marks)**

(b) Goddard's marketing director suggests that it is incorrect to use the same discount rate each year for the leisure project, as the early stages of the investment are more risky and should be discounted at a higher rate. Another board member disagrees saying that more distant cash flows are riskier and should be discounted at a higher rate. Discuss the validity of the views of each of the directors.

**(5 marks)**

**(Total: 15 marks)**

## 5 Capital structure and financing

There are no additional questions on this chapter.

## 6 Dividend policy

### HGT Inc

#### Question

HGT Inc is a UK based multinational company with two overseas subsidiaries. The company wishes to minimise its global tax bill, and part of its tax strategy is to try to take advantage of opportunities provided by transfer pricing.

HGT has subsidiaries in Glinland and Rytora.

| Taxation | UK | Glinland | Rytora |
|---|---|---|---|
| Corporation tax on profits | 30% | 40% | 25% |
| Withholding tax on dividends | – | 10% | – |
| Import tariffs on all goods (not tax allowable) | – | – | 10% |

The subsidiary in Glinland produces 150,000 graphite golf club shafts per year which are then sent to Rytora for the metal heads to be added and the clubs finished off. The shafts have a variable cost in Glinland of $6 each, and annual fixed costs are $140,000. The shafts are sold to the Rytoran subsidiary at variable cost plus 75%.

The Rytoran subsidiary incurs additional unit variable costs of $9, annual fixed costs of $166,000, and sells the finished clubs at $30 each in Rytora.

Bi-lateral tax agreements exist which allow foreign tax paid to be credited against UK tax liability.

All transactions between the companies are in pounds sterling. The Rytoran subsidiary remits all profit after tax to the UK parent company each year, and the Glinland subsidiary remits 50% of its profit after tax.

### Required

The parent company is considering instructing the Glinland subsidiary to sell the shafts to the Rytoran subsidiary at full cost. Evaluate the possible effect of this on tax and tariff payments, and discuss briefly any possible problems with this strategy.

**(10 marks)**

## 7 International investment and financing decisions

### Axmine

### Question

The managers of Axmine plc, a major international copper processor are considering a joint venture with Traces, a company owning significant copper reserves in a South American country. The proposed joint venture with Traces would be for an initial period of four years.

Copper would be mined using a new technique developed by Axmine. Axmine would supply machinery at an immediate cost of 800 million pesos and 10 supervisors at an annual salary of £40,000 each at current prices. Additionally Axmine would pay half of the 1,000 million pesos per year (at current prices) local labour costs and other expenses in the South American country.

The supervisors' salaries, local labour, and other expenses will be increased in line with inflation in the United Kingdom and the South American country respectively.

Inflation in the South American country is currently 100% per year and in the UK, it is expected to remain stable at around 8% per year. The government of the South American country is attempting to control inflation and hopes to reduce it each year by 20% of the previous year's rate.

The joint venture would give Axmine a 50% share of Traces' copper production, with current market prices at £1,500 per 1,000 kilograms. Traces' production is expected to be 10 million kilograms per year, and copper prices are expected to rise by 10% per year (in pounds sterling) for the foreseeable future. At the end of four years, Axmine would be given the choice to pull out of the venture or to negotiate another four-year joint venture, on different terms.

The current exchange rate is 140 pesos/£. Future exchange rates may be estimated using the purchasing power parity theory.

Axmine has no foreign operations. The cost of capital of the company's UK mining operations is 16% per year. As this joint venture involves diversifying into foreign operations, the company considers that a 2% reduction in the cost of capital would be appropriate for this project.

Corporate tax is at the rate of 20% per year in the South American country and 35% per year in the UK. A tax treaty exists between the two countries and foreign tax paid is allowable against any UK tax liability. Taxation is payable one year in arrears and a 25% straight-line writing-down allowance is available on the machinery in both countries.

Cash flows may be assumed to occur at the year-end, except for the immediate cost of machinery. The machinery is expected to have negligible terminal value at the end of four years.

(a) Prepare a report discussing whether Axmine plc should agree to the proposed joint venture. Relevant calculations must form part of your report or an appendix to it.

   **State clearly any assumptions that you make**.

   (**20 marks**)

(b) Explain whether you consider Axmine's proposed discount rate for the project to be appropriate.

   (**5 marks**)

(c) If, once the investment has taken place, the government of the South American country imposed a block on the remittance of dividends to the UK, discuss how Axmine might try to avoid such a block on remittances.

**(5 marks)**

**(Total: 30 marks)**

## 8 Option pricing

### Option valuation

### Question

An investor holds 200,000 shares in D Inc and is considering buying some put options to hedge her investment. D's current share price is $6. The risk free interest rate is currently 12% pa and the recent volatility of D Inc shares has been 30% pa. She requires European put options with an exercise price of $5 for exercise in two years time.

### Required

(a) Calculate the value that the bank is likely to charge for 200,000 put options of the investor's required specification.

**(8 marks)**

(b) Calculate the investor's change in wealth if she buys 200,000 put options to hedge her portfolio and the share price in two years time is a) $3 per share or b) $10 per share.

**(4 marks)**

(c) A friend informs the investor that she could achieve a safer position by selling call options to construct a delta hedge. Calculate the number of call options to be sold to construct a delta hedge.

**(3 marks)**

**(Total: 15 marks)**

## 9 Strategic aspects of acquisitions

### Rayswood Inc

### Question

In a recent meeting of the board of directors of Rayswood Inc the chairman proposed the acquisition of Pondhill Inc. During his presentation the chairman stated that: 'As a result of this takeover we will diversify our operations and our earnings per share will rise by 13%, bringing great benefits to our shareholders.'

No bid has yet been made, and Rayswood currently owns only 2% of Pondhill.

A bid would be based on a share for share exchange, which would be one Rayswood share for every six Pondhill shares.

Financial data for the two companies include:

|  | Rayswood | Pondhill |
|---|---|---|
|  | $m | $m |
| Turnover | 56.0 | 42.0 |
| Profit before tax | 12.0 | 10.0 |
| Profit available to ordinary shareholders | 7.8 | 6.5 |
| Dividends | 3.2 | 3.4 |
| Retained earnings | 4.6 | 3.1 |
| Issued ordinary shares | 40m | 150m |
| Market price per share | 320 cents | 45 cents |

Rayswood 50 cents par value, Pondhill 10 cents par value.

A non-executive director has recently stated that he believes 'the share price of Rayswood will rapidly increase to $3.61 following the announcement of the bid.'

**Required**

Explain whether you agree with the chairman's and the non-executive director's assessment of the benefits of the proposed takeover.

Support your explanation with relevant calculations, including your assessment of the likely post acquisition share price of Rayswood if the bid is successful.

State clearly any assumptions that you make.

**(15 marks)**

## 10 Business valuation

**Predator**

### Question

The board of directors of Predator Inc is considering making an offer to purchase Target Co, a private limited company in the same industry. If Target is purchased it is proposed to continue operating the company as a going concern in the same line of business.

Summarised details from the most recent set of financial statements for Predator and Target are shown below:

|  | Predator | | Target | |
|---|---|---|---|---|
|  | Balance sheet as at 31 March | | Balance sheet as at 31 March | |
|  | $m | $m | $000 | $000 |
| Freehold property |  | 33 |  | 460 |
| Plant & equipment |  | 58 |  | 1,310 |
| Inventory | 29 |  | 330 |  |
| Receivables | 24 |  | 290 |  |
| Cash | 3 |  | 20 |  |
|  | —— | 56 | —— | 640 |
| Total assets |  | **147** |  | **2,410** |
|  |  |  |  |  |
| Equity and liabilities |  |  |  |  |
| Ordinary shares |  | 35 |  | 160 |
| Reserves |  | 43 |  | 964 |
| Shareholders funds |  | 78 |  | 1,124 |
| Medium term bank loans |  | 38 |  | 768 |
| Current liabilities |  | 31 |  | 518 |
|  |  | **147** |  | **2,410** |

Predator, 50 cents ordinary shares, Target, 25 cents ordinary shares.

|  | Predator | | Target | |
|---|---|---|---|---|
| Year | PAT | Dividend | PAT | Dividend |
|  | $m | $m | $000 | $000 |
| T5 | 14.30 | 9.01 | 143 | 85.0 |
| T4 | 15.56 | 9.80 | 162 | 93.5 |
| T3 | 16.93 | 10.67 | 151 | 93.5 |
| T2 | 18.42 | 11.60 | 175 | 102.8 |
| T1 | 20.04 | 12.62 | 183 | 113.1 |

T5 is five years ago and T1 is the most recent year.

Target's shares are owned by a small number of private individuals. Its managing director who receives an annual salary of $120,000 dominates the company. This is $40,000 more than the average salary received by managing directors of similar companies. The managing director would be replaced, if Predator purchases Target.

The freehold property has not been revalued for several years and is believed to have a market value of $800,000.

The balance sheet value of plant and equipment is thought to reflect its replacement cost fairly, but its value if sold is not likely to exceed $800,000. Approximately $55,000 of inventory is obsolete and could only be sold as scrap for $5,000.

The ordinary shares of Predator are currently trading at 430 cents ex-div. A suitable cost of equity for Target has been estimated at 15%.

Both companies are subject to corporation tax at 33%.

**Required**

Estimate the value of Target Co using the different methods of valuation and advise the board of Predator as to how much it should offer for Target's shares.

**Note:** There has been no increase in the share capital of Target over the last five years.

Why is this relevant?

## 11 Corporate failure and reconstruction

### Last Chance Saloon Inc

#### Question

Last Chance Saloon Inc has experienced considerable losses in the last few years, leading to a debit balance on its revenue reserves and thus a deterioration of its cash position. The company has developed a wonder product to revive its fortunes. The wonder product will require a total investment of $7 million. The finance director has drafted a scheme of reconstruction:

(1) Existing shareholders are to be offered a cash payment 25 cents per share to redeem their shares which would then be cancelled.

(2) 10 million new shares 50 cents (par value) are to be issued at $1.20 each.

(3) An increase of $500,000 in inventory (working capital) is required.

(4) The 10% debentures would be repaid immediately.

(5) The bank is willing to provide a $1 million overdraft facility at an increased cost of 9% to replace the existing overdraft. The bank would purchase a $3 million 12% debenture. Both loans will be secured.

If the new wonder product is not launched the company earnings before interest and tax will be a ridiculously low figure from which you should immediately realise that it is over for the company unless it goes ahead will the new product.

If the scheme is organised the earnings before interest and tax is estimated to be $1 million in the first year of trading.

**Summarised balance sheet (statement of financial position) as at 31 December 20X4**

|  | $000 | $000 |
|---|---|---|
| Land and buildings | | 2,200 |
| Plant and machinery | | 6,300 |
| | | 8,500 |
| Inventory | 2,000 | |
| Receivables | 1,500 | |
| Cash | 500 | |
| | | 4,000 |
| **Total assets** | | **12,500** |
| Ordinary share capital (50c shares) | | 3,000 |
| Share premium | | 2,000 |
| Revenue reserves | | (1,000) |
| Shareholders' funds | | 4,000 |
| 10% Debentures 20X5 | | 5,000 |
| Current liabilities | | |
| Payables | 2,300 | |
| Bank overdraft | 1,200 | |
| | | 3,500 |
| **Total equity and liabilities** | | **12,500** |

The realisable values of assets upon liquidation are estimated to be:

|  | $000 |
|---|---|
| Land and buildings | 1,500 |
| Plant and machinery | 3,450 |
| Inventory | 1,000 |
| Receivables | 1,000 |

The current market price of ordinary shares is 22 cents per share. The corporate tax rate is 30%.

### Required

Prepare a report analysing whether the proposed scheme of reconstruction will be successful. State clearly any assumptions that you make.

## 12 Risk management

### Political risk

### Question

The finance department of Beela Electronics has been criticised by the company's board of directors for not undertaking an assessment of the political risk of the company's potential direct investments in Africa. The board has received an interim report from a consultant that provides assessment of the factors affecting political risk in three African countries. The report assess key variables on a scale of −10 to +10, with −10 the worst possible score and +10 the best.

|  | Country 1 | Country 2 | Country 3 |
|---|---|---|---|
| Economic growth | 5 | 8 | 4 |
| Political stability | 3 | -4 | 5 |
| Risk of nationalism | 3 | 0 | 4 |
| Cultural compatibility | 6 | 2 | 4 |
| Inflation | 7 | -6 | 6 |
| Currency convertibility | -2 | 5 | -4 |
| Investment incentives | -3 | 7 | 3 |
| Labour supply | 2 | 8 | -3 |

The consultant suggests that economic growth and political stability are twice as important as the other factors.

The consultant states in the report that previous clients have not invested in countries with total weighted score of less that 30 out of a maximum possible 100 (with economic growth and political stability double weighted). The consultant therefore recommends that no investment in Africa should be undertaken.

**Required**

(a) Discuss whether or not Beela electronics should use the technique suggested by the consultant in order to decide whether or not to invest in Africa.

(8 marks)

(b) Discuss briefly how Beela might manage political risk if it decides to invest in Africa.

(7 marks)

(Total: 15 marks)

## 13 Hedging foreign exchange risk

There are no additional questions on this chapter.

## 14 Hedging interest rate risk

### Murwald (Interest rate hedging)

The corporate treasury team of Murwald plc are debating what strategy to adopt towards interest rate risk management. The company's financial projections show an expected cash deficit in three months time of £12 million, which will last for a period of approximately six months. Base rate is currently 6% per year, and Murwald can borrow at 1.5% over base, or invest at 1% below base. The treasury team believe that economic pressures in the euro zone y will soon force the European Central Bank (ECB) to raise interest rates on the euro by 2% per year, which could lead to a similar rise in UK interest rates. The ECB move is not certain, as there has recently been significant economic pressure on the bank from the governments of euro zone countries not to raise interest rates.

In the UK, the economy is still recovering from a recession and representatives of industry are calling for interest rates to be cut by 1%. Opposing representations are being made by pensioners, who do not wish their investment income to fall further due to an interest rate cut.

The corporate treasury team believes that interest rates are more likely to rise than to fall, and does not want interest payments during the six month period to increase by more than £10,000 from the amounts that would be paid at current interest rates. It is now 1 December.

Euronext.liffe prices (1 December)

**Futures**

£500,000 three month sterling interest rate (points of 100%)

| | |
|---|---|
| Dec | 93.75 |
| March | 93.45 |
| June | 93.10 |

**Options**

£500,000 short sterling options (points of 100%)

| Exercise price | CALLS June | PUTS June |
|---|---|---|
| 9200 | 3.33 | - |
| 9250 | 2.93 | - |
| 9300 | 2.55 | 0.92 |
| 9350 | 2.20 | 1.25 |
| 9400 | 1.74 | 1.84 |
| 9450 | 1.32 | 2.90 |
| 9500 | 0.87 | 3.46 |

**Required**

(a) Illustrate results of futures and options hedges if, by 1 March:

   (i) Interest rates rise by 2%. Futures prices move by 1.8%.

   (ii) Interest rates fall by 1%. Futures prices move by 0.9%.

   Recommend with reasons, how Murwald plc should hedge its interest rate exposure. All relevant calculations must be shown. Taxation, transactions costs and margin requirements may be ignored. State clearly any assumptions that you make.

(b) Discuss the advantages and disadvantages of other derivative products that Murwald might have used to hedge the risk.

## 15 The economic environment for multinationals

---

### Growth of multinationals

---

#### Question

The global turnover of the largest multinational companies is greater than the gross national product of many countries.

Discuss factors that might explain the successful growth of large multinational companies.

**(10 marks)**

---

## 16 International money markets and complex financial instruments

There are no additional questions on this chapter.

## 17 Topical issues in financial management

There are no additional questions on this chapter.

## Test your understanding answers

### Influence on objectives

#### Answer

Non-financial issues, ethical and environmental issues in many cases overlap, and have become of increasing significance to the achievement of primary financial objectives such as the maximisation of shareholder wealth. Most companies have a series of secondary objectives that encompass many of these issues.

Traditional **non-financial issues** affecting companies include:

(i) **Measures that increase the welfare of employees** such as the provision of housing, good and safe working conditions, social and recreational facilities. These might also relate to managers and encompass generous perquisites.

(ii) **Welfare of the local community and society as a whole**. This has become of increasing significance, with companies accepting that they have some responsibility beyond their normal stakeholders in that their actions may impact on the environment and the quality of life of third parties.

(iii) **Provision of, or fulfillment of, a service**. Many organisations, both in the public sector and private sector provide a service, for example to remote communities, which would not be provided on purely economic grounds.

(iv) **Growth of an organisation**, which might bring more power, prestige, and a larger market share, but might adversely affect shareholder wealth.

(v) **Quality**. Many engineering companies have been accused of focusing upon quality rather than cost effective solutions.

(vi) **Survival**. Although to some extent linked to financial objectives, managers might place corporate survival (and hence retaining their jobs) ahead of wealth maximisation. An obvious effect might be to avoid undertaking risky investments.

**Ethical issues** of companies were brought into sharp focus by the actions of Enron and others.

There is a trade-off between applying a high standard of ethics and increasing cash flow or maximisation of shareholder wealth. A company might face ethical dilemmas with respect to the amount and accuracy of information it provides to its stakeholders. An ethical issue attracting much attention is the possible payment of excessive remuneration to senior directors, including very large bonuses and 'golden parachutes'.

## Key answer tips

Should bribes be paid in order to facilitate the company's long-term aims? Are wages being paid in some countries below subsistence levels? Should they be? Are working conditions of an acceptable standard? Do the company's activities involve experiments on animals, genetic modifications etc? Should the company deal with or operate in countries that have a poor record of human rights? What is the impact of the company's actions on pollution or other aspects of the local environment?

**Environmental issues** might have very direct effects on companies. If natural resources become depleted the company may not be able to sustain its activities, weather and climatic factors can influence the achievement of corporate objectives through their impact on crops, the availability of water etc. Extreme environmental disasters such as typhoons, floods, earthquakes, and volcanic eruptions will also impact on companies' cash flow, as will obvious environmental considerations such as the location of mountains, deserts, or communications facilities. Should companies develop new technologies that will improve the environment, such as cleaner petrol or alternative fuels? Such developments might not be the cheapest alternative.

*Environmental legislation* is a major influence in many countries. This includes limitations on where operations may be located and in what form, and regulations regarding waste products, noise and physical pollutants.

All of these issues have received considerable publicity and attention in recent years. *Environmental pressure groups* are prominent in many countries; companies are now producing social and environmental accounting reports, and/or corporate social responsibility reports. Companies increasingly have multiple objectives that address some or all of these three issues. In the short-term non-financial, ethical and environmental issues might result in a reduction in shareholder wealth; in the longer term it is argued that only companies that address these issues will succeed.

### Breckhall

#### Answer

(a) **As there is more than one inflation rate, we must calculate the money cash flows and hence discount them by the money (nominal) rate.**

**Net present value calculation for Breckall Inc**

| Year | 0 | 1 | 2 | 3 | 4 | 5 | 6 |
|---|---|---|---|---|---|---|---|
| | $000 | $000 | $000 | $000 | $000 | $000 | $000 |
| **Receipts** | | | | | | | |
| Sales (5% rise pa) | | 3,675 | 5,402 | 6,159 | 6,977 | 6,790 | |
| **Payments:** | | | | | | | |
| Materials | | (589) | (908) | (1,198) | (1,537) | (1,449) | |
| (10% rise pa) | | | | | | | |
| Labour | | (1,177) | (1,815) | (2,396) | (3,075) | (2,899) | |
| (10% rise pa) | | | | | | | |
| Overheads | | (53) | (110) | (116) | (122) | (128) | |
| (5% rise pa) | | | | | | | |
| Capital allowances (W1) | | (1,125) | (844) | (633) | (475) | (1,423) | |
| **Taxable Profits** | | 731 | 1,725 | 1,816 | 1,768 | 891 | |
| **Tax:** | | | | | | | |
| Corporation tax | | | (256) | (604) | (636) | (619) | (312) |
| Add Capital allowances | | 1,125 | 844 | 633 | 475 | 1,423 | |
| Non-current assets | (4,500) | | | | | | |
| Working capital (W2) | (300) | (120) | (131) | (144) | (156) | (42) | 893 |
| **Net cash flow** | (4,800) | 1,736 | 2,182 | 1,701 | 1,451 | 1,653 | 581 |
| Discount rate (15%) | 1 | 0.870 | 0.756 | 0.658 | 0.572 | 0.497 | 0.432 |
| **Present values** | (4,800) | 1,510 | 1,650 | 1,119 | 830 | 822 | 251 |
| **Net present value** | **$1,382** | | | | | | |

A positive NPV is when the expected return on a project more than compensates the investor for the perceived level of (systematic) risk.

## W1: Capital allowances calculation

| | | W.D.A. | Year |
|---|---|---|---|
| Cost | 4,500 | | |
| W.D.A. year 1 | (1,125) | 1,125 | 1 |
| | ————— | | |
| | | X0.75 | |
| W.D.A. year 2 | | 844 | 2 |
| W.D.A. year 3 | | 633 | 3 |
| W.D.A. year 4 | | 475 | 4 |
| Scrap value | | | |
| Balancing allowance | Balancing figure | 1,423 | 5 |
| | | ————— | |
| **Check Line** | **0** | **4,500** | |
| | | **(Cost – Scrap) =** | 4,500 |

## W2: Working capital requirements

| Year | 0 | 1 | 2 | 3 | 4 | 5 | 6 |
|---|---|---|---|---|---|---|---|
| Total in real terms | 300 | 400 | 500 | 600 | 700 | 700 | |
| Inflation | 1 | 1.05 | $1.05^2$ | $1.05^3$ | $1.05^4$ | $1.05^5$ | |
| Total in money terms | 300 | 420 | 551 | 695 | 851 | 893 | |
| Movement | (300) | (120) | (131) | (144) | (156) | (42) | 893 |

**W3: Sales** - $3,500,000*1.05= $3,675,000

$4,900,000*$1.05^2$ = $5,402,000 etc.

## (b) Calculation of IRR

15% gave a positive NPV, therefore I will choose a higher discount rate to try and achieve a negative NPV, to enable the calculation of the IRR by linear interpolation. Under exam conditions I would simply pick the highest discount rate from the tables i.e. 20%.

| Year | Cashflow | 20% Discount Rate | Present Value |
|---|---|---|---|
| 0 | (4,800) | 1 | (4,800) |
| 1 | 1,736 | 0.833 | 1,446 |
| 2 | 2,182 | 0.694 | 1,514 |
| 3 | 1,701 | 0.579 | 985 |
| 4 | 1,451 | 0.482 | 699 |
| 5 | 1,653 | 0.402 | 665 |
| 6 | 581 | 0.335 | 195 |
| | | | ——— |
| | | | 704 |
| | | | ——— |

The estimate of the IRR by extrapolation: **15 + ((1382/1382 - 704) × (20 - 15)) = 25.20%**

## Goddard Inc

### Answer

(a) The overview – What method should I use to calculate the discount rate for a project in a different industry (different business risk), when the capital structure of our company remains unchanged (same financial risk) post project implementation.

### The Leisure Project

I have assumed the business risk (the beta asset) of the leisure industry can be estimated by de-gearing the equity beta of Cottons plc.

Goddard's existing gearing ratio/capital structure based on market values is:

|  |  | $m | % |
|---|---|---|---|
| Equity | 15/0.5 × 3.80 | 114.00 | **66** |
| Debt | 56 × 1.04 | 58.24 | **34** |
|  | Total | 172.24 | 100 |

Cotton's gearing ratio/capital structure based on market values is:

|  |  | $m | % |
|---|---|---|---|
| Equity | 10/0.25 × 1.80 | 72.00 | **81** |
| Debt | 15 × 1.12 | 16.80 | **19** |
|  | Total | 88.8 | 100 |

(1) Find the business risk asset beta $ß_a$ of the new project/industry.

$$ß_a = ß_e \times V_e / [V_e + V_d(1 - Tc)]$$
$$= 1.3 \times 81 / [81 + 19 (0.70)]$$
$$= 1.12$$

(2) Calculate the equity beta of the **new project**.

$$ß_a = ß_e \times V_e / [V_e + V_d(1 - Tc)]$$
$$1.12 = ß_e \times 66 / [66 + 34(0.70)]$$
$$1.12 = 0.73 \, ß_e$$
$$ß_e = 1.12 / 0.73 = 1.53 - \textbf{Reflects the systematicrisk of the project}$$

(3) $\mathbf{K_{eg}}$

$$R_f + (R_M - R_f) \, ß_e.$$

$$6\% + (14 - 6) \, 1.53 = 18.24\%.$$

**(4)** $K_{dat}$

The investors' required return = $K_d$ = 11%. Therefore to find the current cost of debt adjust for the tax relief on interest.

$K_d(1 - t) = 11(0.70) = 7.70$.

$K_d(1 - t) = 7.70\%$.

**(5) WACC**

$= 18.24\% \times 0.66 + 7.70\% \times 0.34 = 14.66\%$.

**The Publication Project**

I have assumed the business risk (the beta asset) of the publication industry can be estimated by de-gearing the equity beta of Blackwell plc.

Blackwell's gearing ratio/capital structure based on **market values** is:

|        |                           | $m     | %   |
|--------|---------------------------|--------|-----|
| Equity | 30/0.50 × 2.30            | 138.00 | **67** |
| Debt   |                           | 69.00  | **33** |
|        | Total                     | 207.00 | 100 |

**As the gearing ratio/financial risk of Blackwell is almost identical to that of Goddard, there is not need to take out the financial risk (degear) and then put back in the same level of financial risk (re gear).**

**(3)** $K_{eg}$

$R_f + (R_M - R_f)\, ß_e$.

$6\% + (14 - 6)\,\textbf{1.2} = 15.60\%$.

**(4)** $K_{dat}$

$= 7.7\%$.

**(5) WACC**

$= 15.60 \times 0.66 + 7.7 \times 0.34 = 12.91$.

(b) The marketing director might be correct. If there is initially a high level of systematic risk in the packaging investment before it is certain whether the investment will succeed or fail, it is logical to discount cash flows for this high risk period at a rate reflecting this risk. Once it has been determined whether the project will be successful, risk may return to a 'more normal' level and the discount rate reduced commensurate with the lower risk. If the project fails there is no risk (the company has a certain failure!).

The other board member is incorrect. If the same discount rate is used throughout a project's life the discount factor becomes smaller and effectively allows a greater deduction for risk for more discount cash flows. The total risk adjustment is greater the further into the future cash flows are considered. It is not necessary to discount more distant cash flows at a higher rate.

KAPLAN PUBLISHING

## HGT Inc

### Answer

### Key answer tips

What appears to be an amazingly complex question for 10 marks is nothing much more than a relevant cost exercise. That said, the numbers take time and it would be sensible, if short of time, to cover the discussion points with assumed numbers if necessary.

**Under the current scheme:**

|  |  | Glinland $000 | Rytora $000 |
|---|---|---|---|
| Sales | (150,000 units) | 1,575 | 4,500 |
|  |  | ——— | ——— |
| Variable costs |  | 900 | 1,350 |
| Costs from Glinland |  | – | 1,575 |
| Fixed costs |  | 140 | 166 |
|  |  | ——— | ——— |
| Profit before tax |  | 535 | 1,409 |
| Local corporate tax | (40% Glinland, 25% Rytora) | 214 | 352 |
|  |  | ——— | ——— |
| Profit after corporate tax |  | 321 | 1,057 |
| Withholding tax | (Glinland: 10% of 50% of 321) | 16 | – |
| Import tariff | (10% of 1,575) | – | 157 |
| Retained | (Glinland: 50% of 321) | 161 | – |
| Remitted | (Glinland: 321 – 161 – 16) | 144 | 900 |
| UK taxation: |  |  |  |
| Taxable profit |  | 535 | 1,409 |
|  |  | ——— | ——— |
| Tax at UK tax rate | (30%) | 160 | 423 |
| Tax credit | (Rytora: limited to Rytora tax) | 160 | 352 |
|  |  | ——— | ——— |
| Tax paid in the UK |  | 0 | 71 |
|  |  | ——— | ——— |

| Total tax paid | $000 | | $000 |
|---|---|---|---|
| In Glinland | | | |
| Corporate tax | 214 | | |
| Withholding tax | 16 | | |
| | _____ | | |
| | | | 230 |
| In Rytora | | | |
| Corporate tax | 352 | | |
| Import taxes | 157 | | |
| | _____ | | |
| | | | 509 |
| In the UK | | | 71 |
| | | | _____ |
| Total | | | 810 |
| | | | _____ |

**If goods are sold at cost by the Glinland subsidiary** (i.e. at variable cost of 900 + fixed costs of 140 = 1,040):

| | | Glinland | Rytora |
|---|---|---|---|
| | | $000 | $000 |
| Sales | | 1,040 | 4,500 |
| | | _____ | _____ |
| Variable costs | | 900 | 1,350 |
| Costs from Glinland | | – | 1,040 |
| Fixed costs | | 140 | 166 |
| | | _____ | _____ |
| Profit before tax | | 0 | 1,944 |
| Local corporate tax | (25% Rytora) | – | 486 |
| Profit after corporate tax | | – | 1,458 |
| Withholding tax | | – | – |
| Import tariff | (10% of 1,040) | – | 104 |
| Retained | | – | – |
| Remitted | (1,458 – 104) | – | 1,354 |
| UK taxation: | | | |
| Taxable profit | | – | 1,944 |
| | | | _____ |
| Tax at UK tax rate | (30%) | – | 583 |
| Tax credit | (limited to Rytora tax) | – | 486 |
| | | | _____ |
| Tax paid in the UK | | 0 | 97 |
| | | | _____ |

KAPLAN PUBLISHING

| Total tax paid | $000 | $000 |
|---|---|---|
| In Glinland | | 0 |
| In Rytora | | |
| Corporate tax | 486 | |
| Import taxes | 104 | |
| | ——— | |
| | | 590 |
| In the UK | | 97 |
| | | ——— |
| Total | | 687 |
| | | ——— |

The proposed change would result in an overall saving of $123,000 per year.

The proposal might not be acceptable to:

(i) The tax authorities in Glinland, where $230,000 in taxation would be lost. The tax authorities might insist on an arm's length price for transfers between Glinland and Rytora.

(ii) The subsidiary in Glinland, which would no longer make a profit, or have retentions available for future investment in Glinland. Depending upon how performance in Glinland was evaluated, this might adversely affect rewards and motivation in Glinland.

## Axmine

### Answer

**(a)**                  **R E P O R T**

> **To:**        The management, Axmine plc
>
> **From:**      The chief accountant
>
> **Date:**      X-X-20XX
>
> **Subject:**   Proposed joint venture with Traces

#### Introduction

Axmine plc is considering entering into a joint venture with Traces in order to import copper from XX country in South America.

#### Financial analysis

The discounting exercise reveals that the projected cash flows have a positive net present value of £4.71m.

Once this decision has been made public the share price will increase if the market is at least semi strong efficient. Therefore as directors can you can achieve your primary duty, which is to maximise shareholders wealth.

#### Accuracy and completeness of cash flows

#### Be question specific

The price of copper grows by 10% pa in sterling terms. Metals prices are notoriously volatile and the implications of this assumption should be investigated.

The justification of the discount rate is unreliable, i.e. the 16% minus 2%, as this does not appear to reflect the systematic risk of this project.

#### General comments

Purchasing Power Parity Theory can be used as our best predictor of future spot rates, however it **is not accurate** because of the following:

- The future inflation rates are only estimates.

- The market is dominated by speculative transactions (98%) as opposed to trade transactions; therefore purchasing power theory breaks down.

Are the various revenues and costs likely to be subject to the same level of inflation?

Corporate tax rates and tax allowances may change over the project life.

## Risk analysis

### General risk comment

When accepting a project we also accept the risk associated with that project. Thus I would suggest we analysis the project risk in more detail before accepting the project. The level of analysis will depend on the complexity and materiality of the project. The risk can be analysed in a number of ways, i.e. sensitive analysis, scenario analysis, and simulation analysis.

### International risk comment

Axmine should undertaken a political risk assessment, it may adopt both macro and micro techniques to help reach its evaluation. Joint ventures have historically been more at risk of expropriation by host governments than wholly owned subsidiaries (Bradley 1977). A review of economic exposure should also be undertaken.

### Qualitative factors

### The relationship with Traces

Will Traces honour its obligations under the joint venture? What will happen at the end of the four years? Will Traces have acquired all the technical knowledge to be able go it alone? Why is the initial period only for four years? Would it benefit Axmine to have this period extended?

### Communication to sophisticated shareholders

Will our shareholders believe it is a worthwhile project to be undertaken? Does the project fit into our previously communicated strategy? Our shareholders' confidence is crucial to maintaining or increasing our share price.

### Future opportunities

Axmine should undertake a review of all real options.

### Affect on other stakeholders

Employees, creditors, debentures holders and the local community.

### Managerial resources

Have we the in hose managerial resources to deliver this project. What will the impact be, on our current operational capabilities?

### Conclusions and recommendations

It is therefore concluded that the joint venture should be proceeded with in the absence of any more lucrative proposals, subject to clarification of the above reservations.

### Workings

### W1 Estimated future exchange rates: based on PPPT

| Year | Forecast South American inflation% | Forecast UK inflation% | Forecast exchange/rate (pesos/£) |
|---|---|---|---|
| 1 | 80 | 8 | 140 x 1.80 / 1.08 = 233.3 |
| 2 | 64 | 8 | 233.3 x 1.64 / 1.08 = 354.3 |
| 3 | 51.2 | 8 | 354.3 x 1.512 / 1.08 = 496.0 |
| 4 | 41 | 8 | 496.0 x 1.41 / 1.08 = 647.6 |
| 5 | 32.8 | 8 | 647.6 x 1.328 / 1.08 = 796.3 |

### W2 Sales

| Year | Volume | Unit price | Inflation | Exchange rate | Total m pesos |
|---|---|---|---|---|---|
| 1 | 5m | £1.5 | 1.1 | 233.3 | 1,925 |
| 2 | 5m | £1.5 | $1.1^2$ | 354.3 | 3,215 |
| 3 | 5m | £1.5 | $1.1^3$ | 496.0 | 4,951 |
| 4 | 5m | £1.5 | $1.1^4$ | 647.6 | 7,111 |

### W3 Labour and other expenses

| Year | Total | Inflation | Exchange rate | Total m pesos |
|---|---|---|---|---|
| 1 | 500m pesos | 1.8 | – | 900 |
| 2 | 500m pesos | 1.8 × 1.64 | – | 1,476 |
| 3 | 500m pesos | 1.8 × 1.64 × 1.512 | – | 2,232 |
| 4 | 500m pesos | 1.8 × 1.64 × 1.512 × 1.41 | – | 3,147 |

## W4 Supervisors' costs

| Year | Total | Inflation | Exchange rate | Total m pesos |
|------|-------|-----------|---------------|---------------|
| 1 | £.4m | 1.08 | 233.3 | 101 |
| 2 | £.4m | $1.08^2$ | 354.3 | 165 |
| 3 | £.4m | $1.08^3$ | 496.0 | 250 |
| 4 | £.4m | $1.08^4$ | 647.6 | 352 |

## W5 UK tax on foreign taxable profits

Tax has been paid in South America at only 20%. A further 15% is therefore payable in the UK.

Year 2 $\quad \dfrac{724m}{233.3} \quad \times \quad 15\% \quad = \quad £0.47m$

Year 3 $\quad \dfrac{1{,}374m}{354.3} \quad \times \quad 15\% \quad = \quad £0.58m$

Year 4 $\quad \dfrac{2{,}269m}{496.0} \quad \times \quad 15\% \quad = \quad £0.69m$

Year 5 $\quad \dfrac{3.412m}{647.6} \quad \times \quad 15\% \quad = \quad £0.79m$

# Axmine plc

**The net cash flow projections of the proposed joint venture with Traces**

| Year | 0 | 1 | 2 | 3 | 4 | 5 |
|---|---|---|---|---|---|---|
| | Pesos m | Pesos m | Pesos m | Pesos m | Pesos m | Pesos m |
| Sales – **(W2)** | | 1,925 | 3,215 | 4,951 | 7,111 | |
| **Payments:** | | | | | | |
| Labour and other expenses – **(W3)** | | (900) | (1,476) | (2,232) | (3,147) | |
| Supervisors salaries – **(W4)** | | (101) | (165) | (250) | (352) | |
| Capital allowances | | (200) | (200) | (200) | (200) | |
| **Taxable profits** | | 724 | 1,374 | 2,269 | 3,412 | |
| Foreign tax @20% | | | (145) | (275) | (454) | (682) |
| Capital Allowances | | 200 | 200 | 200 | 200 | |
| Machinery | (800) | | | | | |
| **Net foreign cash flow** | **(800)** | **924** | **1,429** | **2,194** | **3,158** | **(682)** |
| **Exchange rate – (W1)** | 140 | 233.3 | 354.3 | 496.0 | 647.6 | 796.3 |
| **£ Cash flow (£m)** | (5.71) | 3.96 | 4.03 | 4.42 | 4.88 | (.86) |
| **UK tax on foreign profits @15% – (W5)** | | | (.47) | (.58) | (.69) | (.79) |
| **Net £ cash flows** | (5.71) | 3.96 | 3.56 | 3.84 | 4.19 | (1.65) |
| Discount rate – 14% | 1 | .877 | .769 | .675 | .592 | .519 |
| Present value | (5.71) | 3.47 | 2.74 | 2.59 | 2.48 | (.86) |
| **Net present value** | **4.71m** | | | | | |

**(b)   Is the proposed discount rate of 14% appropriate?**

The first point is the each discount rate must be bespoke, i.e. calculated specifically for each project and based on the perceived systematic risk of the inherent cash flows of that project. To base the discount rate of the foreign project on the rate for UK mining operations is not satisfactory as the systematic risk of the project may be significantly different.

The logic of the 2% reduction is also questionable:

One argument put forward for overseas expansion is that of risk diversification, i.e. that the income of the combined company will be less volatile as its cash flows come from a variety of markets. However, this is a reduction in total risk, but has little or no affect on the systematic risk.

Will this benefit the shareholders?

Basic answer: No

Shareholders should diversify for themselves, because a shareholder can more easily and cheaply eliminate unsystematic risk by purchasing an international unit trust.

If the diversification is into foreign markets where the individuals cannot directly invest themselves this may lead to a reduction in their systematic risk.

This could be possible for a South American country, where exchange controls and other market imperfections often exist. However, as it gets easier for individuals to gain access to foreign markets the value of this argument has diminished.

(c) **Blocked remittances might be avoided by means of:**

(1) Increasing transfer prices paid by the foreign subsidiary to the parent company.

(2) Lending the equivalent of the dividend to the parent company.

(3) Making payments to the parent company in the form of royalties, payment for patents, or management fees.

(4) Charging the subsidiary additional head office overhead.

(5) Parallel loans, whereby the subsidiary in the South American country lends cash to the subsidiary of another a company requiring funds in the South American country. In return the parent company would receive the loan of an equivalent amount of cash in the UK from the other subsidiary's parent company.

The government of the South American country might try to prevent many of these measures being used.

## Option valuation

### Answer

### (a)  Option valuation

First use Black-Scholes to value the equivalent call.

**Step 1 Calculate $d_1$ and $d_2$**

$d_1 = [\ln (P_a/P_e) + (r+0.5s^2)t] / s\sqrt{t}$

$d_1 = [\ln (6/5) + (0.12+0.5 \times 0.3^2)2] / (0.3 \times \sqrt{2})$

$d_1 = \mathbf{1.21}$

$d_2 = d_1 - s\sqrt{t} = 1.21 - 0.3\sqrt{2}$

$d_2 = \mathbf{0.79}$

**Step 2**  $N(d_1) = 0.5 + 0.3869 = 0.8869.$

$N(d_2) = 0.5 + 0.2852 = 0.7852.$

**Step 3  Plug these numbers into the Black-Scholes formula**

Value of a call option = $P_a N(d_1) - P_e N(d_2)e^{-rt}$

= $6.00 \times 0.8869 - 5.00 \times 0.7852 \times e^{-(0.12*2)}$

= $5.32 - 3.08$

= **2.24**

(Reasonableness check: this exceeds the intrinsic value of $1.00 so it looks ok.)

**Step 4 Then use the put call parity rule to value a put option.**

| | |
|---|---|
| **$2.24** | **$6.00** |
| **Call price** | Share price |
| + | = + |
| **PV of the exercise price** | **Put price** (Balancing Figure) |
| **5.00e$^{-(0.12*2)}$** | |

= $2.24 + $3.93 − $6.00 = value of a put

= **$0.17**

200,000 puts would therefore cost

= 200,000* 0.17

= **$34,000**

(Reasonableness check: this option is out of the money so we would expect a low value.)

(b)

**Shares only:**       Share prices

|  | $3 | $10 |
|---|---|---|
| Share price movement | **-$600,000** | **$800,000** |

**Shares with Put options**

|  | Adverse Exercise* | Favourable Abandon |
|---|---|---|
| Share price movement | -$600,000 | $800,000 |
| Profit on options* | $400,000 | |
| Less premium | -$34,000 | -$34,000 |
| Net | **-$234,000** | **$766,000** |

The hedge would save $366,000 ($600,000 – $234,000) if the share price fell, and would lose $34,000 if the share price increased i.e. the cost of the options that were not exercised.

(c) The investor purchased 200,000 shares and wishes to hedge the position, how many call options would he have to sell to construct a risk free investment?

= 200,000 / 0.8869 = Sell 225,505 call options

## Rayswood Inc

### Answer

### Assumptions:

(1) Share price is the present value of future cash flows i.e. the economic model.

(2) The stock market is weak and semi strong efficient most of the time, therefore once new information is communicated to the market it is rapidly reflected in the share price.

(3) In an efficient market shares are fairly priced i.e. a zero NPV transaction. They give investors the exact return to compensate them for the perceived level of systematic risk of the shares.

(4) If shares are zero NPV transactions, takeovers/mergers could only be successful due to value created as a result of the merger i.e. the synergies.

(5) Therefore it is absolutely essential that one undertakes an exhaustive review to identify all the synergies. In this question no synergies have been identified, therefore before any final advice would be given to the client one would request an immediate review of all synergies.

(6) The question will therefore have to be answered on the basis of the unrealistic assumption that there are no synergies.

### Post acquisition share price:

The Add Company Approach:

| Market values: | $m |
|---|---|
| Rayswood – 40 × 3.2 = | 128.0 |
| Pondhill – 150 × 0.45 = | 67.5 |
| Value of combined company | 195.5 |
| | |
| No of shares: | 65m |
| Share price of the combined company | 3.01 |

Rayswood buys Pondhill in a 1 for 6 shares for share exchange. Rayswood already has 40m shares and buys Pondhill for (150 × 1/6) = 25m shares, thus 65m shares in total.

---

**Tutorial note**

In fact the takeover has been a wealth decreasing decision in relation to the shareholders of Rayswood. The new share price of $3.01 is lower than current market price of $3.20. Which reflects the fact that premium payment to Pondhill's shareholders has reduced the wealth of Rayswood's shareholders.

Calculation of the acquisition premium – Value per one share of Pondhill:

Pondhill shareholders get 1 share in Rayswood ($3.01) for every 6 shares of Pondhill.

$(1 \times 3.01) / 6 = \$0.50$

$(0.50 - 0.45) / 0.45 = 11.11\%$

Therefore before an acquisition premium is paid consideration should be given to ensure that it does not exceed the synergistic effects of the acquisition.

---

**Director's comments:**

'As a result of this takeover we will diversify our operations and our earnings per share will rise by 13%, bringing great benefits to our shareholders.'

**Risk diversification:**

One of the primary reasons put forward for all mergers is that the income of the combined entity will be less volatile (less risky) as its cash flows come from a wide variety of products and markets. However this is a reduction in total risk, but has little or no affect on the systematic risk.

Will this benefit the shareholders?

Basic answer: No. Shareholders should diversify for themselves, because a shareholder can more easily and cheaply eliminate unsystematic risk by purchasing an international unit trust. As the majority of investors in quoted companies have well diversified portfolios they are only exposed to systematic risk. Thus the reduction of total risk by the more expensive company diversification option is generally not recommended. The Director's comment is incorrect.

## Earnings per share will rise by 13%.

Calculation of EPS:

|  | Rayswood | Pondhill | Enlarged Rayswood |
|---|---|---|---|
| Profit available to ordinary shareholders | 7.8m | 6.5m | 14.3 |
|  | 19.5c | 4.33c | 22c |

% increase in the Earnings per share: (22 - 19.5) / 19.5 × 100 = 13%

An increasing EPS does not automatically result in an increase share price, as the P/E ratio may fall to reflect the lower growth potential of the enlarged company.

The P/E ratios:

|  | Rayswood | Pondhill | Enlarged Rayswood |
|---|---|---|---|
| Share price | 320 | 45 | 301 |
| EPS | 19.5 | 4.33 | 22 |
|  | 16.41 | 10.39 | 13.68 |

In the absence of synergy from the acquisition, purchasing Pondhill, with relatively low growth expectations, will depress the growth of the enlarged Rayswood's post acquisition and thus the post acquisition P/E ratio falls.

The Director's comment is incorrect, the increasing earnings per shares does not bring great benefits to the shareholders, in fact it masks a potential decrease in the share price.

## Non-executive comments:

"The share price of Rayswood will rapidly increase to $3.61 following the announcement of the bid."

## Bootstrapping:

A company is able to increase its EPS by merging with a company on a lower P/E ratio than its own. The bootstrapping argument states that the

Share price of the enlarged Rayswood = Post acq EPS × Pre acq P/E ratio of Rayswood.

$3.61 = 22c × 16.41 times

It contends that the market may believe that when that merger is completed that the management team of Rayswood can increase growth potential of Pondhill earnings to the same level as Rayswood earnings. It may then assign the Rayswood's higher P/E ratio to the combined earnings of both companies (i.e. the post acquisition EPS).

There has been some well documented cases of bootstrapping occurring in the 50s and 60s in America however as the stock markets have become more and more efficient it much less likely to occur today. The investors would request a detail analysis of the synergies so they could calculate the present value of future cash flows.

If there are no synergies identified the higher post acquisition EPS simply results in a lower post acquisition P/E multiple as we have seen. Therefore the non-executive is also incorrect in his views.

## Predator

### Answer

**Predator Inc**

The approaches to use for valuation are:

(1) Net asset valuation.

(2) Dividend valuation model.

(3) P/E ratio valuation.

**(1) Net asset valuation**

Target is being purchased as a going concern, so realisable values are irrelevant.

|  | $000 |
|---|---|
| Net assets per accounts (1,892 – 768) | 1,124 |
| Adjustment to freehold property (800 – 460) | 340 |
| Adjustment to inventory | (50) |
| **Valuation** | **1,414** |

**Say $1.4m**

**(2) Dividend Valuation Model**

The average rate of growth in Target's dividends over the last 4 years is 7.4% on a compound basis.

The estimated value of Target using the dividend valuation model is therefore:

Valuation    $113,100 × 1.074 / (0.15 – 0.074)    = $1,598,281

**Say $1.6m**

**(3) P/E ratio Valuation**

A suitable P/E ratio for Target will be based on the P/E ratio of Predator as both companies are in the same industry.

P/E of Predator (70m × $4.30) / $20.04m or 430 / 28.63 = **15.02**

The adjustments: – Downwards by 20% or 0.20 i.e. multiply by 0.80.

(1) Target is a private company and its shares may be less liquid.

(2) Target is a private company and it may have a less detailed compliance environment and therefore maybe more risky.

A suitable P/E ratio is therefore 15.02 × 0.80 = 12.02 (Multiplying by 0.80 results in the 20% reduction).

Target's PAT + Synergy after tax:

$183,000 + ($40,000 × **67%**) = $209,800.

After adjusting for the savings in the director's remuneration.

**The estimated value is therefore $209,800 × 12.02 = $2,521,796**

**Say $2.5m**

## Advice to the board

On the basis of its tangible assets the value of Target is $1.4m, which excludes any value for intangibles.

The dividend valuation gives a value of around $1.6m.

The earnings based valuation indicates a value of around $2.5m, which is based on the assumption, that not only will the current earnings be maintained, but that they will increase by the savings in the director's remuneration.

On the basis of these valuations an offer of around $2m would appear to be most suitable, however **a review of all potential synergies is recommended**. The directors should, however, be prepared to increase the offer to maximum price.

## Maximum price comment

It is worth noting that the maximum price Predator should be prepared to offer is:

The maximum price Predator should pay for target is:

$$PV_{Target\ Company} + PV_{Synergy}$$

The comment on the maximum price is particularly appropriate in this question, as this an example of horizontal acquisition where considerable synergies normally exist.

## Last Chance Saloon Inc

### Answer

### Report on the proposed reconstruction scheme of The Last Chance Saloon

### The scheme of reconstruction is likely to be successful if:

A    It raises adequate finance.

B    If the issue price of the new shares is fair.

C    It treats all parties fairly.

D    No group is worst off under the scheme.

### The reason why the scheme is required

As a result of the recent considerable losses there is inadequate funds available to finance the redemption of the $5m debentures in 20X5.

### Does the scheme raise adequate finance?

| Cash in: | $m | Cash out: | $m |
|---|---|---|---|
| Equity (new shares to be issued) | 12.0 | Scheme funding | 7.0 |
| 12% Debenture issued | 3.0 | Equity (old shares cancelled) 6m × 0.25 | 1.5 |
| | | Stock | 0.5 |
| | | 10% Debentures repaid | 5.0 |
| **Total raised** | 15.0 | **Total Out** | **14.0** |
| Total Out | (14.0) | | |
| **Scheme Surplus** | 1.0 | | |
| **Current cash balance** | 0.5 | | |
| **New cash balance** | 1.5 | | |

## The Capital Repayment position

| | Immediate Liquidation | Cash | Post Scheme Capital Risk |
|---|---|---|---|
| Land and Buildings | 1,500 | | 1,500 |
| Plant and machinery | 3,450 | | 3,450 |
| Inventory | 1,000 | 500 | 1,500 |
| Receivables | 1,000 | | 1,000 |
| Cash | 500 | 1,000 | 1,500 |
| New Assets – (realisable value may be considerably lower) | | 7,000 | 7,000 |
| | 7,450 | | 15,950 |
| Less: Secured creditors | | | |
| 10% Debentures | (5,000) | 5,000 | – |
| 12% Debenture | | (3,000) | (3,000) |
| Bank overdraft | | | (1,000) |
| | (5,000) | | (4,000) |
| Funds available to pay unsecured creditors | 2,450 | | 11,950 |
| Less unsecured creditors: | | | |
| Bank overdraft | (1,200) | | – |
| Other creditors | (2,300) | | (2,300) |
| | (3,500) | | (2,300) |
| Funds available to pay shareholders | nil | | 9,650 |
| Calculation of payment | 2,450 | 70c | |
| in the $ to unsecured creditors | 3,500 | | |

**An estimate of the liquidation expenses to be incurred would be necessary in practice.**

### Is the issue price of the new shares fair?

|  | $000 | $000 |
|---|---|---|
| Profit before interest and tax | | |
| Interest: | | |
| 12% Debentures – 3,000 × 0.12 = | 360 | |
| 9% Overdraft – 1,000 × 0.09 = | 90 | |
| | | (450) |
| | | |
| **Earnings before tax** | | 550 |
| Tax | | (165) |
| | | |
| **PAT** | | 385 |
| Interest cover (EBIT/Interest) = | | 2.2 |

The interest cover is below the minimum acceptable level of 2.5 times and is therefore cause for concern.

E.P.S = PAT / No. of Shares = 385 / 10,000 = 3.85c

P/E ratio: Issue price / E.P.S

   120c / 3.85 = 31.17 times

Assume that the industry average P/E is 16 times. Therefore would investors also be willing to pay 31.17 times the estimated earnings of Last Chance for a share?

The answer is no, they would want to be able to buy the shares at a discount given the fact that earnings would be perceived to be less reliable as a result of its recent poor performance. Therefore the current issue price may be unacceptable to investors.

A discount of 25% would seem reasonable i.e. 16 times × 0.75 = 12 times. Then a more reasonable issue price would appear to be 3.85c × 12 times = 46.2c.

**Conclusion:** The shares could not be sold for $1.20. Thus the financial viability of the scheme is called into question. (As the 12m cash in from the issue of new shares will not occur.)

### Is the scheme acceptable to all parties?

## Unsecured creditors:

In the event of liquidation they would receive 70c in the pound (ignoring liquidation expenses). However under the scheme they should receive a full repayment. The scheme is clearly beneficial to them.

## The Bank:

| | Current position (sunk) $000s | Liquidation $000s | Scheme $000s |
|---|---|---|---|
| Bank overdraft | 1,200 | 840 | 1,000 |

The reality of the situation is that the scheme will be organised (and the overdraft will be $1m) or the company will be liquidated and the bank will only receive $840,000. The current position of an overdraft of $1.2m as denoted in the balance sheet is **a sunk position**.

Thus the bank has a simple choice have $840,000 on liquidation or agree to a reduced overdraft of $1,000,000 under the scheme, which will be secured. If the bank agrees to the scheme the capital loss on the overdraft is reduced from $360,000 to $160,000 – a saving of $200,000.

Thus the bank will probably agree to the reduced overdraft (thus the reduced overdraft does not give rise to a cash flow).

However the low interest cover would be of concern to the Bank, and raises doubts about the company's ability to repay the interest. Therefore the bank may which to scrutinise the company profit forecasts in some details to ensure that they are based on realistic assumptions.

## Existing Shareholders:

| Per share | Current position | Liquidation | Scheme – cash repayment |
|---|---|---|---|
| Capital | 22c – ? | Nil | 25c |

The current share of 22c does not represent a realistic exit strategy of all the existing shareholders, because if a sizeable proportion of shareholders try to sell, this would drive down the share price.

Thus existing shareholders will probably agree to the scheme.

The company may consider offering the existing shareholders a share for share exchange as opposed to offering them a cash repayment as this would reduce the need for financing and allow those existing shareholders who wish to remain the opportunity to do so.

---

**Conclusion (have the reconstruction principles been adhered to):**

(1) The shares appear to be overpriced at $1.20. This need to be reviewed immediately and possibly reduced to a more realistic level.

(2) As the shares are overpriced – the $12m cash inflow from their issue is therefore unrealistic. Thus the scheme in its current form will not raise adequate finance.

(3) The planning horizon needs to be extended beyond one year.

(4) I recommend that the company valuation be taken using the present value of the free cash flows approach, if the information is available. Together with some evaluation of the risk inherent in the scheme. Risk analysis methods, which may be considered, are scenario planning, sensitivity analysis and simulation.

---

## Political risk

### Answer

(a) The consultant's report should not be used as the only basis for the African investment decision, for the following reasons.

   (i) The decision should be taken after evaluating the risk/return trade-off; financial factors (e.g. the expected NPV from the investments); strategic factors; and other issues including political risk. Political risk is only one part of the decision process (although in extremely risky countries it might be the most important one).

   (ii) The scores for the three countries are, giving double weighting to economic growth and political stability:

      Country 1  29

      Country 2  24

      Country 3  28

      Just because previous clients have not invested in countries with scores of less than 30 does not mean that Beela should not. The previous countries may not have been comparable with these in Africa. This decision rule also ignores return. If return is expected to be very high, a relatively low score might be acceptable to Beela.

   (iii) The factors considered by the consultant might not be the only relevant factors when assessing political risk. Others could include the extent of capital flight from the country, the legal infrastructure, availability of local finance and the existence of special taxes and regulations for multinational companies.

   (iv) The weightings of the factors might not be relevant to Beela.

   (v) Scores such as these only focus on the macro risk of the country. The micro risk, the risk for the actual company investing in a country, is the vital factor. This differs between companies and between industries. A relatively hi-tech electronics company might be less susceptible to political actions than, for example, companies in extractive industries where the diminishing bargain concept may apply.

   (vi) There is no evidence of how the scores have been devised and how valid they are.

(b) Prior to investing Beela might negotiate an agreement with the local government covering areas of possible contention such as dividend remittance, transfer pricing, taxation, the use of local labour and capital, and exchange controls. The problem with such negotiations is that governments might change, and a new government might not honour the agreement.

The logistics of the investment may also influence political risk:

(i) If a key element of the process is left outside the country it may not be viable for the government to take actions against a company as it could not produce a complete product. This particularly applies when intellectual property or know-how is kept back.

(ii) Financing locally might deter political action, as effectively the action will hurt the local providers of finance.

(iii) Local sourcing of components and raw materials might reduce risk.

(iv) It is sometimes argued that participating in joint ventures with a local partner reduces political risk, although evidence of this is not conclusive.

(v) Control of patents and processes by the multinational might reduce risk, although patents are not recognised in all countries.

Governments or commercial agencies in multinationals' home countries often offer insurance against political risk.

## Murwald (Interest rate hedging)

(a) The treasury team believe that interest rates are more likely to increase than to decrease, and any hedging strategy will be based upon this assumption. There is also a requirement that interest payments do not increase by more than £10,000 from current interest rates.

**Current expectations**

The current expectation is a £12m deficit in three months' time for a six-month period. At current rates, the company could borrow at 6% + 1.5% = 7.5%. Interest costs at current borrowing rates would therefore be: £12m * 7.5% * 6/12 = £450,000.

**Alternative 1: Futures hedges** (Either March or June contracts may be used, or both. This suggested solution uses June contracts.)

Use June contracts to hedge a deficit of £12 million. To hedge against the risk of a rise in interest rates, the company should sell futures.

**Tutorial note:** We sell futures because if interest rates do rise, the market price of the futures will fall. The company can then close its position by buying futures, and making a gain on the futures trading to offset the 'loss' from higher interest rates in the loans market.

(i) If interest rates rise by 2% and the futures price moves by 1.80%

As a six months hedge is required and each future is for a three-month interest period, the number of contracts will be £12m / £500k x 6/3 = 48 contracts

The tick value is £500,000 * 0.0001 * 3/12 = £12.50

|  |  | £ |
|---|---|---|
| Cost of borrowing at current rate |  | 450,000 |
| Cost if rates rise 2% (£12m × 9.5% × 6/12) |  | 570,000 |
| "Loss" from extra borrowing cost |  | (120,000) |
| *Futures* |  |  |
| Sell 48 contracts at | 93.10 |  |
| Buy 48 contracts at (93.10 – 1.80) | 91.30 |  |
| Gain per contract | 1.80 |  |
| Value of gain 180 × 48 × £12.50 |  | 108,000 |
| Net additional cost with hedging |  | (12,000) |

(ii)  If interest rates fall by 1% and the futures price moves by 0.9%

|  |  | £ |
|---|---|---|
| Cost of borrowing at current rate |  | 450,000 |
| Cost if rates fall 1% (£12m x 6.5% x 6/12) |  | 390,000 |
| "Gain" from fall in borrowing cost |  | 60,000 |
| *Futures* |  |  |
| Sell 48 contracts at | 93.10 |  |
| Buy 48 contracts at (93.10 + 0.90) | 94.00 |  |
| Loss per contract | 0.90 |  |
| Value of loss 90 x 48 x £12.50 |  | (54,000) |
| Net gain with hedging |  | 6,000 |

Based on these futures prices, hedging in the futures market does not allow the company to guarantee that interest costs in the case of a deficit do not increase by more than £10,000.

### Alternative 2: Options hedges

The expectation is for interest rates to rise, therefore put options on futures will be purchased. This will allow the company to sell futures contracts at the exercise price for the options. The company should buy 48 options, since this is the number of futures contracts that might be required. (If interest rates rise the value of the put options will also increase.)

For example using the 9400 exercise price:

(i) If interest rates rise by 2% and the futures price moves by 1.8%

|  | £ |
|---|---|
| Cost of borrowing at current rate | 450,000 |
| Cost if rates rise 2% (£12m x 9.5% x 6/12) | 570,000 |
| "Loss" from extra borrowing cost | (120,000) |

Options

|  |  |  |
|---|---|---|
| Buy 48 puts at | (1.84) | |
| Exercise - sell futures at (exercise price) | 94.00 | |
| Buy 48 futures contracts at (93.10 - 1.80) | (91.30) | |
| Gain per contract | 0.86 | |
| Value of gain 86 x 48 x £12.50 | | 51,600 |
| Net additional cost with hedging | | (68,400) |

In reality the options are likely to be sold rather than exercised. This is because they are June contracts, so they will still have time value that will be reflected in the option price. The gain from the options sale is therefore likely to be higher than the gain from exercising the options and selling futures. However, no data is provided on option prices on 1 March.

(ii) If interest rates fall by 1% and the futures price moves by 0.9%

|  | £ |
|---|---|
| Cost of borrowing at current rate | 450,000 |
| Cost if rates fall 1% (£12m x 6.5% x 6/12) | 390,000 |
| "Gain" from fall in borrowing cost | 60,000 |

Options

|  |  |
|---|---|
| Buy 48 puts at 1.84. Cost =184 x 48 x £12.50 | (110,400) |
| Net additional cost with hedging | (50,400) |

Different outcomes will exist for using options if different put option exercise prices are selected. The best exercise price to select if the put options are exercised will be the 9350 option.

If interest rates rise by 2% and the futures price falls by 180 to 91.30, this will give a gain from the options of:

93.50 − 91.30 − 1.25 = 0.95 or 95 ticks

95 × 48 × £12.50 = £57,000

If interest rates fall by 1% and the futures price rises to the futures price moves to 94.00, the option will not be exercised. The loss from hedging with options will be the premium paid of:

125 × 48 × £12.5 = £75,000

Outcomes with options at 9350

2% increase: £(120,000) + £57,000 = £(63,000)

1% decrease: £60,000 − £75,000 = £(15,000).

Neither futures nor options hedges can satisfy, with certainty, the requirement that the interest payment should not increase by more than £10,000.

## Collar

However, one way to achieve this would be to use a collar option, whereby downside risk is protected, but potential gains are also limited. A collar effectively fixes a maximum and minimum interest rate.

If a company expects to be borrowing and is worried about interest rate increases, a suitable collar can be achieved by buying put options and selling call options, to reduce the cost of protection.

For example a collar could be achieved by buying 48 9400 put options at 1.84 and selling 9400 call options at 1.74, a net premium cost of 0.10 (other alternatives are possible).

Murwald doesn't want interest to move adversely by more than £10,000 for a six month period on a £12 million loan.

In annual terms this is a £10k/£12m × 2 = 0.167%

A put option at the current interest rate (6%) and a total premium cost of less than 0.167% will satisfy the company's requirement. In the above example the total premium cost is 0.10%, and no matter what happens to interest rates Murwald can fix its borrowing cost at 7.6% (= 100 − 94.00 + 0.10 net option premium, plus the 1.5% premium over base rate for borrowing).

This satisfies the requirement. (Interest payments would be £12m * 7.6% * 0.5 = £456,000 which is £6,000 worse than current interest rates.)

The use of a collar is the recommended hedging strategy, but the company should consider the implications of the collar if a cash surplus were to occur rather than a cash deficit.

(i) Alternative interest rate hedges include:

    (i) Forward rate agreements (FRAs).

    (ii) OTC interest rate options - including interest rate guarantees.

    (iii) Interest rate swaps.

(i) A forward rate agreement (FRA) is a contract to agree to pay a fixed interest rate that is effective at a future date. As such Murwald could fix now a rate of interest of 6.1% (for example) to be effective in three months time for a period of six months. If interest rates were to rise above 6.1% the counter-party, usually a bank, would compensate Murwald for the difference between the actual rates and 6.1%. If interest rates were to fall below 6.1% Murwald would compensate the counter-party for the difference between 6.1% and the actual rate.

(ii) OTC options. Instead of market traded interest rate options such as those that are available on LIFFE, Murwald might use OTC options through a major bank. This would allow options to be tailored to the company's exact size and maturity requirements. An OTC collar would be possible, and the cost of this should be compared with the cost of using LIFFE options. Interest rate options for periods of less than one year are sometimes known as interest rate guarantees.

(iii) Interest rate swaps. Murwald expects to borrow at a floating rate of interest. It might be possible for Murwald to swap its floating rate interest stream for a fixed rate stream, pegging interest rates to approximately current levels (the terms of the swap would have to be negotiated). Interest rate swaps are normally for longer periods than six months.

## Growth of multinationals

### Answer

### Growth of multinationals

Multinational companies are normally able to take more advantage of imperfections in product markets, factor markets or financial markets than companies that only operate in a domestic market. Taking advantage of market imperfections gives a competitive advantage and facilitates the organic growth of multinationals. By virtue of their size they are also well placed to grow through acquisition, often in the form of vertical or horizontal integration.

Many market imperfections result from government actions, for example through tariffs, quotas, exchange controls, and investment incentives. Multinationals often avoid government imposed barriers through foreign direct investment, and may take advantage of favourable tax and other incentives.

Multinationals may benefit from locating production in different countries in order to take full advantage of economies of scale and scope, low labour costs, and control of raw material supplies. Economies of scale and scope may be in production (operating at an optimum unit size, and specialising production in those countries where comparative advantages are greatest), purchasing (quantity discounts and use of market power), marketing (utilising an internationally known brand image, and an efficient international marketing structure), research and development (superior technology and/or differentiated products) or financing (access to international financial markets with the potential to raise finance at relatively low cost, and to earn higher yields on financial investments). Multinationals also often have the ability to reduce their global tax payments by locating activities in tax efficient countries, reducing taxable income or shifting tax liability from one country to another through devices such as transfer pricing, royalty fees and management fees, and eliminating or deferring taxation through the use of tax havens.

In many countries multinationals may be in an oligopolistic or even monopolistic situation, which may be exploited to generate abnormally good profitability and growth.

### Internalisation of comparative advantages

Competitive advantage can be maintained by possession of unique information and skills which employees can use to create further advantage through research and development, marketing and other commercial skills. The multinational company is motivated to create an internal market for this information and to keep possession of their unique advantage specific to the firm.

Taking advantage of market imperfections is important, but a prerequisite for a successful multinational is high quality management, and the ability to survive against other multinationals in a competitive world.

# Index

# Index

# Index

# Index

# KAPLAN

## PUBLISHING

**THI**

*SO THAT*        *:RE*

**IN ADDITION TO THE**      **LES YOU TO**
**BENEFIT FROM EXTR,**      **MATERIALS:**

- An online version o     e expandable
  content and view th    s
- Fixed Online Tests
- Test History and Re    s
- Interim and Final A

**And you can access all**      sing your
**EN-gage account.**

## How to access your onl

If you are a Kaplan Financial student       se extra resources will
                               gister again, as this
process was completed when you enrolled. If you are having problems
accessing online materials, please ask your course administrator.

If you purchased through Kaplan Flexible Learning      You will automatically receive an e-mail invitation to EN-gage
or via the Kaplan Publishing website      online. Please register your details using this e-mail to gain access to your
content. If you do not receive the e-mail or book content, please contact
Kaplan Flexible Learning.

If you are already a registered EN-gage user      Go to www.EN-gage.co.uk and log in. Select the 'add a book' feature and
enter the ISBN number of this book and the unique pass key at the
bottom of this card. Then click 'finished' or 'add another book'. You may
add as many books as you have purchased from this screen.

If you are a new EN-gage user      Register at www.EN-gage.co.uk and click on the link contained in the e-
mail we sent you to activate your account. Then select the 'add a book'
feature, enter the ISBN number of this book and the unique pass key at
the bottom of this card. Then click 'finished' or 'add another book'.

**Your Code and Information**      **This code can only be used once** for the registration of one book online.
This registration will expire when the final sittings for the examinations
covered by this book have taken place. Please allow one hour from the
time you submitted your book details for us to process your request.

CHGv-17uj-cOV0-QOlJ

For technical support, please visit www.EN-gage.co.uk